TO THE SHORES
OF TRIPOLI

★ ★ ★

TO THE SHORES OF TRIPOLI

★ ★ ★

THE BIRTH OF THE
U.S. NAVY AND MARINES

A.B.C. Whipple

BLUEJACKET BOOKS

Naval Institute Press
Annapolis, Maryland

Naval Institute Press
291 Wood Road
Annapolis, MD 21402

Originally published by William Morrow and Company, Inc., New York, N.Y.
First Bluejacket Books printing, 2001
ISBN 1-55750-966-2

Library of Congress Cataloging-in-Publication Data

Whipple, A. B. C. (Addison Beecher Colvin), 1918–
    To the shores of Tripoli: the birth of the U.S. Navy and Marines / A. B. C.
Whipple.
      p. cm. — (Bluejacket books)
    Originally published: New York : William Morrow, 1991.
    Includes bibliographical references and index.
    ISBN 1-55750-966-2 (alk. paper)
      1. United States—History—Tripolitan War, 1801–1805—Naval opera-
tions, American. 2. United States. Navy—History—Tripolitan War,
1801–1805. 3. United States. Marine Corps—History—Tripolitan War,
1801–1805. I. Title. II. Series.
E335.W48 2001
973.4'7—dc21
    2001042600

Printed in the United States of America on acid-free paper ∞
08 07 06   9 8 7 6 5 4 3 2

PREFACE

★ ★ ★

This is a book about America's first war with an Arab tyrant. It is the story of the earliest major challenge to U.S. foreign policy, precipitating a congressional debate over the Constitution's restrictions on the war-making powers of the president. It was also the first U.S. attempt to blockade another nation, bombard its capital, and mount a land war across the desert, fighting alongside Arabs against other Arabs. It also reverberates with the implacable religious animosity of a holy war of Muslims against the infidel invaders. In short, it is the story—with its lessons—of how one of the Founding Fathers, President Thomas Jefferson, dealt with a confrontation strikingly similar to what the United States would face 200 years later.

Its cast of characters include dictators ruling in the name of Allah, shady middlemen offering deals of arms for hostages, supercharged American patriots volunteering for suicidal missions, and rugged warriors complaining, not for the last time, that timid diplomacy was surrendering what military might could have achieved.

Four nations along the northern rim of Africa then known as the Barbary Coast—Tripoli, Tunis, Algiers, and to a lesser extent Morocco—under the technical but loose control of the Ottoman Empire, had been terrorizing merchant shippers for centuries, capturing and looting their vessels and imprisoning their crews and passengers for ransom. To the Barbary potentates it was not piracy but a religious war at a tidy profit. (Muslim-owned ships were exempt.) Simmering with anger over what they regarded as Western exploitation of the Arab world since the time of the Crusades, the Barbary rulers took delight in humiliating their Christian captives, enslaving them on the rowing benches of their galleys in earlier centuries, selling them in white slave markets and, in later years, holding them for ransom. Muslim religious hatred, especially along the Barbary Coast, was fueled by the expulsion from Christian Spain of thousands of Moors in 1492; deprived of their livelihood and the homeland they had occupied for seven centuries, the Moors turned eagerly to piracy and became some of the most savagely effective sailors of the Barbary fleets.

The most powerful European governments, especially Britain and France, reacted with the pragmatic if ignominious policy of buying protection, paying annual tribute for safe passage in the Mediterranean. Colonial Americans were shielded from attack under Britain's tribute—until the American Revolution. After Yorktown, Parliament was in no mood to continue defending a nation of rebels who had defeated the British Army. And so the Barbary pirates began to prey on American shipping. They did so with such success that they forced the new United States of America, its government nearly in anarchy, its army and navy disbanded, to confront a vital decision: whether to follow the European practice of ransoming hostages, even paying ransom in advance, or to meet the challenge with force.

Thus a little band of petty despots along the Barbary Coast were in large part responsible for the formation of the United States Navy and Marine Corps, and not least for weaning a new nation from infancy to adolescence. The Barbary War became the first proving ground for U.S. sailors and marines. It was in the Mediterranean, aboard brilliantly designed new frigates built to meet the Barbary challenge, that Americans were blooded in combat and gained the experience without which the nation might well have lost its hard-won independence in the later War of 1812.

The Barbary War has had a distorted press. In its time at the turn of the eighteenth to nineteenth centuries, not a great deal was published in contemporary journals about American hostilities along the North African coast. American political leaders made fewer speeches about the Barbary threat than about what seemed greater menaces. The Royal Navy, the mightiest sea power the world had ever known, was marshaling its forces against Napoleon and kidnapping American sailors in a provocative campaign that would eventually lead to the War of 1812. The French Navy, which had helped the Americans win their independence, was turning on the United States because of its trade with France's enemy England and capturing U.S. trading vessels. So the Barbary threat seemed less important at first. Only when dozens of U.S. ships were captured and hundreds of Americans were thrown into Barbary prisons did Americans take more notice of what was going on in the Mediterranean half a world away. And even then Congress, most of whose members had fresh memories of the grim struggle for independence, refused a formal declaration of war.

● Most U.S. historians have tended to consider the undeclared Barbary War as a sideshow. In the nearly 200 years since then perhaps half a dozen books on the subject have been published in the United States. More has been written about it in rousing historical fiction for boys. Yet the Barbary War was responsible not only for the foundation of the U.S. Navy and Marines; it challenged the infant United States with many of its first major foreign-policy problems, including such tests of national will and morality as tribute versus force, concern for U.S. hostages, and honoring promises made to an ally. Significant foreign policy and naval and military precedents were set in the course of the Barbary War, decisions that have a bearing on similar dilemmas today.

The popularity of the Barbary War as adolescent fiction is understandable; reality was quite as colorful. Though undeclared, the United States' first land-and-sea hostilities were as violent and lethal as any formal conflict before the modern age of technological, chemical, biological, and nuclear slaughter. There were thundering broadsides and naval bombardments, battles of sword against scimitar on the blood-spattered decks of Mediterranean gunboats, and a 500-mile desert march by a foreign legion of mercenaries and marines that is one of history's most bizarre military operations.

The Barbary War also casts a revealing spotlight on America and Americans during a critical early period, especially on the politicians, today revered as Founding Fathers, who struggled with the task of affording to nourish a democracy and defend it at the same time. And it directs a laser beam on a nearly hidden side of Thomas Jefferson—the peacemaker, the secretary of state who counseled against war with a militant revolutionary France, the president who preferred the Embargo to war with Britain, the commander in chief regarded as a crippler of the navy—who proved in fact to be one of the earliest advocates of naval force against the Barbary corsairs and was the first president to use that force.

Not to mention Edward Preble, a tyrant of the quarterdeck in whose "Nursery of the Navy" dozens of young officers learned the harsh discipline of war at sea and went on to cover themselves with glory in the more famous War of 1812. Meanwhile the bombastic but heroic William Eaton, with the help of a little band of U.S. Marines, led a motley, often rebellious mob of Christians and Arabs across the Libyan Desert to a victory that was snatched from him at the last moment. And hundreds of lesser-known but equally authentic Americans became heroes in this first crisis of the new nation.

George Santayana is often quoted as warning that those who do not learn the lesson of history are condemned to repeat it. If only for that reason, the lesson of the Barbary War is as relevant today as it was 200 years ago.

ACKNOWLEDGMENTS

★ ★ ★

No one can write a history of the Barbary War without including the overland expedition led by William Eaton. And no one can fully describe Eaton's exploit without consulting the huge collection of his papers at the Huntington Library. This stately, attractive establishment in San Marino, California, surrounded by remarkable botanical gardens, is a delightful place to work, not least because of the helpful staff who made our research a pleasant task—especially Daniel H. Woodward, John H. Rhodehamel, Elsa Lee Sink, Leona Schonfeld, Sharon Nemechek, Mary Wright, and Bryant M. Duffy. Most of the material in the book concerning William Eaton, his letters and journals, is reproduced by permission of the Huntington Library.

Our work was also made easier by William Eaton himself, who dutifully made copies (in a readable hand) of nearly every communication and kept a daily journal even during his march across the Libyan Desert. Not only was it a fascinating experience to sit in the Huntington's well-appointed reference library studying the original journals written 184 years earlier in Eaton's desert tent, but his meticulous record also enabled me to describe his overland expedition in more detail than I have seen in any published account.

A close contender to the Huntington is the G. W. Blunt White Library at the Mystic (Conn.) Seaport Museum, where the working conditions also are ideal and where Douglas L. Stein, curator of manuscripts, and Paul J. O'Pecko, reference librarian, were especially helpful.

Once again I owe a large vote of thanks to Connie Roosevelt, my editor at William Morrow, for encouragement and, more important, essential editorial guidance. The late Barbara Tuchman and Professor Robin Winks of Yale were most helpful. A thank you, too, to Julian Bach, my literary agent, who originally proposed the subject of the book. And most of all I'm grateful as always for the tireless research of my wife, Jane, and for her equally important index to this book.

CONTENTS

★ ★ ★

PART I

★ ★ ★

THOMAS JEFFERSON

CHAPTER 1

* ★ *

PROLOGUE IN THE DESERT

The night encampment looked like a gathering of ghosts. The tents, row on row and lit from the inside, glowed and flickered in the dark, and ectoplasmic shadows wavered on their walls. Beyond the tents watch fires dotted the area, briefly illuminating the turbaned faces of soldiers passing like specters in the night. Behind the camp rose the thick, dark 30-foot-high parapets of *Burg el Arab*, the Arab's Tower, and beyond it the Mediterranean surf rolled against the shore. Above the distant boom of the waves some 200 camels and nearly 100 asses and Arabian horses nickered, brayed, snuffled, and stomped in their holding areas. The campground murmured with the muted nighttime voices of soldiers and camel drivers on watch. From one of the tents came the sound of a violin.

Dominating the encampment, guarded by four heavily armed Tripolitan Arabs, was the large silk pavilion of Hamet[1] Karamanli, the squat, swarthy pretender to the throne of Tripoli. Hamet was the eldest living son of the deceased bashaw,[2] and had fled Tripoli when his younger brother Yusuf had usurped the throne and threatened his life. A genial, meek young man, still terrified by his rapacious brother, Hamet was nevertheless the central figure in an expedition to overthrow him. The reason was Hamet's companion, a U.S. Army captain named William Eaton, without whose forceful persuasion Hamet never would have considered attacking his brother.

Bashaw Yusuf Karamanli had declared war on the United States, resulting in the dispatch of an American naval squadron to the Mediterranean. Eaton had convinced President Thomas Jefferson that the United States could use Hamet in a plot to overthrow

Yusuf. And now in the desert Eaton was the player and Hamet the pawn.

• Meeting in Hamet's pavilion on the night of March 4, 1805, the two men made their final plans to put into action an agreement both had signed. Eaton had promised the U.S. government's monetary and military support for an armed expedition against Tripoli to be led by Hamet, who in turn promised peace with the United States as soon as he had regained the throne. Bashaw Yusuf had also taken more than 300 Americans as hostages; Hamet guaranteed their immediate release. He also promised to hand over to the Americans his brother and family, as well as the hated chief admiral of Tripoli's navy—if, that is, he could catch them. Not only did the agreement (to which Eaton gave the more imposing name of "convention") promise peace; it even proposed repaying the United States for the cost of the expedition, in a cynical provision pledging future tributes paid by other nations to Tripoli. Eaton was not interested in stopping all Mediterranean piracy, only its attacks on the United States.

Surrounding the silk pavilion where Eaton and Hamet conferred was one of history's most outlandish international brigades, a private mercenary army rounded up largely in the alleys and dives of nearby Alexandria, Egypt: a dozen nationalities including some 40 veteran Greek infantrymen, a 60-man troop of Arab cavalry and 400 foot soldiers, a 25-man team of cannoneers (in charge of a lone two-pound artillery piece mounted on wooden wheels), 21 of Hamet's aides and hangers-on, and an assortment of renegades from England, France, Italy, Spain, Germany, Yugoslavia, Albania, Egypt, and the Levant plus a band of desert Bedouins—all lured by the promise of plunder in the expedition to come.

The real leader of this mixed mercenary army was William Eaton. A veteran of the Continental Army and a Dartmouth graduate, Eaton had been U.S. consul to Tunis, where he had met Hamet in exile and persuaded him, with lavish promises of U.S. help, to undertake the daring mission. Now, in his desert encampment, the 41-year-old Eaton was somewhat fattened by his consular years; but he still could ride a horse all day and live on a bit of goat cheese and a few sips of water. He was a better marksman than most of his followers, and he could throw a knife accurately for 80 feet. Adept at languages, he had learned four Arab dialects plus, of course, the mixture of Arab and European languages that was the lingua franca of the Mediterranean. With an odd ambivalence, Eaton despised the Arab leaders of the Barbary states yet was himself a flamboyant early-day Lawrence of Arabia. He adopted Arab robes and burnoose, and although for this expedition he changed to an officer's uniform, he wore a hat with plumes, carried a crescent-shaped scimitar, and chose for himself a large, imposing Arabian stallion to ride at the head of his foreign legion. At times he was mistaken by some of the soldiers for Hamet.

Eaton was one of only ten Americans in the entire army; with him were a midshipman and eight marines on loan from the U.S. naval squadron in the Mediterranean. They were led by a fiddle-playing marine lieutenant named Presley Neville O'Bannon, a fourth-generation Irishman from the mountains of Virginia who claimed that he and his men were ready to follow Eaton wherever he wanted to go.

Ahead of them was a desert hell of some 500 miles before they could reach their first destination: Derna,[3] Tripoli's largest eastern city. The scheme was to capture Derna, unite the thousands of supposedly disaffected Tripolitans, and march on the capital city of Tripoli. There were no maps of the sandy and rocky terrain they would traverse. They could expect to be vastly outnumbered by the troops of Bashaw Yusuf. But Eaton's boundless optimism infected them all.

On March 8, 1805, with Hamet at his side and Lieutenant O'Bannon and his marines haranguing the motley army into marching formation, William Eaton mounted his Arabian stallion, waved his scimitar, and led the way out into the desert, westward toward the shores of Tripoli. In the excitement of his quixotic mission Eaton probably did not give a thought to the fact that only four days earlier Thomas Jefferson, who had authorized the expedition, had been sworn in for his second term as president of the United States. What Eaton certainly did not consider was that President Jefferson already had betrayed him.

CHAPTER 2

★ ★ ★

RANSOM, TRIBUTE, OR WAR?

Thomas Jefferson was plagued by the Barbary pirates for all of his career in public service. He first confronted them when he was posted to Paris in 1785 to join Benjamin Franklin and John Adams as ministers plenipotentiary to negotiate treaties between the new nation and the European governments. The author of the Declaration of Independence, former governor of Virginia and representative to the Continental Congress, Jefferson at first enjoyed the country he later would regard as a second home. After four or five moves about Paris he settled in a house on the Champs Elysée with a staff of servants, a rapidly expanding collection of antiques, silver, objets d'art, an extensive wine cellar,[1] and dozens of books he had been unable to purchase in still-uncultured America. He went to concerts and the opera and visited Paris's many museums.[2]

Handsome, red-haired, and tall (some called him "Long Tom"; 6 feet 2½ inches was indeed tall in the eighteenth century), Jefferson was welcomed in the best salons and held some of his own, attracting Frenchmen and women who already had been charmed by Franklin and were openly fascinated by yet another sophisticated American. But Jefferson also found time to meet with Franklin and Adams, from whom he learned that Old World diplomacy moved at a frustratingly slow pace. One of the missions assigned to the U.S. envoys was to see what could be done to gain the release of the American prisoners of the Barbary corsairs.

Jefferson would later be known and remembered as the man who preferred peaceful negotiation to war. But there was something about the petty despots of the Barbary Coast that triggered the redheaded Virginian's temper and set his adrenaline pumping. He recognized that his new government was confronted with its first major foreign-policy decision: whether to follow the example of the European nations by paying tribute or to meet force with force. His own choice was force. He was firmly convinced that tribute would purchase only a precarious peace and lead to demands for more and more money from America.[3]

Piracy was as old as the Mediterranean. Homer had Ulysses boast that he was a "sacker of cities." Julius Caesar was taken hostage by Mediterranean pirates;[4] so was Cervantes. Barbary Coast piracy reached its golden age, from the pirates' point of view, with the legendary Barbarossa, who rose to become chief admiral of the Ottoman Empire. By the late eighteenth century, when Jefferson confronted the problem in France, piracy and the white slave trade had become the major industry of the North African coast.

In every city there were regular auctions in which men, women, and children were prodded onto the stump before the assembled buyers, some of whom speculated by purchasing in a glutted market ("Christians are cheap today," was the word when a new cargo arrived) and tossing their purchases into a dungeon until the price rose again—allowing in their calculations for a number of deaths from the many Mediterranean diseases to which foreigners succumbed. The local dey or bashaw would confiscate the strongest men for public works—building roads or aqueducts, reinforcing fortifications—and the educated men as clerks. With the oared galley replaced by the sailing ship, fewer men were consigned to the bench and the lash. The better-looking women were sold as concubines. (And not a few young boys were peddled to well-off pederasts.)[5] An occasional titled or wealthy captive would bring even more money through ransom than in the slave market. The major profiteers of the slave trade were the pirate captains, who became immensely rich, building their own palaces and enjoying luxuries rivaling those of the Barbary rulers. The potentates themselves were also using captives as pawns, holding them for ransom or to enforce a treaty with tribute.

The system was brutally simple. A Barbary ruler would "declare war" on any nation whose trade offered a profitable target or whose citizens could be traded for a lucrative treaty, thereby giving their corsairs a crude form of legitimacy as privateers, licensed to capture enemy ships, rather than as outlaw pirates. In the Barbary powers' view, they were the lords of the Mediterranean; and any nation whose vessels ventured into their sea was a potential enemy.

It was the British government that devised the system of paying tribute as early as 1646, when Parliament voted to send an emissary to ransom the hundreds of Englishmen enslaved in Algiers. Official ransom led logically to regular payments for protection against further enslavement of Englishmen. In 1662 England also concluded a treaty with the bey of Tunis that freed English slaves and provided for annual payments to guarantee against capture of captains, crews, and passengers of English vessels.[6] Similar treaties were signed with Algiers and Tripoli; and other major European nations followed the English example.

The treaties were loftily regarded as nonaggression pacts. The Barbary powers promised not to declare war on their signatories; consuls were posted to Barbary capitals; and an ingenious system was devised to protect their vessels. It consisted of the issuance of "passports" by the Barbary powers. Each passport (Appendix A) declared the possessor immune from attack.[7] Usually it was honored; sometimes it was not. Then there would be protests, recriminations, haggling, threats, perhaps even a show of force by the European nation's navy, before the dispute was settled, usually after healthy bribes to the captain, the Barbary ruler, and the negotiators. It was a far from satisfactory arrangement; but it was better than the unrestrained piracy of earlier years. And the more powerful European powers were quick to discover the secondary advantage of tribute: It lessened competition from the trading ships of nations that could not afford to pay.

Nonetheless, England's decision constituted an important turning point in which the Mediterranean became officially recognized as a Barbary fiefdom. For a century and a half, until the new United States finally disputed it, this cynical arrangement controlled all shipping in one of the world's most important trading areas.

As a first move, Thomas Jefferson asked his sources in Paris for exhaustive reports on the strength of the Barbary navies. They were, he found, designed for the quick thrust of piracy rather than the sustained battle of traditional naval warfare. Even Algiers's fleet, stronger at the time than the others combined, consisted of fewer than a dozen xebecs[8] and only four galleys. Nothing, Jefferson concluded, prevented the powerful European navies from combining to destroy the Barbary pirates but the Europeans' refusal to unite in such a campaign, not least because of the benefit of hindering competition.

● One of the Americans who came to Jefferson's Paris salons was John Paul Jones, who had returned to France to collect prize money due him and his sailors from ships captured during the Revolution. Jefferson had helped Jones recover some $22,000 (after many delaying tactics by the French intermediaries). In their conversations Jefferson found that Jones, too, was outraged at the Barbary pirates, and equally contemptuous of their strength. Urging *"une croisade"* against them, Jones calculated that a small fleet, commanded by him, of course, could wipe out the pirates forever. Elaborating on Jones's scenario, Jefferson estimated that a naval force with no more than 150 guns could be mounted at a cost of about $2 million—considerably less than what the major European countries were paying in official bribes. The United States would need a navy sooner or later, he argued. To his friend James Monroe (then a member of the Continental Congress), Jefferson urged, "Can we begin it on a more honorable occasion, or with a weaker foe?"

Within a year of Jefferson's arrival in Paris, Franklin had returned home and Adams had gone across the Channel to be U.S. minister to Britain. Jefferson replaced Franklin as minister to France, and continued to lobby for a naval assault on the Barbary powers. His vision expanded to encompass an allied U.S.-European campaign, a veritable international navy, which he urged on the Continental diplomats.[9] But the grand project died in infancy when it became obvious that the United States had no warships or much money to contribute to such an armada. In fact, Jefferson's determination to stand up to the Barbary powers had little support at home.

It is difficult in this age of U.S. world leadership (and occasional arrogance) to appreciate how pitifully weak and divided the nation was immediately after winning its independence. In fact, it was scarcely a nation at all. There was no president of the United States. There was no judiciary (except for admiralty courts). A

Continental Congress attempted to preside over the affairs of government, most of which the separate states jealously preserved for themselves. Indeed, the designers of the Articles of Confederation referred to Congress not as a national body but as "a firm league of friendship."[10] And sometimes, as the states feuded over conflicting rights, it was not even that.[11]

Such national necessities as control of interstate commerce, currency, and even the armed forces were left to the individual states. There was no army or navy;[12] both had been disbanded after the Revolution. In the early peacetime years the only army in the United States consisted of separate state militia, most of whom were needed to defend the western settlers against Indian attacks.

There was a more significant reason for abandoning the standing army or established navy. Most Americans felt that they had learned by bitter experience that an armed force was the tool of the tyrant, and they wanted no such threat to their hard-won freedom. There also were well-founded fears of unruly soldiers. In 1783 a disgruntled contingent of Continentals, converging on Congress in Philadelphia and threatening violence if they were not paid, so frightened the congressmen that they fled to Princeton, N.J. (The Continental Congress later moved to Annapolis, Md., and in 1785 to New York.) Nor were Americans willing to submit to the sort of national revenue-raising that had afflicted them with taxes on tea and stamps. So the Continental Congress was denied the authority to raise funds directly from the populace. To pay the post-Revolution war debt, Congress had to plead with the states for money; and the state legislators were unable or unwilling to remit. When in 1782–83 Congress asked the states for $10 million, it received less than $1.5 million. As a result of its inability to tax the people directly, the new nation was virtually bankrupt.

The plight of Congress merely reflected the national mood of Americans, many of whom were uneducated farmers concerned mainly with local matters and convinced that a minimum of government interference was what they had fought for. The only government most of them knew had consisted chiefly of repressive laws, tax collectors, and debtors' prisons. Some states did not even send their representatives to New York, where the Continental Congress was struggling to survive. When John Hancock was elected president of the Congress in 1785, he did not bother to attend.[13] Robert Morris, the superintendent of finance, unable to achieve cooperation between Congress and the states, quit in disgust.

◉ Appalled at the impotence of Congress and the perilous existence of the independence he had helped win, George Washington wrote, "No morn ever dawned more favorably than ours did; and no day was ever more clouded than the present. . . . We are fast verging to anarchy." But Washington and many of the other major players in forging the nation, those who later would be praised as the Founding Fathers, had retired from or were yet to come on the stage. With the Continental Army disbanded, the commanding general had gone home to Mount Vernon. Jefferson was in France and John Adams in Great Britain. Benjamin Franklin preferred being president of Pennsylvania's Executive Council. Alexander Hamilton was practicing law in New York.

The new nation was going through its growing pains locally as well as nationally. Americans considered themselves New Yorkers, Virginians, or Vermonters rather than citizens of the United States. There were disputes over state lines; Pennsylvania and Virginia resorted to arms before finally agreeing on a boundary. When New Hampshire and New York both claimed Vermont (then known as the Green Mountain Commonwealth) as part of their states, Ethan Allen, the famous leader of the Green Mountain Boys in the war, offered the British a treaty making Vermont part of Canada. That and similar threats of secession continued until after the Constitution had been ratified.

In Massachusetts, where merchants had skewed the state laws in their favor and had levied excessive taxes on the farmers, filling the state's prisons with debtors, a Continental Army captain named Daniel Shays led a revolt against farm foreclosures, attacking the state arsenal in Springfield to arm his followers. The revolt was put down by local militia (equipped by Boston businessmen), but Shays' Rebellion was recognized as a manifestation of growing anarchy.[14]

From the Old World, Europeans watched with mixed amusement and contempt. The 13 former colonies comprised a vast area as large as Britain, France, Italy, and Spain combined, and few Europeans believed that so large a land mass could be incorporated into a single government. There was no precedent; not since the

Greek example 2,000 years earlier had a nation successfully managed a political system based on the consent of the governed. Dean Josiah Tucker of England's Gloucester Cathedral confidently predicted of the Americans: "A disunited people till the end of time, suspicious and distrustful of each other, they will be divided and subdivided into little commonwealths or principalities, according to natural boundaries." Dean Tucker's gloomy assessment was shared by many Americans who were realizing that making a democracy work was a more revolutionary undertaking than the Revolution itself.

Meanwhile, however, American shipping merchants were going about their business as if there were no political crisis, quickly resuming the trade that had been halted by the war. Within months of the end of hostilities, the *Empress of China* sailed from New York to Canton. U.S. ships traded in ports all over the Old World, their skippers peddling American merchandise, buying European goods and selling them wherever there was a market. Salem's legendary "Lord" Timothy Dexter reputedly sold coal in Newcastle, bed-warming pans in Bermuda, and cats in Malta. Britain's Parliament (which had not yet bothered to send a minister to the new nation) reacted to the growing American competition in 1783 with an Order in Council banning U.S. trade with British islands in the West Indies. U.S. shippers responded by tapping new markets elsewhere,[15] including the Mediterranean, where the trade was flourishing. As many as a hundred ships, employing 1,200 American seamen, and carrying some 20,000 tons of salted fish, flour, lumber, and sugar, sailed to the Mediterranean annually, bringing back lemons, oranges, figs, olive oil, wine, and opium. Inevitably these traders ran afoul of the Barbary pirates.

In 1784, one year after the colonies had become the United States of America, the Boston brig *Betsey*, en route to Teneriffe, was captured by a Barbary corsair. These pirates happened to be Moroccans, whose emperor, Sidi Mahomet, was more interested in trade than brigandage. He also claimed that he was proud to be one of the first heads of state to recognize the new American nation, and he expressed a desire for diplomatic and commercial ties. He released the *Betsey*, her captain and crew, and announced that he was waiting for an envoy from America.

Only three months later the American schooner *Maria* was taken off Cape St. Vincent, this time by the much more formidable Algerians. And that same week another Algerian pirate vessel captured the American ship *Dauphin* off Cádiz. One of the six crewmen aboard the *Maria*, James Leander Cathcart, vividly described the pirates' methods. Swarming aboard the schooner, the Algerians stripped the *Maria*'s captain and crew to their underwear, seizing their clothes, belongings, and everything of value aboard the ship. A prize crew was put aboard the *Maria*, and the shivering captives were driven belowdecks in the Algerian vessel into a dark, verminous hold already crowded with 36 men and a woman from previous captures. Taken to Algiers, the prisoners were issued lice-infested clothing and paraded through the streets, past mobs of Algerians jeering at the Christian infidels, to one of the city's two prisons. Three days later they were auctioned off at the slave market. Many of them were purchased by the dey's officers for work crews or domestic service;[16] the woman prisoner was sent off to the sultan's harem in Constantinople.

❧ Responding to these captures of American ships, the Continental Congress ignored Jefferson's pleas and voted for "an amicable peace with the Barbary states in the usual way"—i.e., with tribute. Jefferson and Adams were directed to send negotiators to Morocco and Algiers. With no choice but to do as ordered, Jefferson agreed with Adams on Thomas Barclay, the U.S. consul in Paris, whom they dispatched to Morocco. Barclay needed only a month to conclude, in June of 1786, a treaty that with small payments of tribute protected American shipping from Moroccan attack.[17]

The more difficult task fell to John Lamb, whom the Continental Congress sent to negotiate with Dey Mahomet of Algiers, who demonstrated only contempt for the infant nation yet was demanding nearly $3,000 per man for the 21 Americans his pirates had captured—twice as much as he was asking for prisoners of other nations.[18]

While the negotiations dragged on in Algiers, Jefferson in Paris tried an intriguing avenue of approach. The religious order of Mathurins, the Fathers of Redemption, had a long history of helping prisoners in the Barbary states; they had recently bought freedom for 300 Frenchmen at a reported cost of $500 per man. Jefferson asked the Mathurin general if his order would intercede for the American prisoners in Algiers—without revealing that they were dealing for the United States—and offered $200 per man. The general agreed to try. Shortly his representatives sent word that the Algerian slave supply was tight and that prices were rising. Jefferson, who by now had gained the consent of Congress, raised the ante to $550. But then the incipient French Revolution overwhelmed the Mathurins, whose estates were confiscated, and that avenue was closed.

● Yet another possibility arose when John Adams urged Jefferson to come to London for secret talks with a potential middleman. He turned out to be the Tripolitan ambassador to Great Britain, a Mr. Abdrahaman, who suavely suggested that he could arrange treaties with the Barbary states for about $1 million in cash—plus, of course, a hefty commission for himself. There was no promise beyond Mr. Abdrahaman's assurances that the treaties could be arranged so easily. And Jefferson knew that $1 million was out of the question; it amounted to one fifth of the entire U.S. annual budget. In any case, he still believed, despite his orders to deal with the Barbary powers, that U.S. funds would be better spent on a navy.

Adams was at first inclined to bargain with Mr. Abdrahaman. Unlike Jefferson, the frugal New Englander believed that tribute would be cheaper than war. "We ought not to fight them at all," he had written to Jefferson, "unless we determine to fight them forever. This thought, I fear, is too rugged for our people to bear." Besides, he argued, even a naval victory probably would lead to an expensive treaty. In the meantime, Adams argued, the cost of tribute might be partially repaid from the savings in marine insurance, which had skyrocketed since the captures of the American ships. By 1789, when both men had returned home, they still held opposing views. And the negotiations started in Algiers were stalled.

The impotence of the Continental Congress and the resulting national chaos finally led to a Constitutional Convention. Meeting in Philadelphia through the long, steamy summer of 1787, its members represented the same rivalries, state against state, city against farm, North against South, that had riven the Continental Congress. But this time the representatives recognized that the alternative to agreement was national anarchy. So emerged the U.S. Constitution, a compromise that had benefits and drawbacks for every representative. A major contribution to final agreement was the dominating presence of George Washington, whose leadership of the Continental Army had made him a father figure to all Americans. Many of those who voted, however reluctantly, to accept the Constitution in the Convention and later in the states as it was ratified did so because of their trust in the one man they now turned to as the first president of the United States.

Only because Washington was convinced that the new nation he had fought for was headed toward disaster did he agree to stand for certain election. And on April 16, 1789, he wrote in his diary:

> I bade adieu to Mount Vernon, to private life, and to domestic felicity, and with a mind oppressed with more anxious and painful sensations than I have words to express, set out for New York with the best disposition to render service to my country in obedience to its calls, but with less hope of answering its expectations.

His resources had been so depleted by the war that he had to borrow the money to pay for the elaborate equipage in which he traveled to New York.[19] So upset was his wife, Martha, that she stayed behind in Mount Vernon, only grudgingly joining him later.

George Washington had good reason for doubting that he could answer his country's expectations. While he was the first army officer whose success on the battlefield propelled him into the presidency, he was not the last to find that public adulation can rapidly wane and that military expertise does not always translate into political acumen. Nor has any U.S. president since faced the daunting challenges that confronted General Washington as President Washington.

He was quite aware of some of his inadequacies. Though a member of the Virginia gentry, he had never been well-off; so he lacked a formal education. He rarely used one word when three or four would do—no doubt a reflection of his self-education. He had virtually no personal experience abroad; his one trip outside North America had been to Barbados in 1751, where he had caught smallpox.[20] He probably did not recognize his tendency toward pomposity or his lack of a sense of humor. His intimate friends claimed that after a few glasses of champagne Washington could become "quite merry" and even laugh; but few of his fellow Americans caught him at it. Indeed, the gravity of his demeanor added to the stony visage to create the impression of someone more than human; and no doubt he worked at maintaining that impression.

● But for all his haughty bearing, Washington was a sincere democrat. When a group of his former army officers proposed establishing an American monarchy with Washington as king, his reaction was, "What a triumph for our enemies to verify their predictions! What a triumph for the advocates of despotism to find that we are incapable of governing ourselves, and that the systems founded on the basis of equal liberty are merely ideal and fallacious!" Washington was not in the least tempted by power, the drug of so many ambitious Americans of the time. He instead used the considerable power he already possessed to affirm the real power of the people he represented.

Perhaps his major contribution to consolidating a democratic government was his insistence on promoting a consensus, for employing the best talents of the nation and persuading them to work together. Virtually everything the first president did set a precedent for all the administrations to follow; and Washington set the precedent of a consultative body of advisers.[21] More important, he chose the most intelligent and far-seeing men of his day whatever their differing views, and by encouraging them to speak frankly, he fostered an environment that produced some of the great thinkers and movers whom we credit today for the survival of democracy.

George Washington's first Cabinet was no body of yes-men. And Washington showed his administrative genius no more for selecting them than for keeping these strong-willed, contentious geniuses from tearing the administration apart.

Certainly the most ambitious of them all was his secretary of the treasury. Alexander Hamilton was a brilliant, hard-driving autocrat who regarded himself as Washington's prime minister. Hamilton favored British tradition and believed that some sort of monarchist government would be best for the United States. When pressed, he stoutly maintained, "As to my political creed, I give it to you with the utmost sincerity, I am affectionately attached to the republican principle. I desire above all things to see the equality of political rights, exclusive of all hereditary distinction." But one evening, *in vino veritas*, Hamilton betrayed his true sentiments by exclaiming, "The people—your people, sir, is a great beast." Hamilton was a firm believer in the natural superiority of men of property, who should govern their inferiors. He also believed in a strong federal government encumbered by as few states' rights as possible. He was an arrogant man, probably masking an inferiority complex (he was the illegitimate son of a West Indies trader), who had fought his way to the top and knew the value of sound money better than most of his well-born, often profligate colleagues. With his peers he could be charming and ingratiating; and Washington, who had seen Hamilton's capabilities as his aide-de-camp during the war, trusted him as a valued lieutenant.

Hamilton's natural enemy in the Cabinet was Thomas Jefferson,[22] the aristocratic gentleman farmer and standard-bearer for agrarian states' rights. Jefferson came to the Cabinet late. He was still in France when Washington was sworn in on April 30, 1789. Four months later Jefferson finished supervising the packing of 86 cases of books, French antiques, statuary, wine, plants, and scientific instruments and set out for home with his two daughters.[23] At Le Havre they were delayed by a gale that blew for a week; Jefferson used the time to search the nearby countryside for sheepdogs for his estate at Monticello (but found none available). He arrived at Norfolk, Va., on November 23, to find a letter waiting for him from President Washington asking him to be secretary of state. Jefferson protested that he did not want a national public office but would serve if the president demanded, which the president did. After unpacking at Monticello (and marrying off his daughter Martha to Thomas Randolph, Jr.) Jefferson arrived in New York to assume his duties in March of 1790.

He found a Department of State that consisted only of himself, two clerks (with two assistants), and a translator. No sooner had he plunged into the many details that had been awaiting him than he suffered a series of debilitating migraine headaches, at the same time that Washington was incapacitated by pneumonia. Jefferson's headaches may have been caused—certainly they were aggravated—by his discovery that Hamilton, who had been assuming many of the secretary of state's duties before Jefferson's arrival, continued to meddle in foreign affairs. And when the president, on his recovery, followed his practice of submitting most of the administration's important decisions to Cabinet discussion, Jefferson and Hamilton soon were at loggerheads.

When over succeeding months of Washington's first administration Jefferson complained about Hamilton's intrusion into foreign matters, Hamilton blandly replied that he was merely acting because of Jefferson's frequent trips to Monticello; Jefferson believed that he could manage his affairs as well from home as from his New York office. But Hamilton, seemingly always in his office (New York was his home), was ever at hand to make a prompt decision before the matter could be communicated to Monticello. It also became clear that Hamilton did not have a high opinion of Jefferson's abilities. Washington, too, it seemed to Jefferson, tended to side with Hamilton, whose undoubted talents clearly impressed the president.

● Hamilton and Jefferson at first were courteous at Cabinet meetings, though in private they expressed dislike bordering on contempt. Hamilton sneered at Jefferson's pretense of the simple gentleman farmer and threatened to expose him as "a secret voluptuary . . . the intriguing incendiary." Jefferson, for his part, scorned Hamilton as a power-hungry *arriviste* and condescendingly refused to respond, maddening the snobbish Hamilton all the more.

Washington had a difficult time keeping his feuding cabinet members in harness. However much he admired and trusted Hamilton, he had an equally high regard for Jefferson's wisdom and knowledge of Europe. But an avuncular role did not come easily to Washington, and when he wanted to tell his secretaries simply to quit squabbling, it came out like this:

> I will frankly and solemnly declare that I believe the views of both of you are pure and well meant; and that experience alone will decide with respect to the salubrity of measures which are the subject of dispute. . . . I have a great, a sincere esteem and regard for you both, and ardently wish that some line could be marked out by which both of you could walk.

Usually such expressions had little effect on the two warring advisers, and Cabinet meetings often ended with Hamilton and Jefferson sulking and glowering at each other.

Washington favored Hamilton's advice on financial matters largely because, as he freely admitted, he had only a scant understanding of the intricacies involved and had to trust his treasury secretary. But in foreign matters he just as readily depended on his secretary of state. It was at Jefferson's urging that the president sent to Congress in December of 1790 a recommendation on the Barbary pirates that artfully urged force instead of tribute.

The message first reminded the congressmen that a sizable proportion of American trade had gone to the Mediterranean before the Revolution: about a sixth of its exports of wheat and flour and a quarter of its dried and pickled fish, plus a considerable amount of rice. War with Britain had of course curbed these exports, Jefferson pointed out, adding that "our navigation, then, into the Mediterranean has not been resumed since the peace."[24]

To resume trading in the area, Jefferson offered three alternative actions: (1) annual tribute, (2) ransom, or (3) naval force. As for (1), he acknowledged the precedent of the European governments, as he scathingly put it, "counting their interest more than their honor." He presented his best estimates of the cost. Britain was probably paying Algiers alone some 60,000 guineas, or more than a quarter of a million dollars, a year. France's annual tribute came to about $100,000. Smaller nations like Denmark, Sweden, and Venice paid about $30,000 a year. These figures, Jefferson warned, were guesswork, because the European governments were ashamed to reveal the exact sums.

Moreover, Jefferson reminded Congress, Dey Mahomet of Algiers was in his seventies; on his death there would be demands from his successor for lavish gifts from any nation paying tribute; and there was no certainty that present agreements would continue to be honored.

As for option (2), Jefferson argued that ransom would simply lead to more captures and greater demands. That left option (3)—force—which Jefferson favored.

Drawing on his researches in Paris, he presented a quick résumé of the makeup of the Barbary navies: tiny fleets of small vessels adapted to chasing and boarding, and incapable of holding their own against warships. These vessels, he reported, were "sharp built and swift, but so light as not to stand the broadside of a good frigate." Their guns, he added, were "unskillfully pointed and worked. The vessels illy maneuvered, but crowded with men . . . resting their sole hopes on boarding," not engaging in a ship-to-ship battle. The Barbary captains, Jefferson wrote, had no conception of fleet warfare; each pirate craft sailed alone in search of prey. Nor, he added, would they come out of the harbor "when they know there are vessels cruising for them." And they did not come out at all during the stormy winter months. Jefferson suggested a way to combat the pirates more cheaply than taking them on alone. Dusting off his original proposition of a U.S.-European task force, he suggested a simple blockade: with "each performing a tour of given duration, and in a given order, a constant cruise during the eight temperate months of every year, may be kept up before the harbor of Algiers, till the object of such operations be completely obtained."

He recognized, in conclusion, that "it rests with Congress to decide between war, tribute, and ransom, as the means of re-establishing our Mediterranean commerce." And his balance of the three options had the desired effect. The Committee on the Trade of the Mediterranean reported to the Senate less than a week after Jefferson's message that its members "are of the opinion that the trade of the United States to the Mediterranean cannot be protected but by a naval force . . ." The committee, however, added a vital proviso: "it will be proper to resort to the same as soon as the state of the public finances permit." In short, the United States could not bankroll a new navy yet.

Envoy John Lamb's attempts at negotiations with Algiers's Bey Mahomet had made no progress. Then, in 1791, Mahomet died and was succeeded by Alli Hassan, who had been Algiers's prime minister. Captain Richard O'Brien of the captured *Dauphin*, who had worked his way up to become one of the dey's clerks, wrote home suggesting that the United States reopen negotiations. President Washington so recommended to Congress, which in May of 1792 voted for another try, appropriating up to $100,000 for a treaty that would release the prisoners.

Still with no choice but to make a deal for tribute as ordered, Jefferson nonetheless proposed a unique candidate. Remembering John Paul Jones's campaign for *une croisade*, Jefferson proposed appointing him to lead the negotiations with Dey Alli Hassan. Jones, Jefferson knew, had returned to Paris from St. Petersburg in disgrace and disgust, and should be eager for adventure in the Mediterranean. It would be a diplomatic rather than naval mission, but Jefferson calculated that Jones's attitude toward the Barbary pirates was no secret to the dey, and that the appointment of the American naval hero should convey the message that U.S. peace overtures might be backed by force.

● President Washington agreed and signed Jones's commission within a month of Congress's appropriation, appointing him "commissioner with full powers to negotiate with the Dey of Algiers concerning the ransom of American citizens in captivity, and to conclude and sign a Convent thereupon." On June 2 Washington formally appointed Jones U.S. consul to Algiers. In his covering orders Jefferson stressed that despite the wording of Jones's commission "no *ransom* is to take place without a *peace*." This was to be a treaty guaranteeing against further captures of Americans. And he added a further stricture: "We have also understood that peace might be bought cheaper with naval stores [i.e., guns and ammunition] than with money. But we will not furnish them naval stores because we think it not right." No American arms for hostages in the eighteenth century—at least not yet.

Thomas Pinckney had just been appointed minister to the Court of St. James's, so Jefferson entrusted Jones's commission to him to pass along to Jones in Paris. Pinckney did not sail for England until mid-July. But on July 18 John Paul Jones, ill with nephritis and' jaundice, contracted pneumonia and died at 45.[25]

When he heard the news, Jefferson turned to Thomas Barclay, who had successfully negotiated the treaty with Morocco in 1786. But there seemed to be a curse on this commission. So slow was transatlantic communication that Barclay did not receive his orders until January of 1793, half a year after Jones's death—and shortly before his own death in Lisbon. David Humphreys, U.S. minister to Portugal, was preparing to take up the negotiations when the situation was suddenly and dramatically changed, not by American efforts but by a British diplomat in Algiers.

CHAPTER 3

★ ★ ★

SIX FRIGATES
TO FIGHT THE DEY

Charles Logie, British consul to Algiers, had heard that the foreign minister of Portugal, Louiz Pinto de Souza, had expressed interest in a truce with Algiers. Seizing an opportunity to work one out, Logie quickly concluded in October of 1793 a one-year cease-fire, without bothering to notify Pinto de Souza or ask for instructions. In fact, according to one account, the first news Pinto de Souza heard of the truce came from officers of the Portuguese Navy who had run down an Algerian warship only to be shown a copy of the truce.

The Portuguese Navy had been cruising the Strait of Gibraltar, effectively blockading Algerian ships in the Mediterranean. Suddenly the Strait was open, and Algerian pirates swarmed through into the Atlantic. American diplomats in southern Europe reacted with dismay verging on panic. David Humphreys chartered a fast Swedish vessel to speed the word to Secretary of State Jefferson in New York. Meanwhile, on October 6, he fired off a warning to John Marsden Pintard, U.S. consul in Madeira, where many American vessels put in after crossing the Atlantic for southern European ports. The latest intelligence, Humphreys reported, was that eight Algerian ships had already passed through the Strait. "I write you in great haste this information in order that you may take such measures as you shall judge Proper to give our Countrymen the most rapid & extensive notice thereof possible."

A similar warning went off the same day from Humphreys to Michael Murphy, U.S. consul at Malaga, Spain, spreading the word with a circular:

● TO ALL GOVERNORS, MAGISTRATES, OFFICERS CIVIL, MILITARY & others concerned . . .

You are most earnestly desired, as speedily as possible, to give an universal alarm to all citizens of the United States concerned in navigation, particularly to the southern parts of Europe, of the danger of being captured by the Algerines, in prosecuting their voyages to that destination.

Edward Church, U.S. consul in Lisbon, took up the cry. A Portuguese frigate captain had just returned to Lisbon reporting that the eight Algerian vessels were heavily armed. The sharp-eyed Portuguese had counted 44 guns on one ship, 36, 30, and 28 guns on three others, not to mention three xebecs carrying 26, 24, and 20 guns and a brig with 22.[1] Church, too, sent out a warning circular:

CITIZENS OF THE UNITED STATES OF AMERICA
Nine[2] Algerine corsairs are now cruising in the Atlantic, they carry from 22 to 44 guns—They sailed out of the Mediterranean on the 26th [of October] instant, and were seen on the 9th [of November] to capture four American Vessels, and one Genoese.

◆ In fact, so swiftly did the Algerian pirates fan out into the Atlantic that in the two months of October and November after the truce with Portugal they captured eleven U.S. merchantmen.[3] Now, instead of 23 American captives, Algiers had 119.

Consul Church also rushed over to Lisbon's Foreign Office to complain to Pinto de Souza. Behind the foreign minister's diplomatic facade, he was clearly angry at the British. Claiming that he was at that moment writing a letter of explanation to Church, the foreign minister protested that he never would have concluded a truce with Algiers without ample warning to the United States. He had indeed some time ago asked Britain for whatever help she could give Portugal in negotiating peace with Algiers, but he was upset by Logie's action without any consultation with him. The conversation confirmed Church's assumption that the Portuguese government was concerned over losing a lucrative trade with the United States. And indeed, ten days later Pinto de Souza offered Portuguese Navy convoys for American ships in the area.

Algiers's motive for a truce was obvious from the speed with which her pirates rushed into the Atlantic.[4] As for Portugal, she stood to profit from a cessation of attacks on her shipping. But the major reason for the truce, Consul Church was convinced, was treachery on the part of British intent on curbing American shipping competition. For the same reason that she paid tribute and preserved the pirates whom the powerful Royal Navy could easily demolish, perfidious Albion surreptitiously concluded a truce that loosed the pirates against the hated Americans.[5]

At least so believed Consul Church, who wrote to Jefferson, "The conduct of the british[6] in this business leaves no room to doubt, or mistake their object, which was evidently aimed at Us, and proves that their envy, jealousy, and hatred, will never be appeased, and that they will leave nothing unattempted to affect our ruin." Warming nearly to hysteria, he went on, "We are all betrayed and many, many of our Countrymen will fall into the Snare . . . I have not slept since the Receipt of the news of this hellish plot—pardon me for such expressions—Another Corsair is in the Atlantic,—God preserve Us."

Evidently rereading his letter, Church appended a semi-apology: "If by the harshness of some of my expressions I should appear to you to be more strongly prejudiced against the british, or british politicks, than my Countrymen in general, I trust it is only because I know them better."

As for the British Foreign Office, its explanation was that the Royal Navy needed the help of the Portuguese Navy against the growing threat of France and that the truce freed the warships of Portugal, England's ally, from blockade duty in the Strait of Gibraltar. Needless to say, Consul Church—and Secretary of State Jefferson—found Britain's explanation unconvincing. Portugal shortly broke the truce by sending warships back to the Strait. But for the United States the damage had been done.

The story of the 119 Americans in Algiers was told by John Foss in a book he wrote about his captivity.[7] He was a foremast hand aboard the brig *Polly* from Newburyport, Mass., bound from Baltimore to Cádiz with a cargo of grain and flour. In October, immediately after the Strait was opened, the *Polly* was captured by the Algerian brig *Babazera* in the Atlantic.

● After plundering the *Polly* and stripping captain and crew to their shirts and undershorts, the Algerians manned their prize with their own crew and took the 12 Americans aboard the *Babazera*, where the captain, receiving them seated on a mat in his cabin and identifying himself as Rais Hudga Mahomet Salamia, ordered them to help man his brig. When one of them protested against working the deck in his underwear, the captain growled that he would teach them to work naked if need be, and quickly set the tone: All Christians could expect to be treated harshly "for your history and superstition in believing in a man who was crucified by the Jews, and disregarding the true doctrine of God's last and greatest prophet Mahomet."[8]

It was a week before the *Babazera* sailed through the twisting, rock-studded channel into Algiers Harbor. Foss and his shipmates studied their destination. The small harbor was heavily fortified, with a mole leading from the waterfront to an island with a large battery of cannon dominating the city. Stone aqueducts plunged down from the mountains, bringing water to the cisterns and fountains of the city squares. The early November weather was balmy, and the sun sparkled off the white buildings and the green harbor.

Ashore reality was less attractive. The narrow streets, little more than alleyways, stank with filth, and the Algerians who jostled one another to jeer at the Americans and cry out their praise to Allah for delivering the hated Christian captives were mostly in rags. Many had running sores; others were blind. The prisoners were herded to the palace and taken before Dey Hassan, a light-complexioned Turk in his sixties with a flowing beard and a mercurial disposition, who snarled at them, "Now I have got you, you Christian dogs, you shall eat stones."[9] Selecting four ships' boys to be palace servants, the dey dispatched the rest of the crew to one of Algiers's two bagnios, or jails. This one, the Bilic prison, was a large stone fortress with galleries, or wide balconies, built around a center courtyard. The Americans were marched up the steps to the third gallery, where their names were entered in the prison manifest and each man was issued a bundle containing his prison uniform: a hooded jacket, a blouse, a shirt, a pair of pantaloons and slippers, plus one blanket for bedding. They were assigned to a section of the open gallery overlooking the enclosed courtyard below.

By 5 P.M. the other prisoners came clanking back from their

work detail, a seemingly endless chain gang of exhausted men, each of whom was checked off on the prison manifest as he came into the courtyard. The long common chain was unshackled, but each man still carried a chain of his own with a ball at its end, which he had to sling over his shoulder when he walked. Shortly they were served their dinner ration: a small loaf of sour black bread per man. In each section the roster was called out, and every prisoner answered to his name. Foss estimated that there were 600 in his bagnio. At dusk they bedded down with only a blanket to cushion the stone floor.

At 3 A.M. everyone was rousted out, lined up, chained together, and marched off to the base of a nearby mountain for the day's labor. By the first light of dawn they were at work. Each man was freed from the chain gang; but he was still confined by his own chain with the 20–30-lb weight at its end. He was able to work within the radius of his chain, but to move to a new location he had to hoist the weight and move it.

The men in the work detail Foss was assigned to were using pickaxes to dig holes in the rocky base of the mountain, carrying away the debris in baskets. When a hole was completed, the guards inserted powder and touched it off, breaking away 10-to-20-ton chunks of rock, which the prisoners rolled down the mountainside to waiting sleds. Once a week the prisoners were tethered to these timber sleds, hundreds of them in long lines, and were driven with goads like oxen to haul the sleds along a stone-paved highway to the harbor.[10] There the rocks were lifted onto a barge and floated out to the end of the mole to extend it beyond the island.

At 8 A.M. and noon each day the work gang was given a ten-minute break for breakfast and lunch of a chunk of bread with vinegar. The bread, Foss wrote, "was so sour that a person must be almost starving before he can eat it." At a half hour before sunset a white flag rose atop a mosque, signifying time for daily prayers; the prisoners were chained in line and marched back to their prison galleries.

More fortunate prisoners drew jobs along the harbor: careening vessels to clean their hulls of barnacles and worm; fitting out pirate ships for the next cruise; unloading the spoils of returning corsairs. Other prisoners served as beasts of burden; everything portable was transported from one part of the city to another by prisoners carrying their loads at the ends of long poles slung over their shoulders; the alleyways were too narrow for wagons.

✦ Whatever the work detail, the labor was unremitting. On the days when the rocks were sledded to the harbor, the overseers of the sled gangs competed with one another to haul the largest loads. The winner was rewarded by the dey; so each one drove his prisoner team unmercifully, beating those who faltered or stumbled under the heavy ropes. Foss reported one incident in which a father who had been captured with his seven sons watched helplessly as one of them staggered and fell in front of a sled that crushed his legs; the son died the next day. Another prisoner was bitten on the cheek by a tarantula while carrying a timber; despite his complaint, he was driven back to work. By the end of the day his head had swollen to nearly twice its normal size, and he was finally sent to the prisoners' hospital where he died. A few weeks later another prisoner died the same way.

Those who escaped the perils of the work detail were threatened by disease. Periodic plagues swept through the unsanitary prisons. And for those who survived there were innumerable forms of punishment. For such slight offenses as malingering or talking back to a guard, the punishment was the bastinado,[11] a beating of the bare feet; the normal allotment was 150 to 200 bastinadoes.

More serious offenders suffered harsher punishment. A thief's right hand was cut off and hung around his neck while he was paraded through the city riding backward on a donkey so the populace could pelt him with stones and filth. When a few prisoners attempted unsuccessfully to escape, the dey ordered the ringleaders beheaded and the others given 500 bastinadoes. If a prisoner was so rash as—and had the rare opportunity—to seduce an Algerian woman, he was beheaded; the woman was taken to sea, tied in a weighted sack, and thrown overboard. The major crime of disparaging the Koran was punished by roasting alive, impalement,[12] or crucifixion. For the crime of killing a Muslim the dey reserved the most ingenious punishment of all—tossing the offender off the city walls to be impaled on iron hooks where he hung until he died; if he was able to pull himself loose, he fell onto the jagged rocks below.

Not far from the prison Foss discovered a cliff where in earlier times recalcitrant prisoners had been tossed onto the rocks where their bodies were carried to sea by the surf. Half a mile away was the Christian burial ground in a low, sandy area behind a row of dunes over which the waves broke during storms and uncovered the bodies, leaving the beach littered with whitening bones.

It was no wonder that the Barbary prisoners called out to their families and friends, politicians and preachers, to come to their aid. Their captors willingly forwarded the petitions in hopes of the ransom they might bring. In 1792 a group of American prisoners in Algiers sent a plaintive message to Congress, pleading for the legislators to "consider what our sufferings must have been for nearly seven years in captivity." Captain O'Brien of the *Dauphin*, who had become one of the dey's clerks, wrote an emotional appeal to the ministers of New England, New York, and Virginia, asking them to "remember us, your unfortunate brethren, late members of the family of freedom, now doomed to perpetual confinement. Pray, earnestly pray, that our grievous calamities may have a gracious end. . . . We ask you in the name of your Father in heaven, to have compassion on our miseries. . . . Lift up your voices like a trumpet; cry aloud in the cause of humanity. . . ."

The trumpet did sound all along the American coast; and the new United States came face to face for the first time with an excruciating dilemma that would plague it down to the present day: how to free Americans taken hostage in a holy war.

At last Congress faced up to the prospect either of negotiating for short-term tribute to the Barbary powers or of using force, as Jefferson had argued for so long. Some congressmen, especially from New England, were as much moved by insurance rates in the Mediterranean, which had soared from 3 percent to 50 percent. Others were convinced that the hated British were simultaneously stirring up the Indians against the United States at home and the pirates against U.S. shipping abroad.[13] Inundated by a clamor from their constituents, the congressmen began to consider a naval force for the Mediterranean. It became a great debate.

Nearly everyone recognized that Congress was deciding not so much the construction and dispatch of a few frigates as the establishment of a U.S. Navy. And despite the acknowledged pressure of public opinion, many members of the House and Senate remained opposed. The debate grew into a battle largely between the pro-navy northern representatives speaking for the shippers and the anti-navy southerners representing the plantation owners.

All of the arguments against a navy were marshaled in lengthy speeches as well as in the contemporary press. A major consideration was the continuing threat from the Indians. As Representative Jeremiah Wadsworth pointed out, "There had never been a day, from the first settlement of America to the present moment without our being at war with the Indians, in one place or another." The United States, went the argument, could not yet afford both an army to control the Indians and a navy to fight the Barbary pirates. Isolationists who clung to the notion of an America protected by the Atlantic seized on the threat of Indian warfare as a handy excuse to inveigh against a navy. They were joined by the politicians wary of too many men in uniform. Senator William Maclay contended that if the new nation had a standing army and a navy, plus "a host of revenue officers, farewell freedom in America."

The economic case against a navy was also raised. An army could be disbanded when not required; but ships, once built, continued to cost money. Some congressmen pointed to the huge sums expended by Britain and France for their navies, arguing that the United States could not yet afford such an extravagance. At one point a committee came forward with what it considered a less expensive alternative, proposing that the U.S. license privateers to attack Algerian shipping, overlooking the fact that the Barbary states had too little maritime trade to be bothered greatly by privateers.

Statistics, as always, were used to prove whatever an advocate wanted to prove. Tables of trade figures were presented to show that the savings to shipping did not match the cost of naval protection. If most of the European governments preferred to pay tribute, the case went, it followed that tribute must be cheaper. Others warned that approving a small navy was only the beginning; it was in the nature of any military establishment to expand. Still others contended that a U.S. Navy would result in provoking war with some of the European nations, far greater and more dangerous naval powers than the Barbary states. There was the argument that a Mediterranean conflict was the wrong war in the wrong place. The Barbary pirates were close to their supply depots, while an American fleet would be more than 3,000 miles from theirs. And there was the question of the captives whose plight was at the heart of the debate. Might not a naval action put them at even greater risk?

● But the pro-navy congressmen brought their own guns to bear. Alexander Hamilton was quoted against the isolationists who believed they were defended by the Atlantic Ocean. In 1787 he had written a perceptive analysis in the *Independent Journal*:[14] "The improvements in the art of navigation have, as to the facility of communication, rendered distant nations, in a great measure, neighbors." To answer the economic case against the navy, proponents pointed out that current insurance rates could be expected to go even higher if there were no protection for American shipping; the increased expenses would amount to six times the cost of a Mediterranean squadron. And while tribute might be cheaper in the short run, any treaty with the Barbary rulers would be useless if not enforced by a fleet.

As for the supply ports, American warships would be able to use most of the harbors of southern Europe. As for the problem of an ever-expanding navy, its defenders pointed out that Portugal had blockaded the entire Strait of Gibraltar with only three warships; the proposed six-ship American squadron would be quite enough. To those who worried about provoking hostilities with a European nation, the pro-navy congressmen replied that any government tempted to go to war against the United States would have its own reasons, more important than the threat of a few American warships. In fact, nearly every congressman realized that lurking behind this argument was the double menace already evident from France and Britain; the former was threatening to attack American ships, and the latter was already impressing Britons—and many Americans—serving aboard U.S. vessels. Both threats were in fact arguments for an American navy. Not least of the incentives for building the new frigates was a compelling one to any politician then as now: jobs. Thousands of men would be employed in shipyards all along the American coast.

The debate went on for four months before a compromise was reached: an agreement that if peace were negotiated with Algiers— the strongest Barbary power and the one that held the most Americans captive—all construction of the frigates would be halted. Even with this exit clause, Congress only narrowly agreed (the

House by 11 votes) to "An Act to Provide a Naval Armament." President Washington was authorized to build or buy, and $688,888 was appropriated for, three 44-gun frigates and three 36-gun frigates. March 27, 1794, the day on which President Washington signed the bill, became in effect the birthdate of the U.S. Navy.

But building the frigates took time, complicated by innumerable supply problems. Washington, expecting the appropriation to pass, had asked Secretary of War Henry Knox to prepare for the construction of half a dozen frigates. Knox, a rotund, jovial intimate of Washington's, was the son of a ship captain. He had started his own career as a bookseller, and had been lured into the army when he became enthralled by the military and naval accounts in Plutarch's *Lives.* During the American Revolution he had become General Washington's chief of artillery. As secretary of war, Knox had no naval experience, but he knew enough to look for the best ship designers he could find.

The man he settled on, Joshua Humphreys, had built his first ship at 21; he was now 43, had designed warships for the Continental Navy, and was a well-known shipbuilder in Philadelphia. Purely by accident Knox found a partner for Humphreys, a marine architect named Josiah Fox. A wealthy 30-year-old Briton, Fox had been preparing himself for a career in his family shipyard by touring the best yards of Europe; he had come to America in 1793 to survey its timber supply and incidentally visit some relatives. One of them was his cousin Andrew Ellicott, the U.S. surveyor general, who introduced Fox to Knox. The secretary of war was vastly impressed by the young Briton, and promptly hired him to assist Humphreys.

They proved, despite frequent disputes, to be an excellent team. Humphreys provided the overall supervision, and Fox, with the help of a draftsman from Humphreys's yard named William Doughty, did most of the actual designing.[15] A major argument was over the size of the frigates, Fox opting for smaller vessels. It was Humphreys's insistence on a combination of greater size and speed that produced the most efficient frigates of their time. Secretary Knox described Humphreys's intention exactly while the vessels were under construction in 1794. These new frigates, he wrote, "should combine such qualities of strength, durability, swiftness of sailing, and force, as to render them equal, if not superior, to any frigate belonging to any of the European Powers." This combination turned out to be less than perfect for chasing Barbary xebecs over the shallow waters along the North African coast. But Humphreys clearly took a longer view toward possible conflicts with the European navies that already had begun to harass the Americans.

Washington saw to it that the work on the frigates was parceled out to shipyards from Portsmouth, N.H., to Norfolk, Va., to employ expertise all along the coast and provide jobs in as many places as possible. This was the list of frigates and ports that he and Knox agreed on:

The *United States* (44 guns), to be built in Philadelphia, Pa.
The *Constitution* (44 guns), Boston, Mass.
The *President* (44 guns), New York, N.Y.
The *Constellation* (36 guns), Baltimore, Md.
The *Chesapeake* (36 guns), Norfolk, Va.
The *Congress* (36 guns), Portsmouth, N.H.

Long consultations—and not a few wrangles—over the multitudinous ship dimensions took months. The final measurements were not taken off the mold loft floors until the summer of 1795, more than a year after Congress's appropriation. The specifications included the use of live oak, the hardest and most durable wood, for crucial points of stress. American live oak grows in a few southern swamplands where northerners who went to cut it found the climate hot and pestilential. They returned with so little live oak that Humphreys had to order a delay in the construction of two frigates so work on the other four could proceed. Humphreys made the right decision in demanding larger frigates, but he made the wrong one in giving oversight authority to the naval officers who would command the warships. Most of them insisted on too many guns, further complicating and delaying construction.[16] By December of 1795 none of the frigates was more than half-finished. It looked like another year at least before any of them would slide down the ways. And already, with its first vessel only half-built, the new U.S. Navy was threatened by peace.

Joshua Humphreys the shipbuilder was no relation to David Humphreys the diplomat. But the former provided invaluable assistance to the latter in his sporadic negotiations with the dey of Algiers, to whom the work in the American shipyards was no secret. In fact, it was the dey who sent out a peace feeler, suggesting in a message to Humphreys that Algiers might be interested in peace for the price of $2.5 million, plus two frigates. Humphreys dispatched his assistant Joseph Donaldson, Jr., to Algiers. Donaldson at the time was suffering from such a severe case of gout that he was on crutches. He arrived in Algiers in the summer of 1795 and was met by Micaiah Bacri, the dey's chief moneylender, and Captain Richard O'Brien, the American prisoners' spokesman and clerk to the dey. Donaldson limped to the nearest couch and tossed down his crutches, emitting a stream of profanity as he lay down. Bacri could not understand English very well, but was shocked at what he thought he heard. O'Brien reassured him in the local lingua franca: "The Ambassador," he explained, "is only saying his prayers and giving God thanks for his safe arrival." Nodding, Bacri murmured, "His devotion is very fervent."

Donaldson had been briefed by Captain O'Brien, who had risked his neck by sending a frank assessment of Dey Hassan to Humphreys. "If the Dey Gets in his usual Blustering Convulsions of Passion," O'Brien coached, "and orders the Ambassador to be gone from his presence and depart Algiers, Obey these orders Instantaniously"—but, he added, leave someone behind to be on hand when the dey finds his bluff called and inevitably calms down. In short, be prepared in dealing for the prisoners to haggle as in any Barbary bazaar. It did not get to the point of Donaldson having to depart, though the dey did tell him to. Donaldson, in an understandably grouchy mood, gave as good as he got, and perhaps won Hassan's grudging admiration. It was obvious, too, that the dey was well aware of those frigates being built in America.

Captain O'Brien had suggested an opening bid of about $500,000. But after long sessions of angry bargaining,[17] the best Donaldson could do was settle for a lump-sum payment of $642,000 ($240,000 of it for the dey's personal account) plus a promise of annual tribute of $21,600, payable in arms—guns, powder, and shot as well as timber and cordage.

Thomas Jefferson by this time had resigned as secretary of state and had gone home to Monticello. But his friend James Madison sent him regular reports from the capital in Philadelphia. Jefferson must have chafed at this ultimate tribute agreed to by his successor Edmund Randolph and President Washington. They could, of course, rationalize that the "Warlike Stores" provided by the Americans would not be used against them since they bought a peace treaty between the two countries. (And the treaty forbade the dey to sell them to any other Barbary ruler.) But Jefferson could not forget his promise to John Paul Jones only three years earlier that the United States would never trade arms for hostages. Evidently President Washington already had forgotten.

The treaty was signed on September 5, 1795, to the thunder of a 21-gun salute and the raising of the American flag. But the dey temporarily withheld release of the prisoners until he could see the gold and silver coins of at least a down payment. It was a shrewd move on his part because the American diplomats promptly found it extremely difficult to raise cash in Europe. The Bank of the United States sent $800,000 in 6 percent certificates to a London banking house; but it proved nearly impossible to find purchasers of certificates from a new nation whose credit was questionable.

The delays did nothing to improve the dey's mood. He had agreed to let his prisoner clerk, Captain O'Brien, go to London to raise ransom money. But O'Brien reported to Humphreys, "I am sorry to inform you that in London Gold and Silver Can not be procured." Humphreys meanwhile was tapping every other possible European source, so far without success. Months went by while the prisoners waited anxiously and the dey became ever more fretful. Not only had no cash been forthcoming, but none of the promised arms had arrived.

American diplomat Joel Barlow[18] was designated as U.S. consul pro tem, and joined Donaldson in Algiers. Barlow had earlier described Dey Hassan as "the most restless and impatient man in the world." He came to Algiers armed with $27,000 worth of brocaded robes, jeweled pistols, and trinkets as gifts for the greedy monarch. But he soon was reporting that the dey still was as angry as "a petulent child . . . it became impossible to speak to him with safety on the subject." Barlow tried every excuse he could think of. It was probable, he explained to the dey, that the ships carrying tribute had been delayed by bad weather or seized by one of Europe's navies. The dey was not persuaded. "You are a liar," he snarled, "and your government is a liar."

Humphreys was meanwhile trying to reassure the American prisoners, who were understandably verging on hysteria. Some of them had been imprisoned for as long as 12 years; and to be forced to wait more months after the treaty that with such fanfare had supposedly released them was a final twist of torture. Humphreys promised them that "you are neither forgotten nor neglected by your Country," and urged them "to have a little more patience." It must have been small comfort under the circumstances. The dey by this time was firing off angry letters to Humphreys questioning U.S. intentions. Four months had elapsed, he pointed out, since the treaty signing "without the least Ratification on the part of the United States of America; which makes me doubt the authenticity of the said Donaldson's Commission. . . . I cannot help doubting the Veracity of his Credentials."

Humphreys had written the dey to explain one reason for the delay: "it is necessary (according to our Constitution) that [the treaty] should be ratified by the President, by and with the advice and consent of the Senate, before it can become the Supreme law of the Land." (The Senate ratified the treaty on March 2, 1796.) But this sort of democratic constitutional explanation made little impression on the dey, despite the fact that he was using a similar argument, claiming that the members of his own legislative body, the Divan, "are very impatient, and by discontenting them, it is out of my power to remedy the fatal consequences that might ensue"—a doubtful excuse in view of the fact that he had not assembled the Divan during his reign.

What the dey was threatening, and pretending to blame on his Divan, was a repudiation of the treaty. Captain O'Brien in London already had warned, "I am Very apprehensive of some fatal consequences in so much time having elapsed." O'Brien was afraid the dey "will declare the treatie void and send out his Corsairs—try and capture the American Vessels that has [sic] very imprudently entered the Mediterranean"—which many American captains had done as soon as they had heard that a treaty had been signed. By

March of 1796 Humphreys was writing to Thomas Pinckney, the U.S. minister in London, asking him to alert U.S. shippers to "give notice to all Citizens of the United States concerned . . . that they may expose themselves to great danger by attempting to proceed up the Mediterranean." By the next month, nearly seven months after the treaty signing, the dey's patience was finally exhausted; he gave Barlow a deadline of one month, after which he would send his pirate ships out again after Americans. Barlow feared the prospect of having to work out a wholly new treaty and probably for many more captives.

Onto this tense scene came Micaiah Bacri,[19] the astute money manager. Barlow (who identified him only as "Bacri the Jew") had discovered that he was the dey's most highly trusted financial adviser. So Barlow offered him a commission of $18,000 (some of which he could use to bribe influential aides to the dey) for interceding. Bacri agreed and, knowing the dey's passion for warships, proposed that the United States promise him an American frigate in return for waiting a few more months. (He did not have to remind Barlow that the dey had asked for two frigates during the negotiations.) Barlow suggested a 20-gun vessel; Bacri talked him up to 24 guns. Indeed, Barlow wrote, "The novelty of the proposition gained the dey's attention." The dey accepted, after upping the number of guns to 36 and asking that it be considered as a gift to his daughter. Why the dey's daughter needed a 36-gun warship was not discussed; what was important was that the dey had been bought off for a while longer.

And at last Humphreys was able to find some bankers who would buy the U.S. certificates: $400,000 worth in Leghorn and $200,000 worth in Lisbon. He sent word to Barlow in Algiers, who persuaded Bacri to advance enough to temporarily satisfy the dey. Captain O'Brien promptly sailed from Leghorn with half of the specie from the bankers—and was captured by Tripolitan pirates.

Fortunately for the frustrated Americans, Yusuf Karamanli, the bashaw of Tripoli, had a healthy respect for the powerful dey of Algiers, and released the vessel and its valuable cargo when he realized its destination. On July 12, 1796, Joel Barlow finally could write to his superiors, "I have the pleasure at last to announce to you the liberation of our people from Slavery in this place."[20]

The American hostages had remained in prison for nearly a year after the signing of the treaty; six of them had died only a few weeks earlier when a plague had swept through the dey's dungeons. Thirty-one of the original 119 had succumbed to the harsh life of Algerian prisoners. And of the survivors, Barlow reported, "Several of them are probably rendered incapable of earning their living. One is in a state of total blindness; another is reduced nearly to the same condition; two or three carry the marks of unmerciful treatment in ruptures produced by hard labour; and others have had their constitutions injured by the plague."[21]

Following the dey's example—in fact, prodded by the dey, the bashaw of Tripoli signed a treaty with the United States (for a mere $58,000 plus the promise of naval supplies) in November of 1796, and bey Hamouda of Tunis followed suit the next year.[22] The United States at last had peace in the Mediterranean and protection for its rapidly increasing shipping. But the government had paid heavily, including naval arms that could someday be used against Americans. Moreover, at the same time, peace in the Mediterranean meant a possible death blow to the infant U.S. Navy.

President Washington now demonstrated the cunning political mind behind his august facade. Reminding Congress of the clause in the 1794 appropriation for the six frigates mandating an end to their construction if there was peace with Algiers, he pointed out that "it is incumbent upon the Executive to suspend all orders respecting the building of the frigates." But, he slyly added, "inasmuch as the loss which the public might incur might be considerable from the disposition of workmen, from certain works or operations being suddenly dropped or left unfinished, and from the derangement of the whole system, consequent on an immediate suspension of all proceedings under it, I have, therefore, thought it advisable, before taking such a step, to submit the subject to the Senate and House of Representatives, that such measures may be adopted in the premises as may best comport with the public interest."

In short, stopping construction meant the loss of hundreds of jobs. And Washington did not have to remind the legislators that (as he had carefully planned) the work was spread through six states comprising most of their constituencies. If Congress wanted to throw all those Americans out of work, Congress could take the blame. It took the congressmen only 48 hours to authorize the president to continue work on three of the frigates and also grant him discretionary power to continue building the remaining three if and when he found it necessary.

By 1797 the president was John Adams. Although the Constitution provided for the president to serve for as many terms as he could get elected, Washington refused to run for a third term and retired at last to Mount Vernon.[23] Two political parties had formed by now: the central-government Federalists, who had nominated Adams and Thomas Pinckney (recently returned from England), and the states' rights Republicans, who had persuaded Jefferson to stand for president with Aaron Burr as his running mate. Adams had won by three electoral votes, and Jefferson, the runner-up, became vice president.[24]

President Adams sent off three consuls to join those of the other countries that had treaties with the Barbary states. Captain Richard O'Brien, who had been the spokesman for the American prisoners, was appointed consul general to the Barbary states and returned to Algiers. James Leander Cathcart, who like O'Brien had been a captive of the Algerians, was posted to Tripoli. For Tunis Adams chose William Eaton, the former U.S. Army captain who would later mount an overland expedition to overthrow the bashaw of Tripoli. Consul General O'Brien reached Algiers first, in March of 1798, in command of the *Crescent*, the new frigate promised to the dey.[25] Cathcart and Eaton followed aboard the 12-gun brig *Sophia*, arriving nearly a year later.

They were an odd lot. O'Brien, who had commanded a privateer in the Revolution before being captured by the Algerians as master of the *Dauphin* in 1785, was a rough-and-ready first-generation Irishman, poorly educated but blessed with a strong native intelligence. Cathcart was the quintessential entrepreneur. He had immigrated to America from Ireland as a boy, had served aboard a Continental Navy frigate, had been captured by the British, and had escaped from a prison ship in New York. He had been a foremast hand aboard the *Maria* when she had been taken by the Algerians in 1785, and had worked his way up the ladder of promotion among the prisoners to become clerk to Prime Minister Hassan; and when Hassan had succeeded as dey, Cathcart had been appointed his chief Christian secretary. (He had also wangled permission to keep a tavern for Christian prisoners who were permitted to spend their hard-earned pittances on alcohol, and he had used his profits to buy two more taverns.) During the negotiations with Donaldson for the treaty, Cathcart had joined O'Brien in serving both the dey and Donaldson as go-betweens.[26] By the time of his release Cathcart had made enough money from his taverns to purchase a bark to return home to Philadelphia, where he had married a local belle named Jane Woodside.

—● William Eaton, still the gung-ho combatant of the Revolution and the Indian wars, was the least likely diplomat of the three, outspoken and impatient with the time-consuming niceties of international relations. He took the customary bonanza of gifts to the bey of Tunis: four pairs of gold-mounted pistols, a musket set with diamonds, a gold watch, and a snuffbox, both decorated with diamonds, a diamond ring and bolts of satin and brocade. But he found Bey Hamouda ungrateful and brutish. Nevertheless he and Cathcart were able to negotiate changes in the treaty with Tunis to which the Senate had objected. Then Cathcart went on to Tripoli, arriving April 5, 1799.

A grumpy Bashaw Yusuf Karamanli at first refused to see him.[27] But eventually gifts to the bashaw amounting to $21,000 plus $1,500 in bribes to his aides sealed the treaty that Yusuf had agreed to in 1796. Yusuf also claimed that Consul General O'Brien had promised him a frigate. Cathcart knew nothing about this; but he promptly used the claim to further a long-smoldering feud with O'Brien.

Their animosity went back to their captivity in Algiers, where forced propinquity and hardship, far from inspiring comradeship, had instead fostered mutual loathing. When O'Brien had been appointed consul general for the Barbary states, he had tried unsuccessfully to block Cathcart's selection as consul to Tripoli and had succeeded in delaying it. But what had triggered a new, even greater animosity between the two consuls was a woman.

When consuls Eaton and Cathcart sailed to their posts aboard the *Gloria*, Cathcart brought along his bride and a comely 20-year-old English emigrant named Betsy Robinson. Miss Robinson had fled a stepmother in Cumberland and found her way across the Atlantic to Philadelphia, where she had planned to join her brother. Finding him gone on a voyage to China, and with her funds nearly spent, she had accepted a job as a "companion" to Mrs. Cathcart. But evidently she soon found that Mr. Cathcart regarded her as a mere servant, wounding her English pride at such treatment, especially by an Irishman. Moreover, his rough sailor's manners and expletives were too much for her cultured sensibilities.

On arrival in Algiers, she announced that she was staying aboard ship for the return voyage to America, primly explaining that she had expected a great deal more refinement in a gentleman of the diplomatic service. Cathcart's characteristically profane reaction drove Miss Robinson into the arms of Consul General O'Brien— literally, it turned out, because she and O'Brien were married six weeks later. In his best forecastle language Cathcart accused O'Brien of seducing his maid, while Mrs. Cathcart reacted with even greater anger at the prospect of her former servant outranking her socially as the wife of the consul general.[28] Now the two men continued to snipe at each other, mostly in angry letters to Eaton.

Cathcart, a roly-poly, baby-faced man who enjoyed altercation, dutifully reported his activities to Consul General O'Brien, usually in curt, sarcastic messages most of which he forwarded through Eaton. Cathcart took malevolent pleasure in blaming his difficulties on O'Brien's false assurance of a gift brig, maintaining that it cost the United States some $23,000 in bribes to pacify the bashaw and his court. Cathcart frequently addressed O'Brien more in the tone of superior to employee than that of consul to consul general: "You will please forward on my salary as it becomes due in gold or silver. . . . You will likewise send me my journal of our negotiations with the Regency of Algiers." And: "You will please facilitate the payment of the following bills as soon as possible."

O'Brien, for his part, treated Cathcart with stony silence; Cathcart complained to Eaton that O'Brien answered none of his letters. And when Eaton made the mistake of admonishing Cathcart that this squabbling behavior was unfortunate, he elicited a torrent of invective. Claiming that he had treated O'Brien "like a brother" while in Algerian captivity, Cathcart charged O'Brien with ingratitude and treachery, and even hinted at a duel.

"I can not help declaiming," he wrote, "that I view Mr. O'Brien as one of the most ungrateful of men, and shall never be on terms of intimacy with him again until he gives me suitable satisfaction for his conduct towards me, which he may depend I will require from him in a very decisive manner when a proper opportunity offers." After a long litany of O'Brien's iniquities, Cathcart, as if finally out of breath, wrote, "I assure you I feel myself much happier since I have committed my thoughts to writing, especially as I intend this to be the last time I shall ever mention Mr. O'Brien's name except in an official manner"—a promise he did not keep for long.

At length O'Brien did deign to write to Cathcart, by way of Eaton and perhaps at his urging; and the tenor of his reply was predictably characterized by the angry recipient in yet another complaint to Eaton. Thanking him for forwarding the letter, "which I'm sorry you did not open," Cathcart wrote, "I never, in my life, read more malice, ignorance and contradiction jumbled together. His letter is a perfect chaos."

By now Cathcart and O'Brien were feuding with Eaton as well. Eaton accused O'Brien of opening and reading his mail as it passed through the diplomatic pipeline in Algiers.[29] O'Brien, like other Americans in the Mediterranean, worried about Eaton's total disdain of all diplomatic courtesies in dealing with the Barbary powers. Indeed, Eaton's hatred extended to nearly everyone in the Barbary states. "There is not a scoundrel among them from the prince to the muleteer," he raged, "who will not beg and steal." When O'Brien complained that some of Eaton's expostulations sounded scurrilous, Eaton angrily replied, "You complain of my *Scurrility of Stile*—I apprehend it is rather *plain dealing* which offends you."

Consul Cathcart was meanwhile preoccupied with threats of war from the bashaw of Tripoli. Yusuf Karamanli was becoming more disgruntled and increasingly hostile over the disparity between his tribute from the United States and that of the dey of Algiers. Cathcart cautioned the U.S. consul at Leghorn, Thomas Appleton, that American shipping should give Tripoli a wide berth. "Shun this place as you would a whirlpool," he warned. And presciently, it turned out, Cathcart advised Secretary of State Timothy Pickering that while more tribute—say, about $10,000—might temporarily allay the bashaw's indignation at being paid less than the other Barbary potentates, what would be needed in the longer run was a show of naval force. "A well-timed energy will without doubt intimidate the present Pasha and his successors from daring to insult our flag, while too great condescension will seem to indicate that he may commit depredations upon our commerce with impunity."

◑ One of the bashaw's pirate captains proceeded to support Cathcart's contention in October of 1800 by capturing the New York merchantman *Catherine*. Protesting at this violation of the new treaty, Cathcart persuaded the bashaw to release the *Catherine*, but only after she had been rifled of most of her cargo. Cathcart again warned Secretary Pickering, proposing that "two of our largest frigates"[30] be sent to humble the bashaw, maintaining that now was the time "that our natural character ought to be established with this Regency." He sent another warning to all American consuls in the area that the Mediterranean was becoming increasingly perilous for American vessels.

But while Cathcart and Eaton were struggling to deal with the growing greed of the bashaw and the bey, the most flagrant humiliation of the American flag came suddenly and unexpectedly from Algiers.

Dey Hassan of Algiers had concluded the first of the three treaties and had helped with the other two. But Hassan had died, to be succeeded by one Bobba Mustapha, whom Consul Eaton had described picturesquely after his first audience:

> We were shown to a huge, shaggy beast, sitting on his rump upon a low bench covered with a cushion of embroidered velvet, with his hind legs gathered up like a tailor, or a bear. On our approach to him, he reached out his forepaw as if to receive something to eat. Our guide exclaimed, "Kiss the Dey's hand!" The consul general bowed very elegantly, and kissed it, and we followed his example in succession. The animal seemed at that moment to be in a harmless mood. He grinned several times but made very little noise. . . . Can any man believe that this elevated brute has seven kings of Europe, two republics, and a continent tributary to him when his whole naval force is not equal to two line-of-battle ships? It is so.

On the afternoon of September 17, 1800, the U.S. frigate *George Washington* hove to off Algiers harbor. Consul O'Brien and the Algerian captain of the port came aboard. The *George Washington's* commander was William Bainbridge, a 26-year-old from Princeton, N.J., who had been born just too late to serve in the Continental Navy but had risen fast in the merchant marine and then in the new U.S. Navy to the rank of captain. At six feet he was tall for the nineteenth century, with jet-black hair and long sideburns. The *George Washington* was a converted merchantman mounting 24 guns with which President John Adams had hoped to impress the dey when he dispatched her to Algiers with some of the gifts promised in the treaty plus a cargo of coffee, tea, sugar, herring, china, and gunpowder. But Bainbridge made the mistake of letting the captain of the port direct him into the harbor to anchor under the guns of Algiers's fortress. The *George Washington*'s cargo was unloaded and she was taking on a return cargo of grapes, figs, oranges, almonds, and pomegranates when Dey Bobba Mustapha announced that he was requisitioning her for a voyage to Constantinople.

The dey had promised the sultan of Turkey, Selim III, a tribute of specie plus some animals and slaves. As Bainbridge angrily wrote in his logbook, he was nearly ready to sail for home when "we receive a positive command from a Dispotic Dey of Algiers that we must be the porters of savage Tygers & more savage Algerines Ambassadors in Compliment to the Grand Seignor at Constantinople."[31]

Consul General O'Brien and Captain Bainbridge protested. But, as Bainbridge described the exchange in his report to the navy secretary, the dey retorted, "You pay me tribute, by that you become my slaves." Not only was the *George Washington* within range of the fortress guns that could sink her if Bainbridge tried to slip her anchor; but the dey also made it clear that defiance of his order could lead to renewed hostilities.[32] And by now Algiers's navy was formidably supported by the new frigate supplied by the United States as part of the treaty. Already the arms-for-hostages deal had boomeranged.

While Bainbridge watched in fury—and, it was reported, some of his sailors openly wept—the Algerian minister of marine and admiral of the fleet came aboard, hauled down the *George Washington*'s U.S. ensign and replaced it with the crescent of Algiers. Into the frigate's cabin went $800,000 in specie and another $200,000 worth of jewels for the sultan. Into her hold went a Noah's Ark cargo of four lions, four tigers, four antelope, 12 parrots, 25 cattle, four horses, a herd of 150 sheep, and an uncounted number of ostriches. Aboard marched 100 black slaves of both sexes, plus the Algerian envoy to the sultan, with a retinue of 99 aides.

● Bainbridge grudgingly set sail early in the morning of October 19, 1800. As soon as he was out of range of the dey's harbor guns, he raised the American flag above the Algerian ensign. But he dutifully set his course for Constantinople. The frigate was not a passenger ship; with her decks dominated by her guns, she presented little open space. Crowded with 200 passengers besides her crew of 131, not to mention the animals fouling the hold, the 624-ton *George Washington* virtually wallowed in the Mediterranean seas, leaving a redolent fragrance in her wake. The Moslems sprawled about on the main deck, constantly underfoot when the crew tried to work the ship. The sailors became so exasperated that Bainbridge had to order the rum ration cut in half to avoid a drunken confrontation. Five times a day the faithful assembled on deck to prostrate themselves in prayer. Because of storms and head winds the frigate frequently was forced to tack. And Bainbridge no doubt enjoyed his passengers' confusion as they tried to face Mecca. Finally the Algerian envoy stationed a man at the binnacle to watch the compass and signal which direction was east.

The dey of Algiers's humiliation of Captain Bainbridge and the *George Washington* stirred Consul William Eaton to one of his lengthier flights of patriotic loquacity: "Have we not already seen one of our national ships of war navigating the sea, in the view of the world, under the flag of the *pirate* of Algiers? . . . Is not this alone sufficient to awake indignation? Or was the degrading exhibition too far removed from our view to excite an emotion? But this, 'tis said, was the *price of peace*! Are we then reduced to the humility of bartering our national glory for the forbearance of a *Barbary pirate*! I am persuaded that this conception, however compulsory, cannot sit easily on the sensibilities of our government and nation—But the scene has been acted—The impression is made on the world—and it will require a series of brilliant actions to blot it out."

The *George Washington* slipped into Constantinople's harbor under the darkness of November 8, 1800. The next morning she was discovered by the sultan's aides swinging to her anchor and flying a flag never seen before inside the Golden Horn. Sultan Selim III was fascinated by the new warship and by her tall, impressive commander. (He also took it as a good omen that the new flag bore stars, as did the Turkish ensign.) He ordered gifts sent aboard the frigate and the proper salutes fired. Bainbridge was lionized by the sultan, his grand admiral, and his aides,[33] and when the *George Washington* set sail down the Sea of Marmora, Bainbridge took with him a firman from the sultan guaranteeing him respect from all the nations of the Ottoman Empire, including the Barbary states.

By the time the frigate had returned to Algiers's harbor at the end of January 1801, the dey had decided to seize her and throw Bainbridge and his crew in prison. He sent out word inviting Bainbridge to sail into the harbor, slyly promising safe passage out whenever he wished. Evidently reassured by his firman from the sultan—though dangerously, considering his previous experience— Bainbridge anchored again in the harbor and presented himself before the dey, who promptly berated him and threatened to put him under arrest. Bainbridge produced the sultan's firman; and, he later recounted, the "blood thirsting tyrant became a mild, humble and even crouching dependent."

On January 30, 1801, the *George Washington* set sail for home. She arrived in Philadelphia, after a stormy passage, on April 19. Bainbridge was still seething over his experience as he hastened to the new capital of Washington, D.C., to report to the new president, Thomas Jefferson.

CHAPTER 4

★ ★ ★

"CHASTISE THEIR INSOLENCE . . ."

At first it appeared that President Jefferson had forgotten the Barbary pirates. He had not.

For nearly three years as President Washington's secretary of state, he had struggled with the problem directly, frustrated by the rejection of his proposals for armed force and Congress's decision (not contested by President Washington) to follow the European example of tribute. As Adams's vice president, Jefferson had had to watch while the United States continued trying to buy off the Barbary tyrants with little success. Now it was his turn. But for the moment he had even bigger problems at home.

He had won the election in a bitter campaign in which his detractors had condemned him as a subversive "atheist." The election for the first time had been forced into the House of Representatives, where the members had wearily gone through 36 ballots in a six-day session.[1] His opponent, John Adams, supremely confident of reelection, had been shattered. In an embittered gesture of revenge he had spent his last hours as president appointing new judges and officeholders sympathetic to the Federalists. Jefferson faced the prospect not only of firing many of these new appointees but also of denying jobs to hundreds of patronage-hungry Republicans—at a time when the total number of federal workers was 130.

He also had to deal with an angry and divided populace. Federalists and Republicans had savaged one another during the campaign; now the Republicans were greedy for revenge, and the Federalists were convinced that the sacrilegious, revolutionary President Jefferson would plunge the United States into the anarchy from which the conservative President Adams and centralist Secretary Hamilton had saved them.

Washington, D.C., the U.S. capital for only nine months, was hardly conducive to an efficient administration. It was a swampy lowland, raw and cold in winter, a quagmire in spring, and hot and pestilential in summer. The ambitious city plan designed by Pierre L'Enfant was yet to be realized. Most of the town consisted of clusters of huts and small wooden houses amid the trees. Goose Creek, a stream crossing Pennsylvania Avenue, had been magisterially renamed the Tiber; but the town still featured a public whipping post. The capitol, only half-finished, and the "President's House," little more completed, were connected (if that is the word) by an unpaved road that was dusty in dry weather and a rutted bog when it rained. Washington did not even have that edifice usually first to be built in New England, a church; religious services were held on Sundays in the House of Representatives, with a band attempting, not always successfully, to provide music for the hymns.

As vice president, Thomas Jefferson had been living at Conrad & McMunn's Tavern at the corner of New Jersey Avenue and T Street, one of the half-dozen boardinghouses favored by senators and congressmen. Conrad & McMunn's was less than two blocks from the Capitol. And at noon on March 4, 1801, Jefferson walked to his inauguration, accompanied by a ragtag procession of Republican congressmen, a couple of holdover Cabinet secretaries, a company of Maryland artillery (complete with cannon), and a straggling group of Washingtonians. At the north wing of the Capitol, the only section completed, he was greeted by a salute from the local militia and the assembled members of the House and Senate, plus nearly a thousand visitors.

Jefferson had labored over his inaugural address in an attempt to heal the wounds of the election. "Every difference of opinion is not a difference of principle," he had written. "We have been called by different names brethren of the same principle. We are all Republicans. We are all Federalists." And he urged, "Let us, then, fellow citizens, unite with one heart and one mind." Unfortunately he read his address so softly that no one but those closest to him could hear it. Many of those present were more interested in the fact that

Jefferson was the first president to be inaugurated in long pants instead of knee britches.

He and Vice President Burr were sworn in by Chief Justice John Marshall (whom Adams had just appointed and whom Jefferson cordially disliked). The ceremony concluded and the new president walked back to his boardinghouse where 30 other tenants had already assembled around the dinner table. He refused a seat of honor, taking his usual place at the foot of the table farthest from the warming fireplace.

John Adams, though still president until Jefferson was sworn in, had left the White House for his Massachusetts home early on the morning of the inauguration.[2] Jefferson stayed on at Conrad & McMunn's for another two weeks before moving into the presidential residence. It still was far from completed and was sparsely furnished. The walls of the East Room (later to be the main reception room) remained unplastered. The main staircase had not been installed. The slate roof leaked. The entrance was fronted by crude wooden steps. The grounds were bare.

The new occupant settled into the few rooms that were livable. He had some furniture brought down from his former residence in Philadelphia. He chose what is now the Cabinet Room for his office, decorating it with potted plants on the windowsills and filling a desk drawer with his favorite gardening tools. He also had two indoor toilets installed, to avoid the indignity of being seen by all every time he had to visit the presidential outhouse.

He announced that the White House belonged to all Americans, not just to the president, and opened it to anyone who wanted to wander in. Many of those who did were as interested in the president as in his domicile. His red hair turning gray at 60, he often could be seen shuffling about in slippers that had replaced his riding boots after a canter in the countryside surrounding the White House.[3] His informality endeared him to his Republican admirers, but it did not impress the protocol-minded diplomats, especially from the Old World. Britain and France had finally condescended in 1792 to send ministers to Washington. When in 1803 a new British minister, one Anthony Merry, arrived, donned in full military regalia, and presented his credentials to the president, he took it as a calculated affront to his country when he was greeted by Jefferson in baggy corduroy slacks and slippers.

Because Jefferson's daughters preferred Monticello, he usually entertained without a hostess, and most of his dinners were stag. His invitations were readily accepted when it was discovered that the White House chef Julien, whom Jefferson had brought from France, prepared gourmet meals and that the wine cellar was elegant. Though European in content, Jefferson's dinners were held American style at 4 P.M., partly because he preferred evenings alone when he would work and wander about the echoing mansion. His only companion was his pet mockingbird; the president would open its cage so it could fly about the room, settling on his desk or perching on his shoulder to sing for him while he went over his papers. And late each night it would hop behind him when Jefferson trudged up the backstairs to his bedroom.

When summer came, mosquitoes swarmed up from the swamps, malaria cases filled the Navy Yard hospital, and the capital was deserted, Jefferson mounted Wildair, his favorite horse, and rode to Monticello. He liked his carriage, but the roads were so rutted and crossed so many streams that it was easier to make the trip on horseback. He had chosen his old friend James Madison as secretary of state; Madison's estate was only 30 miles from Monticello, so the two men settled matters of foreign policy by riding to each other's homes, away from the distractions of Washington.

As far as Jefferson was concerned, the major foreign-policy decision concerned his old bugbear, the Barbary pirates. Two years earlier the *Journal of the Captivity and Sufferings of John Foss* had been published, confirming the many previous accounts of the barbarous treatment of Christian prisoners by their Muslim captors and arousing the anger of most Americans. The dey of Algiers's impressment of the *George Washington* to carry tribute to the sultan particularly enraged Jefferson and his constituents alike. Shortly after Captain Bainbridge had reported to the president, the new secretary of state, James Madison, wrote to Consul General O'Brien that the incident had "deeply affected the sensibility, not only of the President but of the people of the United States."

But now the question of what to do about the Barbary problem was complicated by two important considerations. John Adams had finally concluded a treaty with France, ending that unofficial war but also providing Congress with the excuse to pass—on March 3, the day before Jefferson's inauguration—an act ironically worded as "providing for a naval peace establishment," which in fact drastically reduced the size of the navy.[4] And Jefferson had promised during the election campaign to cut the costs of government. He had selected as his secretary of the treasury Albert Gallatin, the Swiss-born financier who had been a stalwart Republican in Congress but who also had been a stern opponent of a large U.S. Navy, which he regarded as an extravagance beyond the nation's means. Only ten days after the inauguration, Gallatin presented a financial plan that included deep cuts in the armed forces, the savings to be earmarked for reducing the public debt and permitting the repeal of excise taxes, another Republican campaign promise. Eager to cut government expenses, Jefferson agreed.[5]

By now those frigates authorized by Congress in President Washington's administration had finally been launched.[6] The navy had also been augmented by other vessels built by private subscription—the *Philadelphia* by the merchants of that city, for example, the *New York* by similar backing, and the *Essex*, built by subscriptions raised in Salem and Essex counties in Massachusetts.[7] When Jefferson took office, there were 13 frigates in the U.S. Navy, of which Congress in its cost-cutting mood had mandated that seven should be decommissioned.[8] The cut involved men as well as ships. Congress ordered that the frigates should be manned by two thirds of their wartime crews. The officer corps was reduced to nine captains, 36 lieutenants, and 150 midshipmen; all others were to be discharged.

But Jefferson still had six frigates. And because the United States was at least temporarily at peace with the other European nations, he at last found himself in a position to make the decision he had advocated 16 years earlier in Paris: to confront the Barbary powers with what naval force he had.

On March 9, 1801, five days after his inauguration, Jefferson convened his Cabinet to consider the proposition of sending a naval squadron to the Mediterranean. The assembled Cabinet members had little doubt that he had already made up his mind. Jefferson had complained that the tribute obligations he had inherited from his predecessors were "money thrown away," adding, "There is no end to the demand of these powers, nor any security in their promises." He had written to Secretary of State Madison that "I am an enemy to all these doceurs, tributes & humiliations. I know that nothing will stop the eternal increase of demands from these pirates but the presence of an armed force, and it will be more economical & more honorable to use the same means at once for suppressing their insolencies."

The problem, of course, was the constitutional right of Congress, not the executive, to declare war. At the Cabinet meeting Levi Lincoln, the Massachusetts lawyer and Congressman whom Jefferson had selected for attorney general, warned that American warships could not attack any foreign vessels without a congressional declaration of war. Treasury Secretary Gallatin agreed. But none of the Cabinet members argued against sending a squadron to the Mediterranean. Secretary of State Madison and Henry Dearborn of Maine, the new secretary of war, went further, contending that the president should proclaim openly that he was authorizing the squadron's commander to attack any vessel threatening American commerce.

Four days later Secretary Madison received support for the decision in a report from James Leander Cathcart, the U.S. consul in Tripoli. "The cruisers of this Regency are now fitting out for sea and will sail the beginning of April, probably to capture Americans. I have forwarded circular letters to all our consuls, from Trieste to Lisbon, to detain the American vessels in port, and by no means permit them to sail unless under convoy." Meanwhile Cathcart had warned William Eaton in Tunis: "Our affairs seems [sic] drawing to a crisis; Murad Reis[9] is fitting out, and from the number of water casks he has on board we may suppose, for a three month cruise."

Cathcart had protested to the bashaw against these warlike activities, but his messages had gone unanswered, and the consul in Tripoli had been sending daily messages of anguish to Eaton in Tunis. On March 19 he had written, "I am kept in the most tormenting state of suspense and have not heard one syllable from the Bashaw." By the next day he had almost given up hope: "Adieu, friend Eaton, this is a dreadful anxious moment with me. Alarm our honest mariners. The rest we must trust to Providence. I shall keep the bear at bay as long as possible." On April 17 he had notified Eaton and Consul General O'Brien in Algiers that "the cruisers are nearly ready to sail."

Jefferson's Cabinet members meanwhile continued to discuss the problem for another two months. By May 15 it was finally decided to send the squadron. What neither Jefferson nor his Cabinet knew was that on the previous day Bashaw Yusuf Karamanli had sent his soldiers to the U.S. Consulate in Tripoli to chop down its flagpole, the picturesque Barbary method of opening hostilities[10]—and the first official declaration of war against the new United States. Cathcart left Tripoli ten days later, arriving in Leghorn June 2. And from his post in Tunis, Consul Eaton was moved to one of his more eloquent exclamations. "It is now a fair question whether our treasury shall be opened to buy oil of roses to perfume that pirate's beard," he wrote to Secretary Smith, "or our gun batteries to chastise his temerity."

President Jefferson regarded himself as a strict constitutionalist, quite aware that he needed a congressional declaration of war to attack the Barbary powers. But Congress was in recess. And Jefferson did not call for a special session, even when a few weeks later the news of Tripoli's declaration reached Washington. No doubt he was understandably disinclined to have the legislative branch of the government meddling in the executive's affairs so early in his administration; and there was the possibility that most of the members might not bother to come to Washington anyway. So Jefferson found himself, after urging naval action against the Barbary states for 16 years, as president and commander in chief yet still unable to use the force he believed necessary.

It was one of the earliest tests of what would be debated down the years as the restrictions on the power of the president in time of emergency. In this case Jefferson was convinced that he did have the authority to send a squadron to the Mediterranean, to protect the lives of Americans and the interests of U.S. commerce. In a letter to Bashaw Yusuf Karamanli on May 21, 1801, he was careful to say that the fleet he was sending out was "a squadron of observation"[11] that would "superintend the safety of our commerce, and to exercise our seamen in nautical duties"—a combination of watchdog and training cruise. But Jefferson could not resist a defiant warning: "we mean to rest the safety of our commerce on the resources of our own strength and bravery in every sea." Let the bashaw beware that tribute could if necessary be replaced by naval action.

Jefferson had had considerable difficulty filling the new post of secretary of the navy.[12] Five of his candidates had rejected the responsibility for a force that both Congress and the president seemed to be emasculating. Jefferson had finally persuaded one of them—General Samuel Smith of Maryland, whose only maritime experience had been as a Baltimore shipping merchant—to reconsider and serve temporarily. Smith now wrote out the instructions for the commander of the new Mediterranean squadron. Still unaware of Tripoli's declaration, he warned against blockading any Barbary port unless that state had declared war against the United States. Moreover, U.S. warships should not attack unless attacked; but they were permitted to defend any American vessel under attack. Smith also cautioned, "Any Prisoners you may take, you will treat with humanity and attention, and land them on some part of the Barbary shore most convenient to you." Obviously aware of the hot-blooded temperament of many young U.S. naval officers, Smith also warned, "In all cases of clashing with the vessels, Officers or Subjects of other Powers, we enjoin on you the most rigorous moderation, conformity to right & reason, & suppression of all passions, which might lead to the commitment of our Peace or our honor."[13]

A significant paragraph of Smith's instructions indicated how far President Jefferson intended to stretch his executive powers. If the squadron's commodore found on his arrival in the Mediterranean that any of the Barbary powers had declared war on the United States, he was authorized—despite the lack of a U.S. declaration of war—to "chastise their insolence by sinking, burning or destroying their ships and vessels wherever you shall find them." And if the bashaw of Tripoli had carried out his threat of war, the commodore was directed to "proceed direct to that port, where you will lay your ships in such a position as effectually to prevent any of their vessels from going in or out."

The officer selected to lead the first squadron, Captain Richard Dale, was no hothead. He had been once:[14] At 23 he had been John Paul Jones's first lieutenant aboard the *Bonhomme Richard* nearly a quarter of a century earlier, and he had had won Jones's praise (plus a gold-mounted sword Jones had received from Louis

XVI) for being the first American to board the *Serapis* in the battle off Flamborough Head. (He grabbed a trailing line and swung himself aboard the British warship.) But age seemed to have dampened Dale's ardor for action. When James Fenimore Cooper made his acquaintance after the Revolution, he characterized Dale as "a man of singular simplicity and moderation." Now Dale carried on his epauletted shoulders the rank of commodore[15] and the weighty responsibility of the first squadron of the U.S. Navy sent to protect American shipping in the Mediterranean.

His flagship was the newly launched 44-gun frigate *President*, which had had only a few months' shakedown service. The rest of the squadron consisted of the frigates *Philadelphia* (38 guns), commanded by Captain Samuel Barron, and the *Essex* (32) guns; the *Essex*'s commander was Captain William Bainbridge, who made a fast turnaround after bringing home the *George Washington*. The fourth warship in the squadron was the sloop-of-war *Enterprise* (12 guns), commanded by Lieutenant Andrew Sterrett. The fleet set sail from Hampton Roads at 6 A.M. on June 2, 1801.

The Barbary regency of Tripoli would be a formidable foe. A deceptively balmy country of oleanders, jasmines, and date palms, of antelopes and ostriches, its desert reaching back from the coast into the northern Sahara, its crescent-shaped capital was dominated by the bashaw's fortress castle looming over the white, flat-roofed houses clustered along the waterfront. Once a port of call during the early days of the Phoenician trade, it later had been part of the Roman Empire.[16]

But its history was soaked in blood. The regime of the Karamanlis had begun when the family's ancestor Hamet had massacred its Turkish rulers in 1714, and Constantinople had been forced to accept him as the new bashaw. Hamet added large eastern areas of Cyrenaica to his regency; but in 1745, blind[17] and feeble, he shot himself. After a bitter battle among his heirs, his second son, Mohammed, assumed the throne and ruled for twenty-one years. Mohammed's son Ali inherited the throne and promptly killed off his brothers. It was Ali's son and namesake who became the father of Yusuf the bashaw and Hamet the pretender.

Ali originally designated a third son, Hassan, the eldest, as his successor. But when Ali became weakened by advancing age, doddering into a decline hastened by forbidden brandy, his scheming third son, Yusuf, lured Hassan to a meeting in their mother's apartment. At her insistence both were unarmed. Yusuf swore fealty to his eldest brother, then turned to one of his servants, who handed him a pistol, and shot Hassan dead, wounding his mother in the process.[18]

● Yusuf turned his attention to the middle brother, Hamet, now entitled by primogeniture to the throne, and pretended fealty to him. But shortly, during Hamet's temporary absence from the capital city, Yusuf seized the throne; and Hamet fled to Tunis. With absolute power Yusuf set about emulating the dey of Algiers, whose nation was the strongest of the Barbary powers. Yusuf was enraged by the fact that Algiers had wangled much more tribute out of the Americans, and it was to even this score that he declared war on the United States. It was Bashaw Yusuf's warships and gunboats that Commodore Dale's frigates would confront in the United States' first foreign war.

The mark of a major power in the late eighteenth and early nineteenth centuries was the famous and formidable ship of the line, a floating behemoth some 200 feet long carrying three tiers of cannon that could send half a ton of whirring cannonballs or shrieking lengths of chain, bars, or other metal in one deadly broadside. It was called a ship of the line because its most devastating tactic was to sail in a fleet in single file, concentrating dozens of broadsides on its target. These mammoth battleships, mounting as many as 100 or more guns, constituted the principal weapon of the European navies—"the wooden walls of England," as they were called in Britain. The Royal Navy had more than 100 such ships; there were 27 British ships of the line battling 33 French and Spanish counterparts in the thunderous engagement off Trafalgar on October 21, 1805.

But ships of the line were reserved for the great naval powers, not for a struggling new nation like the United States. That was why Joshua Humphreys, unauthorized to design anything larger than a frigate, had insisted that the new U.S. frigates be larger and more heavily armed than European frigates, as well as fast enough to skip out of range of the more ponderous ship of the line.

Humphreys had also made another break with tradition, designing his new frigates with two gun decks. The customary European frigate of the time had one full deck of guns; its upper deck had bow- and stern-chasers, but most of the space consisted of catwalks across the midsection. By extending the upper deck the length of the vessel, Humphreys provided a sturdy firing platform for a second row of guns over the lower gun deck.[19]

The *President*, Commodore Dale's flagship, was heavily armed with 30 long 24-pounders[20] on the lower gun deck and 20 long 12-pounders on the upper deck. She also carried two long 24-pounders on her forecastle.[21] Like Humphreys's other frigates, the *President* also mounted on bow and stern a couple of carronades—short, squat cannon that could fire a large ball with devastating force at close range;[22] because they were so short, carronades could be loaded, fired, and reloaded more quickly than the long guns. But all this heavy armament—and the large sail area to give the vessel greater speed—made the *President*, like the other U.S. frigates, labor in a heavy seaway, as the sailors aboard her shortly discovered in the open Atlantic.

Some 350 men—able and ordinary seamen, midshipmen, gunner's, surgeon's, carpenter's, and boatswain's mates and marines—were crammed into the 175-foot frigate. The *President* had a stormy crossing, and most of the men were confined below during rough weather. Heavily loaded with her guns and provisions for a year, the ship lurched into the head seas. Her seams worked open and leaked, as did the closed gunports. When off watch, the men hung their hammocks above the guns and swung with the roll of the ship as they slept. Even so, most of them were seasick for the first few days; and the fetid interior of the vessel stank with bilge and vomit. Life aboard a nineteenth-century man-of-war was little better than in a dungeon—though it was not much worse than life ashore in the slums of the nineteenth-century city.

At least everyone was kept occupied with the ordinary duties of the ship and with preparations for the battles to come. The first light of dawn brought reveille and the call to stow all hammocks; anyone who did not tumble smartly to the deck was "started" by an officer's knotted rope. Each man folded his hammock and took it topside to fasten in its assigned place along the gunwales, where in action it would serve as a buffer against flying shells, langradge,[23] bullets, and splinters. Breakfast—usually tea and hardtack (biscuits)—was served first to the men coming off the 4 A.M. to 8 A.M. watch[24] and to the watch replacing them. After breakfast, and every meal, the smoking lamp was lit and the men were given a few minutes to relax with their pipes and cigars or to visit the "head," so-called because the toilet consisted of a grating with a few seats at the bow, a wet and uncomfortable perch in heavy weather and a noisome spot in the best of weather.

Some of the men going on watch were assigned to the pumps that wheezed away as they sucked the day's accumulation of bilge water. Others were set to scrubbing the decks, mending sails (and cleaning and airing them to prevent mildew), hauling the food casks from the hold, adjusting the rigging, scraping masts, reeving tackle, painting and whitewashing, splicing cable, tarring rigging, making gaskets and mats out of used rope, and the hundred other house-keeping details of a ship at sea. A nineteenth-century warship was labor-intensive, mainly because the vessel carried so many sailors to man the guns. The many labor-saving devices that were adopted aboard merchant ships were largely ignored by the navy, which had manpower to spare.

The *President* and her squadron confronted a unique war, unlike the fleet maneuvers and coordinated support of army troops during the Revolution. The Barbary warships fought one-on-one. Their preferred tactics were to close as quickly as possible and attempt to board the enemy. The best defense was an overpowering offense, a devastating series of broadsides that would keep them at bay. So Commodore Dale wasted no time in ordering gunnery practice. A warship's broadside—orchestrating the firing of her two decks of guns simultaneously—was an intricate and meticulous performance perfected over the centuries. The *President*'s crew was divided into six divisions. The first, second, and third divisions manned the big 24-pound long guns; the fourth and fifth were assigned to the lighter guns, including the carronades; the sixth division was com-posed of such nongunners as the sailmaker, the carpenter, the cook, and their mates, and the others who worked the ship that carried the guns.

Each man in each gun crew had his specific assignment, and gun-nery practice was designed to perfect the flawless teamwork re-quired to produce a simultaneous broadside. The "exercise," as it was called, was announced by a roll of drums, at which signal the "powder monkeys," ship's boys wearing flannel slippers to avoid making a spark, rushed down to the powder magazine deep in the hold, where each was given a black, cloth-covered bag of powder to carry up to his assigned gun; without waiting, he ran back below for the next one. Meanwhile the chief gunner of each cannon was making sure that the necessary tools—rammer, sponge, powder horn—were in their appointed places.

The exercise began with the call: "Cast loose your guns," at which the tacklemen loosed the lashings holding the cannon against the bulwarks and coiled them on deck, replacing them with breech lashings that would take up the gun's massive recoil.[25] At the second order, "Level your guns," the crew hefted the cannon barrel so it would fit through the gunport. "Take off your tompions" was the next call, to remove the stoppers that had protected the open muzzle of the cannon. At the order "Load with cartridge," the men assigned to this task shoved the bag of powder into the cannon's muzzle and, using the long rammer, pushed it down the length of the barrel and shoved a wad behind it to hold it in place against the roll of the ship. "Shot your guns" was the signal to load the muzzle with the cannonball or bag of langradge. The big gun was now ready to fire.

"Run out your guns" came the order for the gun crew to put their backs into shoving the heavy gun forward so its muzzle protruded through the port. If every gun crew was working in proper synchronization, the *President*'s outer side suddenly bristled with her protruding cannon, a sight that rarely failed to awe the enemy. As the gun captain checked the tackle falls, the thick ropes secured to cushion the recoil, the order "Prime" was called; and he quickly sprinkled a bit of powder into the touch hole at the base of the cannon. It remained only to aim each gun, which tacklemen and handspikemen did with crowbars and quoins (wedges), making sure the cannon was taking a bead on the target. Now one of the cannoneers knelt by the touch hole, blowing on his "slow match," a long, lighted fuse, to make sure it was glowing hot enough to ignite the powder.

The last call was timed with the roll of the frigate, calculated so the trajectory of the cannonball would hit the enemy vessel. At that precise moment came the order "Fire!" The cannoneer touched his match to the powder hole, the great gun exploded in a deafening blast and leapt backward, and a whirring cannonball flew hundreds of yards out over the water.

It took many such exercises (frequently without cannonballs to save the supply) before every gun crew had synchronized its performance so all the guns fired in unison. The roar of the broadside was still echoing when the call came "Sponge your guns," at which one of the men in each gun crew thrust a sponge on a long staff into a bucket of water and rammed it down the muzzle of his cannon to put out any remaining powder sparks or burning cloth. As he withdrew the sponge, the order came again to "Shot your guns"; and the procedure was repeated until that day's exercise was over. After many hours of practice the gun crews began to appreciate the satisfaction and enjoy the camaraderie of teamwork. The members of each crew boasted that their gun was the best—or the worst—and gave the guns such pet names as Defiance, Spitfire, and Raging Eagle.

Besides perfecting the ship's rapid fire, her crewmen well knew that when the time came for action in the Mediterranean, they would also have to sprinkle sawdust on the deck to absorb the blood of the wounded so the men would not slip as they rushed about their business. The surgeon and surgeon's mates would assemble their instruments, bandages, sponges, and rum for anesthetic in the operating room belowdecks, heating the saws to lessen the shock of cold metal against the flesh. The frigate's marines would climb to their posts in the mast tops, armed with muskets, blunderbusses, cartridges, and even small cannon to fire onto the enemy's deck. Their orders would be to concentrate on the officers on the enemy's quarterdeck. Other marines would be posted at the foot of the companionways, ordered to shoot any deserter who tried to flee below.

If the ship was holed or her masts shattered by enemy shot, certain members of the gun crews were designated to leave their posts for damage control: plugging the holes, clearing the wreckage, and manning the pumps. Each gun crew was somewhat larger than required to make up for those killed or wounded in action or needed for damage control or for manning the guns on the other side of the frigate if she was surrounded. And if the battle reached a point of grappling and boarding, nearly every member of the crew had his assignment.

After each gun practice the big cannon were stoppered with their tompions and lashed against the bulwarks to keep them from getting loose when the ship rolled. Excepting enemy action, few tasks aboard a man-of-war were more difficult and frightening than trying to capture and control a 3¼-ton cannon rumbling back and forth on a pitching deck. With the ship rolling heavily in a stormy sea, men could get killed, and some did, trying to get a line around the cannon and haul it back to its station.

With her guns secured, her powder magazine locked, and her extra cannon packed in tallow (deep in her hold to provide more ballast), the *President* pounded into the stormy seas of the mid-Atlantic. In the waist of the ship her sailmakers fashioned and mended the ship's canvas. The coopers repaired barrels that had been opened for the crew's rations. The sailors took their turns in the barber's chair; they were required to be clean-shaven twice a week. Forward on the starboard gun deck the midshipmen, most of them destined to become officers, were taught in a classroom formed by canvas screens. Frequently the teacher was the chaplain, who, besides conducting church services and presiding over burials at sea, taught the midshipmen arithmetic and navigation. The port side of the gun deck aft of the main hatch was set aside for officers to promenade or read.

The cook and his mates prepared the main meal, which was served at the change of the noon watch. Officers ate in their wardrooms, the crew in separate messes on the gun deck of eight to ten men each. A common pot and cooking utensils were brought from the "caboose," as the galley was called, by an elected member of each mess; and the "president" of the mess would dish out the dinner—salted meat or fish (soaked the previous night), hard bread, peas or beans, potatoes or turnips, and beer.[26] After dinner came the first tot of grog, which the men were required to drink at the grog tub to prevent them from hoarding it in order to get drunk. On Sundays came the high spot of the mess: the dessert known as "duff," made of biscuits, raisins, and "slush," the fat scraped from the cooking pots.[27]

Supper came at the 4 P.M. change of watch, consisting mostly of leftovers from dinner with bread, cheese, tea, and another tot of grog. At 8 P.M. the cook and purser went below to break out the food casks for the next day's meals. And the sailors off duty took their hammocks down from the rails, slung them from the beams over the guns, and lost little time getting to sleep after a long, hard day. Anyone who woke could hear the tramp of the night watch, the master at arms and the marines, patrolling the frigate's decks and keeping a lookout as the *President* plowed eastward toward the Mediterranean.

For service aboard a U.S. Navy vessel the pay ranged from $75 a month for the captain to $9 for an ordinary seaman. The ship's company also shared prize money. The assessed value of an enemy vessel brought into port and adjudged as a prize was apportioned among the men aboard, after the U.S. government had taken half. The rest was divided into 20 shares, of which three went to the captain (four if he was commodore of the fleet); the other commissioned officers received two shares to divide. The warrant officers split another two shares, and the petty officers divided six. The remaining seven shares were apportioned to the rest of the crew.[28]

Nearly as important as the frigate's gunners were her marines, whose duty in battle would be to station themselves on platforms on the masts and lay down a barrage of rifle fire and grenades across the Barbary warship's deck to prevent the pirates from swarming aboard. In fact, the men of Commodore Dale's squadron included two thirds of all the marines who had been recruited since Congress had authorized the Marine Corps in 1798.[29] Each frigate carried a complement of some 40 marines led by a captain and a second lieutenant, a couple of sergeants and corporals, and a drummer and fifer to call the ship's crew into action. Aboard the *President* and the other warships of the squadron there undoubtedly was friction between the marines and the navy; it was almost a tradition.

The essential conflict was over command. Naval officers insisted that the marines aboard their ships be under their direction, but the Marine Corps itself had been established with its own command structure, including a marine commandant in the capital and a marine officer in charge of all marines serving aboard each ship. The marines were generally derided by the sailors as "tin soldiers" because their chief function was to keep order aboard ship. Many of the early marines came from the ranks of the unemployed, runaways, and common criminals; the first marine recruiting station was in a tavern. In earlier times marines were paid about two thirds of what a sailor received. The rosters of Commodore Dale's squadron, however, indicate that the marines' and sailors' pay was the same.

So far most U.S. naval engagements had been at cannon range;[30]

most of the marines would have their first experience of sharpshooting from the mast tops in the Mediterranean. During the Revolution the Continental Marines had proved their usefulness in another of their functions—landing parties—by storming ashore at Nassau, for example, and capturing much-needed cannon and other munitions from one of Britain's principal arsenals. The marines aboard the *President* knew that they might well be called on for similar amphibious operations on the shores of Tripoli.

Throughout the Revolution the marines had distinguished themselves in virtually every naval engagement. But U.S. naval officers and the fiercely independent marine officers were frequently at loggerheads. With the establishment of the Marine Corps in 1798, President Adams appointed a dedicated Charlestonian named William Burrows as the first commandant. Burrows promptly set the tone for the corps by insisting on its independence, and carefully selected an equally independent and dedicated handful of officers.

Burrows saw to it that every marine defended the corps from insult from the navy. A revealing example of his attitude appeared in a letter to one Second Lieutenant Henry Caldwell, who had had an encounter with Naval Lieutenant Charles Jewett aboard the *Trumbull*. Burrows angrily wrote:

> Yesterday the Secretary told me, that he understood one of the lieutenants of the Navy had struck you. I lament that the Capt. of yr. Ship cannot Keep Order on board of her. . . . As to yourself I can only say, that a Blow ought never to be forgiven, and without you Wipe away this Insult offer'd to the Marine Corps, you cannot expect to join our Officers. . . .
>
> It is my duty to support my Officers and I will do it with my Life, but they must deserve it. —On board the *Ganges*, about 12 months ago, Lt. Gale, was struck by an Officer of the Navy, the Capt. took no notice of the Business and Gale got no satisfaction on the cruise: the Moment he arrived he call'd the Lieut. out, and shot him; afterwards Politeness was restor'd.

◊ Lieutenant Caldwell got the message. As soon as the *Trumbull* put into port, he "called out" Lieutenant Jewett, who also got the message and apologized.

The marines' spirit of independence continued to irritate naval officers who considered themselves in charge of everyone aboard their warships. Testy Captain Thomas Truxton, for one, got into a quarrel with the commander of the marines aboard his frigate and wrote to the secretary of the navy threatening to toss all the marines off his ship at the next port if they refused to recognize his authority. He and his fellow captains continued to chafe under the divided command. And the U.S. Marines continued to be regarded as second-class warriors by their navy counterparts. The proud tradition of the U.S. Marine Corps remained for the future. And in the Barbary War that future was not far away.

●The *President* turned out to be the fastest of the new frigates.[31] But the Atlantic storms slowed her crossing. And the sloop-of-war *Enterprise*[32] was even faster. With Commodore Dale's permission Lieutenant Sterrett took the *Enterprise* on ahead, arriving at Gibraltar on June 29, 1801. There he came upon the richest prize of the Barbary navies.

Anchored in the harbor was the flagship of Tripoli's navy. When the Boston brig *Betsey* had been released by the emperor of Morocco, she had been captured again, this time by Tripolitan pirates; Tripoli's high admiral, Murad Reis, had converted her into a schooner, armed her with 28 guns, and rechristened her the *Meshouda*. Many pirate captains liked to decorate their vessels, but the *Meshouda* was a particularly colorful example. Her hull was yellow with a white stripe; her stem was green; painted flowers decorated her stern windows, and a woman's head adorned her transom. The muzzles of her guns were a striking red. She was attended by a 14-gun brig, decorated but drab by comparison.

Sterrett could not attack these vessels in a neutral harbor. He was still eyeing the *Meshouda* with frustration when Commodore Dale brought the *President* into the harbor on July 2, followed by the *Essex* and the *Philadelphia*. Sterrett reported to Dale, who hailed the *Meshouda* and asked if Tripoli was at war with the United States. Tripoli's High Admiral Reis lied that she was not. But as Dale reported to the secretary of the navy, "From every Information that I can get here Tripoli is at war with America." He decided to leave the *Philadelphia* off Gibraltar, instructing Captain Barron to lie in wait for Murad Reis and "take him when he goes out."

William Eaton, fretting in his consular post in Tunis, was constantly writing home urging action against all the Barbary powers.

The antithesis of Thomas Jefferson in many ways,[33] Eaton felt
even more strongly than the president that the only way to deal
with the Barbary potentates was with overwhelming force. With no
compunctions about giving advice for dealing with his fellow consuls' regencies, he freely offered his opinion on Tripoli in a letter to
his friend Congressman Lyman. The United States, he wrote,
could "either buy off the mischief at the Bashaw's price or chastise
the Regency into terms more compatible with our feelings & abilities. Of the former resort what would be the result? Unlimited
tribute; constant harassing of our commerce; frequent enslaving of
our Citizens; eternal bickerings, and perpetual . . . negotiations."

After he heard of Jefferson's election, Eaton wrote to the new
secretary of state, James Madison, in May of 1801: "It is devoutly
to be hoped that under the new Executive a new system in respect
to the African Regencies will be established. A worse than the present would be difficult to frame." At the moment Eaton was particularly exercised by the fact that Tripoli's high admiral, Murad Reis,
in "dressing ship" (i.e., flying the flags of all nations in his rigging)
for a ceremonial occasion, had had the gall to fly some flags higher
than that of the United States "The American flag has been hoisted
on board [Reis's vessel] at the forestay *under the neapolitan!*" he exclaimed. "I swear by the God of my fathers that I will never be
reconciled to this affront until Lisle's head shall be hung in the
same posture." His anger mounting as he wrote, Eaton exploded,
"What! Is there no blood in American veins! Are we incapable of
blushing!"

The news of Murad Reis and his two warships being caught in
Gibraltar delighted Eaton, and when he heard that Captain Barron
had been posted off Gibraltar in the *Philadelphia* to watch for them,
he promptly fired off a message proposing that Barron forget diplomatic niceties and grab the high admiral. "This would be an event
so fatal to the Bashaw of Tripoli," he wrote, "that it would at once
put an end to the war. . . . He can do nothing without the crews of
these two corsairs— They are many of them from the first families
of Tripoli— Their circumstance, if they fall into our hands, would
incite an insurrection in his Kingdom and give us the intire command of terms." Eaton ominously warned that if the navy permitted Murad Reis to escape, "it will prolong the war and be
productive of incalculable mischief."

*   *   *

● Commodore Dale meanwhile sailed eastward, his flagship accompanied by the *Enterprise*. There were other Tripolitan warships to deal with. In recent years Tripoli's navy had grown nearly to the size of that of Algiers. The intelligence reports Dale had received added up to a Tripolitan navy of seven men-of-war, mostly small felucca-type vessels and galleys but armed with more than a hundred guns and manned by some 800 men.

The *Philadelphia* did succeed in bottling up Tripoli's two warships but not her high admiral and his crews. Murad Reis bribed some local boat owners to spirit his 366 men across the Strait to the North African coast, where they marched overland to Tripoli. The high admiral himself persuaded the authorities in Gibraltar (to the annoyance of Dale when he found out) to let him ship out aboard a British vessel to Malta, where he paid another captain to take him home. (Consul Eaton reacted with fury at the news.)

Commodore Dale also felt that he should provide convoy protection for American merchantmen in the Mediterranean and waiting to enter the Mediterranean. He sent Captain Bainbridge in the *Essex* to the major ports in southern Europe, picking up American vessels as he went along and shepherding them to their next ports of call. Once the United States had signed peace treaties with the Barbary powers, American merchantmen had flocked to this part of the world, where they had been making huge profits, chiefly because of the pent-up demand that had not been satisfied while the treaties were being negotiated and U.S. trading vessels had had to keep clear of the Mediterranean. Leghorn, for example, was crowded with as many as two dozen American vessels.

But Bainbridge found that many of the American captains, eager to reap the windfall, were insufficiently worried about the threat from Tripoli, despite Consul Cathcart's warnings. They were luckier than they knew: When Murad Reis had put into Gibraltar, he had been cruising the western Mediterranean for 35 days without sighting a victim. Nonetheless, many U.S. captains continued to risk capture by sailing unescorted. Some broke away from their convoys to take shortcuts to their destinations. One refused to sail from Leghorn with the convoy because he would have missed a party planned for the evening after the convoy's departure. It was surprising that despite these potential prizes roaming the Mediterranean the Tripolitans failed to capture any American vessels throughout 1801.

━● This may be partly because Commodore Dale, after quick courtesy calls at Algiers and Tunis, took the *President* and *Enterprise* to blockade the rest of Tripoli's warships in their harbor. His deep-draft frigate and sloop-of-war could not keep the shallow-draft feluccas from running along the shoaling coast; but the blockade effectively pinned down Tripoli's larger warships. Near the end of July, with the blockade fleet's water supply running low, Dale sent Lieutenant Sterrett in the *Enterprise* off to Malta to refill their barrels. The *Enterprise* had scarcely left Tripoli's coast when early in the morning of August 1, 1801, her lookouts spotted on the horizon what appeared to be a Barbary corsair. Sterrett bore down on her, flying a British ensign.[34] She turned out to be the warship *Tripoli*, 14 guns, commanded by Admiral Rais Mahomet Rous, who, deceived by the British flag, responded to Sterrett's hail by saying that he was cruising for American merchantmen. Sterrett lowered the British flag, raised the Stars and Stripes, and the battle began.

The first major naval action of the Barbary War was a three-hour battle that demonstrated Tripolitan tactics as well as U.S. gunnery. The *Tripoli*'s cannon fire was sporadic, while the *Enterprise*'s gunners fired in concentrated broadsides. Sterrett was a strict young officer who ran a taut ship,[35] and his men promptly demonstrated how well they had been trained. So fast did they load, fire, clean, reload, and fire that the *Tripoli* was soon reeling under the attack.

Admiral Rais proceeded to confirm what Thomas Jefferson had reported 16 years earlier. Unable to match the firepower of the *Enterprise*, which in fact had two fewer cannon than the *Tripoli*, he tried to swing alongside, grapple, and board. Sterrett's marines, led by Lieutenant Enoch Lane, were waiting for him. As soon as the *Tripoli* came within range of their muskets, they swept her deck with fire, cutting down her men like a scythe sweeping grass.

The *Tripoli* bore away, and Sterrett sent more broadsides into her, smashing her masts and holing her above the waterline. The *Tripoli*'s guns ceased, and Rais hauled down his flag. Sterrett's men cheered as the *Enterprise* moved in to accept his surrender—whereupon Rais raised his flag again and reopened fire.

Outraged, Sterrett replied with a broadside that shook the *Tripoli* in the water and showered her with deadly flying splinters. Again

Rais tried to close and grapple; again Lane's marines sprayed the
Tripoli's deck. Rais bore off, followed by a shower of cannonballs
from the *Enterprise*.

Obviously unnerved by the rain of death, Rais tried his surrender ruse again; this time Sterrett was not fooled. Again, in desperation, Rais tried to move close enough to grapple; Sterrett kept
his distance.

Huge clouds of smoke drifted across the sea. The *Tripoli* was
nearly obscured; but between his murderous broadsides Sterrett
could hear the cries of the *Tripoli*'s wounded. Once more Rais
lowered and raised his colors. Enraged at these tactics, Sterrett
gave the command to lower the guns and sink her. With cannonballs smashing holes in his hull at the waterline, Rais at last bent
over his shattered rail in supplication and threw his flag into
the sea.

Lieutenant David Porter, who led the boat crew aboard the
Tripoli, found a shattered ship with 30 of her 80 officers and men
killed and 30 more wounded, including Rais and his second in command. In striking contrast, not one sailor or officer aboard the
Enterprise had even been wounded—a vivid testimony to Sterrett's
supremely trained gunners, to his seamanship in maneuvering out
of the grasp of the *Tripoli*'s grapples, and to the ineffectiveness of
the *Tripoli*'s guns.

The *Tripoli*'s surgeon had been killed, so Sterrett ordered his surgeon and surgeon's mates to tend the enemy wounded. Commodore
Dale's orders had been to "heave all his Guns over board Cut away
his Masts & leave him In a situation, that he can Just make out to
get into some Port." So Sterrett sent his sailors aboard the *Tripoli* to
hoist her guns over the side, chop down what remained of her
masts, and dump her powder, cannonballs, small arms, cutlasses,
pikes, and swords into the sea. They then raised a stubby mast,
rigged a sail to it, and left Rais and his remaining men to get home
as best they could.

Rais made it to Tripoli, where he was greeted by a furious
bashaw who stripped him of command and sent him riding through
the streets mounted backward on a jackass with sheep's entrails
hung around his neck. For good measure the humiliated ex-admiral
was also given 500 bastinadoes.

Sterrett took the *Enterprise* on to Malta, sent his crews ashore to fill the water casks and bring them back to the ship. With a fresh water supply for the blockading fleet, Sterrett returned to join them off Tripoli. Shortly Dale took the *President* to Malta for reprovisioning. By August 15 he was back, bringing 41 Tripolitans he had seized from a Greek ship. He sent a message to the bashaw offering to release them for a price—evidently not concerned that he, too, was engaging in holding prisoners for ransom. The bashaw, apparently no more considerate of his subjects than of his defeated admiral, told Dale to keep them until he could purchase them with Americans—when he caught some.

Disgusted and weary, Dale sent the prisoners ashore and sailed on September 3 for Gibraltar. Finding that Murad Reis and his men had escaped from Gibraltar, Dale sent the *Philadelphia*, no longer needed to watch for them, to join the blockade. He then sailed for home. The *President* was leaking badly; her stores were low; and her men were nearing the end of the enlistment, which Congress had limited to one year.

Dale made his landfall off Norfolk, Va., on April 14, 1802. Shortly he requested promotion to admiral; but there was no such rank in the navy at the time, and Congress, lobbied by Dale to establish the higher rank, refused. So he resigned from the navy and became a Philadelphia merchant. Beyond immobilizing a couple of Tripolitan warships, Dale had accomplished little. In fact, under his command the U.S. squadron had succeeded mainly in making the bashaw more stubborn and contemptuous of Americans than ever. And the situation would soon get worse.

CHAPTER 5

★ ★ ★

"THE COMMODORESS"

Commodore Dale's ineffectual tour of duty in the Mediterranean was especially embarrassing to President Jefferson, who was still struggling with Congress over the authority to make war. Jefferson had seized on the one bit of good news, the triumph of Lieutenant Andrew Sterrett of the *Enterprise*, whose gunners had smashed the *Tripoli* without a single casualty to themselves.[1] He had shrewdly noticed that Sterrett's triumph had caught the public eye. *The National Intelligencer and Advertiser* spoke for most Americans in commenting that "with the fact that not a single individual of the crew of the *Enterprise* was in the least degree injured, we are lost in surprise."

Reporting to Congress on this action, Jefferson added with thinly veiled sarcasm, "Unauthorized by the Constitution, without the sanction of Congress, to go beyond the line of defense, the vessel, being disabled from committing further hostilities, was liberated with its crew." Was it not time, the president asked, for Congress to respond to Tripoli's declaration of war with one of its own? Congress still would not go that far. The same fresh memories of the Revolution that had kept the members from declaring war against a belligerent France now kept them from plunging the new nation into another conflict, this time against a petty city state on the Barbary Coast. But after some haggling, on February 6, 1802, Congress did pass An Act for the Protection of the Commerce and Seamen of the United States Against the Tripolitan Cruisers, which authorized the president "fully to equip, officer, man, and employ such of the armed vessels of the United States as may be judged requisite . . . for protecting effectually the commerce and seamen thereof on the Atlantic Ocean, the Mediterranean and adjoining seas."

In effect the act repealed the earlier restrictions on the numbers of ships and men. And more to the point for the commodore in the Mediterranean, it authorized the president "to instruct the commanders of the respective public vessels aforesaid to subdue, seize and make prize of all vessels, goods and effects belonging to the Bey [sic] of Tripoli, or to his subjects . . . and also to cause to be done all such other acts of precaution or hostility as the state of war will justify and may, in his opinion, require." The new act also extended sailors' enlistments from one year to two. Though not an official declaration of war, it was a practical substitute.

Jefferson had already moved to strengthen the squadron. On January 12 Navy Secretary Robert Smith[2] had ordered the dispatch of five more warships to the area: the frigates *Constellation*, *Chesapeake*, *New York*, *Adams*, and *John Adams*. The frigates *Essex* and *Philadelphia* were still in the Mediterranean, and the sloop-of-war *Enterprise*, which had returned with the *President*, was turned around and sent back, with Lieutenant Sterrett still in command. The new squadron would be far more formidable than Dale's had been. And its commodore, with Congress's authority, would be permitted to take the action to the enemy.

Captain Thomas Truxton was Jefferson's first choice as the new commodore—more because Truxton was next in line on the seniority list than because he was the president's enthusiastic candidate. Truxton was a fighter but could be as contentious with his friends as with his enemies—which he proceeded to prove by replying to Secretary Smith's order on March 3 by claiming to be insulted by not being given a captain for his flagship as was customary. He should have known that these were not customary times; Congress had recently reduced the number of captains in the navy, and there were not enough to go around. As with Dale, the secretary expected Truxton to command his flagship as well as the squadron. Truxton also made the fatal mistake of threatening that unless he could have his captain, he felt obliged to resign his commission. With barely disguised relief Secretary Smith replied, "I cannot but consider your notification as absolute." And while Truxton was still catching his breath, the secretary turned to Captain Richard Valentine Morris.[3]

Smith had also considered Captain Edward Preble. But Preble was ill. Nonetheless, Morris was an odd choice. His selection may in fact have been a bit of presidential prerogative. Morris had considerably better lineage and political influence than naval ability, though he had seen service in the Mediterranean. The son of Lewis Morris, a signer of the Declaration of Independence, a nephew of Gouverneur Morris, a financier of the Revolution and member of the Constitutional Convention, Richard Morris had been promoted to captain during Adams's administration. He also happened to be a brother of Lewis Robert Morris, a representative from Vermont who after thirty-six votes in the congressional balloting between Jefferson and Burr had withheld his vote, permitting Vermont to go for Jefferson. Whatever the president's reasoning, Morris was selected. It would prove to be one of Jefferson's worst appointments. Perhaps the first indication was when Secretary Smith received a request from Mrs. Morris, the new commodore's wife, to be permitted to sail with her husband and bring along her young son Gerard and his nursemaid. Smith compounded the mistake by consenting.[4]

The Morrises sailed down the Chesapeake in the frigate named after the bay, reaching Norfolk, Va., on April 14, 1802, where the new commodore of the Mediterranean squadron was surprised to find the previous commodore. Dale had arrived in Norfolk the same day. In a brief meeting Dale told Morris that he would be presenting a full report to the secretary of the navy and suggested that Morris await any change in his orders. Morris so informed Secretary Smith, and received a curt command to "proceed immediately." If any revised orders were required, Smith promised, they would be sent by the frigate *Adams*. But Morris waited in Hampton, Va., for what he called "contrary winds." Meanwhile, in a perfect example of bureaucratic foul-up, Secretary Smith did write up revised orders, which were forwarded to the *Adams* on April 20. No one noticed that Morris was still in Hampton; so he did not receive them until three months later when the *Adams* caught up with him in the Mediterranean.

The flagship *Chesapeake* finally sailed from Hampton Roads on April 27, into a stormy Atlantic. Within four days she had sprung her mainmast, which, Morris angrily reported, "was rotten." The shipyard workers evidently had slighted their inspection. Meanwhile a *Chesapeake* midshipman named Henry Wadsworth[5] was observing Mrs. Morris and commenting perceptively in his journal that "her knowledge of Geog. History etc. are extensive & a passion for reading is predominant; her person is not beautiful, or even handsome, but she looks very well in a veil." It also became clear that Mrs. Morris had considerable influence over the commodore; indeed some took to calling her the "commodoress."

 The squadron's vessels had sailed separately when each was ready. So the *Constellation*, under Captain Alexander Murray, reached Gibraltar on May 7, three weeks ahead of the flagship *Chesapeake*. On arrival Morris ordered Murray in the *Constellation* to resume the blockade of Tripoli, meanwhile sending the *Chesapeake*'s "rotten" mast ashore for repairs. Further inspection showed many of the flagship's other spars in various stages of deterioration. While waiting for repairs, Morris reported to Secretary Smith on the delay, complaining that the frigate had been sent to sea in such a condition and adding that the flagship also had been "most injudiciously stowed. . . . I never was at sea in so uneasy a ship; in fact, it was with the greatest difficulty we saved our masts from rolling over the side."

While the flagship sat at her anchor in Gibraltar Harbor, Captain Murray aboard the *Constellation* found some Swedish warships also blockading Tripoli; the bashaw's soldiers had chopped down their flagpole, too. But even with Sweden's help, Murray found the blockade ineffective. When he took his frigate after a fleet of Tripolitan gunboats (including the galley of High Admiral Murad Reis, who had made his way home from Gibraltar), the *Constellation* could not follow them into the shoaling waters along the coast, and Murray had to content himself with a few broadsides from more than half a mile away; most of them fell short. The abortive action "had a pleasing effect upon our Young Officers," Murray reported to Morris; but the gunboats got away.

Another five Tripolitan galleys had meanwhile slipped out of Tripoli's harbor and had gone all the way to the Spanish coast, where they made the first capture of an American vessel since the peace treaty: the brig *Franklin* en route from Marseilles to the West Indies. Shrewdly selling the brig to avoid running the blockade with her, the Tripolitans slipped back into the capital with the crew imprisoned in their galleys and paraded them through the city streets. Disgusted and frustrated, Murray protested to Commodore Morris that Tripoli could not be blockaded without more warships, especially smaller, shallower-draft vessels that could sail close to shore.

It is difficult to understand Commodore Morris's subsequent actions. Perhaps he believed that his political influence made him immune from discipline for disobeying orders. Certainly they were clear enough. He was directed to "use our best exertions to keep the enemy's vessels in port, to blockade the places out of which they issue, and to prevent as far as possible their going out or coming in." It is true that his orders contained a clause giving him discretion in case the situation suddenly changed, mainly because of the problem of communications at such distances. Secretary Smith's directive took into account the possibility that "circumstances may arise to induce a frequent change in your position, and we have a perfect confidence that you will provide judiciously against every movement of the enemy." Smith also had made it clear that the "great object of maintaining a squadron in the Mediterranean is the protection of our commerce." On his own, Morris decided that the best "protection of our commerce" was not a blockade of Tripoli but convoying American merchantmen.

Moreover, he also perceived a new threat to his rear. It came from the old Boston brig *Betsey*, renamed the *Meshouda*, which was still languishing in Gibraltar Harbor, deserted by her captain and crew, who had fled home. The emperor of Morocco, who had freed her and her crew when his corsairs had captured her in 1784, was now demanding that she be returned to him—on what legal grounds was unclear; the emperor may have concluded that Tripoli had forfeited ownership of the vessel, but in that case she should have reverted to her American owners. Probably that is why Morris refused to release her; another reason was that the emperor made no secret of his intention of using her to transport grain to Tripoli. Morris was convinced that much as the United States wanted to preserve friendship with Morocco, she did not want Moroccan vessels running the blockade of Tripoli.

But the result of his refusal, Morris now wrote to the secretary, was that Morocco had declared war on the United States. Morris reported that he had sent word to the American ministers in Eu-

rope to warn U.S. captains away from the Strait of Gibraltar. And
he pointed out that because of this new menace he would need
reinforcements. In the meantime Morris waited for the *Adams* and
the possibility of revised orders and dithered over what to do. His
mast and spars had been repaired by June 14; but still he remained
in Gibraltar, coincidentally enjoying with Mrs. Morris the ban-
quets and balls of the diplomatic set ashore.

When the *Adams* at last reached Gibraltar on July 22, two
months after Morris's arrival, she did bring updated orders. But on
the main point they were unequivocal, reiterating the secretary's
original directive that blockading Tripoli was of the first importance. President Jefferson had decided on a combination of negotiation and a show of force. Consul Cathcart, who had gone to
Leghorn after the bashaw's declaration of war, was being directed
to return with an offer of peace. Morris was ordered to send a ship
to Leghorn for him. At the same time the directive read, "It has
been determined to lay our whole naval force under your command
before Tripoli and Mr. Cathcart will accompany the expedition.
Holding out the olive branch in the one hand, and displaying in the
other, the means of offensive operations." Accordingly, Secretary
Smith wrote, "You will proceed with the whole squadron under
your command and lie off Tripoli, taking every care to make the
handsomest and most military display of your force, and so conducting your maneuvers, that in the event of negotiations failing,
you intend a close and vigorous blockade." Moreover, the secretary
warned (in a "P.S." that must not have pleased the commodore), "It
has not been deemed expedient to associate the commanding officer
of the squadron with Mr. Cathcart, in the commission to make
peace."

Secretary Smith had not, of course, received Morris's claim that
the emperor of Morocco had declared war. Nonetheless he did suggest that if the commodore was concerned about saber-rattling from
Morocco, he could leave one warship in the area to continue keeping watch on the *Meshouda*[6] and on Morocco as well. What the secretary did not say, perhaps considering it unnecessary because
Morris should have known, was that Morocco's emperor, Muley
Soliman, was far friendlier to America than his counterparts along
the Barbary Coast, and unlikely to engage in open warfare against
the U.S. Navy.

But despite his explicit orders, Commodore Morris refused to assemble his warships off Tripoli; as he blandly put it, "the idea of a blockade was abandoned." Instead Cathcart was sent to Tripoli to negotiate without any display of naval force, and without success.[7] As Morris tried to explain later, he decided on his own—3,000 miles from headquarters and in supreme command in the Mediterranean—that convoying American merchantmen was more important than blockading Tripoli, which he considered a dangerous and doubtful enterprise. There was also the factor of the "commodoress"; one naval lieutenant in Washington later reported that "the Secretary is much displeased with the conduct of Commodore Morris. His wife it is said commands so much as to lay five months in port." This time the commodore and the commodoress stayed two and a half months in Gibraltar, finally sailing on August 17, shepherding a convoy of American merchantmen to Leghorn. Not until October 12, after dawdling along the southern European coast for another two months, did the flagship finally reach Leghorn, where more festivities awaited.

Nor did Morris send any other warships to support Murray,[8] who finally broke off the blockade and set out for Toulon for provisions and repairs. Since Sweden soon concluded a truce with Tripoli, her harbor went unguarded. And Commodore Morris continued his grand tour of French and Italian ports, entertaining and being entertained, rendezvousing with the warships of his squadron but never approaching the Barbary Coast. Secretary Smith reiterated his directive on August 13. In a message announcing the sailing of the frigate *New York* for the Mediterranean, he repeated, "Let me at this time urge you, to use every exertion to terminate the affair with Tripoli." But Morris did not receive this message until it caught up with him in Leghorn in October. He ignored it.

Many of the squadron's officers were frustrated and outraged, but the commodore's command was unquestionable. Bored by inactivity, some of the junior officers quarreled and challenged one another to duels.[9] One of the encounters was particularly unfortunate because it involved the secretary of Malta's governor-general, upon whose hospitality the U.S. squadron depended for its water and many of its provisions. When the frigate *New York* took refuge from a storm in Valletta Harbor, Midshipman John Bainbridge (Captain

William's younger brother) went on shore leave with some shipmates. He was jostled by the secretary, a Mr. Cochran, who was
with a group of Royal Navy officers at the local opera house and
joined them in taunting the Americans, a favorite pastime of young
British naval officers who regarded the U.S. Navy with contempt.
When Cochran deliberately bumped into Bainbridge for the fourth
time, the midshipman hauled off and flattened him.

⬤ The next day a challenge was delivered aboard the *New York*, and
Stephen Decatur volunteered to act as Bainbridge's second. Hearing that Cochran was an accomplished duelist, which Bainbridge
was not, Decatur used the challenged party's right to demand four
paces instead of the normal ten. Cochran turned out to be overad-
vertised as a duelist, because even at that range he missed his target
twice. Bainbridge, carefully coached by Decatur, blew Cochran's
hat off with his first shot and killed him with the second. The
angry governor-general demanded that Bainbridge and Decatur
stand civil trial; but Commodore Morris hastily sent them back to
the United States, where an investigation concluded that
Bainbridge had not been the aggressor in the affair. Fortunately the
diplomatic furor died down, and the U.S. squadron continued to
receive water and supplies from Malta.[10]

Morris continued on his languid tour of southern European
ports, finally reaching Malta on November 20. Here he sent his
wife and son ashore; she was pregnant, and he made arrangements
for her delivery in a Valletta hospital. His report to Secretary
Smith read like a tourist's postcard. Referring to his last dispatch
from Leghorn, he added that "since that period there has nothing of
importance transpired in this quarter." The *Chesapeake*'s bowsprit
had to be replaced; and when the flagship was ready for sea again,
he blandly remarked, "I shall employ her in cruising, until the arrival of the squadron," most of whose vessels he had sent off convoying American trading vessels in the western Mediterranean.

Not until the end of January 1803 did Morris finally decide to
renew the blockade of Tripoli—whereupon one of the Mediterranean's notorious winter gales drove him back to Malta. And when
he sailed again, he set a course not for Tripoli but for Tunis.

He had been summoned by a warning message from the U.S. consul in Tunis. William Eaton, the undiplomatic diplomat, was no

supporter of Commodore Morris, feeling strongly that the only way to deal with the Barbary potentates was with relentless force. He had been chafing and complaining about Morris's dilatory cruise of the Mediterranean even more than he had criticized Morris's predecessor, Richard Dale. "Who but an American would ever propose to himself to bring a wife to war against the ferocious savages of Barbary?" Eaton asked when he heard that Morris's wife was aboard the flagship *Chesapeake*. "The circumstance carries conviction to the enemy that the object is not fighting." Commodore and Mrs. Morris traveling about the Mediterranean reminded Eaton of Antony and Cleopatra; and he wrote a sarcastic note in the margin of his letter book:[11] "I would recommend to the government . . . to station a company of comedians and a seraglio before the enemy's port." When Eaton found out that Morris was concentrating his forces on convoys rather than the blockade of Tripoli, the consul was furious; he did not believe in convoys because, as he wrote to Secretary of State Madison (Eaton, to the annoyance of Navy Secretary Smith, frequently directed his comments on naval strategy to the secretary of state), "Our merchantmen, impatient at long delay [in subduing Tripoli], will hazard themselves at sea." When Eaton heard the stories of U.S. naval officers' duels, he commented sardonically that they were losing more blood on the dueling ground than on the Barbary Coast.[12]

He had meanwhile been indulging in what might be judged a conflict of interest, considering his consular office, by investing in a few vessels of his own carrying supplies from southern Europe to Tunis. Eaton evidently saw no impropriety in attempting to profit by his location and position. Ever conscious of the fact that he had been a poor man before marrying a wealthy widow, he wrote his wife, Eliza, in June of 1800 that he hoped to make his fortune in the Mediterranean. He proudly announced that he was sending her a chest containing $500, and added that he hoped to return home some $3,000 to $4,000 richer. He did not want, he confessed, to live "on the earnings of another man. It is this pride which has forced me from the bosom of a companion whose bosom is heaven." Promising that the day was not too distant "when we may be happy in the enjoyment of the fruits of our own enterprises," he boasted that he would "demonstrate to the world that it was not Mrs. Danielson's fortune but her *person* that *Capt. Eaton* married."[13] And as his trading business expanded, he sent $5,000 to a New York bank to pay for the education of Eliza's three eldest children.

But Eaton's clashes with Bey Hamouda led to reverses in his trading investments. And when it appeared that he would not make his fortune after all, he wrote his wife in 1802, "Tell me, Eliza, will you be contented to set down on a hard farm with a poor old soldier? With one who loves and honors you for your goodness—with one not void of sensibility if void of cash?"

Clearly Eaton could not resist baiting the bey, who could be counted on to go into a whisker-curling fit of rage when provoked. At one point when the bey threatened to throw him into one of Tunis's dungeons, Eaton defiantly replied, "I came here expressly to be put in chains." The bey's mild response, according to Eaton, was, "You are a hard little fellow." But by the summer of 1802 Eaton was reporting to a friend that "my position is changed and is daily changing here," and blamed the situation on the naval squadron rather than his own provocative attitude. "The unproductive operations of our force, and the ineffectual blockade of Tripoli . . . have induced a sentiment of contempt rather than respect." Disillusioned and frustrated, he wrote to Secretary Madison that "I cannot serve another summer in this station," adding that Siberia or Botany Bay would be preferable to the unpleasantness of Tunis. He also was becoming increasingly suspicious that Bey Hamouda was preparing to join Bashaw Yusuf of Tripoli in declaring war against the United States. "It appears to me manifest," he wrote Cathcart, "that this regency is seeking pretexts for a rupture—and I am well convinced they would be willing to fix the cause on me."

Now, in January of 1803, Eaton apparently thought that, much as he disliked Commodore Morris, the time had come to warn him of the latest crisis. "Affairs of incalculable moment to the United States here," he wrote, "require the assistance of your counsel, perhaps your force." Eaton had just been summoned before Bey Hamouda, who had complained that the U.S. warship *Enterprise* had seized the chartered vessel *Paulina* carrying goods from the Levant to one of the bey's subjects in Tunis. The bey had demanded that the cargo be handed over to him. Knowing that the *Paulina* had been caught trying to run the blockade off Tripoli, Eaton had pointed out that she was a lawful prize; and the bey had slyly countered, "You know I am at war with Naples and Genoa. I will order my corsairs to make reprisals on your merchant vessels entering these ports."

• Reading Eaton's message, Morris realized that the bey was in effect threatening to join Tripoli in war against the United States. Morris knew all about the *Paulina*. She had put into Malta en route home from the Levant, and when Morris had heard that her next port of call was Tripoli, he had sent Sterrett in the *Enterprise* after her. Sterrett had brought her back to Malta, and Morris had found from her papers that two of her passengers were Tripolitans. One, David Vallanzino, owned part of the cargo and was trying to smuggle it home in a neutral ship. So Morris decided he had better call at Tunis en route to Tripoli. His fleet anchored off Tunis on February 22, 1803, his first visit to the regency after nine months in the Mediterranean.

Making sure that he was promised safety ashore, he took a delegation—Cathcart and Captain John Rodgers of the *John Adams* as well as Eaton—to his audience with the bey. Arguing that part of the *Paulina*'s cargo was Tripolitan and not Tunisian, Morris demanded that a court of admiralty in Gibraltar rule on whether or not the ship was a legitimate prize. The bey insisted that the decision be made in Tunis. Morris objected. The bey threatened war. Morris capitulated, and offered to bring ashore the *Paulina*'s papers for inspection, with the proviso that the bey "would waive all pretensions to such property as should not appear bona fide to belong to his subjects." The bey agreed. The papers were inspected by the bey's commercial agent, Hagdi Unis Ben Unis, who found that "a considerable share" of the cargo was Tunisian. Morris promised to return that share to Tunis, keeping the Tripolitan-owned cargo,[14] and wrote to the navy secretary, "I flattered myself that the appearance of the squadron in this Bay, had tranquilized our affairs with the Regency for some time." He was preparing to go back aboard the *Chesapeake* when he was presented with a bill for $34,000.

That, he was told, was the amount Consul Eaton had borrowed from Commercial Agent Hagdi Unis Ben Unis; Eaton had promised to pay it back the next time the U.S. squadron visited Tunis.

The bey announced that Commodore Morris was under arrest until the debt had been paid.

● Astonished and enraged, Morris concluded that Eaton had lured him to Tunis to pay the consul's debts. Eaton protested that he had not made any such promise; he had merely said that "he hoped when the squadron arrived, that he would be able to pay [Hagdi Unis]." Another audience with the bey erupted into an undiplomatic slanging match between the blunt, angry Eaton and the Tunisians. The consul claimed that the prime minister had "robbed me of my property." The prime minister shouted, "You are mad!" The bashaw agreed: "Yes, yes, you are mad! I will turn you out of my kingdom." Turning to Morris, he said, "This man is mad. . . . I will not permit him to remain here. Take him away."

"I thank you," shouted Eaton. "I long wanted to go away."

Morris, trying to restore order, asked if the bey meant what he said. "Yes—he shall no longer remain here," said the bey. After more acrimonious discussion, Morris agreed to arrange transportation for Eaton and to settle his debt. In that case, the bey replied, he would release Morris, and gave him his blessing: "I wish you a good voyage."

That night in a conference with Hagdi Unis a settlement was worked out. Eaton offered to give up the only vessel he owned, the *Gloria*, which was estimated to be worth $7,000. He also put up $5,000 of his own funds. His attempt to make his fortune in the Mediterranean had proved disastrous; as he wrote to Secretary Madison, "I am now totally destitute of funds and credit here, and do not know where to obtain the means of daily subsistence."

He also had lost all credit with Commodore Morris, who agreed to make up the difference of $22,000, which he sent ashore when he returned aboard the flagship. He appointed George Morris (no relation), a naval doctor, to serve as consul. And he sent an angry report to the secretary of the navy, claiming that Eaton had been "an accessory to my detention." Morris would not forget this unpleasant incident when Eaton would later need his support in planning his expedition against the bashaw of Tripoli. In the commodore's considered opinion Eaton was "rash, credulous and by no means possessed of sound judgment."

Morris's fleet finally upped anchor and sailed—again not to Tripoli but to Algiers. The commodore had meanwhile received word that the dey of Algiers was complaining about one of the payments of tribute that had arrived in cash instead of arms as promised. Moreover, Consul O'Brien had decided to retire and return home with his bride, Betsy. President Jefferson had proposed Cathcart as his replacement, but the dey had refused to accept him.[15] "His character does not suit us," the dey explained, "as we know that wherever he has remained, he has created differences." Unable to resolve that dispute, Morris picked up O'Brien and his wife and took them, with Cathcart and Eaton, on west to Gibraltar, where they could find a vessel to take them home. Now the damage was compounded. Not only was Commodore Morris doing little if anything to subdue Tripoli; but two Barbary capitals were without U.S. consular representation and the third, Tunis, had only a temporary replacement. Morris could not be held responsible for O'Brien's retirement or Eaton's and Cathcart's temperaments. But at this point U.S. influence in the Mediterranean was at perhaps its lowest point.

Among Commodore Morris's failings was a refusal to keep Washington informed. He rarely sent in a report, and when he did, it was maddeningly cryptic. In May of 1803 Secretary Smith reminded him with a touch of sarcasm, "I have not heard from you since the 30th November 1802, but I will not permit myself to suppose that you have not written since that period. Yet it is a subject of serious concern that we have not heard from you. I presume it would be superfluous to remind you of the absolute necessity of your writing frequently and keeping us informed of all your movements." To Captain John Rodgers, second in command of the Mediterranean squadron, Smith was more direct about Morris's mission: "He has not done anything which he ought to have done. . . . We besides can obtain from him no information what he is proposing to do." Other reports were, however, coming in from the Mediterranean, and they added up to a condemnation of Commodore Morris's behavior. President Jefferson was gloomily concluding, "I have for some time believed that Commodore Morris's conduct would require investigation. His progress from Gibraltar has been astonishing. I know of but one supposition which can cover him; that is, that he has so far mistaken the object of his mission as to spend his time convoying. . . . We gave great latitude to his discretion, believing he had an ambition to distinguish himself, and [were] unwilling to check it by positive instructions." The president was perhaps all the more embarrassed by the taint of politics in Morris's appointment.

◆ The news from the Mediterranean was an excruciating blow to Jefferson, who against advice from many in his Cabinet and in Congress had stubbornly held to a determination to meet Barbary force with force. Now two of his commodores had failed, and in fact U.S. prestige in the Mediterranean and in Europe was worse than it had ever been. Jefferson could remember his days in Paris when the Europeans had been impressed by the U.S. minister's defiance of the Barbary despots—and the complacent clucking later when the new nation had settled for tribute after all. Now he had tried to restore American resistance, only to have commodores Dale and especially Morris confirm the contempt with which the Europeans, and even the Barbary rulers, viewed the United States.

At a Cabinet meeting on May 8, 1803, Jefferson resignedly asked, "Shall we buy peace with Tripoli?" The affirmative vote was unanimous. Instructions went off to Consul Cathcart to try again for negotiations with the bashaw. But now a scornful Bashaw Yusuf would not let Cathcart anywhere near Tripoli. And in any case Commodore Morris still would not support negotiations with an all-out blockade.

He did finally decide at least to have a look at the harbor of Tripoli. In the spring of 1803, while President Jefferson was agonizing over the failure of the squadron's mission, Morris sent his flagship *Chesapeake* back to the United States for refitting, moved aboard the frigate *New York*, ordered the *John Adams* and the *Enterprise* to accompany him, and set out eastward. Still he was in no hurry. He called at Leghorn and Malta, where he checked on his pregnant wife's condition, and at last set a course for Tripoli—only to be thwarted by a conflagration aboard the flagship.

Early on the morning of April 25, 1803, a gunner's mate stowing signal lanterns in the cockpit storeroom set off a small fire that ignited some powder. The explosion rocked the frigate and started a much larger fire that threatened the nearby powder magazine. Ordered to signal FIRE ON BOARD to the accompanying ships, a rattled quartermaster instead hoisted the flags for MUTINY ON BOARD, bringing the other warships rapidly onto the scene with their crews at battle stations. But a damage-control party led by lieutenants David Porter and Isaac Chauncey, wielding wet blankets and water buckets for an hour and a half, managed to put out the fire before it could reach the magazine and blow the frigate to bits. Fourteen of the *New York's* men, including Morris's secretary, the chief gunner, the surgeon's mate, and the marine guarding the powder magazine, were killed. Again Morris had to return to Malta.

Not until May 20 did the squadron finally sail for Tripoli. A week later, Commodore Morris saw the harbor he had been ordered to blockade for the first time. With his flagship *New York* were the *John Adams*, the *Enterprise*, and the *Adams*. History repeated itself with the swift little feluccas slipping alongshore and avoiding the blockade. The *Enterprise* went after one of them, but even a sloop-of-war drew too much water to cut her out. Lieutenant Isaac Hull, who had replaced Sterrett as commander of the *Enterprise*, fired a broadside that frightened the felucca's crew into running onto the beach and fleeing. But Morris, when asked, refused permission to send ships' boats in after her.

Shortly a ship and nine gunboats were spotted trying to slip into the harbor. Morris took the *New York*, the *John Adams*, and the *Enterprise* after them. For a while it looked like a golden opportunity to move between the enemy and the shoaling harbor waters. But the late afternoon breeze died as it often did, and the U.S. Fleet succeeded only in getting becalmed in such a formation that the vessels were firing on one another more than on the enemy. Silhouetted by the sunset, Morris's vessels made perfect targets for the bashaw's shore batteries until a providential breeze helped them move out of range.

At last came a chance to deliver a telling blow. The *Enterprise* sighted a dozen grain-carrying feluccas sneaking toward the harbor, drove them into a bay west of the city, and trapped them there. This time Morris agreed to send a scouting party into the bay; and on the night of June 10, two boats—one from the *New York* with Lieutenant Porter, Midshipman Wadsworth, and five sailors and one from the *Enterprise* with Lieutenant James Lawrence and five more men—rowed quietly toward shore. There was a bright moon, and they could make out the boats huddled together under the guns of a stone fortress on the beach. They had just got within earshot of their quarry when the gunboats opened fire and the Americans had to retreat. Porter asked Morris for permission to attack. Morris decided to wait.

By morning he had agreed to what became the first U.S. amphibious operation on the Barbary Coast, a combined action of the navy and the marines. Morris put Lieutenant Porter in charge with Lieutenant Lawrence second in command; Lieutenant Enoch Lane represented the marines. By 8 A.M. the attack party of nine boats rendezvoused from the frigates; seven of them carried 50 men and the other two were packed with inflammable material to be set afire and driven onto the grain boats.

The attackers were covered by a barrage from the frigates' guns as they rowed for the shore. From the fortress and barricades on the beach the Tripolitan guns opened up as the attack boats neared the feluccas. And while the two fireboats were guided toward their targets, the other seven raced for the beach, shooting as they went in. As soon as they grounded, the men swarmed ashore with pistols and swords.

The 50 Americans were met by an army of Tripolitans that Morris estimated at nearly 1,000 foot soldiers and cavalrymen, including a dashing officer on a black horse who rode up and down the beach brandishing a rifle until a volley from the attackers sent him tumbling. It was a pell-mell battle, but despite the heavy odds, the Americans gradually fought their way up the beach. Watching through his telescope, Morris noticed that large numbers of the defenders were holding back, apparently waiting to encircle the Americans when they pushed farther ashore.

But Porter knew better. He kept his small force concentrated on the beachhead only long enough for the men in the fireboats to ignite the grain boats. Then he called for retreat, and got nearly all his men back into their boats before he was hit simultaneously in both legs. Crawling into one of the boats, he continued to direct the retreat until he became too weak from loss of blood and called to Lieutenant Lawrence to take over.

Under a hail of bullets the boats raced back to the ships, the sailors and marines watching in satisfaction as the grain boats burned fiercely behind them. They had gone in, done the job, and come out in only two hours. Fifteen of them had been killed or wounded, but they had slaughtered many more of the enemy. As soon as they were out of range, the Tripolitans went to work dousing the fires, considerably hampered by a heavy barrage from the frigates and the *Enterprise*. Morris estimated that the attack destroyed only about half of the grain, which was difficult to burn. But he was satisfied that at last he had struck a direct blow at Tripoli, even if it had been more symbolic than destructive.

• Bashaw Yusuf Karamanli, however, was not particularly moved. When Morris sought to capitalize on the effect of the assault and sent in a message proposing negotiations for peace, the bashaw responded gruffly that he was not impressed by the Americans. "I do not fear war," he boasted; "it is my trade." Nevertheless he appointed his "trusty minister Mohammed Dghies" as his negotiator. Captain Rodgers was rowed into the harbor under a white flag. He negotiated a guarantee backed by the French consul for Morris to come ashore. And despite his recent experience with the bey of Tunis, Morris agreed.

The commodore stayed three days while a flag of truce flew over the house assigned to him. But Morris quickly found that Porter's assault and the loss of the grain boats had not had the effect he had hoped. The bashaw calmly demanded a price of $200,000 for peace, plus an annual payment of $20,000 to maintain it. Morris angrily replied that such a demand was outrageous: "should the combined world have made it, my nation should have treated it with contempt." When Dghies reported Morris's answer, the bashaw shouted, "This business is at an end!" and ordered the white flag hauled down. The French consul responded to this threat by warning the bashaw of retaliation from his navy if his guarantee for the safety of the American commodore was ignored. The bashaw let Morris and his negotiators leave. Clearly the power of Emperor Napoleon meant a great deal more to Yusuf Karamanli than the might of President Jefferson.

Morris decided it was time to end the blockade, and ordered Captain Rodgers to bring the rest of the squadron back to Malta within the month. Meanwhile he hurried to Malta to check on his wife and found that he had a five-day-old second son. Rodgers, after accomplishing nothing more than the destruction of a Trip-olitan poleacre,[16] returned to Malta on June 30. And on July 11 Morris, with his family aboard, set out aboard the *New York* for home. He was nearing Malaga, Spain, on September 9, when his frigate crossed paths with six Royal Navy warships. One of them was the majestic 100-gun ship of the line *Victory*, which Admiral Horatio Nelson had just joined. As the American frigate sailed un-der her looming stern, Morris hailed her quarterdeck and Nelson responded politely. The *Victory* and her squadron continued on the course that two years later would lead to triumph and Nelson's death at Trafalgar.[17] The *New York* continued to Malaga, where Morris found waiting for him an abrupt order from Secretary Smith.

> Sir:
> You will on receipt of this, consider yourself suspended in com-mand of the squadron in the Mediterranean station, and of the frig-ate *New-York*. It is the command of the President, that you take charge of the *Adams*, and that with her you return without delay to the United States.

On his return Morris was summoned before a court of inquiry that convened to study the charge that "a close and vigorous block-ade of the port of Tripoli hath not been made, and all practical means have not been used to annoy the enemy." Morris offered the defense that in his judgment as the commodore on station, "it was deemed most consistent with the true interest of the United States to attend to the great object of securing their commerce and seamen, rather than to hazard, by a literal compliance with the Secretary's instructions, a great and irreparable mischief." In short, while President Jefferson's major target was Tripoli, Morris con-sidered it more important to convoy Americans through the Medi-terranean.

Captain Samuel Barron, chairman of the court, and his fellow members found Morris "censurable for his inactive and dilatory conduct of the squadron under his command" and censured him on a number of specific charges. Their conclusion was that "he did not conduct himself in his command of the Mediterranean squadron, with the diligence or activity necessary to execute the important duties of his station."

That was putting it mildly, in the view of Jefferson, who revoked Morris's commission as a captain. Angrily he now insisted on a new commodore, one who could at last assert U.S. prestige in the Mediterranean.

PART II

★ ★ ★

EDWARD PREBLE

CHAPTER 6

★ ★ ★

DISASTER ON KALIUSA REEF

Edward Preble, the man Jefferson now chose as Mediterranean commodore, was an imposing quarterdeck figure with broad shoulders, piercing blue eyes, the nose of a hawk, and the jaw of a mastiff.[1] He was the third son of 12 children of Brigadier General Jedediah Preble, who had served in the army in the French and Indian Wars.[2] Young Edward was a better athlete than student, and a superb marksman; his schoolmates claimed that he once won a bet by picking off five swallows with five rifle shots. His father had retired to a farm and had put his sons to work planting and digging potatoes. But in 1777, at 16, anxious to join the Revolutionary War at sea, Edward shipped aboard a privateer. General Jedediah, realizing his son would never be a farmer, wangled him a midshipman's berth aboard the 26-gun light frigate *Protector*.

The *Protector* had captured several British prizes in the West Indies and Preble had risen to the rank of lieutenant when in May of 1781 she was captured by two Royal Navy warships. Preble wound up in the hold of the *Jersey*, the Royal Navy's notorious prison hulk in New York Harbor, where he nearly died of typhoid fever. Paroled because of his illness, he recovered and became a lieutenant aboard the 12-gun sloop-of-war *Winthrop*, hunting down British prizes along the New England coast.[3] By the end of the war he was already a hardened veteran at 22.

Joining the merchant service, Preble quickly rose to captain and owner of his own vessel. And when during the Quasi War with France President Adams's navy secretary, Benjamin Stoddert, decided to convoy American merchantmen to and from the Dutch East Indies, Preble was promoted to captain in the navy and given command of the new 32-gun frigate *Essex*, sailing in January of 1800[4] along with Captain James Sever's 36-gun *Congress*. The two frigates had scarcely set out in the Atlantic with their convoy when a gale dismasted both. Sever ran for the nearest port. Preble re-rigged the *Essex* on the run and continued on around the Cape of Good Hope with some of the merchantmen; the *Essex* thus became the first American warship to enter the Indian and Pacific Oceans.

By November of the same year, after encountering more gales and putting down a mutiny, Preble brought the *Essex* and eleven American merchantmen with their cargoes of pepper, sugar, coffee, and tea safely home from Batavia. What impressed Preble's superiors even more was that he did it without losing a man to the dreaded malaria of the East Indies. But the ten who became infected included Preble himself; he would suffer recurrent malarial attacks for the rest of his life. He also had developed ulcers.

In April of 1802, he was offered command of the *Adams* in the Mediterranean squadron; he went to New York to supervise her fitting out, but became so ill that he was unable to take command. Mindful that the navy's officer list had been cut by Congress, he did not ask for sick leave but regretfully submitted his resignation, accompanied by the recommendations of two doctors.[5] But Navy Secretary Smith humanely refused to accept the resignation, instead putting Preble on furlough "until your health should be restored." That time seemed to have come when in May of 1803 Preble reported to the secretary that he apparently had recovered, and was promptly appointed to replace the disgraced Richard Morris as commodore of a new Mediterranean squadron.

President Jefferson had high hopes that Commodore Preble would humble the bashaw as his previous commodores had not. But the president was surrounded by advisers who were convinced that the navy could not succeed in this mission. So he also decided to prepare for the distasteful option of buying peace at a price. In choosing a consul general to replace Captain O'Brien, he turned to a man whose diplomatic talents he had long respected. When he had been President Washington's secretary of state he had been impressed by Washington's personal secretary, Tobias Lear.

Jefferson now asked Lear to accompany Preble to the Mediterranean and stand ready to negotiate a treaty of peace if and when it became the only alternative. But the president was still determined to keep his options open as long as possible. He directed that Consul Lear was not to act on his own; he was to serve under the command of Commodore Preble, who, Jefferson fervently hoped, would make a last all-out attempt at winning the peace by force.

Commodore Preble's flagship was to be the 44-gun *Constitution;* she would be accompanied by the 38-gun *Philadelphia,* whose command had been given to Captain William Bainbridge; three 12-gun schooners: the *Enterprise,* the *Nautilus,* and the *Vixen;* and two 16-gun brigs: the *Argus* and the *Siren,* both newly built to shallow-draft specifications for the shoaling waters of the Barbary Coast.

It was characteristic of Preble that he received his orders on May 19 and reported aboard the *Constitution* at 10 the next morning. He immediately ordered an inspection, found the frigate badly in need of repairs, and ordered them to begin the next day. The *Constitution* was hove down to replace her damaged copper bottom; the work crews labored overtime, from 5:15 A.M. to 7 P.M. with brief interruptions for meals. In the record time of one month the frigate's hull was completely recoppered. Countless other repairs were meanwhile being made and stores were brought aboard for the long cruise. Preble was all over the ship at all hours, urging, haranguing, and driving until everyone was ready to drop from exhaustion.

Preble also had problems signing on his crew, and had to send recruiters to other cities looking for foreign seamen who, fearful of impressment from merchant ships into the British and/or French navies, might be attracted by the promise of protection aboard a U.S. Navy vessel. The recruiter dispatched to New York City had the good fortune to arrive while a Royal Navy sloop-of-war rode at anchor in the harbor; within a day he had signed on 80 men. By the time the *Constitution* had her full complement, her crew included so many foreigners that Preble complained, "I do not believe that I have twenty native American sailors on board."[6]

By August 9 the *Constitution* was ready for sea—just in time for five days of contrary winds that pinned her down in Boston Harbor while Preble fumed and his ulcers flared. Finally, on August 14, the *Constitution* dropped down the harbor and set her course for the Mediterranean. Most of the squadron's vessels, in less need of repair, had already sailed, so the flagship was alone.

❦ Immediately Preble put her on a war footing, issuing formal regulations for the *Constitution* covering every activity of the ship.[7] The log was to be cast to measure the ship's speed every hour. Lookouts were to be posted constantly by day as well as night. The pumps were to be sounded every two hours. Any sighting of another vessel or any change in wind speed or direction was to be reported to the commodore. Cannon and small arms practice would be held twice a week. The frigate's decks were to be washed down every morning and evening. The weather (high) side of the quarterdeck was reserved for the captain or the officer of the watch. Swearing and "immorality" were forbidden. No one was to be excused for illness without the diagnosis of the surgeon. The entire ship's company was to be mustered every evening at sunset; all absent, intoxicated, dirty, or slovenly men were to be reported. No ragged clothes or long hair was permitted. Every man aboard ship was to be shaved and changed into clean clothes twice a week. Daily inspection was to be held with officers checking every hammock and kit bag and reporting to Preble, who personally inspected the ship from bow to stern, top deck to hold, every day.

Preble was stingy with praise, and malingerers or rebels were quick to feel the lash; the *Constitution*'s logbook recorded numerous floggings.[8] But Preble also made sure that the frigate's law-abiding men were cared for. Sundays were days of rest, except for such necessary duties as trimming sails, washing down the ship, dealing with a storm, or sighting a possible enemy. The purser was directed to report to the captain any provisions unfit for the mess. And the traditional rum ration was issued twice a day, at noon and 4 P.M.

In the first week of the *Constitution*'s transatlantic voyage Preble's officers found him a martinet[9] with a temper that was frightening to behold. Plagued by his ulcers, he could erupt at the slightest affront; but the victim of his rages usually found that his outbursts, as one man put it, "did not last long enough for him to take a turn of the quarterdeck"; and he frequently apologized later.

Preble kept to himself,[10] dining with his officers only once a week. He posted a marine sentinel at his cabin door, admitting only senior officers reporting to him on the business of the ship. And when he strode the weather side of the quarterdeck, no one was permitted to approach him unless summoned or bearing an urgent message.

๏ Preble was particularly appalled at the youth of his officers. At 42 he was twice the age of most of them; the oldest commander in the squadron, Captain Bainbridge of the *Philadelphia*, was 12 years his junior. Hardly an officer aboard the flagship was yet 30. Preble complained openly that he had been saddled with "nothing but a pack of boys."[11] But this same band of youngsters—many of whom had fretted at inactivity under Commodore Morris—now, under the stern discipline of their new commodore, became the seasoned veterans who would later cover themselves with even greater glory in the War of 1812. Stephen Decatur, Isaac Hull, David Porter, James Lawrence, William Biddle—all would proudly call themselves "Preble's Boys"; and Preble's Mediterranean squadron would become known as the "Nursery of the Navy."

Preble faced a daunting challenge in the Mediterranean of 1803. The bashaw of Tripoli had suffered hardly at all from the two American squadrons and their feckless commodores. The other Barbary potentates were stirring uneasily, talking of declaring war and joining Tripoli in cruising for U.S. merchantmen. Indeed, the main reason the Tripolitans had captured only one American ship, the *Franklin*, was because most U.S. merchant captains were beginning to steer clear of the Mediterranean, with a huge consequent loss of U.S. trade. Insurance rates for those rare ships that did risk the perilous passage through the Strait of Gibraltar were astronomical.

Captain John Rodgers, who had been given temporary command of the remaining U.S Mediterranean squadron, was quite a different commodore from Dale and Morris. A hotheaded driver eager to attack, he had attempted to renew the blockade of Tripoli; but with his reduced fleet he could accomplish little until reinforcements arrived. And the U.S. effort to subdue Barbary piracy by naval power was still the laughingstock of the Europeans, who were confirmed in their belief that tribute was the most effective deterrent to capture of their ships.

๏ Even the mild-mannered emperor of Morocco, who professed to be the Americans' friend, was tempted to flout their feeble naval presence. When Muley Soliman had wheedled the *Betsey-Meshouda* away from Commodore Morris and had sent her to run the blockade, Rodgers had captured her; so the emperor was making warlike noises again.

  ◉ Preble got his first indication of trouble with Morocco as the *Constitution* was approaching the Strait of Gibraltar.[12] Off the Portuguese coast on September 6, the flagship's lookouts sighted a strange frigate. Closing with the *Constitution*, she turned out to be the Moroccan warship *Maimona*, 30 guns and 150 men. Her captain presented his papers and claimed that he was on a peaceful voyage from Lisbon to Sallee (now Salé). Preble was suspicious. He knew of Moroccan emperor Muley Soliman's earlier threats that supposedly had been dropped when President Jefferson had sent him a gift of American gun carriages for the emperor's army.[13] Why was a Moroccan 30-gun frigate roaming the Atlantic near the Strait of Gibraltar? If Morocco was threatening war again, she could endanger American shipping even more than Tripoli because her port of Tangier was on the Atlantic side of the Strait.

Tobias Lear and his family were aboard the *Constitution*, sailing to the Mediterranean to replace Richard O'Brien as consul general. Lear volunteered to question the *Maimona*'s captain and inspect her papers, and Preble sent him aboard. The *Maimona*'s captain continued to protest his innocence, and his papers were in Arabic, which Lear could not read. Preble had no choice, and let the *Maimona* proceed on her way, though with Lear he shared an uneasy feeling—which heightened when he put into Tangier to call on U.S. Consul James Simpson.

The *Constitution* fired her signal gun to summon Consul Simpson. There was no response. Through his telescope Preble could see seven national flags flying at their consulates but no U.S. flag. Preble went on to Gibraltar,[14] arriving September 12 to find the *Philadelphia*, which had sailed before the *Constitution*, at anchor in the harbor. Her boat came over; Captain Bainbridge climbed the 11 cleated steps of the *Constitution*'s hull, saluted the quarterdeck and reported to Preble that he had caught a Moroccan warship with a captured American merchantman.

Bainbridge had reached Gibraltar on August 24, in time to hear that Moroccan cruisers were harassing American shipping. Setting sail to look for them, he shortly sighted two vessels off Spain's Cape de Gata. The first was the 22-gun Moroccan frigate *Mirboka;* the second was the American brig *Celia* with a Moroccan prize crew on her decks and her own captain and crew imprisoned below. Bainbridge herded both vessels back to Gibraltar, where he freed the *Celia* and held the *Mirboka* in custody. She was still at anchor in Gibraltar when the *Constitution* arrived.

Preble summoned her captain, an ingratiating man named Reis Ibrahim Lubarez who blandly handed over his orders from the alcayde (governor) of Tangier, named Hashash, directing him to seize any American vessels he encountered. They had been sealed orders, he reported, not to be opened until he was at sea. When he had sailed from Tangier, he claimed, he had not heard that Emperor Muley Soliman had made any official declaration of war against the United States.

Had he? The next day the frigate *New York* arrived from Malta bearing ex-commodore Richard Morris home to face his inquiry. It must have been a poignant meeting between the departing commodore and his successor. Both men must have noted with not a little irony that their orders to press the war against Tripoli were threatened by a Moroccan challenger from the rear. Although neither commented on it for the record, Morris, resentful at his abrupt recall, must have felt a smug satisfaction that the new commodore was having the same problem. And Preble must have been frustrated, and perhaps a little embarrassed, over the development that was diverting him from concentrating on the main enemy, Tripoli.

Preble soon learned about the squabble over the case of the Betsey-*Meshouda*, which Morris had surrendered to the emperor of Morocco to help keep the peace.[15] When Captain Rodgers had caught her trying to run the blockade, U.S. Consul Simpson in Tangier had protested and had been put under house arrest. That explained why he had not been able to answer the *Constitution*'s signal gun. Now ex-commodore Morris could supply more detail. And the next day Captain Rodgers arrived with the final piece of the puzzle.

The *John Adams* sailed into Gibraltar's harbor with the *Meshouda* in tow and a full report on her cargo of swords, guns, and cannon as well as provisions from the emperor of Morocco. And to cap it off, Gibraltar buzzed with a rumor that the *Maimona*, which Preble had permitted to go on her way in the Atlantic, had captured four American merchantmen.

● That report later turned out to be false. But Preble was convinced that all the evidence could point only to a Moroccan war against the United States. The treaty that Muley Soliman's father had signed in 1786 provided for a small annual tribute; it looked as if Muley Soliman meant to harass the United States into a more favorable agreement. Preble decided to nip this threat in the bud.

John Rodgers, it happened, was senior to Edward Preble on the navy list of captains, and was quick to remind him of the fact.[16] He could be as prickly as Preble, and the two cordially disliked each other. An aggressive fighter like Preble, Rodgers had chafed under Commodore Morris's inaction, had had a brief taste of command after Morris's recall, and was understandably angry at being superseded. But orders were orders, and Preble had been appointed as the new commodore. So Rodgers reluctantly agreed to serve under him. At midnight on September 16, only four days after his arrival from the United States, Preble set sail for Tangier, where he requested an audience with Muley Soliman.

After innumerable delays—the emperor was off in the countryside; he was delayed by rainstorms and floods; he needed time to recuperate—Preble succeeded in confronting Muley Soliman.[17] It was a mutual sizing-up, an opportunity for Preble to get his first close look at a Barbary Coast potentate and equally a chance for the emperor to take the measure of the flinty, self-confident commodore from the United States.

With Consul General Lear, Captain Rodgers, and two junior naval aides, Preble went ashore to be met by ranks of Moroccan soldiers lining Tangier's narrow streets. The roofs were crowded with townspeople awed by the erect, epauletted American commodore and the flotilla of U.S. warships in the harbor; they had never seen anything like it.

Joined by U.S. Consul Simpson,[18] newly released from house arrest, Preble and his party were ushered into a piazza under the watchful eyes of 50 armed guards. A court attendant arrived—not to lead them to the audience chamber but to put a cushion on the step in front of the main door. Shortly a nondescript little man came out and sat on it.

Midshipman Ralph Izard, one of the Preble party, later wrote home, "I had connected with the idea of the Emperor of Morocco something grand, but what was my disappointment at seeing a small man, wrapped in a woolen *haik* or cloak, sitting upon the stone steps of an old castle." Midshipman Henry Wadsworth, also in the delegation, wrote that "we were very much surprised when the Minister came and told us, 'That's the Emperor.'" One of the emperor's aides ordered Preble to remove his sword. Preble refused. Through his interpreter the emperor greeted Preble and asked him to kneel. Preble refused again.

The emperor asked, "Are you not in fear of being arrested?"

Preble replied, "No, sir. If you presume to do it, my squadron in your full view will lay your batteries, your castles, and your city in ruins."

Emperor Muley Soliman had no way of knowing whether or not the American commodore was bluffing. In fact, Preble had assembled his officers aboard the flagship before debarking. Unlike Commodore Morris, who had blundered into two near-hostage situations, Preble had instructed his officers to "keep the ship cleared for action . . . and if the least injury is offered to my person, immediately attack the batteries, the castle, the city, and the troops, regardless of my personal safety."

In any case Muley Soliman had had a good look at the fleet in his harbor—the frigates *Constitution*, *John Adams*, and *New York*, the sloop-of-war *Nautilus*—all with gunports open, cannon protruding, and tompions removed. The emperor promptly assured Preble that all he wanted was peace with the United States. He blamed the Moroccan Navy's warlike threats on Tangier's Governor Hashash, who had rashly acted on his own and who, the emperor promised, would be punished "more than to your satisfaction."[19] As for the treaty between Morocco and the United States, it was intended to last for 50 years, but he, Muley Soliman, considered it binding forever. He promised a formal reratification and said he would write a personal letter to the president of the United States.

When Preble returned to his flagship, the emperor put on a dazzling display for his visitors. Accompanied by most of his army, Muley Soliman came down to the beach to salute the American squadron. Soldiers lined the shore for nearly three miles. Arabian horses pranced along the beach. The Imperial Moroccan Band serenaded the ships. Boats came out with gifts from the emperor: ten bullocks, 20 sheep, four dozen chickens and ducks, two boatloads of other fresh provisions. Preble called for a 21-gun salute, which was promptly answered from the batteries on the shore.

• Convinced that he had effectively secured his rear from Moroccan attack, Preble returned to Gibraltar, where he wrote to Secretary of State Madison that the 1786 treaty had been reratified and that Muley Soliman had ordered his navy to treat all U.S. vessels as belonging to a favored nation. Preble also reported that the emperor was disappointed because he had not had a letter from President Jefferson for a long time. As a precaution and a warning, Preble left the *Argus* to cruise the Moroccan coast.[20]

Now he could turn to the business he had come to the Mediterranean for, renewing at long last the blockade of Tripoli. Putting into Gibraltar to assemble his squadron, he found a message from the secretary of the navy ordering the frigates *New York* and *John Adams* home; they were long overdue for repair and refitting. But he still had the *Philadelphia*, which he had already sent ahead to Tripoli, plus the smaller craft *Argus*, *Vixen*, and *Nautilus*, which with their shallow draft should be more effective in the shoaling waters off the Barbary Coast. Preble wrote to the secretary, promising, "You may rest confidently assured, there shall not be an idle vessel in my squadron," and buoyantly predicting peace with Tripoli by the spring of 1804. The *Constitution* weighed anchor and sailed out of Gibraltar for the coast of Tripoli. And on November 4, speaking the British frigate *Amazon*, Preble was informed of the worst naval disaster to befall the Americans since the Revolution.

The *Amazon* had been in Syracuse when a trading packet had arrived with a report that the U.S. frigate *Philadelphia* had run aground and had been captured by the Tripolitans.[21]

When Preble had ordered the 38-gun *Philadelphia* and the 14-gun *Vixen* to precede him to Tripoli, he had made it clear to Captain Bainbridge that his frigate and the *Vixen* were to join forces in the blockade, combining the frigate's great firepower with the schooner's shallower draft to "annoy the enemy with all the means in your power." The two vessels arrived off Tripoli on October 7, and spent the next 12 days cruising on and off along the coast without sighting any Tripolitan vessels. Then, on October 19, the *Philadelphia* spoke an Austrian brig whose captain told Bainbridge that two Tripolitan warships were roaming the Mediterranean; presumably they had sailed just before the arrival of the American blockaders. Bainbridge decided to send the *Vixen* looking for them, and ordered her commander, Lieutenant John Smith, to sail west toward Cape Bon, the bulge of Tunis that reaches north to form a narrow passageway with Sicily, and to watch for the enemy ships. Smith took the *Vixen* westward on October 20.

Two days later a gale came out of the northwest; heading into it and tacking back and forth, the *Philadelphia* fought the storm for nine days, gradually drifting about 20 miles east of her blockade post. At nine on the morning of October 31 her lookouts spotted a sail heading for Tripoli. Bainbridge concluded that it might be one of the vessels the *Vixen* was looking for, and immediately gave chase.

In the aftermath of the storm the winds still were strong, and the two vessels raced toward Tripoli Harbor, with the frigate closing on her quarry. Within two hours she was close enough to open up with her bow chasers. The other vessel, now made out to be a xebec, was running as close to the shore as she could, but the *Philadelphia* was converging on her.

A year earlier, when Commodore Morris had arrived in the Mediterranean, one of the bits of advice imparted to him by his predecessor, Commodore Dale, had been, "I recommend that you get a good pilot for the Coast of Barbary. Should you meet with the *Philadelphia*, you may get a very good one out of her." Presumably Morris had done just that, because the *Philadelphia* was sailing dangerously closer to the coast than a good pilot would have advised. Captain Bainbridge evidently was depending on Lieutenant David Porter, who had studied the area during the blockade.

The men in the forechains were casting the lead and calling out the depth: ten fathoms (60 feet), eight fathoms, seven, then back to ten, then back to seven. The *Philadelphia* drew 18-1/2 feet forward and 20-1/2 feet aft, so she still had enough water.

By 11:30 A.M., about four miles east of the harbor entrance, with Tripoli's minarets clearly visible, it became obvious that the xebec was going to reach the harbor before they could catch her. Bainbridge called for a last volley from the bow chasers. The soundings were now showing a steady eight fathoms (48 feet), but the water could be expected to shoal quickly from here on, and the

Philadelphia was thundering along at nearly eight knots. Some of the men were expressing their concern; still, according to one of them (Marine private William Ray), Porter assured everyone that there "was no danger yet."

Bainbridge at last ordered the helm up, and asked Porter to climb to the mizzentop for a good look at the harbor, its vessels, and the city's fortifications as they turned. Porter was halfway up the mizzen shrouds when he heard one of the leadsmen call out less than six fathoms and Bainbridge immediately order the men to brace the frigate's yards about to tack away. It was too late. Porter was almost shaken out of the rigging as the *Philadelphia* struck.[22]

Porter and Bainbridge had been following a chart, but like most other maps and guides to the Barbary Coast it was sketchy and unreliable. The xebec captain had in fact lured the *Philadelphia* inside what the Tripolitans called Kaliusa Reef. It was not indicated on the flagship's charts, but it was known to all the local mariners: a long, shallow sandbank running parallel to the shore with a few narrow passages, also known only to the local seamen.[23]

At first Bainbridge ordered the frigate's yards slanted to the wind in hopes of driving her over the reef. But the reef was too wide and the *Philadelphia* merely shuddered more deeply into the sand, raising her bow some six feet. Noticing that her stern was still in deep water, Bainbridge ordered the sails set aback, attempting to get her off the reef stern first. The frigate did not move.

A boat went over the side to survey the damage. The *Philadelphia* was firm aground in 12 feet of water, six feet less than her draft at the bow, which was now imbedded in sand and rock. The force of the grounding had canted the frigate onto her side. After a quick inspection the ship's boat had to be hauled back aboard. Already the first Tripolitans were coming out of the harbor.

Rushing frantically now, the *Philadelphia*'s men cast loose her guns, trundling some of them aft to bring to bear on the Tripolitans. The others, at Bainbridge's order, were thrown overboard, plunging into the water with booming splashes. The frigate's anchors and other heavy objects were pushed over the side. Bainbridge set more men at the pumps to jetison the *Philadelphia*'s precious fresh water. With the frigate many tons lighter, he ordered her sails trimmed to the wind again. And again she did not move.

● In desperation Bainbridge ordered the foremast cut down. The axes went to work, and in a crashing tangle of yards and rigging the mast went over the side, dragging the main topgallant mast with it. Still the frigate did not budge. Some of the officers proposed kedging her off: taking an anchor astern in a boat and winching the anchor line to pull her free. But the Tripolitan boats were converging on the scene, and would quickly pounce on any boat putting out from the frigate.

By now there were nine of them. And with her remaining guns pointing skyward on the listing deck, the *Philadelphia* was defenseless. Bainbridge ordered a part of the stern cut away, and the men went furiously to work again with their axes. A few of the big cannon were wheeled into place and aimed at the Tripolitan boats. The first salvo flew harmlessly over their heads; and because the guns could not be run out far enough, they set fire to the frigate's bulwarks.

Now the Tripolitans opened up, increasing their fire as they realized that the *Philadelphia* could not retaliate. They aimed at the rigging; they clearly had no intention of hulling their valuable prize. From the *Philadelphia*'s deck they could be seen sitting there, bobbing in the swells, safe from the frigate's guns, patiently waiting like vultures to swoop down on their prey.

After a futile four hours Bainbridge called a council of his officers. He later described their conclusion: "Upon a deliberate consideration of our situation, it was the unanimous opinion that it was impossible to get the ship off . . . and it was unanimously agreed that the only thing left for us to do was to surrender to the enemy."

Midshipman Wadsworth later recorded that there were tears in Bainbridge's eyes as all agreed to surrender "to save the lives of the Brave Crew." The "Brave Crew," however, did not all see it that way. According to William Ray, many of the sailors argued that they should keep trying to get the ship free. And the man who was ordered to haul down the *Philadelphia*'s colors, Ray reported, "positively refused to obey the captain's orders" until a midshipman threatened to run him through, "seized the halyards, and executed the command [himself] amidst the general murmuring of the crew."

In the meantime, at Bainbridge's orders, ship's carpenter William Godby led a team below with bits and augurs to drill holes in the frigate's bottom and scuttle her. Gunner Richard Stephenson

opened a cock to flood the powder magazine. Bainbridge also ordered shot poured into the pumps so the frigate's captors could not
pump her out. His code and signal books were brought on deck,
and Bainbridge tore the pages out, handing them to Midshipman
Daniel Patterson, who set them afire and tossed them over the
side.[24] Other groups of sailors brought up all the frigate's muskets,
pistols, and cutlasses; instead of issuing them to all hands for defense of the ship, the captain ordered them tossed into the sea.

Bainbridge, again according to Ray, mustered all hands and
"read a clause in the articles of war stating that our wages would
continue while we were prisoners of war; encouraged us to hope for
ransom by our country and advised us to behave with circumspec-
tion and propriety among our barbarian captors."

Ray also recalled many of the crewmen preparing for their imprisonment by rushing below, putting on all the clothes they could,
and emerging on deck looking "like Falstaff." The sun was reaching
the horizon as they awaited their captors. But the captors did not
come.

They remained in their boats surrounding the stricken frigate.
No doubt with their pirate's mentality they assumed that the
lowering of the *Philadelphia*'s flag was a ruse. After an embarrassing
wait, Bainbridge sent Midshipman Wadsworth off to announce the
Philadelphia's surrender.[25] Finally, at dusk, the Tripolitans swarmed
aboard, whooping and yelling as they came. They stripped the men
of their pocket money, watches, and layers of clothes, and ran
plundering through the vessel.[26] A few of the sailors slashed back
at their attackers; and when one Tripolitan tried to rip a locket from
Bainbridge's neck (it held a miniature of his wife), the captain angrily beat him off.

But all resistance had ceased by the time High Admiral Murad
Reis climbed aboard. He immediately sent men below to plug the
holes in the frigate's hull. She had taken on very little water,
mainly because she was so high aground. Sneeringly accusing
Bainbridge and his officers of cowardice,[27] Murad Reis ordered everyone over the side into the waiting boats. Through the early evening the *Philadelphia*'s 307 officers and men were ferried ashore.
The seas were still running high, and the Americans, many in their
underwear, were soaked. Like the galley slaves of earlier centuries,
they were forced to row the Tripolitan boats while their cutlass-

wielding captors stood over them. They landed on the shore under the bashaw's fortress. Most were pushed into the water and had to swim and wade through the surf crashing onto the beach. Just before Surgeon's Mate Jonathan Cowdery's boat grounded, two Tripolitans knocked him down, stole his case of surgical instruments and a silver pencil.

Assembled on the beach, the Americans marched in a torchlit procession through jeering crowds that spat at them along the way. The bashaw's palace was guarded by armed soldiers and some 50 dogs. The prisoners were led through heavy, iron-bolted doors into a dark tunnel and out into a paved courtyard filled, Private Ray recalled, with "janissaries armed with glittering sabres, muskets, pistols and tomahawks." Again they filed into a winding passageway leading at last to the reception room where Bashaw Yusuf Karamanli awaited them.

Frustratingly little is known about this wily adversary of the United States. Some of the *Philadelphia* prisoners described Yusuf as in his thirties, overweight but handsome, with a majestic black beard. He enjoyed opulent display, and was dressed for the reception in a beribboned turban and long silk robe embroidered in gold, his ample waist encircled with a diamond-studded belt into which he had stuffed two gold-mounted pistols and a ceremonial saber, chain, and scabbard. His audience chamber of porcelain walls and shining marble floors covered with thick Oriental rugs was dominated by his throne, inlaid with mosaic, lapped with gold-fringed, jewel-speckled velvet, and perched on a four-foot-high dais.

The bashaw was equally ostentatious when he went about his principality, richly caparisoned and usually accompanied by smartly performing guards, obsequious aides, and members of his family. His magnificent display evidently masked a secret terror, the paranoia of the tyrant. Everyone around him was heavily armed at all times. And always in his retinue was a special guard in charge of two strongboxes holding a fortune in gold and diamonds; the bashaw's treasure chests never left his presence, even outside his palace.

Rapacious, stubborn, hot-tempered, superstitious (a fixture of the palace was a crone whose prophecies he swore by), Bashaw Yusuf had one soft spot, his children. The Scotsman Peter Lisle who turned Muslim and adopted the name Murad Reis owed his appointment as high admiral to his wife, Yusuf's eldest daughter. And the other children of the bashaw were the recipients of lavish gifts and favors. Tender father, greedy dictator, paranoid tyrant, Bashaw Yusuf Karamanli deserved closer inspection than history has given him.

It was nearly midnight by the time the *Philadelphia*'s crew had been herded into an old warehouse and her officers had been quartered in the American Consulate that had been vacated by James Cathcart after the bashaw's declaration of war. The pirates had relieved Bainbridge of his sword, his pocket money, and even his epaulets, but he still had his locket.

He promptly demanded permission to talk to the Danish consul, Nicholas Nissen, who came to see him the day after the capture and promised to help in every way he could. Bainbridge then sat down to write an official report to Commodore Preble, which Consul Nissen agreed to forward.

The imprisoned captain acknowledged, "Had I not sent the Schooner [*Vixen*] from us, the Accident might have been prevented . . . but my Motives of ordering her to Cape Bon, was to grant more efficient protection to our Commerce than I could by keeping her with me."[28] He tried to explain his decision to surrender: "Some fanatics may say that blowing up the ship would have been the proper course. I thought such conduct would not stand acquitted before God or Man, and I never presumed to think I had the liberty of putting to death 306 souls[29] because they were placed under my command." He suggested that he had little to live for himself; he realized that the loss of his frigate "strikes the death blow to my future Prospects."

As if any further humiliation were needed, two days after the *Philadelphia*'s grounding another November storm sent huge swells over Kaliusa Reef, lifting her and permitting the Tripolitans to haul her free. In dismay Bainbridge looked out his window and saw her riding at anchor in the inner harbor. Over succeeding days local sponge divers rescued most of the frigate's guns, anchors, and other jettisoned gear. High Admiral Murad Reis now had in his navy the most formidable warship in all the Barbary fleets. With the *Philadelphia* he could play havoc with the American blockaders and perhaps even attempt to capture the only remaining U.S. frigate on station in the Mediterranean, Commodore Preble's *Constitution*.

But the salvaging of the *Philadelphia* inspired Bainbridge with a daring plan. In a report to Preble he proposed that the squadron send in a task force to burn her at her mooring and at least deprive the Tripolitans of their new warship. The bashaw encouraged Bainbridge to write to Preble pleading for ransom. But in his letters Bainbridge employed an ingenious method of reporting to Preble despite the Tripolitan censors. His letters overtly recounted details on the loss and salvage of the frigate and his imprisonment. But in lemon juice[30] diluted with water, between the lines Bainbridge proposed his scheme. The lemon juice was invisible until heated over a flame. The subterfuge fooled the Tripolitan censors, who permitted Consul Nissen to forward Bainbridge's letters along with his regular diplomatic correspondence to the Danish consul in Malta, who sent it on to Preble in Syracuse.[31]

Commodore Preble's first reaction to what he called the "melancholy & distressing intelligence" was a characteristic flare of temper. Writing to Secretary Smith to report the frigate's loss "without a man on either side having been killed or wounded," he raged, "Would to God that the Officers and crew . . . had one and all determined to prefer death to slavery. It is possible such a determination might save them from either."[32] Clearly Preble believed that Bainbridge could have fought off his attackers until a favorable wind helped him off the reef. And remembering his earlier, rosy prediction, Preble gloomily admitted, "Were it not for that loss, I have no doubt we would have had peace with Tripoli in the Spring; but I have now no hope of such an event."

By the time he had received more of Bainbridge's reports, Preble had cooled off enough to write him a placating reply.[33] He, too, had considered destroying the *Philadelphia*. Better to lose her altogether than let Murad Reis use her against the American squadron.[34] Preble immediately set to work on a plan to sabotage her.

CHAPTER 7

★ ★ ★

SINGEING THE BASHAW'S BEARD

The *Philadelphia*'s men resigned themselves to a long incarceration. Nineteenth-century Barbary prisoners at least were not chained to rowing benches of war galleys as they had been for centuries before sail had replaced oars. Nor were the *Philadelphia*'s men sold in the Barbary slave markets; the bashaw was quite aware of their value to him as hostages and bargaining pawns. Nonetheless Tripoli's prison was worse than anything in the United States.

The captives were confined in a 50- by 20-foot stone warehouse that they first had to clean out; it had been used as a smokehouse and still reeked of the fumes. Each morning they were led to work by foremen who seemed to enjoy beating them. The unskilled were put to work on the city's fortifications, especially a new one on the waterfront east of the city which the sailors sardonically called "the American Fort."[1] Some were assigned to a daily water detail, lugging huge buckets from a well to the work gangs. The frigate's cooks were sent to work in the castle. The carpenters and coopers were ordered to the shipyards where xebecs, feluccas, and other vessels were being built. When the *Philadelphia* was salvaged, some of these artisans were assigned to repair the damage they had done in scuttling her and to remounting the guns that had been brought up from the reef. When he heard of this work, Bainbridge objected, without success.

One contingent of prisoners was taken on an intriguing mission. Four of them loaded down with provisions were herded through Tripoli's narrow, winding streets to a passageway that led into a courtyard where the women of a harem (they never found out whose) were sunning themselves on the porches, naked to the waist. Marine private Ray, one of the four prisoners, described the harem women: "their eyelids stained round the edges in black, their hair braided, turned upward and fastened with a broad tinsel fillet. They had three or four rings in each ear as large in circumference as a dollar. Several of them were very delicate and handsome." The women "manifested great surprise at our appearance," Ray recalled, and "were full of giggling and loquacity." They offered the Americans "dates, olives, oranges and milk." But the guards soon whisked the prisoners away from temptation (perhaps on both sides).[2]

The prisoners worked without food from dawn to noon, when they were given a few minutes in which to eat a piece of black bread dipped in olive oil. By late afternoon they were marched back to their prison, counted again, and served the rest of their meager ration. They had been shackled the first night but not thereafter. The warehouse was heavily barred and lit only by a skylight and two high windows. There was scarcely enough room for all the men to lie down on the dirt floor at night. And in the description of one prisoner, "We had nothing to keep us from the cold, damp earth, but a thin, tattered sailcloth; the floor of the prison was very uneven, planted with hard pebbles, and as we had nothing but a shirt to soften our beds, and nothing but the ground for a pillow, and very much crowded into the bargain, the clouds of night shed no salutary repose." The narrow, swinging hammocks of the *Philadelphia* seemed in retrospect like luxury.

For the first few days the guards dispensed rations of salted pork and beef rescued from the frigate, served raw and not soaked to remove the salt. But those supplies soon ran out, and the daily ration per man consisted of one 12-ounce loaf of barley bread with an occasional addition of couscous, a form of coarse barley boiled in oil. The seamen petitioned Bainbridge to demand better food, and he promised to, advising them meanwhile to "conduct yourselves as becoming American seamen and soldiers. Keep your spirits up and hope for better days."[3] Consul Nissen, who visited them regularly, also said he would do what he could; but the diet did not improve. Many of the prisoners became ill. Surgeon's Mate Cowdery was permitted to treat them, but virtually no medicines had been salvaged from the ship. By January of 1804 two of the men had died.

But gradually the others adapted to the diet, and the hard work kept them healthy.

● Their mental reactions were more diverse. Some managed to get drunk. The Muslims disdained anything alcoholic. But there were numerous Christian slaves, mainly Neapolitan, who bought rum, whiskey, or *aguardiente*, a local concoction made from fermented dates, from the city's Jewish merchants and smuggled it into the prison in their robes. One desperate American attempted to cut his throat but was foiled by the guards. Some of the more adventurous tried to dig an escape tunnel; it collapsed, nearly suffocating them. They tried again and again failed.[4]

Gradually they settled into the routine of prison life, learning the ways of saving and swapping food and blankets, the minimum amount of work they could do without punishment, and especially which of their guards were more brutal than others. Nearly every guard was soon given a nickname: Tousef, a not-too-bright renegade Frenchman whom they called the "quid," a current term for a "jerk"; a lame Greek guard who became known as "Bandy"; and "Captain Blackbeard," the head jailer. Everyone did what he could to avoid "Scamping Jack," a Tunisian who seemed always angry; "Blinkard," the doctor who enjoyed torturing his victims; and "Red Jack," the "most barbarous" of the guards.

A few Americans became turncoats, attempting to curry favor with their jailers. Quartermaster John Wilson was particularly despised by his shipmates when he toadied to the guards, persuaded them to make him an overseer, and beat a few men to show his zeal. Wilson outraged the other prisoners on an occasion when the bashaw came to gloat over them. Wearing a white, hooded robe and riding a gray horse ornamented by gold trappings, Yusuf Karamanli was attended by a vast retinue of foot guards, a high constable carrying the three-pronged scepter, the minister of state, an enormous black bodyguard, some of Yusuf's children, dozens of Mamelukes wheeling about on their horses as they brought up the rear, and the ever-present chests containing the bashaw's treasure. When the procession swept before the prisoners whom Wilson and the other overseers had assembled for the visit, Wilson called for three cheers. Most of the sailors were struck dumb, but a few responded by braying like donkeys.

Wilson enraged Bainbridge by telling his jailers that the captain had dumped 19 boxes of silver dollars onto Kaliusa Reef. The Tripolitans greedily dived for the treasure; and when they found nothing, the bashaw submitted Bainbridge to a harsh interrogation. Bainbridge swore that the frigate's money had been left in Malta, but the bashaw did not believe him, and had Bainbridge's cabin boy flogged in a vain attempt to get more information. Bainbridge went to the prison, angrily upbraided Wilson, and promised him that he would be hanged for treason when they returned to the United States. Undaunted, Wilson told the Tripolitans that some of the sailors who had signed a parole promising not to attempt escape if permitted to visit the shops in the town were in fact planning to make a run for it; their parole was canceled.

Wilson's fellow prisoners were tempted to beat him to a pulp; but when one marine did give him a thrashing, he was rewarded with 500 bastinadoes. So the others simply refused to speak to Wilson. He reacted by becoming more Moslem than the Tripolitans, renouncing Christianity, swearing allegiance to Mohammedanism, and wearing Moslem robes. Four other Americans switched faith—or pretended to—and earned the same scorn from their shipmates.

The ironic plight of some *Philadelphia* captives was that they were not Americans but British deserters who had volunteered for service in the U.S. Navy to avoid even worse conditions aboard British men-of-war.[5] Bainbridge estimated that half of his crew was British; perhaps he was exaggerating in hopes of freeing as many men as possible. He asked Preble to urge the British to intercede, and Preble passed the request along to the nearest Royal Navy officer. According to legend, the request eventually reached Admiral Nelson, who coldly replied that the deserters deserved to be hanged.

The *Philadelphia*'s officers fared better than her men. Their prison, the former U.S. Consulate, was a sizable house with a large courtyard. Danish Consul Nissen provided some furniture, but there were not enough beds, and most of the officers slept on mats spread on the tile floor. Nissen also supplied fresh fruit, vegetables, and other food bought in the marketplace to supplement their rations, which consisted of two meals a day: a piece of bread and two eggs for breakfast, camel meat or tough beef, boiled cabbage, and bread for dinner. The only drink was rainwater. The officers' meals were served by European and Maltese slaves.

The officers were not required to work. The consulate had a wide roof on which they could walk for exercise; it also provided an excellent vantage point from which to study the city with its warren of narrow streets, the white houses, the palm trees and flowering hibiscus and the sparkling blue Mediterranean. Tripolitan men could be seen spending their mornings on benches in front of the coffeehouses with their European slaves fanning them and sometimes holding their tiny coffee cups so their masters could converse with both hands. Few Tripolitan women were seen in public, and those who appeared were swathed in robes from head to toe. Tripoli's slums swarmed with people in tatters. Sometimes the city echoed with the din of children sent screaming through the streets; the guards explained that Tripolitans believed the noise would attract much-needed rain.

From the consulate rooftop the officers could also see the city's fortifications. On one occasion they watched with wry pleasure as the Tripolitans—many wearing captured American uniforms—mounted some of the *Philadelphia*'s guns on the city's batteries and in attempting to fire one of the cannon overloaded it; the explosion killed one and wounded four of the bashaw's soldiers. But when after the *Philadelphia*'s salvage the guards spotted Captain Bainbridge studying her through his telescope, all officers were banned from the roof.

Tripoli's foreign minister, Sidi Mohammed Dghies, was a frequent visitor to the consulate, sometimes offering deals for American money. A week after the *Philadelphia*'s capture he announced that he had rescued eight trunks of personal effects from the frigate, which he could return to them for $1,200; Bainbridge declined. Dghies a week later suddenly demanded that Bainbridge order Commodore Preble to return all Tripolitans captured by the U.S. squadron, threatening retaliation against the American captives if he did not. Bainbridge replied that he had no authority to command Preble. The next day all of the officers were taken from the consulate to an underground dungeon. For a day they were confined there with no food; then, with no explanation, they were marched back to the consulate.

Consul Nissen called on them nearly every day, bringing provisions and news and serving as a post office for the captain and the other officers. Nissen also sent the officers two baskets of books from his library. On one of his visits he brought along a load of books he had found in the marketplace; they consisted of most of the volumes from the *Philadelphia*'s library. He had bought them for very little, he said, because they were in English and of no use to anyone else. Bainbridge promptly used them to establish a school for the midshipmen and young officers, with lieutenants Porter and Jacob Jones as teachers. Throughout their captivity the officers studied navigation, naval tactics, and mathematics.

The *Philadelphia* officer who received the best treatment of all was Surgeon's Mate Cowdery, especially after he had been called to the palace to administer to the bashaw's eleven-month-old daughter. Cowdery found her quite ill and her father "much affected." He could do little for her, but when he called the next day, she was greatly improved, and the grateful bashaw offered Cowdery a horse, a servant, and permission to go anywhere he liked. Yusuf suggested that the doctor might enjoy the royal gardens two miles outside the city. Cowdery was also permitted to walk about the streets; and during one of his outings the infamous Murad Reis cordially invited him into a coffeehouse for a cup. Later the bashaw, "with much politeness," asked Cowdery to be the royal physician. Cowdery accepted, and shortly the *Philadelphia*'s officers were permitted to stroll in the nearby countryside—six at a time, under guard. Cowdery's services became popular with the bashaw's retinue, many of whom asked him to treat their eye troubles. The combination of sun, blowing sand, biting insects, and improper care caused blindness among many Tripolitans, as it did all along the Barbary Coast.

A month and a half after the capture of the *Philadelphia* the Tripolitans began to observe the Fast of Ramadan; for 30 days all true believers abstained from food and drink from dawn to sunset. When on January 15, 1804, Ramadan ended, everyone celebrated with the festival of Biaram. And because Ramadan was a time to be charitable to one's enemies, the *Philadelphia*'s officers were invited to the feast at the palace. Bashaw Yusuf received them in his throne room surrounded by his Divan, his bodyguards, his other attendants, and his family. After a serving of coffee and sherbet, they were invited to kiss the bashaw's hand; they refused, but saluted him as they departed. On the way out of the palace Bainbridge noticed three forlorn young men sitting on a stone bench; they had not participated in the festivities. When the captain asked one of the guards who they were, he was told that they were the sons of Hamet, Yusuf's older brother, and that Yusuf had kept Hamet's wife and five children as hostages for his loyalty.

● Dr. Cowdery kept busy with his American and Tripolitan patients. The midshipmen and younger officers had their school, which they called "The University of the Prison." The rest of the officers were bored to distraction. Captain Bainbridge tried to occupy himself writing regular reports, with secret intelligence in his invisible ink, to Commodore Preble. From his window he could see the *Philadelphia* at anchor, constantly reminding him of his humiliation.

The Tripolitans seemed in no hurry to get her ready for sea. They had brought down her topmasts and were still replacing her guns. Bainbridge reported to Preble that because she was partially dismasted it was impossible to "restore this beautiful vessel to our Navy." He also had good reason to remember the treacherous shoals around Tripoli's harbor, and warned Preble, "It would not be possible to take the frigate out, owing to the difficulty of the channel." On February 16 he sent off another intelligence report: "She lays about three quarters of a mile from the shore," and again proposed slipping in and burning her.

That afternoon Dr. Cowdery was asked to look in on the bashaw's eldest daughter, High Admiral Murad Reis's wife. He was leaving her at 5 P.M. when he heard that two British merchantmen had apparently run the American blockade and were approaching the harbor. "At about 11 at night," he wrote, "we were alarmed by a most hideous yelling and screaming from one end of town to the other, and a firing of cannon from the castle." He and the other officers went to a window overlooking the harbor and "saw the *Philadelphia* in flames."

Commodore Preble had established his headquarters at Syracuse, on the island of Sicily. It was farther from Tripoli than Malta,[6] where the hospitable British governor, Sir Alexander Ball, still offered the services of his dockyards. But Admiral Nelson, dogging the French Fleet in the Mediterranean, had virtually denuded Malta of provisions. Moreover, Preble had not forgotten the Royal Navy luring deserters from his flagship at Gibraltar, even though Ball promised not to permit such activities in Valletta. The governor of Syracuse, an obsequious Italian named Marcello de Gregorio, outdid himself in welcoming the Americans, whose presence, he was sure, would deter Barbary pirates' attacks on Syracuse more effectively than the Neapolitan Navy had. Not incidentally, the Americans could be expected to pump many dollars into the city's economy. And no small incentive to de Gregorio was the largess Preble gave him personally, such gifts as port and Madeira, English cheeses and bottles of attar of roses. The governor offered the U.S. squadron the use of Syracuse's navy yard, storehouses, and naval hospital. There was abundant water at the Fountain of Arethusa near the dockyards and fresh produce from the surrounding farms (including partridges for the commodore's table).[7]

• The American presence did stimulate Syracuse's economy. New stores and hotels opened. The Syracuse Opera Company attracted the best Sicilian singers when the word spread that American sailors showed their appreciation by throwing money on the stage. But Preble soon tired of the toadying governor, whose hand was always out and who cadged supplies from the Americans to sell to others. Preble's limited patience was exhausted when a U.S. sailor deserted to a French privateer and Lieutenant Richard Somers went after him. Even more afraid of the French than of the Americans, Governor de Gregorio arrested Somers and his shore party and sent a couple of aides out to the *Constitution* to explain. They made the mistake of arriving at 10 P.M., after Preble had retired.

Midshipman Wadsworth recalled Preble's reaction: "in the rage the tables and chairs and Neapolitan officers' hats flew about the cabin, and when the light was again brought in, it was some time before these unfortunate messengers could be found. They were detained all night and frightened out of their senses." Preble sent them ashore with a curt note to the governor demanding that his men be released immediately and threatening to level the city.

Somers and his shore party were soon back aboard the flagship; but the American deserter remained uncaught.

● Preble joined the U.S. blockaders off the Tripolitan coast in December of 1803, three months after his arrival in the Mediterranean. Accompanying the flagship *Constitution* was the schooner *Enterprise*, with Lieutenant Stephen Decatur in command. On December 23 at 8:30 A.M., nine miles east of the harbor, the *Enterprise* sighted another vessel and gave chase, followed by the *Constitution*. An hour and a half later Decatur caught up with the stranger and found her to be a 64-ton ketch named *Mastico* flying the Turkish ensign. She had sailed from Tripoli, destination Constantinople, with an odd assortment of crew and passengers: eleven Greek and Turkish sailors, two Tripolitan officers, ten Tripolitan soldiers and 42 black slaves—men, women, and children—destined as gifts from Bashaw Yusuf to the sultan in Constantinople.

Although her master contended that she was a Turkish trader, she had two cannon on deck and two more stowed below, as well as an arsenal of muskets and pistols. The *Constitution* rounded up on the scene, and Preble ordered the *Mastico* taken as a prize to Syracuse. There his assumption was confirmed.

Earlier Preble had encountered at Malta a Dr. Pietro Francisco Crocillo, who had been Bashaw Yusuf's physician and had since left Tripoli. Realizing the usefulness of someone with knowledge of the bashaw's palace, Preble had signed on Dr. Crocillo as a surgeon's mate. Now Crocillo attested that he recognized the *Mastico*'s captain as one of the men who had gone out to attack the *Philadelphia*. Another Italian Preble had hired was a 32-year-old trading captain from Palermo named Salvador Catalano who knew Tripoli Harbor; Preble had taken him aboard the flagship as a pilot. Catalano had also been in Tripoli at the time of the *Philadelphia*'s grounding, and he claimed that the *Mastico*'s captain had led one of the boarding parties descending on the frigate. A final clue was provided when a more thorough search of the ketch turned up the sword of the *Philadelphia*'s Lieutenant Porter. Preble condemned the *Mastico* as a legitimate prize of war[8] and renamed her the *Intrepid*.

The capture of the *Mastico* stimulated Lieutenant Decatur to call on the commodore with an idea—the same idea that Bainbridge and Preble had already been considering. Now, Decatur pointed out, they had the perfect vessel for the project, a lateen-rigged ketch that would attract no suspicion when she entered Tripoli Harbor. Pleased at the confirmation of his own thinking, Preble agreed. Decatur begged to command the expedition.

⦁ Preble knew the colorful background of his young lieutenant— indeed it may have figured in his recent decision to transfer Decatur aboard the *Enterprise* and take him east where the action would be, replacing him with Isaac Hull aboard the *Argus* in the western Mediterranean.

Stephen Decatur had been born on January 5, 1779, to Philadelphia parents.[9] A broad-shouldered, curly-haired, handsome ladies' man, young Decatur reputedly had gone to sea at 19 at the urging of attorneys after being acquitted of the murder of "a woman of doubtful integrity." Whatever his reason, he found a berth as a midshipman (no doubt with his influential father's help) aboard the frigate *United States*. While briefly ashore he married an heiress who had fallen in love with him even before meeting him; she had become infatuated with his portrait. But she agreed with his declaration that the U.S. Navy took precedence in his affections. Decatur was not the only young naval officer who felt that way in the early nineteenth century.[10]

Now the young commander of the *Enterprise*, Decatur impressed nearly everyone, officers and men alike, with his quality of leadership. Marine private Ray, who enjoyed being critical of naval officers, wrote, "The intrepid Decatur is proverbial among sailors, for the good treatment of his men, as he is for his valour. Not a tar, who ever sailed with Decatur, but would almost sacrifice his life for him." And Midshipman Robert Spence, who had served with Decatur aboard the *United States*, wrote, "I was struck with a peculiarity of manner and appearance calculated to rivet the eye and engross the attention. I had often pictured to myself the form and look of a hero, such as my favorite Homer had delineated; here I saw it embodied."

Decatur had competition from a fellow lieutenant and former shipmate from the *United States*. Charles Stewart, commanding the sloop-of-war *Siren*, also volunteered to lead the expedition. But Preble shared the others' admiration for Decatur's leadership and zeal.

And he decided that Stewart could serve as well by accompanying the *Intrepid* and rescuing her men after they had accomplished their mission.

It was another testimony to Decatur that when—his voice high-pitched with excitement—he asked the *Enterprise*'s crew for volunteers, every man stepped forward. (A contributing factor may have been the utter boredom of blockade duty.) He selected 62 of the most muscular for the close combat he expected with the *Philadelphia*'s Tripolitan crew.[11] Eight of his selection were marines. Meanwhile work crews washed down and fumigated the *Mastico-Intrepid*, whose hold was alive with vermin. Her guns were taken ashore, and she was made to look more like an innocent trading vessel; her lateen yards were left for the same reason. The *Siren* was painted a different color so she would not be recognized.

Preble's orders to Decatur were clear and simple. His men were to use the *Intrepid*'s combustibles to set fire to the *Philadelphia;* they were not to attempt to bring her out of the harbor. If it looked worthwhile and feasible, Decatur could then set the *Intrepid* afire and send her in among the ships of the harbor, escaping in the *Intrepid*'s boats to the *Siren.* Lieutenant Stewart was directed to lie outside the harbor prepared to send in the *Siren*'s boats to rescue the *Intrepid*'s men if necessary.

Five midshipmen from the *Constitution*, no doubt after much pleading, were added to the *Intrepid*'s force. Most important, Salvador Catalano was enlisted to masquerade as captain of the *Intrepid.* Catalano claimed to know every reef in Tripoli Harbor, and he could speak Arabic as well as the lingua franca used by the traders along the Barbary Coast. The *Siren* was also given a pilot, John Jourvass of the *Constitution.* All hands were assembled in the two vessels. Preble gave a final blessing: "May God prosper you in this enterprise." At 5 P.M. on February 3, 1804, the *Intrepid* and *Siren* set sail on their mission of destruction. Midshipman Ralph Izard left behind a letter: "This evening, Dear mother, I sail for Tripoli . . . for the purpose of burning the Frigate *Philadelphia.* . . . We are certain of success."

By the next day, in mid-Mediterranean en route to Tripoli, Decatur was informed that the meat aboard the *Intrepid* was inedible. Evidently the beef had been packed in barrels that had previously been used for salted fish and improperly cleaned; now it was spoiled beyond human consumption. The ration had to be reduced to biscuits and water. But the weather was perfect, and the two vessels made their landfall off Tripoli in four days. As they approached the coast, they separated so as not to appear to be sailing together. The *Siren's* crewmen were still re-rigging her to look more Turkish and had disguised her gunports. By late afternoon of February 7, under a light breeze, the *Intrepid* hove to and anchored. As dusk fell, Decatur could see the Siren anchoring not far away. Everything was in readiness.

But with the darkness the wind picked up; soon it was blowing a small gale, and the seas were running high. Catalano warned against trying to negotiate the tricky harbor entrance in such weather. Frustrated and impatient, Decatur insisted on a reconnoiter and sent Midshipman Charles Morris and Catalano ahead in a boat. It was dark by the time they returned to report that the wind-driven waves were roaring into the harbor, obscuring some reefs and crashing over others; the *Intrepid* would almost certainly be swept onto the rocks. Besides, it would be impossible to escape from the harbor against such a sea and head wind. As they shouted their findings on the windy quarterdeck, the storm increased. Their boat was smashed against the *Intrepid's* side before it could be hauled aboard. Decatur resignedly headed seaward to ride out the gale.

Aboard the *Siren* Lieutenant Stewart saw the *Intrepid's* stern lights heading into the open Mediterranean and attempted to follow her. He had already put his boats over the side, ready to rescue the *Intrepid's* men if necessary; and the gale-driven seas were running so high that it took a long time to recover them. Then he found that the *Siren's* anchor had dragged and fouled on some rocks. For hours the crew worked on the wet, heaving foredeck trying to hoist it; directing the operation, Stewart was thrown to the deck and injured. But he continued to command, finally ordering the anchor cable cut. Dawn was approaching as the *Siren* went pitching seaward to try to find the *Intrepid*.

The storm continued for a week, driving the two small vessels eastward into the Gulf of Sidra. The ships' lookouts managed to sight each other, but all the two crews could do was fight to keep their vessels afloat. The situation was particularly intolerable aboard the overcrowded *Intrepid*. Decatur and four other officers were crammed into one tiny cabin. Six midshipmen and Catalano were confined to a makeshift platform over the water casks, so close to the deck that, far from standing headroom, there was not even room to sit up. The eight marines were on a similar shelf on the other side of the vessel. The sailors were jammed into a small hold amid crashing barrels and crates, listening to the seas thunder against the hull and wondering when her seams would open or whether the 60-foot vessel would be swamped by the mountainous waves. Worse, it turned out that the fumigators had not done their work well; the hold still swarmed with rats and other vermin. In the heavy seas the ketch shipped tons of green water, and the men frantically worked the pumps to keep her from foundering. As the punishing days went by, exhausted by working the ship in deck-sweeping waves, the men gradually weakened on their meager diet.

Finally on February 15 the winds began to slacken. Decatur called for more sail and a course westward for Tripoli harbor. By 5:30 P.M. both vessels were back off Point Tagiura, just east of Tripoli Harbor. Decatur and Stewart decided to get out of sight of land to avoid detection. At 9:30 they headed back toward the harbor—and could not find it in the darkness.

At 11 A.M. on the 16th Decatur turned toward Tripoli again, towing a drag made of spare wood to slow her in the still-blustery wind. The *Siren* held back while the *Intrepid*, her sails purposely flopping to make her look more like a trading vessel, approached the harbor. The Union Jack flew at her masthead. It was dusk and the wind was moderating as she reached the harbor entrance.

Decatur looked out to sea for the *Siren*, but she was not in sight. At 7 P.M., worrying about the dying wind, he decided to go ahead and hope that the *Siren* would be off the harbor waiting for him when he came back out. The *Intrepid*'s lateen sails were trimmed to the light breeze, and she slipped through the outer harbor entrance.

Studying the sunset and calculating the ketch's speed, Decatur decided that she was moving too fast. Although there was only a breath of wind, the heavy sea of the storm's aftermath was propelling her shoreward. At this rate she would reach the *Philadelphia* too soon. Rendezvous with the *Siren*'s boats—assuming she made it—had been set for 10 P.M., and Decatur needed to wait for her in case his mission required a rescue.

He called for more drags; large buckets went over the side. The *Intrepid* slowed. They were already approaching the narrow, twisting entrance to the inner harbor, and Catalano was studying every reef, which in the darkness boiled white with surf. A crescent moon was high overhead. By 8 P.M., with the breeze continuing to drop, Decatur ordered the drags brought in. At this point some boats could be seen approaching.

Before Decatur could become alarmed, the men identified themselves; they were from the *Siren*, which had reached the outer harbor entrance and anchored. In the boats were 30 men eager to join the *Intrepid*'s crew. Decatur let them come aboard, except for those needed to take the boats back to await their rescue mission. He ordered every man to his hiding place and demanded utter silence.

Huddled in their hideouts, the men reviewed their assignments. All were to rush aboard the frigate at Decatur's signal. No guns were to be used; the Tripolitans aboard the *Philadelphia* were to be dispatched by sword, cutlass, and dagger. Decatur, two other officers, and 14 men were to concentrate on the frigate's spar deck. Other detachments were assigned to the berth deck and forward storerooms, the cockpit, and aft storerooms. A few officers and men were to remain aboard the *Intrepid* to watch for a counterattack. As soon as the Tripolitans in the frigate were subdued, the men aboard the *Intrepid* were to hand up the combustibles to be placed throughout the *Philadelphia*. At Decatur's command everything was to be set alight at once and everyone was to rush back aboard the *Intrepid*.

Nine o'clock. The ketch was barely moving in a near calm. Decatur and his masquerading companions on deck could see the winking lights of the city. Then, silhouetted against them rose the large hull of the *Philadelphia*. The helmsman silently guided the *Intrepid* toward her. As the distance slowly closed, lights showed aboard the frigate. Her gunports were open and her cannon ready. Turbaned heads could be seen passing by the ports. There was no sign of anyone on her high, dark deck.

Nine-thirty. The *Intrepid* was now under the frigate's guns—as well as more than a hundred cannon in Tripoli's shore batteries. The harbor was still except for swells lapping against the ships. Decatur could just make out two gunboats off the frigate's starboard bow. The *Intrepid*'s long lateen boom creaked as she rolled with the swells.

Ten. A voice boomed from the *Philadelphia*. Catalano, who understood Arabic, whispered to Decatur that the lookout was ordering the *Intrepid* to bear off. At Decatur's nod Catalano called out to identify his vessel: He was a trader from Malta; his ketch had lost her anchor in the gale, and he requested permission to tie up alongside for the night.

The lookout's voice indicated his suspicion. He asked what the vessel's cargo was. Catalano's reply seemed to reassure him—until the lookout asked about another vessel just outside the harbor.

Decatur had prepared Catalano for this. She was the *Transfer*, Catalano replied; the Tripolitans, Decatur knew, had recently purchased her and were awaiting her arrival. As the pilot talked, the *Intrepid* drifted closer; she was now only 20 yards from the tall side of the *Philadelphia*. The breeze died, and the *Intrepid* stalled.

Men could be seen climbing down into one of the frigate's boats. They rowed around to the bow, took a line, and turned toward the *Intrepid*. Decatur responded quickly; he did not want the *Philadelphia*'s boat getting too close. At this point the ketch was a sitting duck; one broadside from the frigate would blow her to bits. Softly he called for one of the *Intrepid*'s boats to take a line toward the frigate. The two boats met, and the men spliced their lines.

The *Intrepid*'s boat started back toward the ketch. Decatur whispered orders to the robed men on deck to bring in the line as fast as they could. Some of those hiding behind the bulwarks lent a hand, pulling as well as they could from their prone position. The gap between the two vessels began to close. A stern line went flying over to the frigate, and someone made it fast. At that moment a voice aboard the *Philadelphia* shouted, "Americani!"[12]

Catalano panicked and shouted, "Board, Captain, board!" But Decatur could see that there still was too much water between the vessels, and called down the *Intrepid*'s deck, "No order to be obeyed but that of the commanding officer!" For a few seconds, while the *Intrepid*'s men pulled frantically on the lines and thumping noises of alarm could be heard aboard the *Philadelphia*, the members of the boarding party held their breaths. The two vessels' hulls came together, and Decatur yelled, "BOARD!"

❂ Leading the charge, jumping for one of the frigate's chain plates[13] to climb aboard, Decatur misstepped and nearly fell. Alongside him Midshipman Alexander Laws, grabbing a gunport lid, got his sword tangled. Midshipman Charles Morris was the first aboard, quickly followed by Laws and Decatur. Not realizing that Morris had beaten him aboard, Decatur mistook him in the dark for a Tripolitan and was about to cut him down when Morris gave the password: "Philadelphia."

All along the *Philadelphia*'s side the *Intrepid*'s men were swarming aboard.[14] Within seconds they were pouring down the frigate's deck, slashing with sword, cutlass, and saber as the terrified Tripolitans retreated, most of them diving over the side with scimitars still in hand; the others were cut down before they could retreat. The frigate was taken, without a shot fired, in ten minutes.[15]

The men aboard the *Intrepid* were ready with boxes of tar, lint, shavings, and powder that had been dried out after the storm and that they now passed up to the frigate's deck and through the ports. Everyone aboard the *Philadelphia* was at his station and quickly spread the incendiary debris. Each man carried a small sperm-oil candle, and the leader of each squad carried lanterns slung over his shoulder. Decatur ran along the *Philadelphia*'s deck calling to each squad leader; as soon as all were ready, he gave the signal. The men lit their candles from the lanterns and tossed them into the flammable debris; nearly every fire was lit simultaneously.

The *Philadelphia* was dry as tinder, and her open ports and hatchways provided a surging updraft. She virtually exploded into flame in half a dozen locations. Midshipman Morris and his group, deep in the frigate's cockpit, were almost trapped by the flames above them as they rushed up the companionway to join the rest of the men pouring over the *Philadelphia*'s side into the *Intrepid*. Behind them they left some 20 Tripolitan bodies on the deck to burn with the ship. Hastily making sure everyone had escaped, Decatur jumped and almost went overboard again; he caught the ketch's rigging and slid down onto her deck as she swung away from the burning frigate. Only later did he realize that in the rush he had dropped the *Philadelphia's* Tripolitan ensign, which he had hauled down to take to Commodore Preble as a souvenir.

The entire operation had taken 25 minutes. And now at last the bashaw's shore batteries opened up. In their surprise the gunners were firing wildly. Still, one shell tore through the *Intrepid's* topsail. Desperately pushing away, her men rushed to get clear of the fiery frigate. The flames had already burned through the bowline between the two vessels, but in the confusion no one remembered the stern line. By the time someone did, steaming tar was pouring down onto the *Intrepid*, and gusts of flame were shooting through the frigate's gunports into the ketch, threatening to ignite the barrels of combustible debris intended for use if she were turned into a fireship.

There was no time for that. The immediate problem was getting clear of the burning *Philadelphia*. The stern line was cut, and Decatur called for the sweeps. But the *Intrepid's* long boom caught on the frigate's stern. The fire was singeing the ketch's cotton sails. The *Philadelphia* was now one huge flame towering into the sky and lighting the whole harbor as her blazing lines and yards broke away and fell hissing into the water.[16] The frigate's firestorm was so intense that the *Intrepid* was almost sucked into it. But the boom was finally freed; the oarsmen got to work, and the ketch slowly pulled away from the zone of fire.

She was a perfect target in the light of the flaming frigate, and the bashaw's gunners redoubled their fire. Then the Philadelphia's guns, which had been double-shotted[17] to aid in the harbor's defense, were ignited by the flames. Thundering like gigantic bombshells as each was touched off, the frigate's guns fired a concert of salvos straight into the castle guns ashore, throwing their gunners into confusion. Her seaward guns fired just short of the *Intrepid*. A providential fresh breeze came up to help the men at the sweeps, and the ketch raced out of range toward the outer harbor. At that point the flames reached the *Philadelphia's* powder magazine.

With a volcanic roar the frigate seemed to rise out of the water and nearly disintegrate into a thousand arcing fireworks. The men aboard the *Intrepid* paused in flight, awed by the spectacle they had created.

(•) It was 1 A.M. by the time the *Intrepid* left the outer harbor. Across the water Decatur heard a man call, "*Siren*'s boats, sir. Have you a line?" The *Intrepid* did not need a tow. But Decatur jumped into one of the boats to be rowed to the *Siren* where he reported to Lieutenant Stewart that the mission had been accomplished without a man lost and only one injured.

For an hour the two vessels stood off the harbor while everyone watched the remains of the *Philadelphia* burn. Then, before a freshening breeze they set sail for Syracuse. As dawn began to light the sky at 6 A.M., they could still see the last glimmering flames on the horizon 40 miles away.

Commodore Preble was waiting at Syracuse with mounting anxiety. By February 19 the *Intrepid* and *Siren* were nearly two weeks overdue. His fleet, too, had fought a storm for four days, and Preble began to fear that the gale had driven both vessels ashore on the Tripolitan coast. The *Siren* should have returned if the *Intrepid* had been captured in the harbor. Of course, it was also possible—even probable, considering the *Siren*'s Lieutenant Stewart—that the *Siren* had tried to go to the *Intrepid*'s rescue and had also been captured.

In a report to Secretary Smith on the proposed action, Preble had written, "It will undoubtedly cost us many lives, but it must be done." He had not, however, expected to lose every man aboard both vessels. Agonizing over the fate of his men and two of his favorite lieutenants, Preble became more than usually irascible. He ordered a constant watch at the flagship's masthead. For a week, ten days, 12 days, there was no sign of the *Intrepid* or the *Siren*.

At 10 A.M. on February 19 the lookout reported two sails on the horizon. As they approached, the *Intrepid*'s lateen yards were soon recognized. Preble called for the hoist of signal number 227: "Have you completed the business you were sent on?" There were a few tense minutes before signal flags could be seen in the distance fluttering to the *Siren*'s masthead: a 2, then a 3, then a 2: "I have completed the business I was sent on."

Under a light breeze the two returning vessels scarcely moved.

Impatiently Preble ordered the flagship's boats out to tow them in. And shortly in grand procession the *Constitution*'s boats, the *Intrepid* and the *Siren*, moved through the fleet while sailors and marines lined the rails and yardarms to cheer them home.

Preble listened to Decatur and Stewart's report, in which Decatur made a point of praising "the brave fellows I have the honor to command, whose coolness and intrepidity was such as I trust will ever characterize the American Tars."[18] In a near ecstasy of relief Preble reported to Navy Secretary Smith describing the successful mission and praising its participants: "Their conduct in the performance of the dangerous service assigned them cannot be sufficiently estimated—it is beyond all praise." He wrote a separate letter to the secretary about Stephen Decatur: "The important service he has rendered . . . would in any Navy in Europe insure him instantaneous promotion to the rank of post Captain. . . . I most earnestly recommend him to the President, that he may be rewarded according to his merit." The Tripolitan corsairs, Preble wrote, "stood appalled at his intrepidity and daring." Adding that "Lieutenant Decatur is an officer of too much value to be neglected," Preble formally requested that he be promoted to captain.

President Jefferson—no doubt also in a wave of relief—made the promotion,[19] and Secretary Smith forwarded it to Preble. The commodore also received a letter from an old friend, Charles Goldsborough, the Navy Department's chief clerk, who privately suggested that Preble advise Decatur to decline the promotion, thereby avoiding resentment from the seven lieutenants senior to him over whom he would be passed. Whether or not Preble bothered to mention the suggestion to Decatur, the lieutenant happily and proudly accepted the promotion; at 25 he became the youngest captain in the navy. And Goldsborough was proved correct. Many of Decatur's fellow lieutenants grumbled; one in particular, Lieutenant Andrew Sterrett, who had smashed the *Tripoli* two years earlier without the loss of a man, angrily handed in his resignation.[20]

But there was no anger like the bashaw's. The burning *Philadelphia* had drifted ashore near his castle before exploding, and the concussion had been felt in all the buildings along the waterfront. Even Marine private Ray, deep in his dungeon, heard the blast and the city suddenly coming to life with people shouting through the streets. When the shore batteries opened up, Ray wrote, they "made our prison tremble at its base."[21] The Tripolitans Ray could see reacted in terror. "Tumult, consternation, confusion and delay reigned in every section of the town and castle," he wrote, "and it was verily believed that if we had been at liberty and armed, we might with ease have taken the castle and every fort in the town."

• Frightened and furious, the bashaw ordered the *Philadelphia*'s officers locked in their quarters with some 20 guards posted outside. Not even the favored Dr. Cowdery was permitted to leave his room. A few days after the explosion all the officers, including Cowdery, were taken from their castle quarters to a dungeon next to the palace, a dank holding cell lit only by a skylight. After a couple of days Cowdery asked permission to tend his patients (some of them the bashaw's family members), but his request was refused. It was a month before the bashaw's anger had simmered down enough to permit the doctor to make his rounds, returning each night to the officers' dungeon. When Bainbridge complained at such treatment, Foreign Minister Dghies managed to arrange a daily release for the captain to get some exercise. The bashaw was still in a rage, Dghies reported to Bainbridge. Three bodies of the *Philadelphia*'s Tripolitan crew had washed ashore "covered with wounds. How long has it been," Dghies asked, "since Nations massacred their prisoners?" Bainbridge tried to explain that the sailors undoubtedly had not been taken prisoner but had jumped overboard after being wounded; but the reply did nothing to mollify the bashaw. The *Philadelphia*'s crewmen also felt Yusuf's wrath, being sent for longer hours working on the city's fortifications.

When word of the bashaw's reaction reached Preble, he reacted to Minister Dghies's charge of "massacre" by commenting, "People who handle dangerous weapons in War must expect wounds and Death." Concerned over retaliation against the prisoners, he wrote to Danish Consul Nissen asking him to explain to the bashaw that the *Philadelphia* "was set on fire on my orders," with no complicity by any of the prisoners (conveniently overlooking Bainbridge's recommendation in invisible ink). Preble also sent a letter to Bainbridge via Nissen; and in a covering note to the consul he wrote, "If it is necessary the Minister should read it, I have no objection to his breaking the Seal." Obviously he hoped that Minister Dghies would do just that, because his message to Bainbridge was clearly written for Tripolitan eyes: Preble professed that he could not "conceive why the Bashaw should have changed his conduct by . . . depriving you of the privileges you enjoyed previous to our burning of the Frigate. She was burned by my orders, and without the previous knowledge of any person in Tripoli. I had a right to burn her, but if I had not, the Bashaw would be unjust to punish you for an Act of Mine of which you could have no knowledge or foresight." Eventually the officers were returned to their quarters. But the bashaw angrily announced that the ransom price for the *Philadelphia* prisoners would go up.

Commodore Preble was not concerned with a ransom price at the moment. Flushed with the success of his first foray into Tripoli's harbor, he was laying plans for another attack, this time to destroy the rest of the bashaw's fleet.

CHAPTER 8

★ ★ ★

ASSAULT BY GUNBOAT
AND FIRESHIP

It was some time before President Jefferson received word of the burning of the *Philadelphia*. And before that he made a fateful decision. The first news he heard of Preble's activities off Tripoli was the new commodore's dispatch, received March 19, 1804, reporting the grounding of the *Philadelphia* and including Bainbridge's letter. Jefferson read it with dismay. Two of his commodores had done virtually no damage to the bashaw of Tripoli, and now the third commodore had presented the bashaw with a U.S. frigate and 307 hostages. Preble's covering letter made it clear that it had been an accident (though he implied that it was the sort of accident that would not have happened to him), and Jefferson certainly did not blame Preble personally for Captain Bainbridge's mishap. Nonetheless, it had happened on Preble's watch.

Jefferson had meanwhile been having other problems at home, chiefly over the national budget. His purchase of the Louisiana Territory had been a popular move, but now the bill was coming due. The cost of the interest on the loan was forcing the president to reconsider yet again the expense of the Mediterranean squadron. Secretary of the Treasury Albert Gallatin had redoubled his arguments against the Mediterranean adventure, as he regarded it, to the extent that Jefferson had wearily agreed that if Commodore Preble had not subdued the bashaw by summer, he would reduce the squadron to one frigate and three smaller warships.

But now the United States had suffered its worst naval loss since the Revolution, and there were 307 Americans in Tripoli's prison. The complexion of the undeclared war had suddenly and drastically changed. One day after receiving Preble's report, Jefferson sent a message to Congress:

> I communicate to Congress a letter from Captain Bainbridge, commander of the *Philadelphia* frigate, informing us of the wreck of that vessel on the coast of Tripoli, and that himself, his officers and men, had fallen into the hands of the Tripolitans. This accident renders it expedient to increase our force, and enlarge our expenses in the Mediterranean, beyond what the last appropriation for naval service contemplated. I recommend, therefore, to the consideration of Congress, such an addition to that appropriation, as they may think the exigency requires.

U.S. public opinion at the news was one of national outrage. And the public's representatives in Congress reflected it by taking only six days to pass an act "for the purpose of defraying expenses" for more U.S. naval vessels. Again Congress would not go so far as to vote an official declaration of war, but it did authorize "carrying on warlike operations against the regency of Tripoli, or any other Barbary Powers." And it voted a new tax, specifying that "a duty of two and a half per centum ad valorem . . . shall be laid, levied, and collected on all goods, wares and merchandise" imported into the United States after the following June. It was called The Mediterranean Fund, and it was to cease three months after ratification by the president of a peace treaty with Tripoli, "unless the United States should then be at war with other of the Barbary powers," in which case the tax would cease three months after peace with that power.

A sum of $1 million was set aside from the Treasury to cover immediate expenses; or, the act stated, the president could borrow funds "at a rate of interest not exceeding six per centum per annum, from the Bank of the United States."

Jefferson moved just as quickly to bolster the Mediterranean squadron and get the new warships on their way: a formidable fleet of five frigates. For their commander he chose Captain Samuel Barron. And because Barron was higher than Preble on the seniority list, Jefferson appointed Barron as the new commodore.

It would turn out to be one of his worst decisions, but for reasons Jefferson could not know in the spring of 1804. There was in fact no captain in the United States on the navy roster who was junior to Preble. Barron had seen service in the Mediterranean.[1] And of course all Jefferson knew at the moment was that under Preble's command the Mediterranean squadron had lost the *Philadelphia* and let 307 Americans be taken hostage. It is safe to say, however, that Jefferson would not have made the decision he did had he known what Commodore Preble was at that time doing to turn the tide of the war.

◉ Preble had concluded that blockading Tripoli Harbor was not enough. Shallow-draft feluccas and xebecs continued to evade the blockaders, and the capital city continued to receive supplies from the unblockaded cities to the east. At first he had ambitious plans for cutting off the supply lines to these cities, including an intriguing scheme to make use of Bashaw Yusuf's elder brother, Hamet, from whom Yusuf had usurped the throne. In Syracuse Preble had been visited by a representative from Hamet, then in exile in Tunis, proposing an expedition in which Hamet, supported by the U.S. Mediterranean squadron, would unseat Yusuf. In return for U.S. backing, Hamet promised to release the American prisoners and sign a peace treaty with no tribute. In January of 1804 Preble wrote to Navy Secretary Smith, "I wish earlier notice had been taken of this man and his views." Two months later he was adding, "If I had a vessel to spare, I would send to Alexandria to bring down the Bashaw of Tripoli's Brother, and put him in possession of Derne and Bangaza [Tripoli's two major eastern cities] immediately, from thence he could march to Tripoli, and with our assistance take all."

The notion of this sort of flank attack on Tripoli continued to tempt him. Again he wrote to the navy secretary, "If no additional force arrives before the Middle of May, I shall take Derne and Bengaza, to deprive the Tripolitan Corsairs of a rendezvous there, the Bashaw the revenues of that Beylic [province]; but I shall be obliged to destroy the Towns, unless the Bashaw's brother contrives to march from Alexandria in Season to receive the possession of them from us." But when he considered all the possibilities, Preble decided that with the small force he had he could make the greatest impact by a direct attack on the capital city itself. So for the time being he put aside plans for diversionary activities in Derna and Beanghazi and concentrated on Tripoli.

❶ Tripoli Harbor in 1804 was scarcely a harbor at all in the true sense of the word. A small concavity in the coastline, it lay open to pounding seas from the northeast. A long mole, built over the years by thousands of rock-hauling slaves, protected part of the inner harbor. Outside was a maze of rocks and reefs, shoals and shallows, that protected Tripoli from the deep-draft U.S. warships almost as effectively as her gunboats.

The city was defended by an array of fortifications including a battery on the mole covering the northeast entrance and another on a rocky island to the west of the mole commanding the western entrance, a narrow 250-yard-wide passageway through a jumble of rocks. And the new fort being built by the American prisoners was nearing completion on the shore, soon to add its guns to the others.

In a report to the navy secretary Preble discussed his plans to attack Tripoli's fleet in the harbor and the city itself, and described the harbor's formidable firepower: "batteries judiciously constructed, mounting one hundred fifteen pieces of heavy cannon and defended by twenty-five thousand Arabs and Turks; the harbor protected by nineteen gunboats, two galleys, two schooners of eight guns each and a brig mounting ten guns." It would not be an easy task.

From his prison cell, writing in his invisible lemon juice, Bainbridge had recommended an amphibious assault on the city. The Americans could "destroy the place," he wrote, if the squadron could put 3,000 to 4,000 troops ashore to march on the capital. But he did not say where Preble could find 3,000 to 4,000 troops. Two years earlier Commodore Dale had also suggested landing troops, predicting, "I would be answerable for Tripoli's being taken in two days after the force arrived off there." But he, too, had failed to explain how a couple hundred marines could overcome the 25,000 armed defenders Tripoli was considered to have.

What appealed to Preble under the circumstances was another of Bainbridge's proposals: "A few bomb shells thrown into this Town would do damage and cause great alarm." Bainbridge suggested that the bashaw's gun batteries were not as powerful as they looked; the guns were "in bad order, and they are very bad gunners." Decatur had confirmed this assessment after escaping the batteries when he had set fire to the *Philadelphia*.

Tripoli's best defense was its fleet of gunboats—squat, shallow-draft vessels mounting a cannon or two—in effect small floating batteries. They were most effective in the harbor and just outside, where Preble's frigate and even his sloops-of-war were at risk in the rock-strewn shallows. What Preble needed was his own fleet of gunboats. That is why in the spring of 1804 he decided to sail to Naples in hopes of persuading Ferdinand IV, king of the Two Sicilies, to sell or loan him some Italian gunboats.

But first there was a flurry on the diplomatic front. After the capture of the *Philadelphia* some of the U.S. consuls in Europe had appealed to their host governments to use whatever influence they had with the bashaw of Tripoli to release the captive crew. In Washington President Jefferson reacted with outrage at what his consuls had done. "I have never been so mortified," he wrote to Secretary Smith, "as at the conduct of our foreign functionaries . . . they have hawked us in *forma pauperis* begging alms at every court in Europe." Jefferson was determined to have the United States solve her international problems on her own. In Paris, however, Napoleon Bonaparte reacted favorably; his foreign minister, Charles Maurice de Talleyrand-Périgord, described him as "touched with the most lively commiseration for [the prisoners'] misfortune." At Napoleon's order Talleyrand directed the French consul in Tripoli, one Citizen Beaussier, to "put all in train to alleviate their situation and obtain their deliverance." U.S. minister to France Robert Livingston, still unaware of Jefferson's anger at his request to the French government, sent Preble a copy of Napoleon's order, adding his hope that Preble, "with that aid," might gain the release of "our brave and unfortunate fellow Citizens."

Preble was at Syracuse at the time. He dutifully returned to the blockading fleet off Tripoli, and on March 26 sent one of his lieutenants, Ralph Izard, ashore under a white flag with a letter to the prime minister asking for negotiations to release the *Philadelphia*'s crew. But as he had expected, Napoleon's intercession came to naught. Lieutenant Izard was turned back;[2] and he was followed by Citizen Beaussier with a message that the bashaw might consider a ransom of $200,000.

• To Preble this was a ridiculous demand. He concluded that Citizen Beaussier, perhaps understandably, was on the bashaw's side, not his. He sent the consul ashore, raised anchor, and sailed for Naples. That night, March 28, he wrote in his diary, "I am confident that the French, English and Swedish Consuls are all in the Bashaw's Interest. That the Danish Consul is the only respectable character among them, and he is not permitted to visit us. We must therefore depend wholly on our own exertions."[3]

→ The *Constitution* sailed into Naples harbor on May 9, attracting crowds along the curving waterfront; she was the first of the new U.S. frigates to enter this port. Preble went ashore and called on Sir John Acton, a Briton whom Ferdinand had appointed as his prime minister (partly because Ferdinand owed his throne to British protection).[4]

The Kingdom of the Two Sicilies was, like the United States, at war with Tripoli. So Preble hoped that Ferdinand would be willing to join forces with the U.S. squadron by loaning him some shallow-draft gunboats. Secretary Smith had cautioned Preble not to spend navy funds enlisting men and vessels in the Mediterranean, but Preble hoped to acquire the gunboats at minimal expense. (He had not yet received the news that Congress recently had overruled the secretary by authorizing the commodore to charter gunboats if he needed them.)

Preble's request was for eight gunboats and two bomb ketches, or mortar boats, to fire shells into the city, plus such extra munitions as cannonballs, shells, powder, muskets, and sabers, and 96 Neapolitans who knew how to handle these vessels and their guns; he proposed that they become temporary sailors in the U.S. Navy.

● Four days later Acton responded that the king had agreed; but he could spare only six gunboats and two bomb ketches, with the requested Italian sailors. The vessels and their crews would be made available at Messina. Preble described his new vessels in a report to Secretary Smith. The 25-ton gunboats were to be armed with a long 24-pound cannon in each bow. The 30-ton bomb ketches would each carry a 13-inch brass mortar to throw shells at the fortifications and city. All of these vessels, he wrote, "are constructed for the defence of harbors; they are flat bottomed and heavy, and do not sail or row even tolerably well. They were never intended to go to sea, and, I find, cannot be navigated with safety, unless assisted by tow ropes from larger and better sailing vessels, nor even then, in very bad weather." And of course they would have to be towed across the Mediterranean to Tripoli.

● Expressing his gratitude to the king, Preble sailed back to Tripoli to check on the blockade while the gunboats were being assembled. A scout sent in close to Tripoli Harbor in a small boat scurried back to report that the bashaw now had 17 gunboats, nearly three times the number Preble would send after them.

At the insistence of Consul General Lear, Preble made yet another attempt at negotiations. Lear had received authorization from Washington to offer $145,000 plus a few "gifts" in the right places for the *Philadelphia*'s prisoners. Well aware of how impatient with these diplomatic maneuvers Preble had become, Lear wrote, "Ardent as I know you would be to gather laurels in your own profession, yet I am equally certain that the love of your country would never permit you to sacrifice her peace and interest when they can be preserved with honor and propriety." Preble ignored the veiled suggestion, as only Tobias Lear could revealingly veil it, that the commodore was a war hawk. He recognized that while his job was war, Lear's job was negotiating a peace. But Preble saw no "honor" or "propriety" in paying such a huge ransom, and was convinced that it would simply stimulate the greed of the other Barbary rulers. So he sent in an offer of $40,000—which the bashaw claimed to be insulting. Preble wrote in his journal, "We have now nothing to expect from the justice or humanity of the tyrant of Tripoli but must endeavor to beat and distress his savage highness into a disposition more favorable to our views than what at present he possesses." Preble went back for his gunboats.

He was in Messina by the end of June, impatiently complaining at the delay in fitting out the vessels.[5] From Naples they had been towed across the Tyrrhenian Sea, reaching Messina in May. The next leg had been slow and difficult, through the swirling Strait of Messina (between the legendary Charybdis and Scylla) and down the Sicilian coast to Syracuse. It was July 14 before they were finally equipped, manned, and ready for the long haul across the open Mediterranean to Tripoli.

More barges than sailing vessels, they yawed back and forth as the fleet moved south, the *Constitution* trailing four gunboats and the bomb ketches and the *Enterprise* and *Nautilus* sharing the rest. Putting into Malta for supplies and munitions, the procession then lumbered on for ten more days. On July 25 the flotilla joined the blockaders.

● Preble now had a formidable fleet for his attack: one frigate, three brigs, three schooners, six gunboats, and two bomb ketches, with 144 guns, not counting those aboard the gunboats.[6] He also had added eight extra cannon to the flagship's spar deck and small carriage guns in five of the flagship's boats. On July 27 he held a council of war in the flagship's cabin. Two days later he issued his battle order.[7] The fleet was to form up in two columns, one inshore including the *Argus*, the *Constitution*, the *Vixen*, and the *Siren;* and one offshore including the *Nautilus*, the *Enterprise*, and the *Scourge*. Each commander was given specific orders as to his unit's place in the line of battle.

The next day, July 28, the squadron closed on the Tripolitan coast. By evening every vessel was in place, riding at anchor about three miles off the city. (The gradually shelving Barbary coast makes it possible to anchor many miles offshore, especially since the Mediterranean is virtually tideless.) In the last light of dusk Preble scanned the harbor. He could count 19 Tripolitan gunboats, two schooners, two galliots, and a brig. High Admiral Murad Reis had formed a line of defense two miles long just inside the reefs surrounding the outer harbor. Preble prepared to attack the next day.

The *Admiralty Pilot* for the Mediterranean warns all mariners of the midsummer conditions along the Barbary Coast:

> The wind is at first light from between east and southeast. The wind veers southward and meanwhile a thin veil of cirrus cloud often spreads across the sky from westward. . . . The southerly wind strengthens and veers, with rising temperature, falling humidity, and increasing dustiness; the wind may reach gale force from southward or south-westward, blowing in scorching gusts, with rapid oscillations of temperature and humidity. . . . The rain in these storms frequently carries down a considerable quantity of mud, consisting of fine dust and sand picked up by the wind over the desert.

● On July 28 the wind veered to the northwest instead of south-west; and it came on with gale force. The usual southerly would have been bad enough, but a northwesterly gale put Preble's fleet up against a lee shore. To prevent being blown onto the rocks, he ordered anchors up and took his fleet out into the Mediterranean to ride out the storm. For three days it pounded his vessels, with the clumsy gunboats surging at their tethers and threatening to break away or sink. In a superb feat of seamanship Preble and his officers managed to survive the storm without the loss of a vessel. Not until August 1 did the winds begin to moderate; and it took another two days to repair the storm damage. August 3 was a beautiful day. By noon the fleet was back in formation off Tripoli Harbor.

Murad Reis was waiting for them. He had brought two divisions of his gunboat fleet through the western passage; they were lined up just outside the rocky barrier, ready to protect the harbor—and also ready to slip back inside the barrier if approached by the heavier-gunned brigs or schooners. Through his telescope Preble could also see the city's roofs crowded with spectators. Murad Reis was challenging Preble to a gunboat duel before an audience of Tripolitans. And Preble was ready to oblige.

The commodore signaled for his gunboats to come within hailing distance. He divided them into two divisions and directed the sec-ond division, under Stephen Decatur's command, to attack the northernmost division of the Tripolitans. The first U.S. division, under Lieutenant Richard Somers's command, was to go after the other Tripolitan division. The bomb ketches would meanwhile sneak into the outer harbor east of the rocks and lob their shells into the city. The brigs and schooners would follow the gunboats and protect them by firing at the shore batteries. At 1:30 P.M., under a gentle breeze, Preble gave the signal to advance and prepare to at-tack. The crews of the gunboats and bomb ketches manned oars to aid their sails and started for their appointed targets. Sailing like the barges they were, weighed down with their guns and about 50 men each, they moved slowly even with their sweeps. It was 2:30 P.M. before they were nearing the enemy.

Murad Reis's gunboats sat in line waiting for them to close. The bashaw's shore batteries were silent. Preble raised the signal to at-tack.

❢ The bomb ketches opened up, sending their shells arcing over the harbor into the city; their instructions were to aim for the bashaw's castle. The city's roofs, including that of the castle, suddenly emptied.[8] The shore batteries erupted and cannonballs splashed around the bomb ketches and gunboats. The squadron's brigs and schooners now joined in, concentrating their fire on the shore batteries. Murad Reis's gunboats moved forward to meet the gunboats bearing down on them.

This was just the sort of close action—boarding the enemy and fighting hand to hand—that the Tripolitans favored. Their gunnery was inaccurate, but they were dreaded masters of scimitar, saber, cutlass, and pike. They confidently expected the Americans to fire on them and retreat; and they planned to board any gunboats they could catch. Preble's officers and men, however, were prepared to take the fight to them. As a result, they had the advantage of surprise.

The second U.S. division struck first. Decatur took gunboat no. 4 down on the nearest Tripolitan, spraying her decks with grapeshot and musket fire, felling her captain and sending her crew scampering for cover. Then, to the Tripolitans' astonishment, they were given a bitter taste of their own medicine. A screaming, yelling swarm of Americans jumped aboard the Tripolitan gunboat waving pikes, swords, and tomahawks. The Tripolitans had fired their pistols and muskets at the approaching Americans and were still trying to reload. Unnerved by the assault and the loss of their leader, they retreated before the wave of attackers. Most were cut down; others dived overboard; the rest surrendered. It was over in ten minutes.

Decatur took the enemy gunboat in tow as a prize and went after another to leeward. Again he led a slashing attack down the enemy's deck, and this time nearly paid with his life.

With his men retreating around him, the Tripolitan gunboat captain, a huge Turk, stood his ground. Decatur advanced on him and thrust his pike at the man's midsection. The Turk caught the pike and wrenched it away. Grabbing his cutlass, Decatur swung at the pike; the cutlass broke at the hilt. Decatur was now unarmed, and the Turk slashed at him, cutting his arm. Decatur went for his throat, grappling with and wrestling him to the deck. As they fell, with Decatur on top, another Tripolitan came to his captain's aid, raising his scimitar to chop off Decatur's head.

At that instant a U.S. sailor named Daniel Fraser, wounded in both arms, lunged between the scimitar and Decatur. At the top of its descent the blade only glanced off Fraser's head, cutting his scalp.[9] A moment later another American shot the Tripolitan, and he fell, his scimitar clattering onto the deck.

Thrashing about in an embrace of death, the big Turk rolled over on top of Decatur, pulled a dirk from his sashband, and lunged at Decatur's chest. Decatur grabbed his wrist, and the two heaving men arm-wrestled for a few seconds—until Decatur managed with his other hand to extract a pistol from his jacket. Locked to his adversary, he could aim the pistol only at the man's back. He fired. The Turk collapsed and rolled away. Rising from a pile of bodies around him, Decatur found the pistol ball lodged in his jacket. At the death of their captain the few Tripolitans still standing quickly surrendered.

Calmly relieving the dead Turk of his dagger—an elaborate footlong poniard with a rhinoceros-tusk handle—and lifting a leatherbound Koran from another dead Tripolitan, Decatur bound up his wounded arm and made a quick estimate: 52 Tripolitans killed or wounded, eight prisoners and uncounted men swimming for their lives; only half a dozen Americans wounded. He was preparing to tow his two prizes back to the fleet when another U.S. gunboat came alongside.

Decatur recognized it as the boat commanded by his younger brother James. But James Decatur was not near the helm, and the acting commander, a midshipman named Brown, reported the news that sent Stephen Decatur into a rage. James Decatur had attacked an enemy gunboat, which had lowered its flag in surrender. As James Decatur had stepped aboard to seize the prize, the Tripolitan gunboat captain had shot him in the head.

While Brown took the gunboat with its dying commander onto the *Constitution*, Stephen Decatur, quivering with anger, called for volunteers. Nearly all his men were exhausted by now, but eleven men stepped forward. Casting loose the tows with prize crews, Decatur took his gunboat down on the Tripolitan. Its captain was trying to flee behind the rocks, but Decatur caught him and led a wildly shouting boarding party. Though outnumbered, the Americans fought with the extra strength of outrage. In 20 minutes Decatur had cornered and slaughtered the treacherous captain, at which the crew surrendered.[10]

Decatur gathered up his other two prizes and returned to the flagship.[11] Still smeared with blood and powder, he saluted the quarterdeck and proudly announced to the commodore, "I have brought you three of the enemy's gunboats, sir."

"Three, sir!" Preble snarled. "Where are the rest of them?"[12]

Preble had some reason for his flash of ingratitude. While Decatur had done the enemy great damage, few of the other attackers had. Preble's officers had not handled the clumsy gunboats very well. Lieutenant Joseph Bainbridge (William's younger brother) immobilized his craft by running onto the rocks. A signalman aboard the *Constitution* mistakenly hoisted the Recall flag; it was quickly hauled down, but not before Lieutenant Joshua Blake had turned his gunboat back. He never did manage to bring the unwieldy craft about and return to action.[13] Lieutenant Richard Somers, attempting to attack the Tripolitan second division, ran into heavy fire from nearby shore batteries and was nearly sunk before a lucky shot from one of the American bomb ketches put out the shore battery's guns. Somers attacked and damaged five gunboats but captured none.

Only Lieutenant John Trippe emulated Decatur by sweeping the deck of one of Tripoli's largest gunboats. Boarding and heading straight for the gunboat's captain, a husky Turk more than six feet tall, Trippe, a short man, was cut about the head and chest and driven to his knees. As the gunboat captain came at him for the final thrust Trippe made a lucky lunge with his pike, catching the Turk in the groin and lifting him off the deck. He had hardly crashed down before his men surrendered.[14]

The *Constitution* also drew blood. At first Preble kept her just out of range of the shore batteries; but shortly he took her to within half a mile of the nearest fortifications and let go two broadsides. The shore batteries found her range, and she took a few hits in her rigging; her main yard carried away, and a cannonball penetrated her mainmast. Another Tripolitan cannonball scored a direct hit on a gunport on the flagship's quarterdeck, shattering as it hit the gun and spraying iron fragments that cut an elbow of a marine standing next to Preble and ripped the commodore's uniform. Meanwhile the *Constitution*'s gunners were doing greater damage ashore.[15] The flagship's crew raised a cheer as one of Tripoli's minarets went crashing down.

But the other Americans floundered about in their slow-moving scows. And the clouds of gunsmoke soon obscured the battle scene so that the gunners aboard the brigs, schooners, and the flagship could no longer lend their support. By the time some of the smoke had cleared, most of the enemy gunboats had ducked back inside the rocks protecting the harbor.

By 4:45 P.M. the U.S. gunboats and bomb ketches were back with the main fleet. Preble totted up the accomplishments and the cost: three enemy gunboats captured and three sunk; 44 Tripolitans killed, 26 wounded, 52 taken prisoner, and only 14 American casualties. Many of the Tripolitan gunboats were undoubtedly smashed beyond repair, and all of the American boats, plus three captured Tripolitan boats, would serve the squadron again. Most of all, the Tripolitans had been shown that they could be beaten with their own tactics—boarding and deck fighting. But more than a dozen of Murad Reis's gunboats had escaped.

Stephen Decatur spent that night by the deathbed of his brother, who lingered until sunset the next day. Typically, Decatur is quoted as saying, "I would rather see him thus than living with any cloud on his conduct." James Decatur's remains, sewn in canvas with shot at the feet, were slid into the Mediterranean in a ceremony conducted by Preble, who reported to Secretary Smith, "He was a young man who gave strong promise of being an ornament to his profession. His conduct in action was highly honorable, and he died nobly."

Preble took the squadron six miles off to the northeast for repairs. The brigs and schooners had suffered only minor damage, and the captured gunboats were repaired to be used in the next assault.

The next day a *Constitution* lookout sighted a sail coming out of Tripoli Harbor. At Preble's order the *Argus* gave chase and quickly overtook her. By 1 P.M. she was brought up to the *Constitution*. She was a 4-gun French privateer, the *Ruse*, Captain Pierre Blaise Mercellise, and she had put into Tripoli for water just in time for the excitement. Preble offered to pay Captain Mercellise for returning

to Tripoli with 14 of the wounded enemy prisoners and a letter for
the prime minister, which read:

> The Fortune of war has placed a number of your People in my
> Power, and while I regret the Effusion of Blood, humanity dictates
> that those who are wounded may be soothed by the presence of their
> friends, and by them furnished with fresh provisions, and other nec-
> essities we have not on board— Under these circumstances I am
> induced to improve a good opportunity of sending them on shore,
> and shall leave it altogether to the known Magnanimity[16] of his
> highness the Bashaw whether or not these good Offices are to be
> reciprocal.

● Recognizing that such a prisoner exchange would involve a great
many more Americans than Tripolitans, Preble also proposed a
ransom of $50,000; and he added ominously that the offer would
stand only until the expected arrival of more American frigates, at
which time he intended to destroy the city.

Captain Mercellise took the prisoners and the message into Tripoli Harbor, and on August 6 returned with Yusuf Karamanli's response, forwarded through the French consul. No exchange; and a
defiant promise: "I would rather bury myself under the ruins of my
country than basely yield to the wishes of the enemy." Again Preble was glad to oblige.

Captain Mercellise also reported that Preble's gunboats had indeed
wrecked a large number of Tripoli's ships, including many at anchor in the harbor. So now Preble decided to concentrate on the
city. There was of course the possibility that a bombardment of the
city would endanger the American prisoners. But Bainbridge had
assured Preble that they were safe in their fortress prison.

At 9 A.M. on August 7, Preble sent his gunboats and bomb ketches out again, the latter to a station west of the city and the gunboats to the northern approaches to the harbor. Again the brigs and
schooners—*Argus, Nautilus, Enterprise, Vixen*—moved in to provide
fire support. At 2:30 P.M., with every vessel in position, the
flagship gave the signal and all of them opened up with a thundering salvo that could be heard for miles across the Mediterranean
and the countryside back of the city. As on August 3, the bashaw's

shore batteries responded, and the air was full of shells and cannon-balls.

This time the bomb ketches got the range; they were only about a mile away, and they poured a deadly rain of shells onto the bashaw's castle. The American gunboats meanwhile sent a withering fire into the shore batteries and the vessels in the inner harbor. For a while the bashaw's gunners gave as good as they got. Lieutenant Somers, in U.S. gunboat no. 1, ducked just in time as a cannonball shattered the flagstaff.

Another Tripolitan cannonball made a direct hit on the powder magazine[17] of gunboat no. 9, a Tripolitan prize from the previous gunboat battle. Gunboat no. 9 erupted in a thundering explosion. Lieutenant James Caldwell, the boat's commander, Midshipman John Dorsey, and eight sailors were killed. As the wreckage settled, only the boat's bow section was still afloat. At the bow was Midshipman Robert Spence, who had miraculously landed back on deck. As the bow settled in the water, he and gunner's mate Edmund Kennedy calmly reloaded but were unable to get off another shot before the gun sank sizzling into the water. Perhaps one reason Spence stuck to his post was because he could not swim. But he and Kennedy found pieces of flotsam and hung on until another American gunboat came up to rescue a dozen of no. 9's 26-man crew.[18]

The bomb ketches meanwhile continued their bombardment, leveling some of the waterfront buildings and chipping away at the bashaw's castle. After an hour a division of Tripolitan gunboats slipped through the western passage and headed for one of the bomb ketches. Preble immediately brought the *Constitution* to the rescue; but before she was in range, the Tripolitans skittered back into the harbor.

By 5 P.M. most of the shore batteries had been silenced. Half an hour later the wind hauled into the northeast and Preble, fearful of being driven too close to shore, ordered the recall. The gunboats, under sail and oars, moved ponderously away from the harbor entrance. The bomb ketches were taken in tow. By 6:30 P.M. the squadron was moving offshore, leaving clouds of smoke rising from the bombarded city.

Still, Preble was disappointed. He had lost one gunboat, its commander, and most of its crew. Many of the bomb ketches' shells had landed without exploding.[19] And now he found that he had far worse news to contend with.

(●) In the midst of the action that afternoon a sail had been seen approaching from the western Mediterranean. Again the *Argus* had been sent to intercept. When she had reached the stranger, she had signaled that it was not an enemy. A freshening northeaster slowed them; not until 8 P.M. did the *Argus* return with the new frigate *John Adams*, fresh from the States, Master Commandant[20] Isaac Chauncey on her quarterdeck.

Chauncey bore good news and bad news. The *John Adams* was in the van of five frigates dispatched to strengthen the Mediterranean squadron: the *President*, the *Congress*, the *Constellation*, and the *Essex* were to have left the United States five days after the *John Adams*. The new arrival also brought welcome stores, munitions, and, more important, letters from home. But the bad news for Preble was in one of the letters, which informed him that he was about to be relieved of command.

The letter, dated May 22, 1804, was from Navy Secretary Smith. It reported President Jefferson's reaction to the loss of the *Philadelphia*: "The president immediately determined to put in commission and to send to the Mediterranean a force which would be able beyond the possibility of a doubt, to coerce the Enemy to a peace upon terms compatible with our Honor and our Interest." The secretary explained that Samuel Barron had been chosen as commodore because there was no navy captain available who was junior to Preble on the seniority list. "Be assured, Sir," Smith wrote, "that no want of confidence in you has been mingled with the Considerations which have imposed on us the necessity of this measure."

The U.S. Navy's seniority list was sacrosanct; every officer could quote the order of names and knew exactly where he was on the list. Certainly Preble already knew that he was junior to the available captains. He also realized that when he had pleaded with the secretary to send more frigates he had been asking for captains senior to him. But the president had already bent the rules to appoint him over Captain Rodgers; and if that had not been feasible a second time, Preble had hoped that the problem could have been solved by designating two squadrons in the Mediterranean with one of them under his command. He also realized that neither Secretary Smith nor the president had been aware of his recent successes when they had superseded him. Nonetheless Preble was deeply shocked. That evening he wrote in his journal: "how much my feelings are lacerated by this supercedure at the moment of Vicotry [sic] cannot be described and can be felt only by an Officer placed in my mortifying situation."

● By morning he had recovered somewhat. He kept Secretary Smith's letter to himself. He could guess the angry reaction of such officers as Decatur, Somers, Hull, and perhaps even Bainbridge. Moreover, the arrival of the *John Adams*, he discovered, did not bring the advantage in firepower he had expected. The *John Adams* had been designated as the transport of the new fleet and had crossed the Atlantic *en flute*,[21] her gun decks cleared to make room for the supplies she was carrying to the Mediterranean. Most of her guns were aboard, packed in tallow in her hold to help serve as ballast; but their carriages were coming over in the holds of the *Congress* and the *Constellation*. So she was useless to Preble in his campaign against the bashaw. Preble, well aware that provisions were easier to acquire in the Mediterranean than gun carriages, bitterly wrote in his journal, "Had the John Adams brought out her gun carriages, I . . . can have no doubt that the next attack would make the arrival of more ships unnecessary for the termination of the Tripoline war."

Since the other frigates had presumably sailed only a few days after the *John Adams*, they could be expected any day.[22] Preble asked Chauncey to delay going on to Syracuse for a while. He—or Barron—might be able to use her guns on his own carriages to replace any destroyed by enemy fire. He also could use the *John Adams*'s boats, as well as some of her officers and men. With the squadron's water supply running low (the *John Adams* had consumed most of hers crossing the Atlantic), Preble sent the *Enterprise* to Malta for more. He repaired the damage to the fleet from the latest engagement. As he gloomily confided to his journal, "I cannot but regret that our naval establishment is so limited as to deprive me of the means of glory of completely subduing the haughty tyrant of Tripoli while in the chief command; it will, however, afford me satisfaction to give my successor all the assistance in my power."

But the days went by with no sign of Barron or any of the new frigates. And while Preble had resigned himself to handing the command over to his successor, he had no intention of sitting on his quarterdeck waiting for him. First he decided to gauge the effect of his attacks by making a final offer for the *Philadelphia*'s prisoners.

He had brought along with him Richard O'Brien. The former consul general's wife, Betsy, was pregnant, and they had decided to postpone crossing the Atlantic until the baby was born. Meanwhile O'Brien could be useful to Preble because he could speak the lingua franca used along the Barbary Coast. Now Preble sent O'Brien into the city under a white flag with a letter to the French consul offering an $80,000 ransom plus a gift of $10,000 to be paid by a new consul to Tripoli.

O'Brien returned with a counteroffer from the bashaw: He would accept $150,000. Preble responded with a counter-counteroffer: $100,000, "plus ten thousand dollars to the Prime Minister and other officers for their interest in influencing the Bashaw to accept of the only terms I have it in my power to propose."[23] Preble had not forgotten that Consul General Lear had authorized as much as the $150,000 that the bashaw was now asking. But he still considered the figure too high. Moreover, when Barron arrived with the new frigates, there was still a chance of forcing the bashaw to free the prisoners at no cost, or at least for a lot less than $150,000.

But not even bribes for the bashaw's aides helped moved Yusuf at this point. A week passed with no indication of Barron's arrival. Summer was waning, and the stormy autumn weather would soon endanger the squadron in its exposed position. There was little more time to be lost unless the squadron was giving up; and Preble had no intention of that. He wrote to a friend, "You will have observed that Commodore Barron supercedes me in the command in the Mediterranean. I hope to finish the war with Tripoli first."

Bainbridge, in one of his many messages, had suggested a night bombardment as likely to give the city's populace and the bashaw a good scare. So at 8 P.M. on August 24 Preble assembled his fleet off the harbor again. The city's lights could be seen flickering beyond the mole. At midnight Preble signaled, and the bomb ketches' escorts started towing them toward the harbor entrance. The gunboats, under sail and oars, slowly followed. At 2 A.M. on the 25th a rocket from the *Constitution* ordered the attack.

For more than two hours the cannonballs and shells poured into the city. Terrified Tripolitans fled into the countryside, as did most of the foreign consuls and personnel (except Danish Consul Nissen, who refused to leave). Preble detailed the damage in a report to Secretary Smith: His fleet "fired upwards of three hundred round shot, besides grape and canister, into the town, Bashaw's castle, and batteries. We silenced the castle [guns] and two of the batteries for some time. . . . The gunboats fired upwards of four hundred round shot, besides grape and canister, with good effect. . . . The Tripolitan galleys and gunboats lost many men and were much out."

As Bainbridge had promised, the heavy-walled prison of the *Philadelphia*'s hostages withstood the pounding. But Bainbridge himself, in the former consulate, was nearly killed. A 36-pounder crashed through the wall, bounced off the inner partition of his room, and ripped the blankets from his bed. He was buried in debris but was dug out; for weeks afterward he limped on a bruised right ankle.

Not until 6 A.M., with dawn breaking, did the bombardment cease. By then the gunboats had fired every ball in their racks and lockers. The brigs and schooners swept in, took them and the bomb ketches under tow, and the squadron moved away from the burning city.

But this was only a softening up for the assault that followed. On August 27 Preble brought his squadron back—a majestic procession of warships: the *Constitution* leading the *Siren, Argus, Vixen, Nautilus, Enterprise,* and the gunboats, with the *John Adams* standing farther offshore to lend what support she could with her boats and crew. Near her were two of the bomb ketches that would not be in action this time. The concussion of the many hours of firing had collapsed the mortar platform of one and sprung the seams of the other, and they were still under repair.

At first the wind was favorable from the north, though Preble still was wary of getting too close to a lee shore. But gradually the wind worked eastward. Preble called his ship commanders to another conference in the *Constitution*'s cabin. As they talked, the flagship plowed ahead, on a reach under a freshening breeze, to within two and a half miles of the harbor's eastern entrance. At 5:30 the *Constitution* anchored and the officers returned to their vessels. But the wind was increasing, so Preble signaled to wait. He well knew the danger of the notorious late summer gales along the Barbary Coast.

◢ By midnight the wind began to slacken. And at 1:15 A.M. Preble ordered the gunboats to move in. By 3 A.M. they were in position off the western entrance.[24] Another rocket soared into the sky from the flagship and another bombardment commenced, with the brigs and schooners adding to the hail of metal into the harbor and town. The beleagured Tripolitans still had some fight left; shore batteries and warships in the harbor answered the attack. But soon the battery on the mole was silenced; and a galliot and a galley in the harbor were smashed and sunk.

The night sky was alight from the flashes of cannon fire and burning buildings. The bombardment kept up until dawn, at which time, evidently in a desperate attempt to put a stop to it, Murad Reis sent a detachment of his gunboats out from the inner harbor. Watching from the *Constitution*'s quarterdeck, Preble called his gun crews to action and took the big flagship straight down on the emerging Tripolitan gunboats and into the fire from the shore batteries.

As she came winging down under full sail, he signaled his gunboats to retire. They backed off, their crews cheering as the *Constitution* swept past them. One gunboat crewman recalled the scene later as "the most ellegant sight I ever saw; she had her tompions out matches lit and batteries lighted up all hands at quarters standing right under the fort." The flagship rounded to only 400 yards from the mole and fired a broadside. The one withering hail of ball and grape sank one Tripolitan gunboat and sent the others ducking back behind the mole, some of them with burning sails. Then, despite the heavy fire from the shore, Preble sent 225 rounds of broadsides into the city, each one making a cloud of mortar fly from the shattered buildings. The batteries' guns tried to home in on her at this close range, but all she suffered was the loss of a few shredded sails and some smashed yards[25] before the batteries were silenced.

● By September 2, while Preble was planning his next assault, a

Spanish vessel came out of Tripoli Harbor and spoke the *Constitution*. She had been in the inner harbor during the August 27 bombardment, and it had taken her nearly a week to repair her damaged spars and sails.[26] Her captain reported that the last assault had wreaked massive destruction in the city and had killed a "vast number" of people.[27]

➤● Preble went ahead with his next bombardment, sending his gunboats into the harbor's eastern entrance. A division of Tripolitan gunboats sortied from the inner harbor, and the Americans opened up on them. He meanwhile sent his repaired bomb ketches to the western entrance, where they pounded the city throughout the afternoon. Again he took the flagship into enemy fire, pouring 200 rounds—eleven rapid broadsides—into the bashaw's castle. The *Constitution*'s gunners could not tell amid the smoke how much damage they had done, but the *Philadelphia*'s Dr. Cowdery in his Tripoli prison recorded that they damaged the castle and several houses (and leveled the home of a Spanish carpenter who built most of the bashaw's gunboats). Only a wind change to the north forced the squadron to retire. And now Preble planned a final attack, one he hoped would be unexpected and devastating.

The most dreaded weapon in the days of fighting sail was the fireship—a vessel loaded with flammables and set afire, her guns shotted, aimed toward the enemy and cast loose with her helm strapped down, descending on her victims like a fiery monster, her guns firing as she came. Preble's idea was to combine the devastation of the fireship with something even worse. He called it an "inferno," a huge floating bomb that would flatten everything in its vicinity. And he intended to send it right into the fleet inside Tripoli's harbor.

His choice was the *Intrepid*—the former *Mastico* that had taken Decatur and his arsonists in to set the *Philadelphia* afire. Under Preble's supervision she was rebuilt. Her forward hold was planked over and packed with five tons of black powder. On top of the powder were loaded a hundred 13-inch mortar shells plus several tons of shot and pig iron (normally used for ballast) and fifty 9-inch shells. The carpenters built a small tunnel aft to a section loaded with powder, shavings, lint soaked in turpentine, and pitch and other highly flammable materials. A powder train would be laid through the tunnel connecting the two compartments. Two musket barrels were laid down, containing two fuses that could be lit just before the *Intrepid* was cast off; the fuses were set for eleven minutes, allowing only enough time for the crew to get safely away. The fuses would touch off the combustibles in the waist of the vessel, turning her into a roaring fireship. And as she approached her target, the fire racing along the powder trail in the tunnel would ignite the powder and mortars in her forward hold, exploding in a gigantic eruption.

Virtually every officer and man in the fleet volunteered for the mission. Preble selected as commander Master Commandant Richard Somers, who had complained about missing the glory—and promotion—that Decatur had earned for firing the *Philadelphia*.[28] Preble also chose Henry Wadsworth,[29] by now promoted from midshipman to lieutenant, as the other officer. The crew of ten was a carefully picked group.

Somers and Wadsworth together selected the two fastest ship's boats in the fleet for their getaway. They and their crew went carefully over every detail of the mission. They would sail the *Intrepid* (which some were now calling the *Infernal*) into the harbor in the darkness, slipping past the gunboats and heading for the walls of the castle. Everyone was given his assignment: tying the helm so she would stay on course; lighting the fuses; going overboard into the boats. And each man was assigned his place at the oars.

By 8 P.M. on September 3 a thin haze had settled over the harbor, cutting horizontal visibility to a couple of hundred yards. The stars could be seen overhead and the tallest minarets of the city were visible, but the harbor itself was obscured by drifting fog. Preble decided that these were ideal conditions.

The *Intrepid* was brought alongside the *Constitution*. Somers, Wadsworth, and ten seamen climbed down onto her deck—plus one more, a lieutenant named Joseph Israel who came aboard overtly to deliver a farewell message from Preble and entreated Somers so earnestly to let him join the crew that Somers consented.[30] Whether or not Somers stopped to consider that Israel raised the *Intrepid*'s complement to 13 is not recorded—or whether he cared; not all mariners were superstitious.

At 8 P.M. the *Intrepid* slipped away, trailing her two escape boats as she headed for the harbor's western entrance. Shortly the *Argus*,

Vixen, and *Nautilus* spread their sails and followed. They would anchor just outside the rocks at the entrance to wait for the *Intrepid*'s escaping boats. Meanwhile the *Siren* moved eastward to station herself off the northern entrance in case the *Intrepid*'s men chose that exit. Preble ordered the flagship to up anchor and sail in as close as possible to the harbor.

As the *Nautilus* approached the harbor, the *Intrepid* could be seen ghosting under a light easterly through the passage. Then she disappeared in the haze.

Everyone aboard the fleet waited. The harbor was as still as it was dark. After an eternity of about ten minutes, the shore batteries suddenly opened up, and the watchers could see the guns' flashes stabbing through the fog. The harbor was lit momentarily as if by lightning each time a cannon fired, and everyone tried to pick out the *Intrepid.*

Aboard the *Siren* a Lieutenant Carrel, standing in the gangway and straining his eye through his glass, thought he did see the *Intrepid*'s ghostly shape in the mist. A light was moving along her deck, perhaps a man carrying a lantern. Carrel pointed it out to Lieutenant Charles Stewart, who thought he saw it, too. The light stopped, then disappeared. In less than a minute—at exactly 9:47 P.M.—the harbor exploded.

It was an ear-shattering, sky-lighting eruption. The concussion was felt aboard the *Constitution* more than a mile offshore. Lieutenant Robert Spence later described "a vast stream of fire, which appeared ascending to heaven." Some of the watchers claimed that they saw the *Intrepid*'s mast soaring skyward like a missile; darkness came so quickly that they did not see it descend. And with darkness there was utter silence. The awed gunners in the shore batteries ceased fire. And outside the harbor's two entrances there was no sound.

The watchers were struck dumb. But all were wondering what had gone wrong. The *Intrepid* could not have reached the anchored Tripolitan Fleet in so short a time. Evidently she had exploded in the harbor's western entrance.

The brigs and schooners put out their boats, which spider-legged to their waiting positions along the rocky passageways. They sat there rolling in the swells all night, while periodically a rocket flared into the sky from the *Constitution* to guide any survivors back to the fleet. By dawn there was no sign of any of the *Intrepid*'s men.

Taking the *Constitution* in as close as he could, Preble studied the harbor. He could make out the *Intrepid*'s mast, tangled in her rigging, on the rocks of the western entrance. But her hull seemed to have disappeared.

What happened to the *Intrepid* remains a mystery. Perhaps one of the shore battery gunners scored a direct hit. Perhaps the *Intrepid* ran aground in the fog and came under fire from one of the gunboats. But there was the evidence of Lieutenants Carroll and Stewart—supported by a midshipman named Ridgely who also thought he saw the wavering light from his lookout in the rigging of the *Nautilus*. The *Intrepid* might have encountered an enemy gunboat, and Somers, in order to keep the Tripolitans from capturing all that powder and ammunition plus 13 more prisoners, might have touched off the explosion, sacrificing himself and his crew.

Preble chose this explanation, partly because he thought he could make out three badly damaged Tripolitan gunboats being towed ashore and partly because Somers had told him beforehand that he and Wadsworth planned to blow up the *Intrepid* if attacked. "They expected to enter the harbor without discovery," he wrote in his report on the incident, "but had declared that should they be disappointed, and the enemy should board them, before they reached their point of destination, in such force as to leave them no hopes of a safe retreat, that they would put a match to the magazine and blow themselves and their enemies up together."

Preble concluded, as he wrote Secretary Smith, that four enemy gunboats had come down on the *Intrepid*, that the Tripolitans of the first gunboat had boarded her, and that Somers had touched off his explosive cargo, taking the first Tripolitan gunboat with him and the *Intrepid* and severely damaging the other three. In his report Preble could not resist a lightly veiled dig at Bainbridge when the *Philadelphia* had been surrounded. Emphasizing the point in italics, he wrote, "The gallant Somers and heroes of his party, observing the other three boats surrounding them, and with no prospect of escape, determined, at once, to prefer *death* and the *destruction of the enemy* to *captivity* and *torturing slavery*, to put a match to the train leading directly to the magazine, which at once blew the whole into the air, and terminated their existence."[31]

● The charred remains of the *Intrepid*'s hull were found by the Tripolitans on the rocks near the harbor entrance. Twelve of the 13 bodies were eventually recovered. Two were in the hold of the *Intrepid*, and one was in one of her two boats, which drifted ashore on the city's waterfront. The others washed onto nearby beaches or were picked out of the water.

● On September 6 the bashaw permitted Captain Bainbridge and Lieutenant Porter to visit the beach and identify six of the bodies that had come ashore. Bainbridge wrote, "From the whole of them being so much disfigured it was impossible to recognize any known feature to us, or even [a revealing phrase] to distinguish an officer from a seaman."

As for Preble, the tragic and useless loss of 13 of his finest officers and men finally seemed to take the heart out of him. He prepared for yet another bombardment, but bad weather forced a postponement. With autumn the weather would only get worse. And his ulcers were as painful as ever.

He ordered the gunless *John Adams* and some of the smaller vessels to tow the vulnerable gunboats and bomb ketches back to Syracuse. He would remain on station off Tripoli with his flagship, the *Argus*, and the *Vixen* to await the arrival of the new commodore.

And as the *John Adams* led the slow flotilla back toward Syracuse, Bashaw Yusuf gave a banquet of thanksgiving to Mahomet in gratitude for saving his city.

On September 9, three days after the gunboats had left for Syracuse, the *Argus* signaled to the *Constitution*, about 15 miles off Tripoli: "Discovering strange ship N.E." Preble took the *Constitution* over, and both gave chase. A morning haze obscured the horizon to the north; Preble could see the *Argus* but not the other vessel. It was Sunday, and he went below for his weekly dinner with his wardroom officers. When he came back on deck, he was told that the *Argus* had been signaling the approaching ships and that they were not blockade runners but the frigates *President* and *Constellation*. Commodore Barron had finally arrived. Tacking upwind, the *Constitution* slowly closed on the *Argus* and the newcomers. Preble ordered his long commodore's pennant hauled down. A boat was lowered, and he was rowed over to the *President* to greet his successor.

♦ Plagued by head winds in the Atlantic but evidently in no great hurry, Barron had taken more than a month—aboard the fastest of the frigates[32]—to reach Gibraltar. There he had found warnings from Consul Simpson in Tangiers that Emperor Muley Soliman was threatening again. So Barron had left the *Congress*, with Rodgers in command, and the *Essex*, with his brother James Barron, to watch Morocco and the western Mediterranean. Calms had further delayed Barron's progress eastward for nearly another month.

For five days the retiring commodore briefed the new commodore as they cruised off Tripoli. Then Barron ordered Preble to take the war-battered *Constitution* to Malta for repairs; and Preble was gratified when Barron decided to give the refurbished *Constitution* to Captain Stephen Decatur.[33]

Secretary Smith, Preble discovered, had expected him to stay on the Mediterranean station. But Preble had no intention of serving as third in command, especially under John Rodgers, the second in seniority, whom Preble continued to dislike—"He never shall command me while I have command over myself," Preble had written. At Barron's urging, Preble agreed before returning home to use his influence in persuading the king of the Two Sicilies to loan the U.S. squadron more gunboats so Barron could continue the attacks on Tripoli. On September 13 the *Constitution*, with Preble on her quarterdeck but no commodore's pennant at her masthead, sailed for Malta.

Barron assigned the *John Adams*, with Isaac Chauncey still in command, to take Preble to Naples and then across the Atlantic. There were delays in Malta over repairs to the *Constitution* and restoring the *John Adams*'s gun carriages. There were courtesy visits for the retiring commodore to make at Syracuse, Messina, and Palermo. The *John Adams* did not reach Naples until December 6. There Preble met more delays before being politely informed that, because of new threats from France, King Ferdinand needed all his gunboats for his own protection. Preble sent a report[34] to Barron, urging him to try to build or buy gunboats in Malta and promising to lobby for U.S. gunboats for the squadron as soon as he got home.

The *John Adams*, her guns finally mounted, reached Gibraltar on January 6, 1805, and took aboard dispatches from the squadron and the U.S. consuls in the Mediterranean. Richard O'Brien, his wife,

Betsy, and their new baby boarded for the return voyage to the United States. On January 10, three and a half months after Preble had handed over his command, the *John Adams* sailed through the Strait of Gibraltar, with Preble aboard as a passenger.

The *John Adams* had a bad weather crossing during which everyone had to be put on short water rations because of leaky water casks. Accordingly, Chauncey headed for the nearest port, New York. Preble dutifully went first to Washington to report before returning to his home in Portland. He arrived in Washington on March 4, the day of President Jefferson's second inauguration, but that did not prevent Secretary Smith from taking Preble to the White House to be greeted by the president.[35]

Word of Preble's campaign off Tripoli had reached America ahead of him, and he received a hero's welcome. Everywhere he went, especially in Washington, he was met with cheers from the people in the streets.[36] Secretary of State Madison asked him over for a game of cards. He was invited to dinner at the White House with the president, who must have been having second thoughts about superseding Preble simply because the other captains were senior. As well as anyone, Jefferson knew that had he been determined, he could have made an exception and kept Preble in command.[37]

At Jefferson's urging, Congress passed a resolution thanking Preble and his men and authorizing a special medal for Preble "emblematical of the attacks on the town, naval force and batteries of Tripoli." But Preble no doubt valued even more a letter praising his command and regretting his retirement, signed by 53 of his officers—Preble's Boys, who at first had been appalled by him and had grown to revere him. At the top of the list was the signature of Captain Stephen Decatur.

President Jefferson even considered appointing Preble secretary of the navy. The scuttlebutt quickly spread to the Mediterranean, and some of Preble's Boys wrote to the president urging the nomination. But Secretary Smith, who had wanted to be attorney general, was persuaded to remain as navy secretary for another term. (He did not get around to making the official presentation of Preble's Congressional Award until 1806.)[38]

Instead Jefferson gave Preble the mission of supervising the construction of gunboats for the U.S. Navy; his account of their usefulness against Tripoli impressed the president, who thought they would also be invaluable for protecting American harbors.[39] Preble was not convinced, believing that gunboats were practical only in special situations. But he carried out his orders, going from one shipyard to another studying plans, designing new models and overseeing construction. His chief hope was to supply some of them to the squadron in the Mediterranean.

At last he returned to Portland and gradually put his Mediterranean years behind him. He relaxed by hunting,[40] fishing, and enjoying uninterrupted time with his wife, Mary. In February of 1806 their only child, a son they named Edward Deering Preble, was born.[41] From the apples on his farm Preble made a special cider, barrels of which he sent to Secretary Smith and other friends.[42]

There was more communication with Washington. Secretary Smith wanted Preble to make a tour of U.S. naval installations in Europe. The superintendent of the Washington Navy Yard considered retiring, and Preble was recommended as his successor. Nothing came of either project. Meanwhile Preble started construction on an impressive new brick mansion in Portland.[43] He did not live long enough to move in.

Besides his ulcers and latent malaria he also had contracted tuberculosis, a rampant nineteenth-century disease (often called "consumption") that was usually terminal. Preble considered moving to a warmer climate, but Mary Preble refused to leave Portland because she was the only daughter of her ailing mother. Preble settled for short cruises around Casco Bay, in the popular belief that sea air was the best restorative.

On July 6, 1807, angered by increasing British impressments of Americans, he wrote to Secretary Smith, "Should the late events lead to war, I pray you to order me early into actual service at sea, and I will cheerfully obey, even if my health should be such that I must be carried on shipboard in my cot." It was a last forlorn gesture. By August of 1807 he was so ill that he did have to be carried aboard his boat, and he was even weaker when he came ashore. To an old shipmate who visited his bedside, Preble muttered, "To die on [a] bed of glory would be something. But to die of a stinking consumption is too bad." On August 25, at 5:15 P.M., he died.[44] The "Old Man" was 46.

* * *

Consul William Eaton, who had not tried to hide his contempt for commodores Dale and Morris, wrote to a friend about Preble in the Mediterranean: "The enterprize of this judicious and gallant commander has effected astonishment. . . . With the small force under his command he has stamped an impression on the Barbary mind which will not be erased this generation and has restored the character of our arms to its proper consideration among the neighboring nations." Always the superpatriot, Eaton professed that after Preble's command in the Mediterranean, "an American is no longer ashamed of the American uniform."

Preble, for his part, had been one of the few navy officers who approved of Eaton's project to replace the bashaw with his older brother. Now Preble had died. But the project had not. A passenger aboard the frigate arriving in the Mediterranean with Commodore Samuel Barron was William Eaton, newly commissioned as "Navy Agent for the United States of America on the Barbary Coast," a title that masked his real mission. The naval war in the Mediterranean was now moving onto the land.

PART III

★ ★ ★

WILLIAM
EATON

CHAPTER 9

★ ★ ★

A FOREIGN LEGION OF MARINES AND MERCENARIES

William Eaton, who was about to lead America's oddest military expedition, is one of the lost heroes of U.S. history. Many Americans who remember Daniel Shays and Betsy Ross, Parson Weems and Dolley Madison, have never heard of William Eaton. Yet in his brief strut across the stage of the Barbary War, he altered U.S. foreign policy and nearly accomplished with a small band of marines what four U.S. Navy squadrons had not.

He was a great bulldog of a man—in appearance and personality. The second son of 13 children of a Mansfield, Conn., farmerschoolmaster, he early discovered that his father would excuse his slacking of chores if he spent the time reading. It was Plutarch's *Lives*, he later claimed, that concentrated his interest on military history, and he determined to become a soldier—which he did at the age of 15 during the American Revolution. Running away from home and lying about his age, he enlisted in George Washington's Continental Army, only to find himself assigned to waiting on tables and washing dishes. Ill, lame, and discouraged, he returned home in a year. But he still found the army irresistible and reenlisted, this time rising to the rank of sergeant by the end of the war.

Self-educated in Latin and Greek, he was admitted to Dartmouth College, where he paid his way by tutoring fellow students. His classmates later remembered him as a bit eccentric, sometimes melancholic, a popular campus figure and a track star.[1] He was also remembered as brave to the point of foolhardiness. When the local police cornered a college thief who took cover behind a shed armed with a dagger and two pistols, Eaton went after him bare-handed, wrested the dagger away, and knocked him sprawling before he could use his pistols.

At Dartmouth the young man nurtured on Plutarch's *Lives* now memorized Caesar's *Commentaries* in Latin and became an authority on and an admirer of Alexander the Great. He courted one of the local girls and on graduating asked her to marry him, warning her that he intended to pursue a military career. When she hesitated at the prospect of being a soldier's wife, Eaton's classmates claimed, he promptly kissed her cheek and announced with precocious pomposity, "My dear . . . No man will hereafter love you as I do—but I prefer the field of Mars to the bower of Venus."

For a few years he taught school in Vermont. He found a more accommodating soldier's bride—Eliza Danielson, the wealthy widow of General Timothy Danielson. He became a promising young politician, but only until he could persuade an influential patron, Vermont's Senator Stephen R. Bradley, to wangle him a captaincy in the new U.S. Army, whereupon Eaton happily went off to join the troops of General Anthony Wayne fighting Indians in the Ohio Territory.

In the army Eaton's supreme self-confidence, bordering on arrogance, won him protectors and detractors alike. His exploits in the Indian wars attracted the admiration of his superiors in the capital, the most influential of whom was Secretary of War Timothy Pickering, who encouraged Eaton to send him confidential reports from the front, to the understandable annoyance of Eaton's immediate superiors in the field.

One of them, Lieutenant Colonel Henry B. Gaither, under whom Eaton served in Georgia in 1795, had him court-martialed on charges of insubordination and the misappropriation of army stores. Eaton persuaded Pickering that Gaither was making him a scapegoat because he would not join the colonel and other officer cronies in a land speculation scheme.[2] The charges against Eaton were dismissed, and when Pickering shortly became secretary of state, he nominated Eaton as one of the nation's first consuls to the Barbary states—in his case, Tunis.

Eaton's tenure in Tunis was one of utter exasperation.[3] The bluff, no-nonsense army captain was no diplomat; flattering and toadying to the petty tyrants of the Barbary Coast went against everything in his nature. Proud, stubborn, effusively patriotic, he regarded every slight to his country as a personal affront. What particularly outraged him was the humiliation of the United States at the hands of men whom he regarded as little more than animals. In a letter to Congressman Samuel Lyman, Eaton complained bitterly that "the freedom of our Commerce, the character of our nation and the personal liberty of our fellow Citizens should be put at issue on the pretensions of so despicable a horde of sea robbers."

Eaton took up his consular post in 1799, armed with a veritable cornucopia of gifts for Bey Hamouda, who regarded such presents as tokens and expected much more, pointing out that the dey of Algiers was continually bragging about the much greater largess he was receiving from the United States. Tunis was a pleasant post for most consuls, who enjoyed generally fair weather and a countryside luxuriant with flora and fauna: lemon, orange, and olive trees, dates, grapes, and colorful flowers, plus an exotic rural landscape inhabited by pheasants and ostriches, lions and monkeys. The city, swarming with Turks, Moors, Arabs, Jews, and Christians, was encompassed by a high five-mile-long wall with five gates. It boasted 35 mosques, nine colleges, and many other schools. But Eaton's major reaction to his surroundings was capsulized in his contrast of Tunis with the ancient capital: "Carthage! Once the rival of the world, proud mistress, now buried in the ruins of two thousand years! . . . How transient is human glory."

Besides baiting the bey, dabbling in Mediterranean trade, and offering unsolicited advice to a succession of commodores, Eaton spent much of his time hatching plots to overthrow the potentate in neighboring Tripoli who had had the effrontery to declare war on the United States. One elaborate scheme involved kidnapping the bashaw, which Eaton described somewhat incoherently. If a U.S. warship could capture Tripoli's high admiral, Murad Reis, he proposed, Reis "might be used to get the Bashaw himself into an American frigate. I have the plan already digested." (He seemed to put too much confidence in a doubtful assumption that the bashaw would stop at nothing to rescue his high admiral.) Eaton also wrote to Secretary Madison that a Danish commodore had assured him "that the most effectual way of reducing Tripoli would be to land troops south of the town. . . . He thinks 3,000 men an ample force . . . but two heavy pieces of ordnance . . . and some light artillery would be requisite." The U.S. squadron, however, had little land artillery, and by most accounts Tripoli's defenses were quite strong enough to defeat such an amphibious assault.

❂ But the most tempting scheme of all came when the bashaw's elder brother, Hamet, fled from Tripoli to Tunis and walked right into Eaton's tangled web of intrigue. The idea actually originated with fellow consul Cathcart, who proposed that the United States back Hamet with money and military support in return for peace with Tripoli when Hamet won the throne from his brother. Eaton seized on the plot and promptly made it his own. As soon as he met Hamet, Eaton wrote to a friend that the "rightful Bashaw," as he called the elder brother, "gave me such assurances of the feasibility of the measure . . . as left scarcely a doubt of its success." Eaton also convinced himself that Bashaw Yusuf was in a weaker military position than the Americans supposed. His supporting army, Eaton argued, was "greatly exaggerated . . . the whole number of fighting men whom he can bring to his obedience cannot exceed ten or eleven thousand . . . it is impossible to keep them in the field any considerable time for want of provisions . . . they are terrified at the appearance of artillery."

Moreover, Eaton argued, Bashaw Yusuf had become such a hated tyrant that many thousands of his subjects were only waiting for an excuse to rally to Hamet. In fact, he pointed out, Hamet had received many letters assuring him that "they will support his cause the moment they see his position formidable." Eaton also made the point that the United States was combating not only the Barbary tyrants but "the commercial policy of all Europe. It is not only then in Barbary that we are about to fix a national Character, it is in the world! Yield but in this instance and we are humbled, perhaps for ages—and our European commercial rivals will exult not less in their intrigue than in our own weakness." And while Eaton was arguing the case for Hamet, he also began to lend him money.[4]

It was not long before Bashaw Yusuf learned of the plot. Yusuf countered with an enticing offer to his brother: the governorship of Derna, Tripoli's easternmost city, plus safe-conduct from Tunis. In fact, he sent 40 of his soldiers to serve, Yusuf claimed, as his brother's bodyguards. Eaton immediately suspected that the body-guards' mission was to assassinate Hamet before he reached Derna. He cautioned his new friend, "Remember that your brother thirsts for your blood." He handed over another $2,000 to Hamet to help him resist the temptation. But his conspiracy was interrupted when his doctor ordered him to leave Tunis's hot, damp climate temporarily for his health. Reluctantly Eaton sailed for Leghorn.

⚫ Hamet Karamanli was a diffident, easily influenced young man, the antithesis of his ambitious younger brother. Without Eaton on the scene to bolster his nerve, he began to waver. Eaton soon got word in Leghorn that Hamet had agreed to sail to Derna, and rushed back to Tunis. He arrived to find Hamet "on the point of departure." Under the consul's frantic persuasion Hamet again changed his mind. But at this point Bey Hamouda complicated things—"whether suspicious of what was on foot," Eaton wrote, "or from what other motives I know not"[5]—by refusing any further aid and sanctuary to Hamet.

Eaton realized that he could be the next to be expelled—as in fact he was when Commodore Morris visited Tunis a few weeks later. The consul meanwhile urged Hamet to sail to Leghorn and "put himself into the hands of Mr. Cathcart" until Eaton and Cathcart could persuade Washington to support their proposed expedition. But Hamet was afraid of trying to give Yusuf's soldiers the slip. So Eaton came up with a complicated subplot.

He knew that Daniel McNeill, the crusty captain of the *Boston*, was somewhere in the vicinity. McNeill's stubborn independence and haughty disdain of the U.S. commodore had appealed to Eaton. He was well aware of the fact that most of the naval officers in the Mediterranean disapproved strongly of his plot, if only because they were still smarting from his outspoken criticism of their lack of success against the bashaw. But he hoped that McNeill would approve. So he proposed that Hamet and his "bodyguards" set sail for Derna; McNeill, tipped off in advance, would capture Hamet's vessel. As Eaton delicately put it, Hamet "expressed a desire by some means to be thrown into the hands of the Americans." Eaton suggested that Hamet head for Derna by way of Malta—to avoid the U.S. vessels blockading Tripoli, whose officers might not approve of the plan. And if by chance McNeill missed him, Hamet should wait in Malta, delaying his departure until McNeill or some other sympathetic American could persuade Malta's governor to let him rescue Hamet from the clutches of his brother's soldiers.

Hamet cautiously questioned the soldiers; they agreed, evidently anxious themselves to steer clear of the blockading ships off Tripoli's coast. Hamet sailed. Eaton sent his trading vessel *Gloria*, commanded by a Captain Bounds, to look for Captain McNeill and the *Boston*. Bounds found him. And for once Captain McNeill proposed checking with the commodore.[6]

By the time Bounds reported back to Eaton, it was too late to catch Hamet's ship en route to Malta. In desperation Eaton sent Bounds to Gibraltar with a plea to Commodore Morris to send a naval officer to Malta to rescue Hamet. But Morris was not at Gibraltar when Bounds arrived. Alexander Murray, the deaf, autocratic (and considered old at 47) captain of the *Constellation* was there. And when Murray read Eaton's message, he sternly "discarded the project," as Eaton unhappily reported, "and dismissed my ship with marks of pointed disapprobation." Murray gruffly ordered Bounds to stop acting like an officer in a private navy, and wrote Eaton, "I believe you will find you were unauthorized in employing the *Gloria* on Public account."

Eaton's reaction was to refer to the *Constellation*'s captain as "Old Woman Murray." Complaining to Secretary of State Madison, he sneered that the United States "might as well send out Quaker meeting houses to float about the sea, as frigates with Murray in command." Eaton was convinced that without U.S. intervention Hamet would be forced to go on to Derna. "He goes to certain death," Eaton wrote Cathcart, "and with him our project goes to annihilation! . . . I weep in unavailing concern that we are thus fallen— We are contemptible in the view of these Regencies— We have merited the contempt!" And it was at that point that he, too, was expelled by the bey. Eaton set out for the United States still determined to lobby the secretaries and the president to support his proposition and send him right back to the Barbary Coast he had only recently been so eager to leave.

Then, while Eaton was heading home, the whole complexion of affairs changed—because, unaccountably and to everyone's surprise, the timid pawn in the struggle suddenly asserted himself. Hamet first dismissed the bodyguards; how he got them to leave remains a mystery, but they must have been getting restive and homesick. Then Hamet sent a message to Commodore Morris, describing the proposed mission and asking for U.S. support. Morris typically ducked by advising Hamet to apply to the U.S. government in Washington.

Shortly Captain Murray happened to call at Malta. Hamet got to him, and proved so persuasive that Murray changed his mind. But Murray first proposed that the U.S. Navy support Hamet by delivering him to Derna to accept his brother's proffered governorship. Whether Murray believed that the show of U.S. force would protect Hamet or whether it was his own plot to get rid of Hamet he did not say. But Hamet, without Eaton on hand to counsel caution, evidently believed that U.S. naval support for him would give his brother pause. Hamet sailed for Derna late in 1802.

As Eaton had predicted, Hamet was greeted with acclaim by Yusuf's disenchanted subjects. As Eaton had not predicted, Bashaw Yusuf did not try to assassinate him—yet. So on January 20, 1803, the "rightful Bashaw," flushed with his newfound power, wrote a letter to President Jefferson. If he could have the support of the U.S. Navy, he announced, he planned to march on Tripoli's capital "with a hundred thousand men."

By this time Eaton had arrived home and had immediately set about lobbying members of Congress, Secretary of State Madison, Navy Secretary Smith, and President Jefferson. The scheme had already precipitated considerable debate in the United States. Most of the naval officers in the Mediterranean had argued against it—except one important naval officer, Edward Preble, whose support obviously carried a great deal of weight in Washington. Jefferson was preoccupied with the intricacies and expense of the Louisiana Purchase; but he was tempted by Eaton's scheme, especially when the ex-consul argued that it would pay for itself as soon as Hamet Karamanli regained the throne and reimbursed his U.S. supporters.

For a while Eaton fretted over the ambivalent attitude in Washington. "The President becomes reserved," he angrily wrote; "the Secretary of War believes we had better pay tribute. Gallatin, like a cowardly Jew,[7] shrinks behind the counter." And Eaton's cause was not aided when word reached Washington that Hamet, right after boasting of his impending attack on Tripoli, had precipitously fled to Egypt when threatened by his brother's soldiers. Nonetheless Jefferson finally decided to give the project his formal approval, directing that artillery, arms, ammunition, some marines, and $40,000 be allocated to the operation.

● Many State Department officials had been wary of the plan from the start. It had long since lost the advantage of secrecy: Commodore Preble had warned the bashaw of it during his attacks on Tripoli.[8] But Secretary Madison followed his orders, writing a wary directive with a carefully worded rationale:

> Although it does not accord with the general sentiments or views of the United States, to intermeddle in the domestic contests of other countries, it cannot be unfair, in the prosecution of a just war, or the accomplishment of a reasonable peace, to turn to their advantage, the enmity and pretensions of others against a common foe.

A key phrase, of course, was "a just war"; Tripoli had declared war, but the U.S. Congress had not. Instead it had authorized the president to take whatever measures he thought necessary to protect American lives and commerce in the Mediterranean. Did that authority include subverting a foreign government? Jefferson obviously thought so, but he remained uneasy about it.

An important opponent of the scheme was the new commodore, Samuel Barron.[9] Quite a different commodore from his fiery predecessor, Edward Preble, Barron was a cautious man, and did not have the imagination to appreciate such an audacious plan as Eaton's.

But Eaton accompanied the new commodore to the Mediterranean as a passenger aboard the flagship, and he used the time for persuasion. In his letter book, datelined "At Sea 1804, Aug. 21," he recorded, "Delivered my opinion to Com. Barron concerning the apparent advantages of cooperating with Ahmet Bashaw [Hamet] against Tripoli—and the possible disadvantages of acting without his cooperation." Some of his arguments: Attack by land would cut off the bashaw's retreat into the countryside. The fear of retaliation from Hamet's army would keep the bashaw from mistreating the *Philadelphia*'s prisoners. The capital city's besieged inhabitants would rise against their hated tyrant. Hamet could be counted on to make a favorable peace treaty with the United States, and might even hand over his brother and High Admiral Murad Reis to the American forces. Even if the expedition failed, the United States would be no worse off than at present. And—most important to Eaton as he saw it—overthrowing the bashaw and keeping faith with Hamet would uphold the honor of the United States.

Eaton was well aware of the main arguments for relying on naval action alone. He noted that he had tried to counter them with what he termed "the probable disadvantages of this strategy." Even if naval bombardment destroyed the city, the bashaw could flee and return to fight again. Certainly he would take his American captives with him; thus the United States would still confront a hostage situation, this time with greater risk to the American prisoners, with no target like the city of Tripoli and with the prospect of a land engagement after all. And even if the bashaw should be defeated and the prisoners released, there was no assurance that Yusuf would abide by a new treaty any longer than he was compelled to by an ever-present American force.

The commodore proved difficult to persuade. From Malta after their arrival in the Mediterranean Eaton wrote on September 18 to Secretary Smith: "Co. Barron declared he does not consider . . . the Pres's instructions will justify him in furnishing cash, arms & ammunition to Hamet Bashaw"—obviously in hopes that Smith would order the commodore to obey the commander in chief's directive. But Barron, it developed, was not as stubborn as Eaton, who doggedly refused to stop arguing his case. Bombarded for another month by Eaton's persistent pleading—and no doubt influenced by ex-Commodore Preble's enthusiasm for it—Barron at last relented to the extent of promising some naval support to the expedition.

Certainly he had the forces to spare. Commodore Barron commanded the largest naval fleet the United States had ever put to sea. Besides the *President* (44 guns),[10] his squadron included the frigates *Congress* (36 guns), now commanded by Stephen Decatur; the *Essex* (32 guns), Captain James Barron (the commodore's younger brother); the *Constellation* (36 guns), Captain Hugh Campbell; and the *John Adams* (36 guns), Master Commandant Isaac Chauncey; not to mention the *Constitution* and half a dozen brigs and schooners already in the Mediterranean. But the new commodore did not plunge all his warships into action as his predecessor had;

indeed, among the intriguing "What if's" of history is the question of what Commodore Preble would have done with such a fleet.

Samuel Barron, it turned out, was a sick man. But while Preble's ulcers had driven him to action, Barron's liver disease seemed to take the fight out of him. It had flared up on his arrival in Gibraltar; and by the time he had reached the squadron's base in Syracuse, he was spending much of his time ashore in the naval hospital. Without the commodore on his quarterdeck, and with no battle orders from Syracuse, the campaign against Tripoli went into doldrums. There were no more bombardments of the harbor and the city. There were no more attacks by gunboat, because King Ferdinand had taken back the ones he had loaned Preble, and Barron had so far been unable—or not persistent enough—to find more.

In fact, the only movement against Tripoli, other than a halfhearted continuation of the blockade, was William Eaton's project. When he finally consented to lend naval support, Barron called a conference with Eaton and Isaac Hull of the *Argus* (now promoted to master commandant). The commodore handed Hull written orders to sail to Alexandria, Egypt, and provide a convoy for any American merchantmen waiting to return to Malta. Then he issued verbal orders for a different mission. Both Eaton and Hull later described them in a memorandum for the record:

> Sir: the *written orders* I here hand you . . . are intended to disguise the real object of your expedition; which is to proceed with Mr. Eaton to Alexandria in search of Homet Bashaw, the rival brother and legitimate sovereign of the reigning Bashaw of Tripoli; and to convey him and his suit [e] to Derne or such other place on the coast as may be determined the most proper for co-operating with the naval force under my command against the common enemy. . . . The Bashaw [Hamet] may be assured of the support of my squadron at Bengazi or Derne; where you are at liberty to put in, if it be required, and if it can be done without too great risque. And you may assure him also that I will take the most effectual measures with the forces under my command for cooperating with him against the usurper, his brother; and for re-establishing him in the regency of Tripoli. Arrangements to this effect with him are confided to the discretion with which Mr. Eaton is vested by the Government.

Commodore Barron had selected Isaac Hull for the job because of Hull's mature judgment. Born in Derby, Conn., on March 9, 1773,[11] he was the second son of Joseph Hull of a prominent local family. Isaac's parents had intended him for Yale and law school, but he had proved less eager as a student[12] than as a seaman, signing on a schooner in the West Indian trade in his teens. By the 1790's he had risen to captain and had applied for service in the new U.S. Navy. In 1798, at 25, he had been a lieutenant aboard the *Constitution*. By 1803 he had been a lieutenant commander in command of the *Enterprise* in the Mediterranean. Commodore Preble had assigned him to the popular *Argus*[13] for much the same reason Commodore Barron was now selecting him to work with William Eaton on the logistics and support of the overland expedition.[14]

But there were weeks of delay while Barron sent the speedy *Argus* on one errand after another about the western and central Mediterranean. And during this time there was a significant change of personnel: The commander of the *Argus*'s marines, Lieutenant John Johnson, was promoted in October to frigate service aboard the *Constitution*. His replacement was Lieutenant Presley Neville O'Bannon, who came aboard at Malta.

Lieutenant O'Bannon was 29 at the time. A surviving portrait of him depicts a handsome, clean-shaven young man with almost delicate features.[15] But he was a rawboned veteran of the American frontier, the fourth generation of Irish ancestors who had settled in Virginia nearly a century earlier; the Marine Corps attracted many American Irishmen. O'Bannon was tough and resourceful, brave to the brink, a natural leader, and almost blindly devoted to William Eaton. "Wherever General Eaton leads, we will follow," O'Bannon said in the typical bravado of the time. "If he wants us to march to hell, we'll gladly go there. . . . He is the great military genius of our era."

Not until November—and then evidently at the urging of Preble—did Barron free the *Argus* for her mission to Alexandria. With Hull on her quarterdeck, O'Bannon at his station and Eaton aboard,[16] she sailed from Syracuse on the evening of November 14, and under a gentle breeze set a course southward.

En route she put into Malta on November 18, where Eaton sent off a note to Barron in Syracuse. Although the original plan had been to take Hamet and his retinue aboard the *Argus* and land them on the Tripolitan coast, Eaton reported that he was now considering an overland expedition. But first he had to find Hamet.

A norther was blowing and a heavy sea was running into the harbor when the *Argus* reached Alexandria on November 26. Hull cautiously sailed off and on along the coast until the next day, when the wind moderated. Entering the harbor, Hull ordered a salute to a Turkish warship flying an admiral's flag. The admiral's vessel responded. Both Eaton and Hull noticed a French and a Spanish warship at anchor, neither of which raised the customary courtesy flag.

The Turkish admiral welcomed them with the usual tiny cups of strong coffee. The British consul, Samuel Briggs, was even more cordial, especially since the ever-obliging governor-general of Malta, Sir Alexander Ball, had given Eaton a letter of introduction to Briggs. Hamet Karamanli, the Americans learned, was not in Alexandria; he had joined a band of Mamelukes in a settlement on the Nile above Cairo. The diplomatic Consul Briggs did not have to tell Eaton that this development posed a problem.

Egypt in 1804 was in a state of chaos. Napoleon, on his way to India to take advantage of a revolt by Tippoo Sahib and weaken the British Empire, had conquered most of Egypt in 1798, only to have his supply lines cut by Admiral Nelson's defeat of the French Fleet in the Battle of the Nile. Returning to France, Napoleon had left Egypt to the British, who in turn had departed in 1803. The country was now under nominal Turkish rule but contested by rival Mameluke beys whose ancestors had ruled the nation for centuries, and by marauding bands of Albanian janissaries originally imported by the Ottoman Empire. The Turkish viceroy, Khourschet Ahmet Pasha, governed Cairo and the surrounding area, and his soldiers were battling the Mamelukes in the countryside.

Reaching Hamet among his Mamelukes above Cairo and bringing him safely through the Turkish-controlled area around Cairo therefore could be a dangerous mission. Eaton was well aware of the hazards involved. In a letter to Hull on January 8 he wrote, "We shall have three perils to encounter; danger of robbery & assassination by the wild Arabs; danger of falling into the hands of the Turks, and being murdered as enemies; and danger of being executed as spies by the Mameluke Beys." But he was stubbornly determined to go after Hamet whatever the risk.

On November 29 he set out for the Rosetta Mouth of the Nile, accompanied by Richard Farquhar, whom he had met in Alexandria, and two midshipmen from the *Argus:* George Mann and Eaton's stepson Eli Danielson. Also in the party was the *Argus*'s new commander of marines, Lieutenant Presley O'Bannon.

At Rosetta they found British Consul Misset, who had come here from Cairo and who, prodded by another letter from Malta's governor-general, offered his assistance but also cautioned Eaton that it could be a perilous undertaking. With Misset's help Eaton chartered two *marches*, Nile riverboats, and set out for Cairo. One of the craft carried Eaton, Farquhar, the two midshipmen, and Lieutenant O'Bannon, with a janissary interpreter named Selim Comb, another interpreter named Ali, and six servant-bodyguards. Aboard the second boat were a Captain Vincents, who was Consul Misset's secretary, and Dr. Francesco Mendrici,[17] an old friend of Eaton's from Tunis who was now the chief physician to Turkish viceroy Khourschet and thus likely to be useful to Eaton's purpose. Eaton's *marche* flew the American flag, the second boat the Union Jack. Both riverboats and everyone aboard were armed against the notorious pirates along the Nile.

They soon were using their deck guns and muskets. On December 7, approaching Cairo, they watched pirates sack a riverfront settlement and fired their guns in warning. Evidently the pirates got the message: They attacked other boats nearby but kept away from Eaton's party.

Evidently with the help of Consul Misset's secretary, Eaton got word to the viceroy that he was approaching Cairo, with the result that he was met by a welcoming committee of carriages, and the Americans and Britons swept through the city gates in a veritable parade, attracting a crowd of curious onlookers. They settled in the British Consulate and put out word that they were American tourists (probably the first) come to see the glories of the ancient city. Eaton did not want to tip his hand to Hamet's enemies in a city filled with intrigue.

The viceroy proved more than hospitable. Inviting them to an audience—in the evening because it was the Ramadan period when food and drink were proscribed until sundown—Khourschet

Ahmet Pasha sent an escort astride six ornately decorated Arabian horses. Again Eaton and his party attracted a crowd as they rode to the palace, where long lines of soldiers in dress uniforms stood at attention for their grand entrance. The viceroy received Eaton warmly and seated him on the royal purple sofa at his right while peppering him with questions about the new United States of America. How big a country was it? When had it become independent? He also wanted to know all the latest news about the Napoleonic war. Then, with Eaton relaxed and talking freely, Khourschet curtly waved away everyone but the interpreter and said he was sure that Eaton was no tourist. What was his real mission?

• Though no diplomat, Eaton knew how to lay it on when he had to, especially on his favorite subject. He launched into a soliloquy on the project, first taking advantage of the viceroy's interest in America by proclaiming that his nation was interested not in conquest but in justice, in this case restoring the rightful ruler to the oppressed people of Tripoli. Sensing the viceroy's assent, he even tried a religious ploy. Christianity, he argued, was not so different from Mohammedanism because, unlike so many others, both religions believe in one God. He was rising to full eloquence when the viceroy, who evidently had had enough, interrupted to say that he thoroughly approved of the mission.

In fact, Khourschet claimed, he had met Hamet Karamanli and had tried to help him. But he no longer knew where Hamet was. Of course, the viceroy purred, if Hamet had joined Khourschet's enemies the Mamelukes, there would be certain difficulties. Eaton tried a riposte by suggesting that if indeed that had happened, it must have been because Hamet was in dire distress, unctuously adding that in both of their religions it was more blessed to pardon than to punish.

To Eaton's relief the viceroy agreed—or at least said so. What Eaton already knew, and hoped the viceroy did not know, was that Hamet had indeed joined a group of Mamelukes and was surrounded by Turkish Army forces. In fact, the day before his audience with Khourschet, Eaton had found Mahmoud, Hamet's chief aide, hiding out in Cairo. Mahmoud had told Eaton that Hamet and some 3,000 Mamelukes were in Minyeh, a settlement 120 miles up the Nile, besieged by 8,000 Turks. Eaton had written a letter to Hamet[18] and Mahmoud had promised to send it to Minyeh by courier. So Eaton was surprised and pleased when the viceroy volunteered to sign a firman permitting Eaton and Hamet to pass through any lines of Turkish soldiers.

• At this gesture of apparent magnanimity Eaton decided to come clean. He told the viceroy that he had reason to believe that Hamet was in Minyeh, and was surprised again when Khourschet, apparently carried away by his own generosity, announced that he would send his own soldiers to Minyeh and bring Hamet to Cairo.

Eaton instantly realized that this was a dismaying turn of events. He had innocently maneuvered Hamet into a trap. If the viceroy's soldiers attempted to rescue Hamet, the Mamelukes would surely kill him. Eaton thanked his host and returned to the British Consulate, gloomily contemplating yet again the apparent doom of his project.[19] And at this point he was accosted by Eugene Leitensdorfer.

A picaresque soldier of fortune, Leitensdorfer was a native Tyrolean who claimed military experience in the Austrian, French, and Turkish armies. (He had deserted from all three.) In a short but dazzling career he had also been a watch peddler, coffee-shop proprietor, theater impressario, novice Capuchin friar, magician, Bedouin tribesman, dervish, faith healer, interpreter, and bigamist.[20] Leitensdorfer was the most recent of the many names he had assumed; and he had had the good timing to turn up in Cairo, looking for new adventures, while Eaton was there. He promptly volunteered to join the expedition; and when he claimed to be fluent in Arabic, Turkish, and half a dozen other languages, Eaton took him on. He explained his problem, and Leitensdorfer with his usual bravado volunteered to beat the viceroy's soldiers to the rescue. First, however, he just happened to be badly in need of funds; could Eaton possibly advance him $50?

Leitensdorfer proved worth the investment. With one companion he set out immediately for Minyeh. Riding night and day, napping on the backs of their dromedaries, they quickly outdistanced the viceroy's soldiers. At Minyeh Leitensdorfer had no trouble ingratiating himself with the Mamelukes' leader. Shortly he found the opportunity to take Hamet aside, identify himself as Eaton's emissary, and quietly propose that Hamet slip off into the desert, where Leitensdorfer would join him and lead him to Eaton. Within days they were on their way down the Nile.[21]

Eaton was meanwhile finding Cairo unpleasant. Food shortages had led to riots, and the streets were unsafe. The French consul, a Piedmontese named Drouetti, was trying to stir up more trouble by charging that the American visitors were spies for the British. Eaton was also getting messages from Hull, who was anxious to return and report to the commodore. Hull was candid about his concerns. In one of the letters he wrote, "You must be satisfied that it is my wish to do every thing in my power before we return [to Malta], but when I look at the situation we are sent here in, I loose [sic] all patience."

Finally, on January 8, 1805, a letter arrived from Hamet reporting that he was on his way to join the expedition. On January 19, Eaton left for Alexandria. En route he and his party were arrested by some Turkish soldiers who had heard of the French consul's accusations. For a tense day Eaton and companions were held in polite but firm custody until their captors had checked with the viceroy—who indignantly demanded their immediate release.[22]

In Alexandria the Turkish admiral announced that he would not permit Hamet Karamanli, who had consorted with Mamelukes, to enter the city. After arguing to no avail, Eaton went to Damanhūr to intercept Hamet. And there on February 5 they were at last reunited. Eaton received his new partner with what little hospitality he could arrange: Hamet was escorted to "a handsome Pavilion pitched for the purpose," where refreshments were served.

Hamet had brought out a retinue of 21 followers, some of them loyal Tripolitans who had accompanied him to Tunis, Malta, Derna, and Egypt. To reward Leitensdorfer for his feat of rescuing Hamet, Eaton appointed him his adjutant. And Eaton and Hamet began making plans for their assault on Yusuf's Tripoli.

As he had written to Barron, Eaton had been considering an overland march instead of the originally contemplated transport of Hamet and his aides to Derna or Benghazi. So he was not surprised when Hamet proposed the same change of plans. While both were convinced that Tripolitans nearly everywhere were waiting to rise to Hamet's banner, both agreed that an army should be recruited in Egypt. And although Hamet did not admit it in so many words, it was clear that he feared the army would never complete the 500-

mile march across the desert without him and Eaton at their head. Eaton used the occasion to promote himself from captain to general; the agreement signed by him and Hamet (Appendix B) stipulated that Eaton "shall be recognized as General, and Commander in Chief" of the expedition and that Hamet "engages that his own subjects shall respect and obey him as such." No doubt Eaton felt that only an exalted title would win the necessary respect of the Arabs. But it was not out of character for Eaton to consider himself worthy of exalted rank.

Lieutenant O'Bannon, who had preceded Eaton in returning from Cairo and had gone back aboard the *Argus*,[23] rejoined the growing army on February 19, bringing with him a sergeant and six enlisted men[24] from the brig's marine contingent, plus one midshipman, Paoli Peck.[25] Shortly O'Bannon and Eaton went back to Alexandria to enlist every mercenary they could find, while Hamet set up camp at the Arab's Tower, eleven miles outside the city. Soon the camp was swarming with men of a dozen nations. There was a dashing cavalryman who claimed to be a noble Bourbon refugee but was actually a bastard son of the late Marie Antoinette's chambermaid. There was a barbarous Bulgarian and an ex-Serbian soldier on the lam. There was a wild band of Arab cavalry and a contingent of Greek artillerymen with one piece of artillery. Lieutenant O'Bannon and his marines were attempting to instill some military order in this raffish group, so far without much success. But O'Bannon himself caught the attention of most of the mercenary army—European and Arab alike—who were fascinated by his hobby. The marine lieutenant had brought along his violin, which of course he called a fiddle and on which he serenaded the group with a repertoire of Irish jigs and such hillbilly tunes as "Hogs in the Corn."

It took two days of constant haggling to arrange for 190 camels to carry the food and equipment; the owner of most of them was a wily and tireless negotiator named Sheikh el Taiib,[26] who also was co-commander of the Arab cavalry. With a show of great reluctance, el Taiib settled for $11 per camel, a fraction of his asking price. And in the midst of the endless dickering, Eaton discovered, or at least claimed, that Richard Farquhar, the Englishman from Malta whom he had hired to handle materiel, had pocketed $1,350. Farquhar protested that he had spent the money plus some of his own on recruiting; but Eaton refused to believe his account, and dismissed him.

◊ By now Eaton had the equivalent of $53 left, and he had committed his government to nearly $100,000. He had been warned before leaving Washington that the government would not honor any claims beyond $40,000. But with characteristic optimism he expected to redeem his pledges with plunder from Tripoli and Hamet's promised payoff when he became bashaw. So Eaton glibly assured his greedy followers that their money awaited them when they rendezvoused with the U.S. Navy for supplies and support before the attack on Derna.

Money was not the only problem. The mercenary army seethed with religious intrigue. The soldiers and suppliers, attendants and camel drivers divided themselves into Christians—including the Greek fighting men as well as the European soldiers of fortune and the American leaders—and Muslims—comprising the Arabs and Turks. The encampment itself was divided, with the Christians' tents separated from the Muslims'. From the start, religious animosity, suspicion, and jealousy continually threatened to break into open hostility.

Even between Hamet and Eaton there was an initial undercurrent of wariness. Hamet had written to Commodore Barron to check on Eaton's claim of authority for the ambitious expedition; the commodore had replied that the project was indeed authorized. Thus assured, Hamet regarded Eaton as a conduit for unlimited funds, an attitude for which Eaton himself was partly to blame. While trying to overcome Hamet's earlier fears, Eaton had assured him that it would be a strongly supported operation, and had written, "Do not think about money, for the occasion demands heavy expenditure. It is a matter of making war, and war calls for money and men." Now Hamet was parroting to his top aide, "Whoever wishes to make war must spend without thought and take no account of the money," meanwhile claiming that Eaton was being too stingy.

There also were Arab officials and sheikhs everywhere looking for bribes. On March 2, with final preparations being made, Turkish soldiers swooped down on a contingent of Hamet's retinue who were, in Eaton's phrase, bringing "sundry articles of baggage" (probably stolen goods) out of Alexandria. By the time the news reached the camp, it had been fanned into a rumor that a Turkish army was advancing on the Arab's Tower. Hamet, convinced that the Turks had been set upon him by his brother, was about to run for his life again when Lieutenant O'Bannon managed to convince him that the U.S. Marines were quite capable of protecting him. Eaton shortly discerned that the real problem was with the local "supervisor of the revenue" who, he noted in his journal, "had not yet been bought." More baksheesh changed hands; Hamet's men and their baggage were freed; and Eaton's currency supply dwindled further.

● Local Turkish authorities now protested that Eaton's recruiters had kidnapped some Turkish soldiers; Eaton soothed them by releasing the men in question. There also was trouble with one Robert Goldsborough, whom Hull had assigned to help with Eaton's preparations but who, according to Eaton, "behaved disgracefully" by brawling in public, insulting Arab women by lifting their veils, "bilking his Courtezan in a Brothel," and—worst of all—cheating at cards. Goldsborough, protesting his innocence, was sent back to the *Argus*.

Hamet and his retinue were meanwhile worrying about rumors that his brother Yusuf had sent an army to attack them. Hostility within the camp was already near fever pitch, aggravated by the lack of communication among so many languages. Despite his years as a consul, Eaton still did not fully understand the Byzantine workings of the Arab mind.

He went aboard the *Argus* to report the change in strategy. Hull was relieved to hear that the *Argus* would not be a troop carrier. He agreed to return to Syracuse for supplies and to meet the marchers at the Gulf of Bomba, the only good bay near Derna. The *Argus* would be joined by the *Nautilus* and the *Hornet* in the attack on Derna. Returning to the Arab's Tower, Eaton changed from the Muslim robes he had favored to an army uniform with the epaulets of a general. The cannoneers, foot soldiers, and escorts were formed up into units. The officers were assigned their horses and Hamet's retinue their camels. A hundred camels and a couple dozen asses were loaded with arms, provisions, and tents. O'Bannon and his marines were everywhere ordering men into line and loaded camels to the rear. Sheikh el Taiib chose this time to ask for more money for the camels he was supplying. Eaton was annoyed, but, he later wrote, "Pacified him with promises." El Taiib went grumbling back to his camel train.

♦ Finally, on March 4, Eaton sent off a copy of the "convention" he had signed with Hamet to the secretary of the navy with the announcement "The camp moves tomorrow morning for Derne." Four days later, on March 8, 1805, "General" Eaton, the "Rightful Bashaw," Hamet, Lieutenant O'Bannon, his marines, and the motley Christian-Arab army set out across the Libyan Desert on one of history's most extraordinary military adventures.

At about this time Dr. Jonathan Cowdery of the *Philadelphia* wrote in his Tripolitan prison diary that some of the American prisoners had been put to work packing armaments and rations for an army that Bashaw Yusuf was recruiting to march against that of his brother. Yusuf, Dr. Cowdery wrote, rode out of the city gates with the army to see it on its way. Cowdery also reported that Bashaw Yusuf took the precaution of holding many of the officers' family members hostage to make sure of the army's loyalty.

Cowdery noted, "It was said that his highness had received a letter, stating that the Americans were making great preparations to attack Tripoli. A tent was pitched on the battery of his castle, and orders given to keep watch all night, and every night afterward. Orders were also given to make every preparation to repel the Americans."

CHAPTER 10

★ ★ ★

RENDEZVOUS AT BOMBA

Seen from above by the vultures, which must have watched hungrily, a long, straggling line of men and beasts stretched across the Egyptian desert. Eaton on horseback led the procession, followed by Hamet and his officers on horses, marines in their blue and scarlet—O'Bannon had ordered full uniform to impress the Arabs—soldiers mounted on camels, files of foot soldiers, and a plodding pack of loaded camels and asses, their herders at their side, gradually falling behind. The way led over expanses of sand that stretched off into the horizon to the south and west, with the Mediterranean sparkling on the north. Technically this area is desert steppe, not the utterly empty waste of the Sahara to the south. The winter's rainy season was ending, and a few vivid flowers still dotted the empty landscape. Here and there were patches of grass.

The early morning was cool, but Eaton and O'Bannon had not been able to get everyone into marching order before 11 A.M., by which time the sun was baking the sand and everyone was sweating in temperatures climbing toward 90 degrees F. The first day's march covered only a dozen miles to an oasis where Eaton decided to camp for the night. The officers, soldiers, cannoneers, and camel drivers drank from the spring. The camel train's tents went up. The first rations were distributed; like the Arabs, Eaton sat cross-legged on the ground, eating with his left hand. O'Bannon posted a marine to guard the supplies and warned the other marines to sleep on their rifles to prevent them from being stolen. Hamet and his aides retired to his silken pavilion, and his bodyguards took their posts. In his tent Eaton sat writing the journal he would keep throughout the expedition. The first entry: "Marched at 11 A.M.,

fifteen miles[1]—camped on an elevated bluff upon the sea bord.
Good water near the shore."

The next day's march covered only nine miles. And when camp
was pitched for the night, a delegation of camel drivers came to
Eaton's tent demanding more money. Eaton managed to put them
off. The next morning they were back, and it soon became clear
who the ringleader was: el Taiib, the sheikh who owned most of the
camels. As Eaton described it, he "had insinuated a suspicion
among them that if they performed their services before being paid
the Christians would be apt to defraud them." "Never trust a
Christian" seemed to be el Taiib's philosophy.

Eaton had no intention of upping the fee, far from doing so in
advance; he considered the agreed-upon price of $11 per camel ex-
orbitant as it was. He turned to Hamet for support, but Hamet
"seemed irresolute and dispondent—Money—more money," Eaton
wrote in his journal that night, "was the only stimulus which could
give motion to the camp."

He decided to call what he was sure was an Arab bluff. He
announced that if the camel drivers would go no farther, the expedition was over. He and Hamet would return to Alexandria. And
there would be no more pay for man or beast. It was an equal bluff
on his part, but it worked—this time. The camel drivers returned
to their charges. But most of the day had been consumed by haggling, so the army remained in camp that night. The next day,
however, they marched 20 miles. On March 12 they made 21
miles.

They were going through "low sand vallies and rocky desert
plains," Eaton recorded. O'Bannon warned Eaton about riding out
ahead of the column in such country. Marauding Bedouin bands
infested the area, and the rocky outcroppings provided perfect
cover for snipers. As Eaton led the way past a stony ridge, two rifle
shots were fired at him; both missed. (O'Bannon suspected one or
two of their own Arabs, probably in the pay of Bashaw Yusuf.)

They came upon the ruins of an ancient castle; it was deserted
and there was no water supply, so they marched on. Their sweat-
stained uniforms rubbed raw sores on their arms and legs. The
powder-fine sand, swirling in the hot winds from the south, penetrated their eyes and nostrils and turned their food gritty. It also
infiltrated their clothing, and their sores began to fester. When the

breeze died, they were attacked by clouds of black flies. But on the afternoon of March 12 their spirits were raised by the arrival of a lone rider who identified himself as a courier from Derna, their destination. The townspeople, he announced, had risen against the governor and put him in jail. They were eagerly awaiting the arrival of their deliverer, Hamet Karamanli.

• The news later proved to be false. But it was welcomed by the marchers with an outburst of joy. "Feats of horsemanship and a *fire de joie* were exhibited in front of the Bashaw [Hamet]," Eaton wrote. While Hamet's Arabs were wasting valuable ammunition, the lagging camel train caught up with them.[2] Hearing the gunfire, the camel drivers immediately assumed that the army had been attacked by Bedouins, and reacted by rushing up to join the attack and share in the loot.

As they bore down on the soldiers, a Greek sentry sounded the alarm, and the Greek cannoneers quickly formed a line of defense. Hamet ran and hid. Eaton's horse had just been unsaddled, but he vaulted onto its back and raced to meet the oncoming Arabs. He found a swirling mass of Greeks and Arabs shouting at each other. Riding into their midst, waving his scimitar over his head, he shouted in the lingua franca both would understand, "Stop! I will cut off the head of any man who dares to fire a shot!" Awed by the spectacle, the men fell silent, and order was restored long enough for the camel drivers to understand what had happened.

The marchers moved on, looking for water, which they found that night in some deep wells originally drilled through the rock centuries earlier by Roman legionnaires; Eaton described it as "water of pretty good quality." With their goatskin canteens filled, they were able to make 25 miles the next day and 26 the next.

They were now crossing what Eaton called a "barren rocky plain." To keep from losing direction, he was following the coast. Along the shore on March 14 they passed "some vestiges of ancient fortifications," no doubt another memento of Roman occupation. Again they found a water supply, this time "a cistern of excellent water." They made 25 miles the next day, and found a huge natural reservoir carved out of the rocks over the millennia by the driving downpours of the North African rainy seasons—one of which inundated the camp that evening. In fact, it rained all night, with lightning streaking the sky and thunder shaking the tents. More squalls continued the next day, making it impossible to get on the march. By morning the campground had begun to flood; by afternoon the tents had to be struck and moved to higher ground on a nearby plateau. In the confusion, with the watchful marines preoccupied, a musket, a bayonet, and some rounds of ammunition disappeared. Unable to keep moving on, Eaton sat gloomily in his tent listening to the torrents drumming on the canvas and marveling at the extremes of drought and flood in the desert.

● His spirits were not raised when some of the camel drivers again came to his tent the next morning demanding more money. Again he managed to put them off: "Reconciled them with promises," he wrote. That day the sodden army made only 12 miles, partly because they came upon a ravine alive with plants and bushes that provided fodder for the hungry animals. And after the day of rain there was no water shortage. It looked to Eaton that everything was back on track, if they could just cover more distance each day.

Fifteen miles the next day brought the army to the first site of human habitation. Eaton wrote that it was "called by the Arabs Massouva." (Today it is known as Marsa Matruh.) Antony and Cleopatra swam here in huge stone baths more than 1,800 years earlier. Now, in March of 1805, it was the home of a sheikh, surrounded by the tents of Bedouins who had flocked there for a few market days. Eaton was struck by the location, set between a stony desert and high dunes blocking the view of the sea. "In this valley," he wrote, "are four vestiges of ancient fortifications, gardens, mansion and pleasure houses, evidence of former cultivation and improvement. . . . Now all lies buried in ruins" except for a few patches of "badly cultivated wheat and barley." What was more important to Eaton's followers were the sheep and goats, butter, dates, and milk offered for sale by the Bedouins. The army's supplies were augmented somewhat, but Eaton had little money left and could purchase only a few necessities.

He shortly needed more money. Again a delegation of camel drivers led by el Taiib presented themselves at Eaton's tent, this time announcing that they had completed their march; they demanded the rest of their pay and planned to turn around and go home. El Taiib assured Eaton that Hamet had contracted for them to accompany the army only to this settlement. Confident that the price covered the entire march, Eaton went to Hamet and was astonished to have him confirm the drivers' claim; Hamet had agreed with el Taiib that the contract covered only the first leg of the march. His rationale was that he had expected by this time to have attracted so many followers with their own beasts of burden that he would no longer need the camels of el Taiib and his fellow drivers. The Bedouins in this settlement were too peaceful to join the expedition, Hamet explained; but he assured Eaton that he expected to find some Arab tribes only a few miles farther west who were sure to rally to his cause.

Hamet suggested that Eaton pay el Taiib and his men for another two days' journey, by which time Hamet was confident that he would find his new recruits. With no other choice, Eaton made the offer and el Taiib grudgingly accepted it. Because he had only a few sequins ($2.25 per sequin) in his possession, Eaton was forced to take up a collection from the marines and other Christian officers and soldiers, promising repayment at their rendezvous with the *Argus* at Bomba. The total collection amounted to just under 300 sequins ($673), which Eaton gave to el Taiib to distribute among the camel drivers. That night about 60 of the 100 drivers, with money in hand, slipped away into the desert. And next morning the remaining drivers refused to continue with them because there were not enough camels left for the tents and other supplies.

Hamet had another suggestion: Why not leave most of the supplies in the sheikh's castle, push on to meet the tribes he expected to recruit, and send their camels back to retrieve the tents and food? Eaton wrote in his journal, "This I rejected; being now destitute of cash, to proceed without provisions would be throwing too much on contingency." He had only Hamet's assumption that these tribes were just over the horizon. That night the rest of the camels disappeared, and the expedition was left with no transport for its supplies.

Eaton was now beginning to suspect a "complot," as he called it, between Hamet and many of his followers, especially when he discovered that there had been a meeting in Hamet's pavilion—from which he had been excluded—to discuss a new piece of intelligence. From the crowd of Arabs swarming about the temporary marketplace emerged a man who claimed to be a pilgrim en route from Morocco to Mecca. While traveling through Tripoli, the man reported, he had heard that the bashaw had dispatched some 800 troops to defend Derna against Hamet's army; these soldiers had already passed Benghazi, two thirds of the way between the capital and Derna. The news had thrown Hamet into a fright, and he had agreed with the proposal of his Arab chiefs that they go no farther until they were sure that American reinforcements awaited them at Bomba.

Furious over what he considered treachery, Eaton marched to Hamet's pavilion and confronted him and his assembled chiefs. If the report of Yusuf's 800-man army were true, he pointed out, "this urged acceleration rather than delay." But Hamet clearly was terrified, and insisted on sending a courier ahead to Bomba.

Eaton angrily responded that he could send a courier—but this one to ask for "our naval detachment to come to our relief." He would meanwhile take his marines and the other Christian officers and soldiers into the sheikh's castle along with the remaining food and supplies, and leave Hamet and his Arabs to make their way home as best they could. But his threat seemed to have little effect. As he put it in his journal, "I left the Arab chiefs in the Bashaw's tent . . . and reclined to my own marquee and reflections."

He had much to reflect on, and in somber self-pity he sat at his table writing:

> We have marched a distance of two hundred miles, through an inhospitable waste of world without seeing the habitation of an animated being or the tracks of man, except where superstition has marked her lonely steps o'er burning sands, and rocky mountains.

He soon realized that he had no choice, with his transport gone and his central figure threatening to desert as well. It was nearly midnight, but he returned to Hamet's pavilion and agreed to send a rider ahead to scout the Bomba coast and report back—on the understanding that the missing camels and their drivers be persuaded to rejoin with the army for another two days. The next day, as if by magic, 50 camels were back, and their drivers agreed to Eaton's offer. His suspicion of a "complot" seemed confirmed.

At about this time in Tripoli Dr. Jonathan Cowdery of the *Philadelphia* was recording in his prison diary, "The Bashaw sent his son-in-law[3] into the country for troops to protect Tripoli." The city was alive with rumors, among them a report "that the Americans had been to Alexandria in Egypt, where they had gotten the ex-Bashaw and four thousand Egyptians and carried them to Syracuse, where they were to be landed to act in concert with the Americans against Tripoli. I perceived many councils," Cowdery wrote, "and long faces amongst the Turks."

• Evidently Bashaw Yusuf expected a two-front attack, against Derna and Tripoli itself, perhaps simultaneously. And he must have been far from encouraged when his son-in-law returned to report that the bashaw's subjects were refusing to supply more men to defend the capital because of his excessive demands for money.

The only compensation from Yusuf's point of view, Cowdery reported, was another rumor that Commodore Barron had died; evidently, however, the rumor had been started by the bashaw himself when he complained that he had not had any peace feelers from the commodore for a long time. Another story apparently spread by the bashaw was that Hamet, too, had died. In Cairo Eaton had heard that Yusuf had sent his hired assassins to kill Hamet; evidently they had returned and, fearful of Yusuf's wrath if they admitted defeat, had claimed that their mission had been accomplished.

On March 21 William Eaton's expedition finally set out again, up and across a plateau of stony plain for 13 miles until they found "good cistern water," where they pitched camp for the night. The next day they trudged on across the plateau, which dipped down toward the coast. And there, as Hamet had promised, were the camps of thousands of Bedouins. "There were vast herds of camels, horses and cattle," Eaton wrote, "and innumerable flocks of sheep and goats." The crucial question was, would some of these tribal chiefs join the expedition? Meanwhile, by his agreement with Hamet, Eaton was forced to set up camp, send off a courier to Bomba, and wait for his report.

The Bedouins were fascinated by the Americans. "We were the first Christians ever seen by these wild people," Eaton recorded. "They laughed at the oddity of our dress [especially, no doubt, the blue and red uniforms of O'Bannon's marines], gazed at our polished arms with astonishment." Evidently the Bedouins assumed that Eaton's epaulets and uniform buttons were pure gold, and expressed their surprise "that God should permit people to possess such riches who followed the religion of the devil!" O'Bannon meanwhile discovered that his marines were taking advantage of this supposition by bartering their brass uniform buttons for food and presumably other favors from the Bedouin women, and decreed a fine of a day's pay for every missing button.[4]

The Bedouins offered Eaton's army dates and other food as well as gazelles and ostriches, but the Americans had no money, so they bartered some of their dwindling rice supply for more substantial food. They had spent four days in this desert encampment reprovisioning, resting, and waiting for the courier from Bomba when a messenger did arrive. It was not the one sent to Bomba but a man from Derna with the news that a force of some 500 cavalrymen and uncounted foot soldiers sent by Bashaw Yusuf were only a few days' march from Derna.

That was 300 fewer men than in the earlier rumor. But Hamet again was terror-stricken and openly talked about turning back. Eaton argued that his army, with support from the U.S. squadron, was more than enough to handle Yusuf's troops, and he finally persuaded Hamet to continue. Eaton's arguments, it happened, were aided by the fact that Hamet had been successful in recruiting the Bedouins; some 80 horsemen and 150 foot soldiers had asked to join the expedition. At first they had demanded pay in advance. ("Cash, we find," Eaton groaned, "is the only deity of Arabs.") But they agreed to accept Eaton's promise of pay at Bomba. And the owners of 90 camels agreed to the same fee of $11 a day, also payable at Bomba.

So when el Taiib surfaced again on March 26, threatening to remain in the settlement until the courier returned with definite news of U.S. warships at Bomba, Eaton was ready for him. Curtly he informed el Taiib that he and his camel drivers could return to Egypt, and good riddance. El Taiib stormed out of Eaton's tent "in a rage," Eaton wrote, "swearing by all the force of his religion to join us no more."

El Taiib persuaded about half of his camel drivers to leave with him; and when Hamet heard of it, he urged Eaton to send an officer after el Taiib pleading with him to return. "I answered that no consideration whatever could prevail on me to ask as a favor what I claimed as a right," Eaton wrote in his journal. "The services of that chief were due to us:—we paid for them;—and he had pledged his faith to render them with fidelity." Hamet worried that el Taiib and his followers might turn on them, perhaps joining forces with Bashaw Yusuf. "Let him do it," Eaton replied. "I like an open enemy better than a treacherous friend," adding angrily that he was ready for him: "I have a rifle and saber," he threatened. "Carry this message to the chief."

● It was March 27, and the army had been in this settlement for five precious days. With Eaton impatiently urging them on and O'Bannon mustering everyone out, the army took up the march again. At noon a horseman came pounding up from the rear with a message from el Taiib: He was rejoining the march, and he asked them to wait for him. Eaton was in no mood to, but Hamet was insistent. They halted for an hour and a half, whereupon a long column of camels appeared. El Taiib had brought back all the deserters. He seemed quite satisfied with himself, and approached Eaton boasting, "You see the influence I have among these people."

"Yes," said Eaton. "And I see also the disgraceful use you make of it." He turned and ordered the march resumed. Because of the delay, they made only five miles that day.

The next day Hamet was still worrying about his brother's troops. Eaton reproached him and, he recorded, "high words ensued." Still, Eaton got the army marching westward again, for 12 miles this time to an ancient castle, its rough stone ruins standing about ten feet high. It was an excellent campsite. "The situation is enchanting," Eaton wrote; "vast plains, capable of high cultivation; good well water; enclosed gardens of small fig and palm trees." But his enthusiasm was short-lived, because by evening when the camel train had caught up with the soldiers, Eaton discovered el Taiib's latest treachery: He had persuaded most of the Bedouin camel drivers, who had just joined them, to desert.

Hamet immediately dispatched his most trusted aide, Hamet Gurgies, to find them. Gurgies did not return that night or the next morning. Eaton waited in mounting exasperation, but he could not continue without what supplies he had left. By 4 P.M. Gurgies was back with the deserters, including el Taiib. Evidently Eaton refused to speak to the trouble-making sheikh; there is no notation in his journal about what certainly would have been an angry exchange.

• Trying to make up for lost time, Eaton ordered a start next morning at 6 A.M. But Hamet and his men were not ready. In the hope of hurrying them, Eaton assembled his Christians and their baggage and set out. And as Hamet's group slowly formed up to follow them, another dispute erupted. This time the troublemaker was Sheikh Mahomet, one of the camel drivers, who had just discovered that at the outset of the expedition el Taiib had pocketed part of the money advanced him for Mahomet's camels.

Mahomet refused to go on, despite Hamet's entreaties. He also persuaded three other camel owners and some of Hamet's sheikhs to join him. Again Hamet sent Gurgies after them, meanwhile racing ahead to inform Eaton.

It was 2 P.M., and Eaton's group had covered 15 miles before Hamet caught up with them. The sheikhs who had defected to Mahomet, he argued, were essential to their cause. They would be influential with important tribes around Derna, and it would be foolhardy to leave them behind.

Eaton resignedly turned about—"it was necessary to retrograde," he wrote in one of his favorite military phrases—and marched back three miles to a campsite where there was water. While Hamet went off to join Gurgies in pleading with his sheikhs, Eaton sat in his tent venting his frustration in his journal.

> From Alexandria to this place we have experienced continual altercations, contentions and delays among the Arabs. They have no sense of patriotism, truth or honor; and no attachment where they have no prospect of gain.

But as his anger began to wear off, Eaton's odd ambivalence concerning the Arabs returned: "With all their depravity of morals they possess a savage independence of soul, an incorrigible obstanicy [sic] to discipline, a sacred adherence to the laws of hospitality and a scrupulous pertinacity to their religious faith & ceremonies." Despite his contempt for what he considered the Arabs' utter lack of morals, he admired and empathized with their fierce independence. Even so, what he now did seems extraordinary. After nearly a month of constant prodding to keep his army on the march, Eaton abruptly relaxed and spent five days wandering among the Bedouin camps in the area, visiting, admiring the people, and discussing their different religions. Far from chafing over the delay, he obviously enjoyed the intermission, and during the long evenings in his tent he filled his journal with his observations on these tribal desert people, their lives, and their beliefs.

> Their young men, young women & children are perfectly well made, and though copper colored, are handsome . . . The women do not veil:—have nothing of the affected reserve and biggoted pride of the Turks; yet in their general deportment modest and bashful. I took dates in the tent of their principal sheik—One of his wives served them in an ozier pannier, and seemed elated with the visit. I complimented her elegant proportion . . . She smiled and said there [were] much handsomer young women in the camp than herself. I doubted it. To give me proof, sundry fine girls and young married women were invited in. I admitted they were very handsome; but could not give up my first opinion.

Whatever the local dialect, Eaton apparently mastered it; his journal mentions no interpreter. Eaton also engaged in a religious discussion with some Bedouin sheikhs who complimented him on taking up Hamet's cause and lamented "that so good a man should go to hell." Eaton tried to convince them that his Christian religion also had a heaven. "They doubted my story." Musing on the discussion, Eaton wrote that the Bedouins "confessed they would be very glad to see me in their paradise; though they doubted whether Mohammed would permit me to come there, even on a visit, except I confessed him and became a true believer. A good Christian would have given me the same admonition," he observed. "How frail is human reason! How absurd is the pride of bigotry!"[5]

Obviously the spartan, healthy life of the nomad appealed to Eaton. "A desert their patrimony.—a wretched hut their dwelling;—a blanket their wardrobe:—a wooden bowl & spoon their furniture;—and milk and roots their food . . . The climate of the desert is pure and healthful. Though placed under an arid sun, it has a constant refreshing sea breeze by day and land breeze by night . . . We seem not to sicken here and only to die by easy and tranquil declination of age.—They consider seventy to eighty years the usual turn of life; but I have seen men and women who count upwards of an hundred, and such very common."

While Eaton's officers, soldiers, and marines waited—and while

Bashaw Yusuf's army raced to defend Derna—"General" Eaton was spending his time in the tents of the local Bedouins socializing and debating the merits of differing religions and alone in his own tent contemplating life in a desert environment. During much of this time intermittent storms swept the encampment; it would have been difficult to make much mileage in such weather. Hamet had convinced Eaton that the army could not push on without those influential sheikhs. Still, a few days earlier Eaton could have been expected to send his own riders after them or to march on toward Bomba without them. Instead he seemed abruptly content to enjoy a pause in the midst of his crusade, to sit in his billowing, rain-soaked tent composing his thoughts on the implacable animosities of Arab and Christian—the soldier turned philosopher, the man of action turned introspective.

He was brought rudely back to reality by his nemesis el Taiib, who suddenly returned to the camp, stormed into Eaton's tent, and demanded larger rations for the camel herders. "I refused," Eaton wrote. "He menaced. I reproached him as the cause of all our delays in the march and with a total failure of all his engagements with me." El Taiib tried to shift the blame to Hamet and his sheikhs. Eaton defended them. El Taiib accused him of favoring Hamet and his Arabs. Eaton responded that it was el Taiib who was to blame, "For I could place no reliance on anything he said or undertook." El Taiib became threatening. No increase in rations, he warned, could trigger an insurrection; and he added, "in a menacing tone: 'Remember you are in a desert and a country not your own. I am a greater man here than either you or the Bashaw [Hamet].'"

Eaton exploded. "I have found you at the head of every commotion which has happened since we left Alexandria," he shouted. "Leave my tent! but, mark;—If I find a mutiny in the camp during the absence of the Bashaw, I will put you to instant death as the fomentor of it."

El Taiib stalked out. Eaton did not mention it in his journal, but he must have been relieved. With the new Bedouins and their camels, he did not need el Taiib's transport. But now he was worrying about Hamet, who had not returned. It was another rainy, windy day, with the rain darkened by blowing sand. Sitting in his tent as it tugged at its pegs, Eaton considered the possibilities. Hamet could have got lost in the poor visibility of the rain- and sandstorms. He could have been captured by desert marauders or even by agents of his brother Yusuf. Eaton waited and worried through the afternoon until 5 P.M., when there was a bustle in front of his tent as someone approached.

• It was el Taiib again. He came meekly into the tent, offering apologies and "eternal obligations and attachment," Eaton recorded in his journal. The blustering sheikh was now the obsequious camel driver asking for forgiveness and promising to show his loyalty. Eaton must have been tempted to order him to leave the expedition, but he did not. "I replied that I required nothing of him but trust fidelity to the Bashaw [Hamet], pacific conduct among the other chiefs, uniformity and perseverance in this conduct. These he promised by an oath, and offered me his hand."

Eaton was still wondering how long el Taiib's good conduct would last when at 6 P.M., to his relief, Hamet returned. He had found the fleeing sheikhs and persuaded most of them to rejoin the caravan next day. Eaton was even more encouraged by Hamet's assertive resourcefulness in riding all night through thunderstorms to find the sheikhs and talk them into returning.

They straggled back into camp during the early afternoon of the next day. At 7 P.M. Eaton held a council of war in his tent. "I exhorted them," he wrote later that night, "to union and perseverance, as the only means of success to the important enterprise in which we were engaged; to which they gave pledge of faith and honor;—and orders were accordingly given to resume the line of march at reveille beating tomorrow." Not only had Hamet and his sheikhs returned, but the number of Bedouin volunteers had risen to 200, attracted by the promise of U.S. money when they reached Bomba plus the lure of loot at Derna and the capital of Tripoli. With some 600 fighting men in the ranks, the expedition now looked more promising than ever.

Miraculously the march got under way the next morning at 6 A.M. So many of the Bedouin recruits had brought along their families, who joined the camel caravan in the rear, that the long column of marchers and riders numbered more than a thousand. They had crossed from Egypt into Cyrenaica by now, and the army stretched out for miles across the rising sandy plain. But the march had progressed for only ten miles when Eaton discovered some of the Arabs calling for their tents and setting up camp alongside a cistern. He rode back to investigate and was told that they had decided to rest here while sending a supply party inland to a settlement known for its good supply of dates.

Eaton tried to point out that plenty of food awaited them at Bomba, which was only a few days' march away. The chiefs reminded him that he could not be sure; his courier to Bomba was long overdue. By now resigned to haggling, Eaton bargained with them all afternoon. At one point he resorted to a threat to move on with Hamet and their own supplies, leaving the Bedouins behind. Finally, he recorded, "They pledged themselves" at his promise to send a supply party inland while they continued the march; the supply party could catch up with them along the coast. By then another day had been wasted, and they camped for the night.

There was a nomad encampment nearby, and again Eaton used the opportunity to mix with a Bedouin tribe. The occasion for the camp, it turned out, was a Bedouin wedding. Eaton was alerted to the festivities by the sound of rifle fire. Riding over to the scene, he found a procession of wagons decorated with multicolored cloths draped over wooden hoops. He was welcomed and told that one of the wagons contained the bride. The procession included young women on foot—the adult unmarried girls of the tribe, he was told—and men on horseback. The women, he later wrote, were "chanting a kind of savage epithalamium; the men performing feats of horsemanship."

The colorful parade circled the camp and stopped at what was described as the bridal tent, where the bride "was precipitated head first into the tent," while the members of the wedding party chanted a prayer. The procession resumed with the young girls performing a dance with what Eaton primly described as "the most lascivious gestures." He noticed one elderly man and an "officious" elderly woman whom he took to be the bride's parents; they turned out to be the bridegroom and one of his wives. The bride, Eaton was told, was 13. She would remain in the bridal tent, attended by her matrons of honor, for a few days "before consummation."[6]

The next morning, April 4, Eaton had his army on the march again at 6 A.M., and this time they kept on the move until 4 P.M., when they found two deep wells. The going had been slow, over rocky ground, and they had made only 18 miles; the water supply was a welcome discovery. The wells, Eaton wrote, were "sunk through solid rock" by some ancient civilization that had departed many years ago. There were "vast sums of masonry scattered in different directions, the superstructures totally effaced by time." Selim Comb, Eaton's Egyptian interpreter now promoted to captain of cannoneers, had brought along his favorite greyhound, which proceeded to run down and kill a desert wildcat. Eaton described it as five feet long, sable, with brindled ears; "it eat [sic] very well," he concluded.

The next day's march made 12 miles to the remains of a stone castle and surrounding buildings that reminded Eaton of Carthage, whose ruins he had seen in Tunis. Inside the roofless walls of the castle was a huge cistern hewn out of rock and connected to a water catchment outside. But apparently the rainstorms that had drenched Eaton's army had missed this area, because the cistern was dry.

So Eaton urged an early departure next day in hopes of finding another water supply. During the night some nomads slipped into the outskirts of the camp and stole nine of the horses. Eaton sent a scouting party into the desert after them and ordered the column on the march again. By noon they had found a 70-foot-deep well. The water was saline and barely potable, but the remaining horses, which had not had a drink in 48 hours, crowded around the well in a neighing, jostling melee in which one horse was trampled to death.

Eaton forced the refreshed horses and men to keep on the move until 3 that afternoon, when they camped on a sandy plain about four miles from the coast. Stretching his legs after the long ride, Eaton walked to the shore and studied the terrain ahead. A wide bay curved westward under the tall bluffs of a mountain that stretched inland. They would have to climb the mountain next day to continue their course for Bomba. But Eaton calculated that Bomba was now only about 90 miles away.

It took them ten hours to trudge to the summit, where they found a small valley with some wild grass for the horses—but no water. The following morning, April 8, after three hours descending the western side of the mountain, they finally came upon a ravine with a cistern filled with fresh water that was still rushing down the mountainside; evidently it had rained here recently. "This was a precious repast to our thirsty pilgrims," Eaton wrote.

He took a few officers riding on ahead to reconnoiter the countryside and select the best route. Returning, he found tents going up; it was not yet 10 A.M. When he demanded an explanation, Hamet explained that everyone was exhausted from climbing the mountain and needed a day's rest. As Eaton argued with him, it became clear that Hamet's greatest concern was the fact that the courier to Bomba had not returned. Hamet proposed that another be sent and that they wait here by a good water supply until he returned with definite assurance that the warships were waiting for them at Bomba.

Water they had, but, Eaton argued, their food was running out. They had only six days' ration left, all rice; the bread and meat were gone. They could not afford to waste any more time. Hamet refused to budge. Eaton angrily responded that if the Arabs "preferred famine to fatigue, they might have the choice." He ordered the food supply locked up. Frustrated and angry, he decided that if he could not persuade them to march, he would starve them into it.

By 3 P.M. Hamet's men were seen taking down his silk pavilion—not to resume the march, Hamet told Eaton, but to return to Egypt. And at that point the seething Arab-Christian hostility, fanned to a flame by the threat of starvation, erupted into open mutiny. A group of Arabs attempted to storm the supply tent.

Lieutenant O'Bannon had anticipated some such move and had reinforced his marines with other soldiers, including Selim Comb's Greek cannoneers. At Eaton's command, they quickly formed a line of defense in front of the supply tent. The charging Arabs pulled up, and the two groups faced each other. For an hour there was a tense confrontation, until Hamet managed to persuade the Arabs to dismount and disperse. He called for his tent to be pitched again. Eaton breathed a sigh of relief, and then made a major miscalculation.

To impress the Arabs and forestall any repetition, he ordered O'Bannon to perform the manual of arms. O'Bannon gave the commands, and his marines smartly executed the manual, smacking their rifles as they raised, shouldered, and pointed them.

"In an instant," Eaton recalled, "the Arabs took an alarm, remounted and exclaimed, 'The Christians are preparing to fire on us!'" Hamet, too, jumped on his horse and "put himself at their head." An army of some 200 Arabs wheeled their horses and charged.

• Eaton called to O'Bannon to hold his fire until the last instant. With the horde rushing at them, yelling and waving their rifles and scimitars, O'Bannon and his line of marines and soldiers stood their ground. Their bluff called, the horsemen broke off a few yards away and circled back into a milling tangle of horses. Some of them aimed their rifles at the marines, and there were shouts of "Fire!"

Surprisingly no one did. Perhaps the sight of the marines' rifles had a cautionary effect.[7] O'Bannon and his marines held their fire but remained stonily unmoved in front of the supply tent. A few of Eaton's aides—Dr. Mendrici, Chevalier Davis (Eaton's aide-de-camp), and others—began to edge away toward their tents. Realizing that the first sign of fright would encourage the more hotheaded Arabs, Eaton made a bold show of authority by dismounting and walking straight toward the milling ranks around Hamet. As he approached, he later wrote, "a column of muskets were aimed at my heart . . . A universal clamor drowned my voice. I waved my hand as a signal for attention." At that imperious command some of Hamet's officers "rode between us with drawn sabres." Eaton was now cut off from his marines and soldiers.

But he immediately realized that Hamet's officers were in fact interposing themselves between Eaton and the mutineers. Seizing the moment, Eaton walked up to Hamet, who clearly was dithering over which way to move, asked him to dismount, took him by the arm, and led him away from the tumult. One Arab protested; Hamet smacked him with the flat of his scimitar. The shouting increased as Hamet followed Eaton. As soon as he could be heard, Eaton calmly "asked him if he knew his own interests and friends. He relented, called me his friend & protector—said he was too soon heated and followed me to my tent—giving orders at the same time to his Arabs to disperse."

Eaton noticed that Hamet was nearly breathless from such a close call. In the comparative quiet of the tent Hamet apologized and proposed that Eaton rescind his order and issue some rice. Eaton countered that he would reissue rations only on the condition that the Arabs agreed to march next morning. Hamet promised.

→ Eaton ordered a ration distributed; and, he wrote, "the camp again resumed its tranquility."

• That night he described the near-disaster in his journal. One shot fired would probably have touched off a bloodbath in which the vastly outnumbered Americans would have been slaughtered. "The firm and decided conduct of Mr. O'Bannon,"[8] Eaton wrote, "as on all other occasions, did much to deter the violence of the savages by whom we were surrounded." His view, he reported, was evidently shared by a remorseful Hamet, who went to O'Bannon, "embraced him with an enthusiasm of respect, calling him *The Brave American*." Eaton gave little credit to his own courageous act that had stopped the rebellion. As much in sadness as anger, he wrote, "We find it almost impossible to inspire these wild biggots with confidence in us or to persuade them that, being Christians, we can be otherwise than enemies to Mussulmen." In the understatement of the expedition he added, "We have a difficult undertaking!"

The next morning, April 9, Eaton and O'Bannon had the army up and marching by 5:30. They had gone ten miles when they came to some crumbling ruins that fortunately included a cistern with water in it and patches of shrub to provide food for the horses. Closer inspection revealed two corpses at the bottom of the cistern—"probably pilgrims murdered by the Arabs," Eaton guessed. "We were obliged nevertheless to use the water."

The half rations were beginning to take their toll; the men were too weak to march further that day. The next day they also made no more then ten miles, fortunately to another cistern surrounded by sparse feed for the animals. Eaton described the place as "a beautiful valley between two ridges of desert mountain and calcarious [sic] rock and flint stone." But while there was some bare sustenance for the animals, the men were reduced to half rations of rice and water. That afternoon the men Eaton had sent after the horse thieves returned empty-handed. And in his journal that night Eaton reported a disturbing conversation with Hamet: "An idea has been insinuated into the mind of the Bashaw that we aim only to use him for the purpose of obtaining a peace with his brother" and that the U.S. plot was to hand him over to Yusuf in return for a treaty freeing the *Philadelphia*'s prisoners. Eaton had argued that the idea was absurd, but was not sure he had convinced him.

That evening Eaton was visited by another delegation of Arabs refusing to push on until they were certain that supply vessels awaited them at Bomba. Eaton managed to work out another agreement: He promised to halt after two more days if the courier had not arrived with news from Bomba. Hamet was warning that his followers would desert the expedition if they thought they had to attack Derna by themselves in their half-starved condition.

By now Eaton was also worrying. For the past ten days they had been taking a direct route inland from the curving shore. If Hull in the *Argus* was out there looking for them, he would not see them. Their only hope was that he—or some other naval officer sent to reprovision them—was waiting patiently at anchor off Bomba.

"We have only three days half ration of rice and no other supplies whatever," Eaton wrote in his journal. "And what renders our situation truly alarming, we can get no information of any vessels having appeared off the coast, as we now plainly perceive their arrival alone will prevent a revolt among our Arabs." That evening at 7, one of Eaton's officers came to his tent to report a more ominous development. Not only the Arabs but also the Christian cannoneers were about to march on Eaton's tent to demand a full ration before proceeding toward Bomba.

Eaton realized the fatal significance of this latest threat. If he were defied by the Christians as well as the Arabs, the expedition would disintegrate. He quickly ordered the officer to confront the cannoneers. "I told him to endeavour by gentle means to suppress the mutiny," and if that failed to warn them "on pain of death, not to appear in arms to make any remonstrance with me." As soon as the officer had left, Eaton sent for the commissary officer to get an accounting of exactly how much rice was left. Half an hour later there was a great stir in the camp. The long-lost courier arrived from Bomba with the news that there were indeed navy vessels off the coast. "In an instant," Eaton wrote, "the face of everything changed from pensive gloom to enthusiastic gladness.—Nothing more heard of the mutiny. The Arabs resumed confidence.—And the Bashaw promised to face the residue of our march to Bomba." The expedition had been saved at what might have been the last moment. Eaton gave the order for resuming the march early next morning. And that evening Hamet became ill, vomiting through the night.

Eaton refused to wait, insisting on marching at 6 A.M. They made only five miles before it became obvious that Hamet could not go on. But by 6 P.M., to Eaton's immense relief, Hamet seemed to be recovering. The next day they made a more respectable 25 miles. But they found no water or food. The last of the rice ration was issued; with no water or wood for cooking fires, the men had to eat it raw, the fine sand crunching in their teeth.

That day in Tripoli Captain Bainbridge wrote to Commodore Barron that the bashaw was threatening reprisals against the *Philadelphia*'s prisoners if the Americans supported Hamet's expedition against him. And on April 13, Dr. Cowdery wrote in his journal that the bashaw had declared that if the Americans attacked Tripoli, he would put every American prisoner to death.

On April 13 Eaton's army made only seven and a half miles before the men became too exhausted and famished to continue. Facing starvation, they killed one of the camels. Another Bedouin tribe was camped nearby with a small flock of sheep. Hamet swapped another camel for a few sheep, and for the first time in days the army had an invigorating ration of meat. The next day the marchers made 15 miles before setting up camp in a valley where there was some shrubbery for forage plus a cistern with welcome water. But, Eaton wrote, "we were totally destitute of provisions."

He took heart at the realization that they must be nearing Bomba and should reach it within the next couple of days; there the squadron's supplies would be waiting for them. Besides, Bomba had the only good harbor between Alexandria and Derna, so there must be a town where they could trade more camels or horses for food. Then came good news when a couple of nomads approached them from the west and reported that there were two ships at anchor in Bomba Bay,[9] and "very well described the brig *Argus*."

But by next morning, April 15, the foot soldiers were barely able to walk. The march started at 7 A.M., in straggling disorder as the men scattered through the valley grubbing for wild fennel, sorrel, and anything else they could find "to appease the cravings of hunger." Eaton and O'Bannon, with their destination just over the horizon, managed by sheer willpower to keep the stumbling, starving army on the move.

At last at 4 P.M. they came over a hill and the bay of Bomba stretched out before them sparkling in the Mediterranean sun. "But what was my astonishment," Eaton wrote, "to find at this celebrated port not the first trace of a human being, nor a drop of water—And what my mortification to find no vessels here."

CHAPTER 11

★ ★ ★

BETRAYAL AT DERNA

● While "General" Eaton was urging his straggling army across the Libyan Desert, Thomas Jefferson was losing heart for the Barbary War. Ever since the dispatch of the first squadron, a running "Battle of the Mediterranean" had been going on in the president's Cabinet. The battle lines had been drawn between Treasury Secretary Albert Gallatin, who from the start had inveighed against what he regarded as the excessive cost of a large navy, and Navy Secretary Robert Smith, who felt even more strongly than Jefferson himself originally had, that the only way to curb the Barbary rulers was by force, and that in the long run a naval force would be cheaper than continual tribute.

Gallatin, preoccupied by the budget and the necessary domestic expenses of the new nation—especially with the huge loan payments for the Louisiana Purchase—held forth at Cabinet meetings with dire prophecies of the United States being sucked into ever-growing commitments in the Mediterranean. Relentlessly he warned the president against what he clearly regarded as folly. "Our object," he wrote in one of his many memos as early as August of 1802, "must clearly be to put a speedy end to a contest which unavailingly wastes our resources, and which we cannot, for any considerable time, pursue with vigor without relinquishing the accomplishment of the great and beneficial objects we have in view. . . . I sincerely wish you could reconcile it to yourself to empower our negotiators to give, if necessary for peace, an annuity to Tripoli."

Navy Secretary Smith's response, as self-serving as Gallatin's, was couched in a similarly pragmatic argument: "A superior force in the Mediterranean will insure us an early peace and will enable us to dictate the terms that will be the most honorable and beneficial to us. A feeble force, on the contrary, will subject us to the necessity of purchasing a peace on the same terms that have from time to time been imposed on the small powers of Europe." Smith countered Gallatin's case for economy by claiming, "A formidable force displayed at this time will make a favorable impression, will repress every disposition hostile to us, and will thus save us great trouble and much expense. . . . With a less force the war may continue for years, which would be playing a hazardous game."

President Jefferson was constantly whipsawed between these opposing points of view. Meanwhile the U.S. squadrons he had sent to the Mediterranean had accomplished little. Even Commodore Preble's concentrated bombardments and gunboat attacks had failed to force Yusuf's surrender. Confronted with mounting expenses at home and the apparently never-ending costs of the Mediterranean squadrons, Jefferson had begun to lose faith in his original determination to meet force with force.

By the spring of 1805 the president still had had no good news from his new commodore, Samuel Barron. And at this point he did not know that Eaton, O'Bannon, and the "Rightful Bashaw" were on the march. The best hope for the United States, it seemed, was for Consul General Tobias Lear to negotiate the cheapest settlement he could make, if only to rescue the 307 American hostages from the *Philadelphia*. So Jefferson decided to give Lear "full power and authority to negotiate a treaty of peace with the Bashaw of Tripoli." The president also began to make plans to call home all but one frigate and one or two smaller warships. Those remaining on the Mediterranean station would confine their activities to blockade duty. "Such a blockade," Jefferson rationalized, "will cost us no more than a state of peace, and will save us from increased tribute, and the disgrace attached to them." From one viewpoint he appeared to be trying to eat his cake and have it too: making a deal for the hostages and leaving a token force in the Mediterranean to continue the posture of force instead of bribery. From another viewpoint he was at last facing the realization that a hostage situation can rarely be settled without negotiation.

Besides, Jefferson added, "There is reason to believe the example we have set, begins already to work on the disparities of the powers of Europe to emancipate themselves from that degrading yoke. Should we produce such a revolution there, we shall be amply rewarded for what we have done." There it was again: the notion he had first advanced as minister to France 20 years earlier, that a consortium of American and European navies could combine to suppress the Barbary powers.

● But this time he had more reason for his optimistic analysis. Many European leaders had indeed been impressed by America's combativeness during the tenure of Edward Preble. Although virtually no European head of state was ready to say so openly while still paying tribute, it was significant that Malta's influential governor-general, Sir Alexander Ball, had confessed in a commendatory letter to Commodore Preble on his retirement (though he was careful not to speak for his government), "If I were to offer my opinion, it would be that you have done well not to purchase peace with the enemy. A few brave men have, indeed, been sacrificed, but they could not have fallen in a better cause, and I even conceive it advisable to risk more lives rather [than] to submit to terms which might encourage the Barbary states to add fresh demands and insults." The spectacle of the young American nation standing up to the arrogant Barbary powers had indeed stirred admiration in Europe.[1] Nonetheless, the prospect of an allied European-American fleet was remote, not least because Britain and France were at war.

● In the bay of Bomba William Eaton faced a more immediate crisis. If there had ever been a settlement on this shore, all traces of it were gone. To the west Eaton could see only the sweeping curve of the bay and a long, empty beach. Behind it to the south was more desert. And to the north the Mediterranean was empty to the horizon.

The Arabs' shock at finding no support at Bomba quickly turned to angry threats. Eaton called Hamet and his sheikhs together in an attempt to keep order. The American ships would come, he promised; and since they now would be marching along the shore, they could watch for the sails. But Hamet and his followers were unpersuaded. "They abused us as imposters and infidels," Eaton recorded; "and said we had drawn them into that situation with treacherous views."

While feigning an air of optimism, Eaton knew in his heart that his army was too weak to continue. He sent a few men to a hill behind the beach with orders to light signal fires and keep them burning through the night. There was little sleep in the camp on the beach, with the Arabs holding an angry meeting in Hamet's pavilion and Eaton periodically studying the horizon for an answering rocket or the lights of a ship. His greatest fear, as he gloomily wrote in his journal, was that Hull and the *Argus* "had left the coast in despair of our arrival." He could blame Hamet, his sheikhs, and especially the wily camel driver el Taiib for the many delays; but recriminations were no help now.

● On the morning of the 16th the Mediterranean still was empty. The fires on the hill were burning down to coals, and the fire-tenders returned to the beach. At about 8 A.M. one of Hamet's aides climbed to the peak for a hopeful look, and came running back into the camp shouting that he had seen a sail. "Language is too poor," Eaton wrote, "to paint the joy and exultation which this messenger of life excited in every breast."

Eaton quickly ordered the fires on the hill fanned for smoke signals. Shortly the vessel could be seen from the beach; she answered with her own signals. By midmorning she was close enough to be identified as the *Argus*. She came closer, hove to, and dropped her anchor. A boat swung out and came to the beach. And by noon Eaton was aboard, happily greeting Master Commandant Hull and making arrangements to send ashore the *Argus*'s provisions: 30 hogsheads of bread, 20 barrels of peas, 100 sacks of flour, 10 casks of rice, a hogshead of brandy, a bale of cloth—and $7,000 (for which, at Commodore Barron's order, Hull demanded a receipt in duplicate).

Eaton spent the night of the 16th aboard the *Argus*. The next day he sent orders ashore to move the camp a few miles westward where a cistern of good water had been discovered. The *Argus*'s provisions were going ashore in her boats when the *Hornet* arrived with more. Returning to the beach, Eaton reconnoitered the bay, found a more convenient landing beach with an even larger cistern surrounded by a good grazing area some 20 miles farther west, and moved his army there to receive the rest of the new supplies.

While Eaton's army had been struggling across the desert, Hull had returned to Malta. Commodore Barron was there, ashore in his sickbed again. He had delegated command of the squadron to Captain Rodgers, but he still wanted to direct the squadron's support of the overland expedition. He ordered the new sloop-of-war *Hornet*[2] to accompany the *Argus* in taking supplies and money to meet Eaton at Bomba. The *Hornet* was to be commanded by Lieutenant Samuel Evans, and Hull was to direct the operation. They were delayed by an easterly gale but got away on March 28.

● Hull and Evans were off Bomba by April 8. Eaton at this point was still a week's march away, and the landing party Hull sent ashore found no one in the area. The next day Hull tried again, and the landing party found a single nomad; they paid him to go along the shore eastward looking for the army.[3] Fearful of the Mediterranean's sudden onshore winds, Hull decided not to anchor and wait for Eaton but to sail along the coast, returning to Bomba every few days. On the night of April 15 he saw over the southern horizon the light in the sky from Eaton's signal fires, and he turned and headed for them. Lieutenant Evans in the *Hornet*, cruising farther out to sea, apparently also saw them and followed suit.

Commodore Barron had written Eaton a long letter detailing the next movements as he saw them. He complimented Eaton on his success so far: "I cannot but applaud the energy and perseverance that has characterized your progress through a series of discouraging diffuculties[4] to the attainment of the object of your research— an attainment which I am disposed to consider as a fair presage of future success." He added pointedly that "I did not lose a moment" in sending off the needed provisions.

But then, in some contrast to the praise and optimism of the introduction, Barron got down to the business of the letter, which obviously was intended to go on record and cover his rear. He first expressed a hope that by the time Eaton rendezvoused with the *Argus* "you will have been enabled to form a correct opinion as to the prospect of ultimate success and thence to estimate the advantages likely to result. . . . Should you have encountered unexpected difficulties which place the chances of success upon more than precarious grounds, your own prudence will suggest the propriety of not committing these supplies and the money uncontrolledly to the power of the Bashaw."

By "the Bashaw" Barron of course meant Hamet. So Eaton, despite his previous experience with Barron's waffling, must have been surprised at the seeming contradiction of his next warning.

Barron obviously had read the agreement signed by Hamet and Eaton in Egypt; Eaton had sent it to him to forward to Secretary Smith just before setting out on the march. And the commodore had immediately sensed that Eaton had put him—and the U.S. government—out on a limb with some of his promises. "I fear," Barron wrote, that in the agreement "a wider range may have been taken than is consistent with the powers vested in me for that particular object. . . . I feel it my duty, to state explicitly that I must withold [sic] my sanction to any convention or agreement committing the United States or tending to impress on Hamet Bashaw a conviction that *we have bound ourselves to place* him on the Throne." The U.S. squadron, Barron continued, fully intended to support Hamet in attacks on Derna and even Tripoli, "but should the Bashaw [Hamet] be found deficient . . . or that it appears that we have been deceived with regard to the disposition of the inhabitants, he must be held as an unfit subject for further support."

To any reasonable man Barron's backpedaling would have been a clear signal that the overland expedition was in grave danger of being compromised. But Eaton was not a reasonable man, especially when it came to the project he had set his heart on and had completed successfully so far against nearly impossible odds. So he refused to take warning. With his boundless optimism and determination he had convinced himself that Hamet Karamanli would, under his dogged command, succeed in unseating his usurping brother. As for Barron's concern about "the disposition of the inhabitants," Eaton remained convinced that most of Tripoli would rise to Hamet's banner as soon as it was made evident that he had some chance of success.

Certainly by now Eaton had his own evidence that Hamet was a weak reed. But the "general" had kept him going so far, and he was convinced that he could continue to. Eaton surely saw through Barron's stilted phraseology to recognize that the commodore was protecting himself—already a tradition in the U.S. armed forces (not to mention the State Department). And Eaton could also detect the hand of Consul Lear, who, Eaton had noticed earlier, was dead set against the overland expedition and could be expected to poison Barron's mind against it. But Eaton reminded himself that the project had the backing of Lear's boss, Secretary Madison, as well as Barron's commander in chief. So with the confidence of his own conviction that he would succeed, Eaton was not dissuaded by Commodore Barron's clear warning.[5]

For all his claims of supporting Eaton, Barron had been parsimonious in loaning manpower. Eaton had originally asked for a hundred marines; all he received were the eight whom Hull lent on his own authority. And in his letter to Eaton Barron wrote that not only had it been "impossible for me to comply with your requisition for one hundred marines," but that "as we are short of officers the service of all will be called for on board the respective ships as soon as we enter on offensive measures"[6]—i.e., he wanted all his personnel back aboard the *Argus* before the attack on Derna. Barron did add, "Should you conceive however that any serious disadvantage may result from those with you, I have no objection to their remaining as volunteers," a clear signal to the men with Eaton that their continuing to stay with the overland army could be at the displeasure of the commodore.

That did not prevent Lieutenant O'Bannon from promptly writing a note to Hull: "Sir, Unwilling to abandon an Expedition, this far conducted, I have to request your permission to continue with Mr. Eaton during his stay on land, or at least untill we arrive at Derne." Evidently O'Bannon's marines also volunteered, and Hull gave his permission. Two of the *Argus*'s midshipmen changed places: Pascal Paoli Peck, who had marched across the desert to Bomba, went back aboard the brig and was replaced in Eaton's ranks by George Washington Mann.

Eaton also needed artillery.[7] In a request to Hull he wrote that "besides the terror that Cannon impress on the undeciplined [sic] Savages we have to dispute with, they will be our best resort against the Walls of Derne;" he asked for "two of your 24 lb. carronades," plus powder, ammunition, and more muskets. Hull felt he could not spare them, but he assured Eaton that the schooner *Nautilus*, by prearrangement with Barron, was en route to Derna with two field pieces (for which Barron also demanded a receipt).

Conferences on the strategy for the assault on Derna, the unloading of supplies, the recuperation of Eaton's half-starved men—all took nearly a week. On April 23 a Mediterranean gale forced Hull and Evans to take their vessels away from the lee shore. Eaton's army was now refreshed and ready to move, and the "general" was anxious to cover the last 60 miles to Derna.

Confident of victory as he was, he nonetheless wrote—as an addition to the note to Hull requesting artillery—an informal will: "in case I see you no more, I beg you will accept my cloak & small sword as marks of my attachment. The Damascus sabre you will find in my chest please give to Captain James Barron [the commodore's brother]—it is due to his goodness and valor . . . My gold watch and chain give to Danielson [his stepson]. Everything else please deliver over to Mr. Charles Wadsworth, my Executor." On April 23, despite the wind and rain, Eaton had the drum sounded to continue the march on Derna.

On April 19, while Eaton and Hull were conferring on their plan of attack, an obviously worried Bashaw Yusuf summoned Dr. Cowdery from his prison cell and, as the doctor confided to his journal, "interrogated me concerning the force of my country; he asked me how many marines the United States kept in pay. My answer, for good reasons, was ten thousand! How many troops? he asked.— Eighty thousand, said I, in readiness to march to defend the country, at any moment; and one million of militia are also ready to fight for the liberty and rights of their countrymen. At this his highness assumed a very serious look, and I returned to my room."

While Cowdery's figures were pardonable hyperbole, the United States was at the time sending a small contingent of reinforcements to the Mediterranean. On the day after the doctor's interrogation, Secretary of State Madison wrote a letter to Consul Lear reporting that the frigate *John Adams* would sail early in May with 600 men, that nine gunboats, each with 20 men, would sail May 1, and that two bomb vessels would sail June 1, all destined for attacks on Tripoli.

The terrain west of Bomba was as bad as the weather. In the wind and slashing rain Eaton's army climbed a rocky mountainside and after ten miles were too exhausted to go on. They found a spring and set up camp beside it. The next day they made 15 miles across a broad plateau and through a stand of red cedar trees; Eaton marveled that they were "the first resemblance of a forest we have seen in a march of nearly six hundred miles." They came into an inhabited and cultivated countryside. When they pitched their tents on the afternoon of April 24, in a valley by a stream surrounded by fields of barley, a local herald came through the camp calling out, "Let no one touch the growing harvest. He who transgresses this injunction shall lose his right hand."

That night another stranger arrived, a messenger from Derna with the news that Bashaw Yusuf's army had not yet reached the city but would probably arrive next day. "Alarmed consternation seized the Arab chiefs, and despondency the Bashaw," Eaton wrote. They gathered again in Hamet's tent and refused to let Eaton join them.

At 6 A.M. on the 25th Eaton ordered the drum for resuming the march. It was answered by Eaton's old nemesis el Taiib, his fellow camel driver Mahomet, and a group of Arabs who announced that they were deserting. They rode off to the east. The rest of the Arabs refused to leave their tents.

Eaton must have been surprised that el Taiib had remained with the army after being paid off at Bomba, and presumably he considered the sheikh's defection as good news. But he obviously needed the rest of the Arabs, and he quickly found the means: cash. With the money delivered by the *Argus* he went among the chiefs offering extra pay to those who would continue. It cost him $2,000, but by noon he had them on the march again. At 2 P.M. they reached the western edge of the plateau, just in time for el Taiib and Mahomet to come riding back with the other deserters and the camels.

From this last camp they could look down on their target. A green plain rolled down to the outskirts and the walled city of Derna. Studying his objective, Eaton could see orchards surrounding the city, the Wadi (river) Derna running down the mountain and through the heart of the city, the narrow alleys, a mosque, and the governor's palace. There was a fort at the harbor's edge. Barricades had been thrown up along the eastern side of the town. And the windowless walls of the houses at the perimeter were pierced with holes for musket fire. He could make out what looked like a howitzer on the terrace of the palace and light cannon in the fort. But out on the Mediterranean there was no sign of the warships that were supposed to support the attack on the city.

The evening was tense with expectation. A delegation of Derna's sheikhs came to the camp to pledge their fealty to Hamet. They reported that two thirds of the people in the city were ready to support him, but that the third loyal to Governor Mustapha numbered about 800, all well-armed. The eight cannon in the harbor port were nine-pounders, and the governor's forces were ready to deploy in the breastworks outside the city. But most important, Bashaw Yusuf's army had not arrived; it was about a day's march away.

Eaton was jubilant, but the news of the 800 defenders had a different effect on Hamet: "I thought the Bashaw wished himself back in Egypt," Eaton wrote. Hamet hid his anxiety as well as he could; and Eaton had no intention of letting him back out at this stage.

He realized that he faced a cruel decision—whether to wait for his naval support, which he considered essential, or to attack the next morning before the arrival of Yusuf's army. In the meantime he sat down and spent most of the evening writing a 2,500-word "Proclamation to Inhabitants of Tripoli," recounting the founding of the United States, listing a litany of American accusations against Bashaw Yusuf and asking for support for the "rightful Bashaw Hamet." He also wrote a brief letter with what he called the "terms of amity" to Governor Mustapha.

His Excellency the   Environs of Derne
Governor of Derne   April 26

Sir, I want no territory. With me is advancing the legitimate Sovereign of your country. Give us a passage through your city; and for the supplies of which we shall have need you shall receive fair compensation. Let no difference of religion induce us to shed the blood of harmless men who think little and know nothing. If you are a man of liberal mind you will not balance on the propositions I offer. Hamet Bashaw pledges himself to me that you shall be established in your government. I shall see you tomorrow in a way of your choice.

                                        Eaton

The next morning a courier went off under a flag of truce with both documents. He promptly returned with Mustapha's answer scrawled at the bottom of the "terms of amity": "My head or yours."

→● Through the morning Eaton scanned the horizon across the Mediterranean. He ordered smoky fires lit on the highest ground. He was considering how much time he had left to attack that day when at 2 P.M. he saw a sail. As the vessel approached, it was made out to be the *Nautilus*. Eaton put off the attack for the next day.

By 6 P.M. a boat was on the shore and Master Commandant Dent of the *Nautilus* came up the hill to report that he had two artillery pieces but that they were too heavy for his boats. The *Argus*'s longboat could handle them, though, he assured Eaton, and the *Argus* should arrive any hour.

After an anxious night the *Argus* did appear at dawn, along with the *Hornet*. The *Argus*'s longboat rowed over to the *Nautilus*. The field pieces, carriages, cannonballs, powder, and equipment were swung over the side, and the longboat was rowed toward the shore. But the officer in charge could find no landing spot out of range of the governor's guns on the rocky coast except at a precipice 20 feet high.

With a block and tackle Eaton's and the *Argus*'s men strained to lift the first cannon and carriage up the cliff. They finally got the gun ashore; but they had taken so long that Eaton impatiently decided to leave the second one. Some of the governor's soldiers were already marching out of the city, and it looked as if they might attack before Eaton's army could. He sent the longboat back to the *Argus* with the message that he was attacking as soon as possible, and asked for the prearranged naval support.

Already the *Hornet*, under a light onshore breeze, was drifting to an anchorage only a hundred yards off the harbor fort. The *Nautilus* had dropped anchor about half a mile off the town, and the *Argus* hove to a little farther out. While Eaton was still forming up his troops for the attack, all three warships let go their broadsides.

Eaton had divided his army into two units: a small contingent of marines, Greek cannoneers, other Christian mercenaries, and a few Arab foot soldiers, numbering about 50, all under the command of Lieutenant O'Bannon; and several hundred of Hamet's Arabs, most of them on horseback with Hamet in the lead. When the warships started laying down their barrage, O'Bannon's unit opened up with musket fire on the defenders at the barricades. Hamet's horsemen raced out around the southeast corner of the city, where they found a deserted castle, which they occupied as a base of operations. While Eaton watched with pleased surprise, Hamet, evidently transformed by the adrenaline of battle, led his horsemen in an enveloping movement to attack the city from the south.

The *Argus* and *Nautilus* were meanwhile lobbing their cannon-balls into the center of the city, while the *Hornet* was concentrating on the fort and silencing her guns one by one. O'Bannon and his marines and mercenaries were meanwhile pinned down by a with-ering fire from the soldiers at the ramparts east of the city. Their situation was not helped when one of the cannoneers manning their one piece of artillery forgot to extricate the rammer before the gun was fired; the long-handled plunger went soaring into the city with the cannonball, and the cannon was useless thereafter.

The Hornet's bombardment had its effect as most of the gunners in the fort broke and ran; but they joined the defenders at the barri-cades, increasing the firepower opposing O'Bannon's and Eaton's force. Some of the mercenaries started to falter, and Eaton saw the makings of a retreat and rout. "Our troops were thrown into con-fusion," he later wrote, "and, undisciplined as they were, it was impossible to reduce them to order." Characteristically he decided that the only thing to do was charge.

He ordered the bugler to blow the signal, and he and O'Bannon, shouting exhortations, led their 60-man army straight at the hun-dreds of defenders in and around the city. With O'Bannon and his blue-and-red-clad marines in the lead, they charged the ramparts. Caught up in the rush, the other mercenaries followed. Eaton, dashing into the firestorm, estimated the odds at ten to one.

Confronted by the insane bravado of the attackers, the governor's troops faltered, then retreated into the cover of the city, stopping only long enough for an occasional potshot as they backed off. One of the random shots caught Eaton in the left forearm, fracturing his wrist and rendering his rifle useless. But he wrapped his wound in a rag, grabbed his pistol with his good hand, and resumed the charge.

O'Bannon and his marines wheeled and—"through a shower of musketry," Eaton wrote—dashed for the fort, where they routed the few remaining gunners and found to their delight that the guns had just been loaded for a barrage at the warships. O'Bannon turned the guns on the town, but not before hauling down the

Tripolitan flag and replacing it with the Stars and Stripes, which he just happened to have with him.

All three warships were now concentrating their fire on the inner city. But shortly they had to slack off because Eaton's charge, aided by the naval bombardment and O'Bannon's fire from the fort, had succeeded, and the attackers were swarming into the center. In the meantime Hamet's horsemen, with him still in the lead, had raced around to the western section of the city and, sweeping all before them, had captured the governor's palace.

After 52 days and more than 500 miles, Derna was taken in two and a half hours. Two of O'Bannon's marines were killed, and one was wounded.[8] Hull sent in the *Argus*'s boats to bring out the wounded to be tended by his surgeon; Eaton, despite the pain in his arm, refused to leave the city until he and O'Bannon had made sure there was no further threat from the governor's troops.

As for Governor Mustapha—"My head or yours"—he had slipped out of his palace just before Hamet's cavalry had taken it. The governor first took refuge in a nearby mosque; then, evidently afraid that the infidel Christians would not respect the sanctuary of a mosque, he fled to the harem of one of the city's prominent leaders, Sheikh Masreat.

Eaton was angry and frustrated. He knew that Mustapha was Bashaw Yusuf's cousin and brother-in-law, and he had hopes of using the governor as a hostage while approaching Tripoli, perhaps bargaining to exchange him for Captain Bainbridge. But, as Eaton later reported to Barron, the Muslim harem was "the most sacred of sanctuaries among the Turks." He confidently predicted, however, that "we shall find means to draw him thence."

He soon discovered that, as he complained in his journal, "neither persuasion, bribes nor menace could prevail on the venerable aged chief to permit the hospitality of his house to be violated. He urged that whatever may be the weakness or even the crimes of the Arabs there was never an instance known among them of giving up a fugitive to whom they had once accorded their protection. And should he suffer himself to transgress that sacred principle, the vengeance of God and the odium of all mankind would jointly fix on him and his posterity."

And now Bashaw Yusuf's approaching army had to be contended with. At Eaton's request Hull agreed to keep two of his warships off the city for the time being to help defend it. The *Hornet*'s guns had shaken loose her plank shear (the deckboards' supports), and she could not fire a broadside until they were repaired. Hull sent her back to Malta on May 1 with reports from him and Eaton on the capture of Derna for Commodore Barron.[9]

Eaton set about strengthening the defenses of the city and established his headquarters in the harbor battery, which he named Fort Enterprise. As he reported to Barron, he "raised parapets & mounted guns towards the country to be prepared against all events."

Hassen Bey, the commander of Bashaw Yusuf's army, had taken his time; his forces did not reach Derna until May 8, eleven days after Eaton's capture of the city. Hassen also was in no hurry for a frontal attack. He stationed his army on the hillside that Eaton had used and spent the next few days recruiting Governor Mustapha's followers. It shortly became clear that the governor was cooperating from his sanctuary.

Eaton reacted with fury. Announcing that Mustapha was violating the rules of sanctuary, he marched 50 men to Sheikh Masreat's house and demanded that the governor be turned out. On his heels came a "deeply agitated" Hamet, warning Eaton that everyone in the city would rise in rebellion against a Christian profaning a Muslim harem. Eaton reluctantly gave Masreat a day to decide. That night the governor slipped out of the city and joined Yusuf's army. Thereupon Sheikh Masreat came to Hamet and pledged his fealty, chiding him nonetheless for attempting to violate sanctuary and reminding him that when he had been governor of Derna and feared his brother's assassins, Masreat had given him sanctuary in the same harem.

On May 13 Hassen made a probing attack. Repulsed, he assembled some 1,200 troops, attacked next day, and quickly overran Hamet's Arabs. They were closing on the palace, obviously intent on capturing Hamet, when they were met with a barrage of musket fire from the townspeople. O'Bannon's cannoneers joined in from the fort, and Hull's two ships added their broadsides. One nine-pound shell crashed into the castle courtyard just in time to turn them back, and they retreated. Some 20 attackers were killed, and Hamet's forces suffered a dozen casualties.[10] O'Bannon was itching to go after them with his marines, but Eaton did not want to leave Fort Enterprise unprotected as the governor's gunners had.

Hassen's troops retired to their camp, and a couple of deserters reported to Eaton that the attackers were refusing to march against the guns of the fort and the ships. It became a siege, with Hassen's soldiers surrounding Derna, appropriating the countryside's food and cutting off supplies to the city.

Hull sent provisions ashore from the warships' rapidly diminishing larders.[11] Apparently resigned to a long siege, he decided to send the *Nautilus* to Malta for more supplies; she sailed on May 18. Two days later Hamet came out to the *Argus* to beg for money to pay his soldiers; Hull told him they would have to wait for the return of the *Hornet* or the *Nautilus*. In his journal Hull wrote, "I told him to give the people of Derne to understand if they were faithfull to him they should be satisfied otherwise we shod. turn the guns of the fort and ships on the Town and destroy every house in it."

For the next three days the city was swept by a succession of North Africa's dreaded siroccos. To Hull aboard the *Argus* it was like a sandstorm at sea: "our riging [sic] and spars were covered with sand," he wrote. It was almost impossible to look to windward "without getting our Eyes put out with dust." It was worse in the city. Eaton recorded that the winds were of hurricane force and that the flying sand "resembled the smoke of a conflagration and turned the sun in appearance into melted copper." The heat was so great that his table and all the books warped. "The heated dust penetrated everything," he wrote, "through our garments; and indeed seemed to choak the pores of the skin." Water glasses were too hot to hold, and the fine, gritty sand sifted up their noses, nearly suffocating them. The wind blew away tents and the flying sand drifted over men and camels huddled before the gale. The sirocco's hot, wind-driven sand "had a singular effect on my wound," Eaton reported, making his broken wrist burn as if by fire.

The stalemate continued for a fortnight, each side wary of attacking the other. Hassen offered a reward of $12,000 for Eaton or $6,000 for his head. There were reports from deserters who slipped into the city that Hassen had also bribed a woman in town (with, Eaton reported, a "brilliant solitaire" diamond) to poison Eaton, who put out an order not to accept any food from the townspeople.

● On May 28, still fretting under the inaction, O'Bannon got Eaton's permission to lead his marines and some of the Greeks in a foray against an enemy outpost; but they accomplished little. Hassen feinted again next day but quickly backed off. Meanwhile reinforcements could be seen joining his army, and Eaton was told that a major assault was being planned.

On June 1 the *Hornet* returned with welcome supplies—and most unwelcome news for Eaton. A letter from Commodore Barron, dated May 19, reported "my candid opinion that the present moment is a moment highly favorable to treat of peace." Accordingly he had ordered Consul Lear "to meet the overtures of the reigning Bashaw," who had sent out peace feelers. Lear was sailing in the *Essex* to meet with Yusuf or his emissaries. If, as the commodore expected, the negotiations were successful, the Americans should be prepared to evacuate Derna and return to Malta. In the meantime, Barron wrote, "our supplies of money, arms and provisions are at an end," and Hamet "must now depend on his own resources and exertions."

Eaton had of course been warned that Commodore Barron was worried about promising to put Hamet on the throne. He also had apparently heard reports from Tripoli that there were some negotiations going on. But the official notification that the commodore was preparing to terminate a successful military action—and desert Hamet Karamanli—filled him with dismay. He sat at his sirocco-warped table in Fort Enterprise and wrote Barren a long, anguished letter of protest.[12]

First he angrily refused to take part in such a betrayal of Hamet. "I cannot persuade myself," he wrote, "that any bonds of patriotism dictate to me the duty of having a chief agency, nor indeed any, in so extraordinary a sacrifice." He reminded the commodore that obviously "the moment [Yusuf] entertains serious apprehension from his brother" he could be expected to offer some kind of deal. "This may happen at any stage of the war most likely to rid him of so dangerous a rival, and not only Hamet Bashaw, but everyone acting with him must inevitably fall victims to our *enemy*!"

Arguing that military success was on the horizon, Eaton urged the commodore not to falter now. The overthrow of Bashaw Yusuf "would very probably be a Death blow to the Barbary system," while relaxing now "would as probably be Death to the Navy and a wound to the national honor."

The expedition could not continue without U.S. support, Eaton wrote. Hamet could hardly "levy contributions" on the very people he was trying to deliver from burdensome taxation. Next came the appeal dear to Eaton's zealous patriotism. The aim of the United States, he chided Barron, was "to chastise a perfidious foe, rather than to sacrifice a credulous friend." He was certain that abandoning Hamet went against all "those principles of *honor* and *justice*, which I know actuate the national breast."

Barron had written, no doubt quoting Consul Lear, that backing Hamet was a doubtful gamble. Eaton had seen Hamet at his worst during the desert march and at his best in the attack on Derna; he maintained his confidence in him, and pointed out to Barron that he was not alone. "It is a general belief among the Gentlemen who have acted with me that Hamet Bashaw possesses talents sufficient to our purpose."[13]

Eaton also tried to appeal to Barron's patriotism. Striking the flag with victory in sight would appear to the enemy as defeat. "Certainly they and perhaps the world will place an unjust construction on this retreat . . . a *retreat of Americans!*" It would be better to lose militarily than in negotiations: "the consequence to our national character would be *more honorable.*"

As for Barron's—and Lear's—argument that the overland expedition was becoming too expensive, Eaton professed to be "apprehensive that the ultimate expence of maintaining a peace with Joseph Bashaw will be *more* burthensome to the United States than that accruing from this co-operation." And he added pointedly that "this expense will be reimbursed"; Hamet, as the agreement spelled out, promised to repay the United States for its support as soon as he was on the throne. (Eaton conveniently neglected to mention that Hamet, with his approval, planned to make the repayment by extortion from other nations.)

Eaton could not resist a shot at Consul Lear as a civilian meddling in matters of war. In a paragraph dripping with sarcasm he reported, "It is insinuated to me that the Consul General is opposed to [the expedition]. It is possible that he may have better information from whence to form an opinion of this issue than we who have thus accomplished the expedition; but it is not probable; has he any agency in *War?*"

And the angry "general" even hinted that the commodore might be overruled by his superiors; after all, the president had approved the project. "I cannot but still indulge the hope," he warned, "that Additional instructions from Government will arrive in season to enable you to furnish the means of prosecuting the cooperation to effect, of chastising the temerity of our Enemy, and of preventing the melancholy and disagreeable events which present Appearances threaten."

After a few dire warnings that the United States would be responsible for the desertion of Hamet's supporters in Derna— "havoc & slaughter will be the inevitable consequence; not a soul of them can escape the savage vengeance of the enemy"—Eaton wound up with a flowery peroration:

> Viewing the present posture of Affairs therefore, either as relative to our national honor and interests, or the situation of the Bashaw [Hamet] and people here, I consider it due to the confidence of Government and a bond imposed by all the injunctions of humanity, to endeavour to hold this post to the last moment, in hopes that some happy occurrence may take place to secure our own & at the same time to assist the interests of our friends; and I must devoutly pray heaven that the blood of innocence May not stain the footsteps of us who have aimed only to fight the Enemies of our Country.

The problem was that Eaton's eloquent appeal could not be delivered to Commodore Barron until one of the warships returned to Malta. Meanwhile they were needed to help fight off Hassen's army. By June 5 Eaton heard that a messenger from Bashaw Yusuf had reached Hassen confirming that negotiations had started and promising that once the bashaw had a treaty with the United States, "he should know," as Eaton put it, "how to dispose of his *internal* enemies." More reinforcements continued to come into Hassen's army from the west.[14] By June 11 Eaton estimated Hassen's forces at nearly 3,000; Hull's count was closer to 5,000. And that day Hassen brought the army swarming down the mountainside in an all-out attack.

Again Eaton was happily surprised at Hamet's stubborn resistance, fighting off the attackers in a swirling melee of pounding horses and slashing sabers until the guns of Fort Enterprise and the warships opened up in support. Hull's 24-pounder carronades did not have the range, but his 12-pounders did, and they were extremely effective. After a two-hour pitched battle Hassen's troops retreated. Hamet's cavalry went after them, cornering them at the base of a bluff. Hassen's horsemen escaped by dismounting and climbing the wall of the cliff, leaving their horses for Hamet's cavalry to round up and take back to the city. O'Bannon meanwhile was eager to lead his marines and Greeks into the fight, but Eaton held them back, again afraid that they would leave the fort unguarded against a flank attack.

In his journal that night he praised Hamet: "I have lately had good reasons to correct the unfavorable opinion at one time entertained of his military enterprize," and added that "the victory was decidedly his." But some 50 of Hamet's men had been killed or wounded (Hassen's casualties were about the same). And Hull sent his surgeon ashore to treat the injured. The defense of Derna was proving far more costly in lives than the taking of it.

But the defense was showing signs of success. More deserters from Hassen's army slipped into the city with news that much of his force was starting to melt away. In fact, one of Hassen's commanders, Abdel Selim, sent word that he and his 150 men would join Eaton if he could promise to protect them from Yusuf's vengeance.

The way to Tripoli might soon be open, Eaton concluded—if he were not blocked by Lear's negotiations. Eaton conferred with Hamet, whose strong reaction to the negotiations Eaton reported to Barron: *"to abandon him here is not to have cooperated with him, but with his rival."* In his letter—still waiting for a means of delivery—Eaton urged Barron not to betray him, and pleaded, "I am extremely anxious to learn the issue of the negotiations."

He did not have long to wait. On June 11 another storm came up, this time from the north with a heavy sea rushing into the bay and threatening to drive the warships onto the beach. Lieutenant Evans put out more anchors to protect the *Hornet*, but Hull took the heavier *Argus* to sea to ride out the storm. That afternoon, despite the high seas, the frigate *Constellation* moved grandly into the bay and anchored. Captain Hugh Campbell sent an officer ashore with the devastating news that on June 3 Consul Lear had signed a treaty with Bashaw Yusuf.

The United States had promised a ransom payment of $60,000; and the *Philadelphia's* prisoners had been released. Campbell had orders from Commodore Barron to take Eaton, O'Bannon, the marines, and Hamet aboard the *Constellation*. He also brought a message from Bashaw Yusuf granting "amnesty" to everyone in Derna who would swear loyalty to him—one of the stipulations of the treaty.

The next morning, still seething with anger, Eaton sent for Hamet and O'Bannon and told them the news. O'Bannon was as outraged as Eaton, and Hamet was crushed. He had suspected betrayal while crossing the desert; but now he was flushed with his defeat of Hassen's cavalry and was for the first time beginning to feel a sense of power and to entertain serious thoughts of regaining the throne. But with the fatalism gained from many reverses, he accepted the inevitable. Knowing the Arab mentality, he warned Eaton that the news must not get out to anyone else, or they would be slaughtered by the followers they were about to abandon.

Eaton agreed and set about deceiving them. He issued an alert to prepare to attack the besiegers. The *Constellation*, he told his troops, had brought reinforcements who would shortly be landed. He distributed new ammunition and rations. He dispatched scouts to reconnoiter the enemy's positions—they discovered that the arrival of the *Constellation* had had its effect on Hassen, who had retired some 15 miles inland. Late in the afternoon Eaton inspected the troops, telling them to be "in readiness to advance at the word."

At 8 P.M. O'Bannon put his men to patrolling the waterfront. The boats of the *Constellation* were at the wharves. At 10 P.M. O'Bannon ordered the Greek cannoneers and foot soldiers to march to the wharves. To deceive the rest of the army he left fires burning in the fort so it appeared still to be occupied. The Christians were ordered to get into the boats, which they did swiftly and silently, Eaton recorded, "but with astonishment."

With the marines still at their posts, Eaton sent a message to Hamet "requesting an interview." That was the signal. Hamet and a selected group of his sheikhs went to the waterfront; the *Constellation's* boats had returned and were waiting for them. Eaton followed. At his order, O'Bannon summoned his marines and herded them into the boats, which immediately set out for the frigate.

Eaton was last to leave; he had his own boat waiting. His oarsmen bent to their work, and were not more than a hundred yards away when the plot was discovered. Eaton described the scene as "the shore, our camp and the battery were crowded with the distracted soldiery and populace; some calling on the Bashaw; some on me; some uttering shrieks; some execrations! Finding we were out of reach, they fell upon our tents and horses, which were left standing; carried them off, and prepared themselves for flight . . . Before break of day our Arabs were all off to the mountains and with them such of the inhabitants of the town as had means to fly, taking away with them every living animal fit for subsistence or burthen which belonged to the place."

It was 2 A.M. before Eaton and all the followers he could save were settled aboard the *Constellation*,[15] which remained at anchor next morning while a boat under a white flag went ashore to deliver Bashaw Yusuf's amnesty offer. Eaton wrote that the crewmen returned to report that "nothing but despair depicted itself in the visages of the few wretched inhabitants who remained; that they rejected Joseph Bashaw's terms of pardon, declaring that they knew his perfidy too well to suffer themselves to be ensnared by it; and that they were resolved to defend themselves to the last moment from their terraces and walls of their houses against his troops."

Eaton's picture of the defiant townspeople was self-serving. Most of the Tripolitans who feared retaliation had fled into the countryside. The remaining population resignedly accepted the amnesty—which did not prevent Hassen and Mustapha from slitting the throats of those they deemed disloyal.

Eaton could be excused for his bitter and nearly maudlin musings that day as the *Constellation*'s anchor rose and her sails were sheeted home. "In a few minutes," he wrote, "we shall lose sight of this devoted city, which has experienced as strange a reverse in so short a time as ever was recorded in the disasters of war; thrown from proved success and elated prospects into an abys of hopeless wretchedness . . . we drop them from ours into the hands of their enemy, for no other crime but too much confidence in us! The man whose fortunes we have accompanied thus far experiences a reverse as striking. He falls from the bright flattering prospects of a *kingdom*, to *beggary!*"

And before reaching Malta Eaton was writing a letter to Captain John Rodgers, the new commodore: "The duties understood to be annexed to my appointment in the navy department having ceased with the war, I have no reasons for remaining any longer in this sea:—I request therefore you will have the goodness to allow me a passage in the first ship of war of your squadron which you may dispatch to the United States."

PART IV

★ ★ ★

THE PRICE
OF PEACE

CHAPTER 12

★ ★ ★

A PRESIDENTIAL
CHANGE OF MIND

Tobias Lear should have been the quintessential diplomat. The son of a prominent Portsmouth, N.H., shipmaster, an honor student at Harvard who did postgraduate studies in Europe, he became at 23 George Washington's private secretary before the Revolution. He continued as Washington's military secretary during the war with the rank of colonel, a title he enjoyed using ever thereafter. He was Washington's presidential secretary as well, in which post he caught the eye of Secretary of State Thomas Jefferson.[1]

Lear stayed on in Washington's service after his retirement to Mount Vernon and right up to the time when, clasping his devoted secretary's hand, the Father of the Country died. Lear idolized Washington even to the extent of fancying that he bore a resemblance to his hero. Now in the Mediterranean as President Jefferson's consul general, Lear was accompanied by his new wife, his third, who herself was distantly related to Washington.

Lear had recently served the United States well in a difficult post as U.S. commercial agent in San Domingo. And he was eager to prove that he could bring peace to the Mediterranean where others had failed. When he had come to the Mediterranean to replace Consul General Richard O'Brien, Lear had been under the command of Commodore Preble, and his attempts to persuade Preble to negotiate with the bashaw of Tripoli had failed. But some months ago Lear had been informed that President Jefferson had vested Lear with "full power and authority to negotiate a treaty of peace." And negotiating a peace treaty with Tripoli, in Lear's view, was the current mission of the United States in the Mediterranean. Not the defeat of Tripoli; a peace treaty with Tripoli.

Tobias Lear accordingly regarded the activities of the U.S. squadron as primarily a means toward a treaty: by humbling the bashaw, the navy would put him in the proper frame of mind. As for the Eaton-Hamet expedition, Lear considered it beneath contempt. He had never met Hamet Karamanli, but all he had heard about him was unfavorable. Such informants as the Chevalier Beaussier and Danish Consul Nicholas Nissen had told him that Hamet was unreliable and a coward. The fact that Beaussier's and Nissen's analyses might be self-serving did not impress Lear, if it occurred to him. He had no illusions about the tyrannical Bashaw Yusuf, but as he put it in practical terms, "I shd place much more confidence in the continuance of a peace with the present Bashaw, if he is well beaten into it, than I shd have with the other, if he should be placed on the throne by our means." And as for William Eaton, the pragmatic Tobias Lear regarded him as a hopeless romantic gratifying his ego in a project that clearly was insane.

Nonetheless, Lear could see that Eaton's operation might threaten his negotiations if by chance it showed signs of success. He was quite aware that Secretary Smith had given Commodore Barron full authority to support or cancel the overland expedition; Barron's instructions specifically read, "The subject is committed entirely to your discretion." So Tobias Lear set out systematically to sabotage Eaton's project.

Certainly he had the perfect opportunity. All during the autumn of 1804 and through the winter and spring of 1805, Commodore Barron's illness worsened, with only brief periods of recovery. Most of his time was spent ashore in the Syracuse naval hospital, and he made only a few short visits to Malta. On November 3 Barron wrote to Captain Rodgers from his bed in Syracuse, "I am so unwell to Day I can scarcely write at all & am totally unfit for business—God knows how it will end." Master Commandant Dent recorded that the commodore's health was such "as to disqualify him from transacting any business, his mind being so much impaired as scarcely to recall anything that transpired from one day to another." Dent wrote that when he tried to discuss the squadron's business, Barron often lost the thread of the conversation.

Even in good health Commodore Barron had been persuaded only by Eaton's persistence to approve the Hamet expedition. Now, in his debilitated state, he was an easy mark for Lear, who, as soon as Eaton had gone east to locate Hamet, began an unremitting campaign to turn the commodore against the operation. Lear spent ten days of October in Syracuse making his case, then went to Malta but continued to bombard Barron with his arguments. And whenever the commodore visited Malta, Lear was there to remind him.

● Perhaps the consul felt he had no time to lose; he wrote to Consul John Gavino in Gibraltar that Barron was ill enough "to make his life despaired of." Lear knew that it would be far easier to persuade the enervated Barron to negotiate with the bashaw than to attempt to talk the fiery John Rodgers, Barron's logical successor, out of an all-out war against Tripoli.

But he propagandized both of them through the autumn and winter. He repeated all the criticisms he had heard of Hamet, adding a new one: that Hamet had lost all credibility with Tripolitans by allying himself with Christians against a Muslim nation. Lear delightedly welcomed the disgruntled comments of Richard Farquhar, whom Eaton had dismissed for embezzlement. "We have heard from Mr. Eaton," Lear wrote, "by a man by the name of Faquier [sic] . . . who has returned to Syracuse, having quarrelled with Mr. Eaton, and left him. He writes to the Commodore, that Mr. E. is a madman—that he has quarrelled with the ex-Bashaw etc. etc. etc."

Lear marshaled a litany of arguments against the overland expedition. He was convinced that Eaton was wildly overestimating his chances for success, and that the bashaw's forces were far too formidable for Eaton's army to overcome. Meanwhile he was persuading Barron not to bolster Eaton's forces with more men and armaments from the squadron. Yusuf Karamanli, Lear was convinced, would fight to the bitter, bloody end, and even if confronted with defeat would escape into the interior with the *Philadelphia*'s prisoners as hostages; if cornered, he would slaughter them.

The bashaw could never surrender his prized prisoners without at least a token ransom, Lear argued. To do so would not only lose face with the other Barbary rulers; it would also invite a coup by his own army. Even in the unlikely event that a coordinated attack by Eaton-Hamet and the navy should succeed in placing Hamet on the throne, Lear believed, Yusuf would promptly counterattack and throw his weaker brother out again, proceeding to wreak vengeance on U.S. shipping as soon as the U.S. squadron departed. Far better, Lear argued, to threaten the bashaw with more naval bombardments like Preble's and frighten him into negotiations favorable to the United States.

● For a while Barron withstood the onslaught. When Hull returned from Alexandria to report that the overland expedition was on the way, Barron agreed to the rendezvous at Bomba with supplies and to naval support of the attack on Derna. When early in the spring his health improved, he wrote to Rodgers, still on blockade station off Tripoli, that he hoped to be well enough to join him in an all-out attack on Tripoli in May. Temporarily worried over the prospect of possible postponement if not elimination of negotiations, Consul Lear sent a cautionary note to Rodgers hoping to keep him in check: "I see no prospect," he warned, "of our forces being concentrated and ready to act against Tripoli sooner than the beginning or middle of June; so that I must regret that you will not have your just and sanguine wishes accomplished of seeing us ready to act before that time." To Lear it probably seemed only a friendly and time-saving admonition; to Rodgers it must have smacked of civilian interference in naval matters.[2]

In any case Commodore Barron had offered no explicit plans for an assault on Tripoli, if indeed he had any. Rodgers was anxious to follow up Preble's bombardments of the city and attacks on the bashaw's navy, if only to keep the pressure on him until more U.S. warships—and those promised gunboats—arrived; with a larger fleet he hoped finally to force defeat on Yusuf. Barron, however, seemed to have no overall strategy. And certainly there was no planned coordination with Eaton's overland expedition except for the promised naval support if and when he and his army reached Derna.

By now, finally, word of Preble's attacks on Tripoli and the bashaw's navy had reached Washington, heartening Jefferson and Madison over the prospect of victory after all. Madison wrote to Commodore Barron on April 20, 1805, expressing his hope that the United States could indeed force peace without tribute on the bashaw, what with "the spirited attacks made on the enemy by Commodore Preble" and the hope of more to come from Commodore Barron. In the same letter Madison announced that American gunboats were at last on the way to the Mediterranean; nine would sail on May 1, followed by two bomb vessels on June 1. The letter—and the gunboats and bomb vessels—would not reach the Mediterranean until too late.

And Barron's recovery had been short-lived; soon he was back in the naval hospital paying little attention to the affairs of the squadron. Except for the blockade fleet under Rodgers's stern command, squadron discipline relaxed. Through the winter, upkeep of the warships had been neglected, and morale had sagged. In early May Barron wrote to Rodgers putting off action against Tripoli until mid-June. His excuse was that the hoped-for gunboats from the United States had not yet arrived and that it made sense to wait for them.[3] The real reason was that the commodore was too ill to think about fighting.

As Barron's condition worsened, Lear kept up his drumfire for negotiations. Already he had been receiving peace feelers from various middlemen purporting to act for the bashaw. Barron had received some of these overtures but so far had rejected them. Lear, however, became even more convinced that the time was ripe for peace and ransom talks, especially when Captain Bainbridge wrote in his invisible lemon juice that "the Bashaw is very anxious for peace and has great apprehension of the intended attack, and was a negotiation to be attempted I think it very probable that it would succeed." Lear, too, believed that the threat of assault could be as productive of favorable peace terms as the assault itself.

Bainbridge and Lear were right about the bashaw's fears. The fury of Preble's attacks was fresh in his memory, and he expected even worse to come. He may not have known the extent of Barron's illness and its effect on the squadron, but he did know that a determined Captain Rodgers was clamping a tight blockade on his city; he had only to look out his castle windows to see the formidable array of American warships off the harbor.

He also, it happened, had been reading translations of some of the American newspapers he had permitted Consul Nissen to pass along to the *Philadelphia*'s prisoners. One item that had caught his eye was a report on the "Mediterranean Fund" enacted by Congress. Treasury Secretary Gallatin had estimated that the tax would raise $550,000 annually; comparing this figure with the amount of money he could raise with the most draconian taxes, the bashaw was impressed by the wealth of the United States.

He tried to bluster by sending a message to Captain Rodgers:

> I know that the exertions of your squadron this summer will be sufficient to reduce my capital; but recollect that I have upwards of three hundred of your countrymen in my hands; and I candidly tell you that, if you persevere in driving me to the last extremity, I shall retire with them to a castle about ninety miles in the interior of my country, which I have prepared for their confinement and my own security.

This, truly a hostage crisis, included using the hostages as human shields. Lear had no doubt that Yusuf meant it.[4] He encouraged Bainbridge to give him more supporting evidence for his argument against force and for negotiations. On March 24, 1805, he wrote, "I can only say, my dear Sir . . . that you may depend that you will not be left a moment longer in the situation you now are, than you can be relieved with propriety," adding somewhat unctuously, "Mrs. Lear unites with me in every wish for your speedy deliverance."

Bainbridge responded with more ammunition against Hamet and Eaton, whose expedition he considered a danger to himself and the other captives. Bashaw Yusuf, he pointed out, was recognized as the legitimate ruler of Tripoli in Constantinople as well as in most of the capitals of Europe. Bainbridge pleaded for the Americans not to get involved in "such an impolitic & extraordinary measure" as backing Yusuf's brother. In fact, Bainbridge wrote, Bashaw Yusuf was well aware of the Eaton-Hamet operation and "is greatly enraged and so is all his people. I am certain the event will prove what I have already said that any connection with him [Hamet] will be against our country's interest." Even Consul Nissen, the respected friend and helper of the American captives, weighed in with the warning that the bashaw "is now very attentive upon your transactions with his Brother" and was threatening dire consequences.

Then came the news from Derna. Ironically, the very expedition that Tobias Lear had been deploring and attempting to sabotage for half a year now made his task easier. Reporting the capture of the city to the bashaw, Governor Mustapha, mortally afraid to admit that he had been defeated by such a small force, vastly inflated the number of attackers. To Yusuf this meant that large numbers of Tripolitans were indeed rallying to Hamet's banner. He did not have to be reminded of his inability to recruit troops in the countryside, or of their bitter complaints against his regressive taxes. As he confided to his "family physician," Dr. Cowdery, the war was no longer over ransom money but over the throne itself. With the usurper's fear of being usurped, Yusuf concluded that if he wanted to keep his despised brother from replacing him, he had better negotiate the release of the American prisoners on the best terms he could get.

More ironically, the news from Derna had the opposite effect on Commodore Barron. Unlike Mustapha's account to Yusuf, Eaton accurately reported the operation. And, finally convinced by Tobias Lear's incessant arguments against the Eaton-Hamet expedition, Barron chose to notice not the extraordinary success of the attack on Derna but the city's strong defense. Hamet, the commodore concluded, had not attracted most Tripolitans to his cause as Eaton had promised. He and his army had had to fight for Derna and were still fighting to keep the city.

Barron now foresaw a long, costly, probably futile land campaign that would inevitably call for more men and resources than he could afford. Derna was proving difficult enough; Benghazi, in the path to Tripoli, could be an even bigger obstacle.[5] As he had informed Eaton, Barron did not want to spare more than a handful of marines for an overland expedition. With a naval officer's natural antipathy to land warfare, the commodore had no intention of mounting or even supporting with troops and armament a major army-type operation against Tripoli.

Had Hamet roused an overwhelming army of Tripolitans for such an invasion, Barron would have been willing to lend the support of naval bombardment; that, he considered, was what they had agreed on in the November conference. But after reading Eaton's accounts of the march from Egypt and the battle for Derna, Barron wrote to Lear that "from their tenor and the knowledge I have within a short time obtained of certain features in the character of Sidi Hamet Bashaw [most of this knowledge from Lear], I must candidly own that I have no longer the same expectations which I once entertained of the result of the Cooperation with him." He complained of Hamet's "want of energy and Military talents" and "his total deprivation of means and resources." The expedition, Barron wrote, had already been expensive and now threatened to be even costlier; "a sum far exceeding both the resources placed at my disposal and the powers vested in me by my Instructions compel me to relinquish the plan."

He reiterated the argument that Hamet's invasion had not caused a landslide of Tripolitan support, even after the capture of Derna. "If the Bashaw," Barron wrote, "having received the first impulse from our strength and being put in possession of Derne . . . has not in himself sufficient means to move on with firm steps towards the Usurper's Residence whilst we second his operation by sea. He must be considered as no longer a fit subject for our support and Cooperation."[6]

So, to complete the irony, the overland expedition against which Lear had argued now became his most persuasive argument for negotiations in the opinion of both Commodore Barron and the bashaw. Thus the commodore's letter to Eaton disavowing any U.S. promises to put Hamet on the throne of Tripoli. Moreover, Barron was by now facing the realization that he would not be well enough to lead any summer attack on Tripoli; in fact, his illness had reached the point that he knew he would have to hand over formal command of the squadron to Captain Rodgers.

But first he made the all-important decision to agree to negotiations for ransom for the *Philadelphia*'s prisoners. He dispatched Tobias Lear in the frigate *Essex* (with the commodore's brother James Barron in command) to join the blockade force off Tripoli. They arrived on May 26, with Lear carrying a letter to Captain Rodgers officially appointing him commodore of the squadron.

Lear was aware that the new commodore remained his last obstacle; no doubt it had been at Lear's urging that Barron had made the decision to negotiate before handing the command over to Rodgers. Lear knew that Rodgers, now that he was in charge, would want to attack first and talk later.

Rodgers was no supporter of the Eaton-Hamet operation. He still had unpleasant memories of being detained with Commodore Morris by the Bey of Tunis because of Eaton's debts.[7] Moreover,

Rodgers and Lear had been friends since 1801, when they had met in San Domingo while Lear had been commercial agent there. But friendship, in Lear's view, was no impediment to outmaneuvering Rodgers if he could. So he planned to get the talks started before Rodgers had time to assemble his forces for the attack.

Lear had another reason for haste. Danish Consul Nissen had sent along a message to Commodore Barron from Tripoli's foreign minister, Mohammed Dghies. The minister, Nissen reported, "was personally desirous of a reestablishment of peace with the U.S. of America and wishing to contribute whatever may be in his power to the Conclusion of it." Lear knew from Bainbridge's reports that Dghies was the Americans' best friend in the bashaw's court; he had acted as go-between and had often persuaded the bashaw to relax some of his harsher punishments. Dghies claimed in fact to be the only member of the bashaw's Divan to have voted against declaring war on the United States in 1801.

What now made his overture urgent was Dghies's failing health. He suffered from eye troubles, which Dr. Cowdery had unsuccessfully tried to cure, and he was preparing to spend the summer in his country villa in hopes of recovery away from the filthy air of the city. Once he was out of touch with the castle, he pointed out, he could not use his benign influence. Nissen added his own opinion that Dghies was serious, and Bainbridge also reported Dghies's eagerness to pave the way to a treaty.

As if to add to the urgency, Lear now heard that the bey of Tunis was saber-rattling again, warning of war over a Tunisian vessel and two prizes captured by Rodgers while trying to run the blockade. To Lear this was another argument against delay.[8] So when the Spanish consul to Tripoli came out to the blockade fleet under a white flag and announced that he was delegated by the bashaw to make a new offer, Lear was ready for him—and outraged when Commodore Rodgers rejected the offer.

It was for a ransom of $200,000, which Rodgers considered unacceptable. He also recognized the Spanish consul, Don Joseph de Souza, as a toady to the bashaw.[9] In Rodgers's opinion, the bashaw would be a lot more amenable to peace talks after a summer of bombardment. But Lear refused to pass up this opportunity to open negotiations. Asserting his new authority, he sent de Souza back with a counteroffer: $60,000 for the release of the captives, and a new treaty with no future tribute.

❍ For three days there was no reply; the weather was stormy, and Lear hoped that was the reason for no sign of a boat leaving the harbor. Rodgers was meanwhile complaining, only half in jest, that he could personally collect from his officers the $200,000 the bashaw had demanded if it could be used to ransom the *Philadelphia* prisoners without calling off the war. He would follow up, he promised, with a series of bombardments worthy of Preble.

On May 29 de Souza was rowed out through the choppy waters to the *Constitution* where Lear and Rodgers waited. He reported that the bashaw had reduced his demand to $130,000. Lear was now convinced that he had the bashaw on the hook. He coldly ordered the Spanish consul to deliver an ultimatum: an exchange of American prisoners for Tripolitans in American hands, and $60,000 ransom to compensate for the difference in numbers—the squadron had roughly one third as many Tripolitan prisoners. The United States, Lear declared, would not go higher than $60,000. If it were refused, naval action would commence.

De Souza went ashore and promptly returned with the bashaw's acceptance. But Yusuf insisted on the Tripolitan prisoners being handed over first. Lear said no. At this point Consul Nissen entered the negotiations and urged the bashaw to agree. Finally convinced that he could do no better, Yusuf acquiesced.

Nissen now became the intermediary. On June 2 he brought Bainbridge out with him to assist in the details. A preliminary treaty was quickly spelled out; and while they labored over the wording, the flagship's carpenters fashioned a spar into a flagpole to replace the one chopped down by the bashaw's soldiers at the consulate four years earlier.

Nissen and Bainbridge went ashore with a treaty. The bashaw accepted it, and everything went with a rush. On June 4 Consul Lear was rowed ashore in the *Constitution*'s barge flying the American flag. Waiting to greet him were the officers of the *Philadelphia* and a crowd of curious Tripolitans. Lear wrote to his wife that he "was met by thousands of people on the landing. . . . The people here are very much pleased with the peace, as they gain nothing but lose much by the war; and it matters not to them whether it is favorable to their leader or not."

→ • Whatever the actual feelings of the populace, the bashaw was all courtesy. When the Stars and Stripes rose again over the U.S. Consulate at 10:30 that morning, he ordered a 21-gun salute. The *Constitution*, followed in stately procession by the *Constellation*, the *Essex*, and the *Vixen*, sailed into Tripoli Harbor and dropped anchor while the flagship boomed its own salute. On a nearby shore could be seen the charred ribs of the *Philadelphia*.

After a consultation with Minister Dghies, Lear sent a heady message out to Rodgers in the *Constitution* promising that "our peace will be so unusually honorable, that we must not expect it to be fully relished by all the Representatives of the European Nations here, which is already manifested." He also reported that the *Philadelphia*'s officers were about to be ferried out to the squadron. The sailors, however, would be delayed for another day "as intoxication of Liberty & Liquor had deranged the faculties as well as dresses of many of the sailors and Capn B. wishes them all on board quite clean and in Order." After 18 months in prison Bainbridge was not going to herd a drunk and disheveled mob of sailors out to the squadron's ships. The next day a haggard, hung over but spotless crew stepped smartly to the landing and aboard the squadron's boats to be rowed to freedom at last.

Eleven of them were missing. Of the 307 officers and crew only six had died, none of them officers. When the survivors were about to be released, the bashaw sent for the five renegade sailors who had professed to turn Muslim. Yusuf offered them the opportunity to renounce their conversion and return to the squadron. Only one, the troublemaking John Wilson, elected to remain a Muslim and stay in Tripoli. The others chose to leave; one of them had a wife and four children at home. But the bashaw, evidently regarding their Muslim masquerade as an insult to his religion, promptly called the guards and had them marched away. "We had a glimpse of them as they passed our prison," marine private Ray recalled, "and could see horror and despair depicted in their countenances." They were never heard from again. Consul Lear chose not to protest.

At Lear's direction Rodgers took the *Constitution* to Malta to pick up the Tripolitan prisoners and $60,000 in cash. By June 10 the treaty was ready for ratification. At noon Lear was ushered into the castle's audience chamber, where Bashaw Yusuf motioned him to the seat of honor on his right. Lear handed him his copy of the treaty; "great order and solemnity were observed," he reported. The bashaw passed the treaty to Minister Dghies, who read it aloud in Arabic to the members of the Divan. There were a few questions, which were answered by the bashaw. Two copies of the treaty went ceremoniously to each Divan member, who dutifully affixed his seal. The bashaw added his and handed Lear his copy "in a solemn manner," Lear recalled, "and with many expressions of friendship." A week later the *Constitution* returned from Malta with the $60,000 and 89 Tripolitans, largely blockade runners; and peace was restored with Tripoli.

The treaty was carefully written to save face for Bashaw Yusuf— and Consul Lear. The $60,000 was described as ransom for the American prisoners beyond the number of Tripolitans who could be exchanged,[10] thus permitting Yusuf to maintain that he had exacted a payment. But it was not a price for peace, nor was any further tribute promised, thus permitting Lear to claim that the United States had not bought an end to hostilities. Perhaps more important to Yusuf—and a concession Lear readily agreed to—was a promise by the United States to abandon Derna and induce Hamet to withdraw.[11]

Understandably pleased with his accomplishment, Lear wrote Eaton a somewhat patronizing letter, which went to him aboard the *Constellation* along with Barron's order to disband his expedition. Datelined "Tripoli, in Barbary, June 6th, 1805," Lear's letter proudly recounted the negotiations and added what he obviously considered a mollifying note: "I found that the heroic bravery of our few countrymen at Derne, and the idea that we had a large force and immense supplies at that place had made a deep impression on the Bashaw." Eaton must have gagged at Lear's casual reference to "immense supplies," when he was convinced that Lear had done all he could to see that supplies to Derna were curtailed. What did stick in Eaton's throat was Lear's lordly paragraph: "I pray you will accept and present to Mr. O'Bannon, and our brave Countrymen with you, my sincere congratulations on an event which you and your heroic behavior has tended to render so honorable to our country." Signing his letter, Lear was careful to append his full title: "Commissioner of the United States for negotiating a peace with the Bashaw of Tripoli."

Eaton's acid reaction, in a letter to Secretary Smith, was:

> After having subscribed to a treaty, the conditions of which, under the then existing circumstances, reflects a wound on our national dignity;—and after having seized an occasion to use me as an instrument to the attainment of this acquisition, as he seems to think it, he evidently flatters himself he shall absorb my just sense of indignation and chagrin in a plausible paragraph of fulsome adulation.

The unhappy little band from Derna left the *Constellation* at Syracuse. Most of the cannoneers and other mercenaries drifted back eastward. Eaton persuaded Commodore Rodgers to give Hamet a temporary allowance of $200 a month for his retinue, and left for home.

He sailed aboard the navy's supply brig *Franklin* from Syracuse on August 6. The situation aboard the brig was tense; Eaton was surrounded by naval officers who felt that his overland operation had threatened to steal their thunder. In any case Eaton spent most of the time in his cabin writing a long letter of protest to Secretary Smith. He started it, as his dateline indicated, "At Sea, Mediterranean, August 9, 1805." Still simmering with anger, he reiterated all the arguments against canceling his operation. He denounced Lear's peace treaty and Lear himself. More than anything else, Eaton felt betrayed. When Commodore Barron had agreed to support his expedition with Hamet, Eaton argued, "no idea was suggested of making this co-operation an instrument only to the attainment of peace with the reigning Bashaw of Tripoli. Nothing was then talked of but chastisement." Only when Tobias Lear came onto the scene was the strategy changed. Eaton complained that "it was not until Commodore Barron despaired of recovering his health in season for activity and not until a man who had no authorized agency in the war, had intruded himself into his confidence, and gained an ascendancy over his resolutions" did the overall plan change.

Commodore Barron, Eaton pointed out, had written him praising the success of his expedition. But, he added, "The instant the

effect of our success discovered itself, through the alarmed solic-
itude of the enemy, a messenger of peace [one can hear him hissing
the phrase] is sent to meet the overtures of the panic-stricken
JOSEPH BASHAW, and bid him to be under no apprehensions;
while our too credulous ally is sacrificed to a policy, at the recollec-
tion of which, honor recoils, and humanity bleeds."

The more he thought and wrote about it, the angrier Eaton became. He did not, he wrote, blame his betrayal on the ill commodore.[12] "It is the work of a Macheavelian commissioner into
whose influence the commodore had yielded his mind through the
infirmity of bodily weakness." It was Tobias Lear's hypocrisy,
Eaton charged, that turned the original U.S. strategy of war into
one of deceit: "We are still to amuse the exile [Hamet] with an idea
of *cooperation and union of operation on the coast*, at the very moment
that a pending negotiation necessarily suspends all hostile operations."

The result, Eaton complained, was that he had been left "to per-
ish with the Mohametans under my command, or desert them to
their solitary fate, and abandon my post like a coward!" And all
while "we had in our power, being actually in our possession, the
capital of the largest province of his [Bashaw Yusuf's] dominions,
containing between twelve and fifteen thousand souls. Could not
this have been exchanged for two hundred prisoners of war? Was
the attempt made?" He did not explain exactly how it might have
been done; perhaps he felt that the United States could have offered to evacuate the captured city of Derna in return for the release of the *Philadelphia*'s prisoners. That, of course, was part of the
very deal worked out by Consul Lear that Eaton was now belabor-
ing. And this argument was inconsistent with the contention he
made to Secretary Smith and others that he and his army were on
the point of marching on to capture the capital.

In his letter to the secretary Eaton assured him that his forces
had "beaten the enemy's army in that province and opened our way
to the gates of Tripoli." As he put it in another letter to a friend, "I
firmly believe we would have entered Tripoli with as little trouble
as we did Derne."[13]

Suppose they had. Tobias Lear had argued that Hamet Karamanli was an unreliable foundation on which to base U.S. hopes
for peace, and that it was safer to make a deal with a humbled

bashaw who still controlled his regency. Scornfully attacking this proposition, Eaton wrote, "If patricide, fratricide, treason, perfidity to treaty, already experienced, and systematic piracy, be characteristic guarantees of good faith, Mr. Lear has chosen the fittest of the two brothers for his man of confidence."

♦ He concluded with the argument that Consul Lear and the United States had succeeded only in making matters worse. "Thus, though it was our business and though we had most amply the means to dismantle the enemy, instead of this, we have established him in a more safe situation to do us and mankind mischief, than he possessed before the war; or than he could have possessed without the war; for by expelling his rival, we have relieved him of his most dangerous adversary. He has gained a kingdom. What have we gained by the war?"

And to rub it in, Eaton appended a "P.S." listing the U.S. naval forces that were ready to attack Tripoli in mid-July of 1805: five frigates, four brigs, two schooners, one sloop, and 15 gunboats.[14]

All William Eaton could hope to accomplish by his anguished appeal was censure of Tobias Lear. It was too late to reverse the course of events. His army was disbanded; the treaty was signed; the U.S. Consulate was reopened with the Stars and Stripes flying atop its flagpole again. For the moment Eaton was merely venting his wrath. But he also had two larger goals: to repay Hamet Karamanli for his efforts; and, if possible, to convince the government to repudiate Tobias Lear and possibly the treaty itself. Eaton realized that his last hope lay in Washington, where President Jefferson had originally approved his expedition and might be persuaded to denounce Consul Lear for subverting it.

What Eaton did not realize was that Jefferson had changed his mind. In his second inaugural address on March 4, 1805, the president had said, "We are firmly convinced and act upon that conviction that with nations as with individuals our interests soundly calculated will ever be found inseparable from our moral duties." Jefferson's initial approval of Eaton's plot with Hamet could be said to have compromised the United States' "moral duties." Now, by betraying that operation, he may have considered that he was confirming the message of his inaugural address. But from Eaton's point of view *that* was the immoral act: abandoning a pledge to an ally and settling for tribute instead of defiance.

*   *   *

Commodore John Rodgers saw to it that even in the Mediterranean July Fourth of 1805 was properly celebrated. The flagship *Constitution* and every other warship in Valletta Harbor were dressed for the occasion, their rigging festooned with flags. At noon the harbor resounded to the crash and boom of a 16-gun salute from every American man-of-war. That night Rodgers presided over a banquet for most of Malta's notables—who debarked, according to the ship's log, with "6 silver spoons a number of Glasses and Many other articles too tedious to Mention" as souvenirs.

But Rodgers was thirsting for the action that had been denied him by Consul Lear's diplomacy. Ironically, at the very time his government agreed to pay for a treaty, he commanded the largest naval force the United States had ever sent overseas.[15] So his reaction was predictable when Bey Hamouda of Tunis let it be known that he was considering a declaration of war against the United States. He may have been salivating over the $60,000 that the United States had just paid to his neighbor. And he claimed to have a just grievance in Rodgers's capture in April of an eight-gun Tunisian xebec and two merchant ships it had captured when they had attempted to run the blockade of Tripoli.

Rodgers had sent them all to Malta as prizes of war, and Bey Hamouda had been demanding their return ever since. The U.S. consul to Tunis, Dr. George Davis, had been resisting the bey's demands, and now Hamouda was threatening to follow the example of Tripoli's Bashaw Yusuf by sending his cruisers out after American shipping.

Commodore Rodgers was delighted to find employment for his enlarged squadron. At the end of July he assembled the frigates *Constitution, Constellation, Congress,* and *John Adams,* along with the smaller warships *Vixen, Siren, Nautilus, Franklin, Enterprise,* and *Hornet* plus some of the newly arrived gunboats and set out for Tunis. On August 1 Bey Hamouda looked out his palace windows to see the largest flotilla ever massed in a Barbary Coast harbor, some 16 warships moving grandly in double file, dropping anchor, furling sails, and presenting their rows of bristling gunports to the city.

The bey resisted at first. When a message arrived from Commodore Rodgers, he refused to see him. Consul Davis went out to the flagship and returned with an ultimatum. Did the bey want peace or war? If the latter, the commodore was ready to provide it. He demanded an unequivocal answer within 36 hours.

● Rodgers soon learned that virtually nothing was unequivocal along the Barbary Coast, especially in only 36 hours. The bey protested against the Americans invading his harbor with the entire U.S. squadron. Rodgers ominously replied that it was not the entire squadron; another frigate, a brig, eight gunboats, and two bomb ketches were on the way. The translators asked for more time, which Rodgers grudgingly granted. The bey requested that the dispute be forwarded to Washington for adjudication and volunteered to send an ambassador to plead his case. Rodgers replied that he would agree on the condition that the bey give an official guarantee of peace with the United States while the judgment was discussed. The bey refused.

― By this time Rodgers's 36-hour ultimatum had been stretched to six days, and his patience was exhausted. He ordered Consul Davis to come out to the flagship next day by 4 P.M. if no guarantee had been promised by Bey Hamouda. The bey still refused, and Davis packed up and left. Rodgers sent part of his fleet outside the harbor to set up a blockade and waited for the bey to sweat it out.

One reason that Rodgers did not simply pour a broadside into the city was that he had brought Consul Lear to preside over the new treaty he expected to exact from the bey, and Lear no doubt influenced him to withhold his fire for the moment. Indeed, the blockade had its effect. Realizing that his harbor was closed to all shipping, Hamouda agreed to talk. Consul Lear, accompanied by Chaplain Cruize of the *Constellation*, went ashore on August 12 for negotiations. Within two days they had reached an agreement. Rodgers would provide transportation to the United States for the bey's ambassador. The bey guaranteed peace at least until the dispute over the prizes was resolved. Surgeon Dodge of the *Constitution* was appointed to replace Consul Davis, whom Bey Hamouda had come to loathe. The U.S. squadron loosed sail and returned to Malta, where Hamouda's ambassador, Sidi Suliman Mellimelli, was put aboard the *Congress*, which Captain Decatur was taking home.[16]

More U.S. warships were leaving the Mediterranean. The ill ex-commodore Barron sailed for home aboard the *President* as a passenger with his brother James in command. Captain Bainbridge, after demanding an immediate court-martial in which he was cleared of culpability in the loss of the *Philadelphia*, also went home. Tobias Lear and his wife toured southern Europe buying gifts for the dey before returning to Algiers. The *Constellation* left in August, followed by the *Nautilus* and the *Franklin*. One by one most of the frigates returned. Jefferson was winding down not only the Mediterranean squadron but the U.S. Navy as well, laying up warships and pensioning officers, despite the threat of war with England, which he still hoped to avoid.

Commodore Rodgers maintained the base at Syracuse and kept busy convoying American merchantmen and showing the flag. The American presence had at least aided U.S. shipping in the Mediterranean. Trade with Italy, for example, had tripled, and insurance rates in the area had dropped by a third. Most of the *Constitution*'s crew, their enlistments long since expired, had been relieved by the crew of the *President* and had gone home. Finally, in May of 1806, President Jefferson ordered Rodgers home, too. The president was increasingly concerned over the risk of U.S. warships in the European area becoming embroiled in the Napoleonic War. On May 26, 1806, after closing down most of the U.S. base at Syracuse and leaving a skeleton crew, Rodgers relinquished command of the squadron and turned the *Constitution* over to Captain Hugh G. Campbell. She remained the last of the many U.S. frigates that had been sent to the Mediterranean, until the spring of 1807 when Commodore Campbell was told that the *Constitution* would be relieved by the *Chesapeake*, which was about to depart from Hampton Roads to continue a small presence in the Mediterranean.

Captain James Barron, who had brought his ailing brother Samuel home, was appointed commodore of what was left of the Mediterranean squadron in May of 1807. He went down to Norfolk, Va., where he found the 38-gun *Chesapeake* scarcely ready to go to sea. Her crews had not been assigned to their stations; her decks were cluttered with unstowed gear; most of her guns were unmounted, and her cannonballs, rammers, and other arms were scattered about the ship. But Barron was anxious to be on his way, so on June 22 he gave orders to sail, planning to get everything shipshape as soon as they were at sea. He had heard that some Royal Navy men-of-war were in the Hampton Roads area, but he expected no trouble from them, despite the fact that there had recently been a dispute over some British deserters.

With the Napoleonic War an increasing drain on Royal Navy manpower, British press gangs had become more and more aggressive. American vessels had been stopped and searched off the U.S. coast, and many American sailors had been seized on the pretext that they were British deserters. Aboard the *Chesapeake* were four men who had run away from the British frigate *Melampus;* all four claimed that they had been impressed into the Royal Navy from a U.S. merchant ship even though they were American-born. Three could prove their U.S. citizenship; a fourth could not but swore he had been born in America. Accordingly, the U.S. government had refused to relinquish them when the British minister had demanded that they be returned to the *Melampus.*

The *Chesapeake* was about 50 miles off the coast and out of sight of land when the Royal Navy frigate *Leopard,* 50 guns, came up with her. An officer called out asking if the *Chesapeake* would carry some dispatches to Europe. Barron consented; it was a courtesy both navies frequently extended to each other. While the *Chesapeake* backed her sails, a boat came across from the *Leopard,* and a Royal Navy officer climbed aboard. What he brought was not a packet of dispatches but an order from the commander of Britain's North American Station directing all British warships to stop the *Chesapeake* and search for the four deserters who, the British charged, had taken refuge aboard the frigate.

Commodore Barron politely but firmly directed the British officer to reply to his captain that the *Chesapeake* was a warship of the United States, whose government did not permit such searches. The officer climbed down into his boat and was rowed back to the *Leopard,* whereupon the *Chesapeake* was hailed again by an officer identifying himself as Captain Salisburg Humphreys. Barron had already ordered the *Chesapeake* to resume course, and could not make out what Captain Humphreys said. The next thing he knew, the *Leopard* fired a round shot across the *Chesapeake*'s bow.

Captain Barron called the crew to quarters, but few knew their stations. Most of the frigate's guns were still lying on the deck without their carriages; and powder, flintlocks, wads, and matches were nowhere to be found. As the officers and sailors rushed about in confusion, the *Leopard* came alongside at close-up range—about 200 feet—and let go a withering broadside.

For a quarter of an hour broadside after broadside poured into the staggering *Chesapeake*, hulling her 21 times, splintering her masts, shredding her sails, and sending her men running for cover. One brave officer, Lieutenant William Allen, raced to the galley, seized a live coal, and ran, juggling it in his bare hands, to one of the mounted guns to touch off the only shot the *Chesapeake* fired in return. With that lone response the *Leopard* ceased fire. Three of the *Chesapeake*'s men were dead, eight were near death, and ten, including Captain Barron, were wounded. Barron ordered the *Chesapeake*'s flag hauled down in surrender.

Captain Humphreys sent over a couple of lieutenants with a boarding party. At their demand the *Chesapeake*'s crew was mustered, and the four alleged deserters were found and herded into the *Leopard*'s boat; one of them had been hiding in the *Chesapeake*'s hold throughout the attack. As a final humiliation, Captain Humphreys refused to accept Captain Barron's sword, explaining that he did not consider the *Chesapeake* a prize since Britain was not at war with the United States.

The *Chesapeake* was too crippled to continue across the Atlantic; Captain Barron took her back to Norfolk. When the news of the *Leopard*'s attack spread through the United States, there was a rash of war fever.[17] President Jefferson refused to ask Congress for a declaration of war. But he sent orders to the Mediterranean to bring the squadron home. Clearly the dangers in the North Atlantic had become far greater.[18]

The news of the *Leopard-Chesapeake* encounter reached the Mediterranean before the orders recalling the squadron. Commodore Campbell found out about it in a newspaper in Malaga, Spain. His immediate reaction was to strengthen the armament of the *Hornet* with four 32-pounders from the *Constitution*, in case there was war with Britain before he could be notified. He also decided for the time being to steer clear of Gibraltar and other British ports.

When the sailors aboard the *Constitution*, at anchor in Malaga, heard that the *Chesapeake* was not coming to relieve them after all, they grumbled with threats of mutiny. A cool-headed petty officer requested permission to present their views to the commodore, and Campbell delegated Lieutenant Charles Ludlow, who was well liked by the crew, to hear their complaint. When Ludlow reported to the commodore that there could be serious trouble, Campbell ordered the flagship immediately readied for sea before there was a flood of desertions.

● At eight bells the next morning when the boatswain's pipe summoned all hands, the sailors refused to work the ship, sending word that they would go to their stations only to return home. Campbell ordered all his officers and the flagship's marine detachment onto the quarterdeck, armed for combat. He called for the signal for all hands to assemble on the larboard gangway. This time they complied, and found themselves facing two long 12-pounders aimed to sweep the deck. While the crew watched, midshipmen loaded the guns with grape and canister, took off the touch-hole covers, and blew on their matches. The officers repeated the call to man the ship, and under the threat of imminent slaughter the crew complied. The *Constitution* put to sea. And before the sailors could organize another mutiny, the orders arrived summoning them home.

On August 18 Commodore Campbell received his instructions to close down the Mediterranean squadron. He sent the *Hornet* to Syracuse to arrange the packing and shipping of U.S. stores in the warehouses, and to Leghorn to take aboard the squadron's money that was banked there. The *Constitution* departed on September 8, arriving at Boston October 14 after four years in the Mediterranean. And she was not even home before Algiers's pirates were again roaming the Mediterranean; that autumn they captured three American vessels.

Algiers's Dey Mustapha had been assassinated in 1805; his successor, Dey Achmet, tried a war against Tunis but found that fighting on land was not Algiers's forte; so he turned his navy loose. Consul Lear, pointing to the treaty supposedly still in effect, persuaded him to release two of the captured American ships—Dey Achmet suavely explained that he did not expect the mere capture of a few American ships to interfere with continuing U.S. tribute. The third vessel never made it into Algiers; she was the schooner *Mary Anne* of Boston, and her captain, Ichabod Sheffield, and his men managed to overpower the Algerian prize crew, killing four and setting the other four adrift in a boat. Sheffield then took the *Mary Anne* to Naples. The Algerians in their open boat did not make it to Algiers either; and Dey Achmet angrily demanded

$16,000 in reparations for his prize crew, threatening to jail Lear if he did not pay. It was as if no U.S. squadron had ever been sent to the Mediterranean. Lear may have wondered if his treaty had squandered any respect the Americans had won. In any case he had no choice but to pay.

● Lear's Tripoli treaty had meanwhile set off a firestorm in Congress. Navy Secretary Smith had been leery of it at the start. When the first reports reached Washington in September of 1805, Smith wrote to the president, "I must say I had expected a treaty of a different character. And informed as I am now, I wish that such a peace had not been made." Later, however, after talking to some homecoming *Philadelphia* prisoners who remained convinced that they would have been killed without ransom, Smith changed his tune, announcing that it was the most favorable treaty any nation at war with Tripoli had achieved in more than a century.

Jefferson submitted the treaty to the Senate for ratification on December 11, 1805. For more than four months, in the Senate and in the press, there was a public outcry against selling out to Tripoli. Senators rose to ask why ransom should have been paid, why the full power of the U.S. squadron had not been used first, why the Eaton-Hamet expedition had been abruptly canceled, and why the United States had let its image be smeared by the betrayal of Hamet Karamanli. It proved to be one of the most unpopular treaties in U.S. history. But it was a *fait accompli;* the bashaw had been paid, the *Philadelphia*'s prisoners were home, and there was no retreat except by an even more ignominious decision to renege on a formal agreement. By the time the treaty had finally, reluctantly, been ratified on April 17, 1806, Tobias Lear, who had hoped to make his name as a diplomat in Tripoli, had achieved a public unpopularity from which he never recovered. And a major reason for the stormy reception of Lear's treaty was his nemesis William Eaton, who was finally having his revenge.

CHAPTER 13

★ ★ ★

"TREASON AGAINST THE CHARACTER OF THE NATION"

When William Eaton landed in Hampton, Va., in the autumn of 1805, the news of his dramatic exploit had preceded him and he was received as a hero.[1] He went straight to Washington, where the November 18 *National Intelligencer* proclaimed:

> On Monday arrived in this city, our gallant and distinguished countryman, GENERAL EATON [a title he always used thereafter] in good health. His achievements merit, and we entertain no doubt will receive, the respectful attention of his fellow citizens in every part of the union.

Eaton was given a White House dinner by Jefferson, another by Chief Justice John Marshall, and the president sent a message to Congress on December 3, praising his expedition:

> An operation by land by a small band of our countrymen and others, engaged for the occasion in conjunction with the troops of the ex-Bashaw of that country, gallantly conducted by our late consul, Eaton, and their successful enterprise on the city of Derne, contributed doubtless to the impression which produced peace.

Perhaps "doubtless" was the key word of the presidential message, given Jefferson's ambivalent attitude toward the expedition. But greater accolades came from Capitol Hill. Senator Stephen Bradley of Vermont, Eaton's early patron, introduced a resolution to reward Eaton, Lieutenant O'Bannon, and his marines "who for the first time spread the American Eagle in *Africa*, on the ramparts of a Tripolitan fort and thereby contributed to the release of three hundred American prisoners from bondage." Bradley proposed setting aside a township six miles square in which Eaton and O'Bannon would be granted 1,000 acres each and the surviving marine enlisted men[2] would each receive 320 acres; the town would be called Derne. The measure was talked to death in the Senate—though, strangely, few of the arguments against the motion protested against U.S. support for an expedition to overthrow a foreign ruler with whom officially the United States had not been at war.

Eaton seized on all the adulation to launch his campaign against Tobias Lear, urging Congress to impeach the consul general for disgracing the nation by settling for ransom. He readily won the outspoken support of many senators and congressmen, especially Timothy Pickering, who had been Eaton's patron as secretary of war and state and was now a vituperative member of the opposition as a senator from Massachusetts, gleefully using the occasion to denounce Tobias Lear and attack President Jefferson for shielding him. Eaton meanwhile kept up a drumfire of diatribe against Lear, pursuing congressmen and senators even into the barrooms of Washington, where his intemperate accusations, fueled by alcohol, began to bore most of his listeners. His accusations soon amounted to overkill, turning otherwise disinterested—and some formerly sympathetic—congressmen and senators against him. When Congress considered a motion to award Eaton a Congressional Medal, such influential politicians as John Randolph and Henry Clay argued that the capture of Derna was insufficient cause—again not because it was illegal or immoral. The proposal lost.

Besides attacking Lear, Eaton was pleading for money. He calculated that his expedition had cost a total of $39,108, much of it paid for out of personal funds for which he asked to be reimbursed by Congress. Not until 1807 did the members finally study Eaton's accounting and agree to pay him $12,636.60, which was considerably less than the $40,000 the president had originally pledged somewhat more than what Eaton would have been paid as an army captain on active duty for two years; this was partly in recognition of the fact that Eaton had volunteered to serve without pay on his expedition. In fact, Eaton was more successful lobbying for Hamet Karamanli than for himself.

*   *   *

In contrast to Eaton's bitter denunciations, Hamet's post-Derna reaction was surprisingly forgiving, perhaps reflecting a Middle Eastern philosophy of the inevitability of fate as well as Hamet's own
experience of many reversals of fortune. As early as June of 1805,
when Eaton had been leaving for home, Hamet had expressed only
gratitude for Eaton's and America's aid in the aborted operation.
Even then, with the U.S. betrayal fresh in his mind, Hamet had
written to his "friend and brother William Eaton late General and
Commander in Chief of our allied forces" a letter that reflected a
surprisingly candid reappraisal of the expedition:

> Without placing in view the misfortunes which have so long pur-
> sued me, I cannot forbear expressing to you, at this moment of our
> final separation, the deep sense of gratitude I feel for your generous
> and manly exertions in my behalf— Be assured that in whatever
> situation the will of God shall place me, I shall always bear the
> impression of gratitude on my heart— On returning to your own
> happy country, to which I wish you a safe passage, I request you
> will express to your sovereign my cordial thanks for his manifesta-
> tions of friendship towards me— Had it been ordained that mea-
> sures might have been carried forward to the attainment of my
> wishes, the restoration of my rightful domain, to me it would cer-
> tainly have been cause of everlasting gratitude. But it is true my own
> measures were small, I know, indeed, that they did not answer your
> reasonable expectations. And this I am ready to admit is a good
> reason why you should not choose to persevere in an enterprise haz-
> ardous in itself and, perhaps, doubtful in its issue. I ought therefore
> to say that I am satisfied with all your nation has done concerning
> me—I submit to the will of God; and thank the king of America and
> all his servants for their kind dispositions towards me.

Eaton and Hamet kept up a correspondence over succeeding
years, and soon Hamet's letters became piteous. He had stayed on
at Syracuse, subsisting on the $200 a month granted him by Com-
modore Rodgers. But after paying for the support of his retinue he
was left with about $1.50 a day for himself; and getting rid of re-
tainers was a difficult task for one so unforceful as Hamet. Nearly
destitute, he appealed to Eaton, who managed to convince President Jefferson to submit a request to Congress.

Jefferson worded it with great care, describing the overland expedition as perfectly feasible and a worthy cause at the time he had approved it, and adding an important qualifier: The operation had been approved "without binding either to guarantee the objects of the other." He did not attempt to explain the inconsistency between this protective clause and his approval of the original plan, which was to put Hamet on the throne of Tripoli—unless he wanted to convey the impression that he had not agreed to go so far and that Eaton had exceeded his authority (which in some details Eaton had). "In operations at such a distance," Jefferson maintained, "it becomes necessary to leave much to the discretion of the agents employed." By slyly shifting the blame onto Eaton, Jefferson managed to ask for monetary relief for Hamet without admitting that the U.S. government owed him anything. Nonetheless a congressional committee did look into the matter, and came to a conclusion that gratified Eaton in its scathing denunciation of Consul Lear.

The United States had entered into an agreement with Hamet that was known to President Jefferson,[3] the committee concluded. This agreement had not been fulfilled, and the villain in the process was Tobias Lear. The report continued:

O   However unpleasant the task, the Committee are impelled by obligation of truth and duty to state further that Mr. Lear . . . appears to have gained a complete ascendency over the Commodore [Barron], to have dictated every measure, to have paralyzed every military operation by sea and land; and finally, without displaying the fleet or squadron before Tripoli, without even consulting the safety of the ex-Bashaw or his army, against the opinion of all the officers of the fleet . . . and of Commodore Rodgers, to have entered into a convention with the reigning Bashaw, by which contrary to his instructions [this must have been news to Jefferson], he stipulated to pay him sixty thousand dollars. . . . The Committee forbear to make any comment on the impropriety of the order issued to General Eaton to evacuate Derna . . . nor will the Committee condescend to enter into consideration of pretended reasons assigned by Mr. Lear to palliate the management of the affairs of the negotiation. . . . They appear to the Committee to have no foundation in fact, and are used rather as a veil to cover an inglorious deed, than solid reason to justify the negotiator's conduct.

• Eaton could have put the case more succinctly but not more convincingly. The committee's report even went on to state its members' belief that if the November plan, agreed to at Syracuse in the autumn of 1804 to combine the squadron's naval operations with the overland expedition, had been carried out, the *Philadelphia's* prisoners might well have been rescued without any ransom payment or danger to their lives. And the committee concluded that Hamet Karamanli had indeed been betrayed. Accordingly, he deserved financial compensation—if only to make sure that no Muslim nation could claim a breach of faith by a Christian nation. That a Christian nation had authorized a military expedition against a Muslim nation without a declaration of war seems to have escaped the committee's attention.

Hamet was duly voted an appropriation of $2,400 and a pension of $200 a month. It was a year before the news and the $2,400 reached Hamet; and as soon as the naval agent in Syracuse heard of it, he cut off the allowance from Commodore Rodgers.

Hamet had a more emotional request, and one for which Tobias Lear could justly be blamed. The treaty with Bashaw Yusuf called for Hamet to leave Tripoli and promised in return: "In case he [Hamet] should withdraw himself as aforesaid, the Bashaw engages himself to deliver up to him his wife and children now in his [Yusuf's] power." Lear had written to Eaton that he had tried "to make an arrangement favorable to [Hamet]," carefully adding, "who, altho' not found to be the man whom many had supposed, was yet entitled to some consideration from us. But I found this was impractical, and that, if persisted in, would drive him to measures which might prove fatal to our countrymen in his power." But, Lear promised, "if his brother withdraws himself quietly from his dominions, his wife and family should be restored to him."

In his letter on their departure Hamet had raised the question. "Situated as I am," he wrote, "you must allow me to ask another expression of your friendship. You tell me that in your treaty with Joseph Bashaw, my perfidious brother, he has promised me to restore my family—I pray you will use your influence with your admiral to permit one of your vessels to go and ask for them; and he will give me the means of repairing with them."

But months went by with no sign of Hamet's family being released. And the U.S. naval authorities in the Mediterranean seemed unhelpful despite appeals from Hamet. Understandably he suspected another betrayal. At his behest Eaton persisted in urging U.S. pressure on Bashaw Yusuf; but it was not until May 7, 1807, two years after the signing of the treaty, that the new U.S. consul, Dr. George Davis, transferring from Tunis to Tripoli to replace the *Philadelphia*'s surgeon Dr. John Ridgeley, discovered why there had been such a long delay in returning Hamet's family.

• Only when Dr. Davis presented President Jefferson's formal request that Hamet's family be released was Davis told that there was a secret clause in the treaty, permitting Bashaw Yusuf to keep Hamet's family as hostages to Hamet's good behavior for at least four years. Yusuf, it was found, had calculated that he could deal with Hamet on his own without American interference after that period; by then the squadron would probably have gone home. Lear had agreed to this condition. A clause separate from the rest of the treaty, contradicting the clause promising to return Hamet's family, had been signed by Yusuf and Lear, who had not included it with the treaty he had sent to Washington; he had kept it a secret until its discovery two years later.

Even then, under pressure from Consul Davis, Yusuf delayed, pretending he could not find transportation for the family. Not until October 7, 1807, could Davis write to Hamet announcing that his wife, three sons, and one of his daughters were finally on their way to rejoin him (aboard the same vessel with the letter). Hamet's married daughter elected to stay with her husband; he was her cousin, Yusuf's eldest son, Mahomet.

Under further pressure from Davis, Yusuf also agreed to grant Hamet an allowance. Davis cautioned Hamet, however, that this support would depend on "the dictates of his [Yusuf's] breast," and that all financial aid from the United States would now cease. "Should the provisions allowed you by your brother be unequal to your expectations," Davis wrote, "or should it at any further period be totally discontinued, you are not thence to found any claim upon the American government." The United States was finally washing its hands of the embarrassing problem of Hamet Karamanli.

But Eaton did not. He continued to hear from Hamet, who by 1808 was reporting that Yusuf had cut off the allowance. "I have had faith in your goodness to represent my cause & support justice," Hamet wrote; he remained confident "that you would not abandon me & my family to wretchedness. Write . . . I pray you . . . to the American consul in Tripoli."

Consul Davis did manage to persuade Bashaw Yusuf to reappoint his brother to the governorship of Derna two years later. But within another two years Yusuf had forced him out again, and again Hamet and the remainder of his family fled to Egypt.

Almost a quarter of a century later, in October of 1832, a man called at the U.S. Consulate in Alexandria, Egypt, announcing himself as Mohammed Bey, the eldest son of Hamet Karamanli. Hamet, he claimed, had died some years earlier, and his impoverished family was living in Cairo. There is no record that the U.S. government did anything to relieve them.

Not surprisingly the news of Lear's secret agreement to let Yusuf keep Hamet's family sent William Eaton into a towering rage. Ignoring the fact that Jefferson had not been informed of the hidden clause, Eaton lashed out in a partisan political attack, declaring, "The President connived at the fraud." Tobias Lear, Eaton snarled, "while he amuses our *Republican* President and Senate with the apparition of an honorable treaty, cedes at his discretion, and in conclave with the enemy, the honor of the Government and of the people of this nation by making them ignorantly accessory to a fraud!" Labeling Lear a "diplomatic swindler," Eaton charged that he had "bartered away the proud claim we had established in that sea to military honor," and had "sold for drachmas the proud claim of the nation to political integrity and good faith! And are we," he cried, "so bankrupt in talent and so debased of soul as to be compelled to employ such agents, and to countenance such duplicity?" Angrily accusing Lear of "treason against the character of the nation," Eaton jabbed again at the president: "he who gives it his countenance is an accomplice in the crime."

But by now Eaton's outbursts were embarrassing even his supporters in Congress. He had finally returned home for the long-awaited reunion with his wife, but he could not resist more visits to Washington, where he went from one saloon to another attempting to buttonhole any senator or congressman who would listen to his litany of complaints against Lear, Jefferson, and the administration. He drank more, took to dressing in his old Muslim robes and showing off his wounded arm to bored audiences who drifted away as gracefully as they could.

Hearing of Eaton's diatribes, Samuel Barron, still ailing but energetic enough to rise to his own defense, wrote to Eaton and to Navy Chief Clerk Goldsborough protesting at the implication that he was also to blame. His prose style undiminished by his illness, Barron complained at Eaton's "remarks which cannot pass unnoticed as it seems to reflect on a character which hitherto the Breath of Slander has never dared to Sully." Barron asked for an explanation and even hinted at demanding "satisfaction," the nineteenth-century buzzword for a duel, though such a match certainly would have finished him off.

Eaton, however, hastened to assure the former commodore that his fulminations were directed not at Barron but at Lear. Barron's inactivity, about which Eaton had protested, was not the commodore's fault, Eaton wrote, because of "the general debility of your system over which you could have no control." And as for settling for ransom rather than forcing the issue, Eaton wrote, "The bad management, which no sophistry can veil, and the reproach due to the inglorious manner of finishing the war with Tripoli, I meant should affix to our commissioner of peace. I then believed and still believe him the Author and the agent of our national disgrace."

Barron was satisfied. But Eaton's neighbors were also becoming disillusioned. They had welcomed him home and honored him by making him a justice of the peace. The Commonwealth of Massachusetts had awarded him 10,000 acres in Maine (then a part of Massachusetts), and local politicians approached him to run for Congress. He replied that he refused to run as a nominee of either party; party labels, he protested, which "split the affections of our countrymen, ought to be lost in the proud name of *American*." So pious a statement from a man playing partisan politics struck his Massachusetts supporters as hypocritical, and he was not nominated. His fellow townsmen elected him to the state legislature, but they did not reelect him. And then came the devastating incident with Aaron Burr.

Listening to Eaton's denunciations of Jefferson and his administration, Burr concluded that here was a likely ally. Narrowly defeated by Jefferson in his bid for the presidency, ignored by

President Jefferson during his vice presidency, in public disrepute after killing Alexander Hamilton in the famous duel, brooding over his thwarted ambitions, Burr became easy prey to Spanish attempts to split the union by denying it part of the Louisiana Territory. Rounding up support for what he called a crusade to drive the Spanish out of the Territory, Burr approached the wealthy Danielson family. And when he proposed that Eaton lead the army forces, the self-styled general rose to the bait.

● But then Eaton intercepted a letter from Burr to one of the Danielsons in which Burr's real mission became clear, a plot to divide the Louisiana Territory from the rest of the United States. Confronted with treason, Eaton found that his patriotism overcame his new dislike of Jefferson, and he took his evidence straight to the president.

He got a chilly reception. Jefferson obviously had been deeply hurt by Eaton's accusations, and was no longer disposed to believe anything he said. The president coldly replied that he had no such evidence himself of treasonable activities on Burr's part, and had Eaton shown out.

Eaton angrily swore a disposition against Burr. Gradually other evidence mounted; and in January of 1807 Burr was tried for treason. A grand jury could not agree, and he was freed. But the accusations would not die, and at the end of May Burr went on trial again. It was conducted in Richmond, Va., and Eaton was called as a witness.

He enjoyed being back in the limelight, and again took to parading about in Bedouin robes and Turkish trousers, regaling everyone with tales of his desert march and the capture of Derna. In the courtroom, however, Burr's clever defense lawyer, Luther Martin, demolished Eaton's credibility, even bringing up the old case of his court-martial (not mentioning the fact that Eaton had been exonerated). Burr was found innocent.

Utterly disillusioned, Eaton went home to Brimfield, Mass., and virtually retired from public life. In 1808 he made a halfhearted appeal to return to army service. Writing to his old friend and mentor Senator Bradley, he asked about the possibility of a commission:

> In case of an augmentation of the Army, and I could obtain a brigade, I will pledge myself to a persevering discharge of the duties of that trust. I cannot take a regiment; because young men who have been my subalterns would probably rank and command me.

Nothing came of it.

● His drinking increased. He had spent much of his wife's fortune and was forced to sell half of his land grant in Maine at a sacrifice price of 50 cents an acre. His favorite stepson, Eli Danielson, who had been with him in the Mediterranean, was killed in a duel with another young naval officer.

Gout and rheumatism made Eaton an invalid. He had considered writing a book about his adventures and had asked a local editor, Charles Prentiss, to help him with what he tentatively titled *A History of the Tripolitan War*, in which he, of course, would be the hero. He also considered publishing a newspaper. But with increasing illness he abandoned both projects.[4]

In January of 1810 Eaton wrote to a friend whom he had known in Tunis, "Fortune has reversed her tables. I am no more Eaton. I live, or rather stay, in obscurity and uselessness." He rambled on about the tragedies of his life and his country, and metaphorically reported his physical condition: "Death has laid himself alongside and thrown his grapplings upon my quarter and forecastle, but I keep him off amidships yet." And as if to show that he still had at least a black sense of humor, he wrote some specifications for his funeral and his coffin: "Let me beg of you not to make it pine, for I cannot bear the smell of it; and take care not to place me on my back, for in that position I am very subject to nightmares."

The funeral came shortly. At 9 P.M. on June 1, 1811, he died, aged 47. He was buried with military honors, but few newspapers recorded his death. A quarter of a century later the *New Hampshire Patriot & State Gazette* belatedly recognized Eaton's death, describing him as "a victim of the ingratitude of his country."[5]

The same year that William Eaton died, his comrade-in-arms Presley Neville O'Bannon was presented with a ceremonial sword by his native state of Virginia. The sword was patterned after a scimitar that Hamet Karamanli had given O'Bannon as a gesture of gratitude at their parting in Syracuse. Adorned with jewels, it had been Hamet's prized possession from his days with the Mamelukes above Cairo. The Virginia sword memorialized O'Bannon's success in the attack on Derna—and misspelled his name. The inscription on the hilt read: "Presented by the State of Virginia to her gallant son Priestly N. O'Bannon."

After the evacuation of Derna, O'Bannon had gone back to duty aboard the *Argus*. There is no further record of him until the secretary of the navy accepted his resignation in March of 1807. O'Bannon returned to his wife in Virginia and shortly moved to Kentucky, where his brother John was running a distillery in Woodford County. There were reports, but no hard evidence, that O'Bannon was embittered at not receiving sufficient recognition from the Marine Corps for his part in the overland expedition. His wife gave birth to a son whom they named Eaton O'Bannon; the son apparently died young. The ex-marine lieutenant was elected to both houses of the Kentucky Legislature, and died—at the venerable age of 74—at Russellville, Kentucky, on September 12, 1850.

In 1920 his remains were moved to Frankfort, Kentucky's capital, and buried under an inscription that misstated his rank: "As Captain of the United States Marines he was the First to plant the American Flag on Foreign Soil." Not until 1917, during World War I, did the U.S. Navy recognize O'Bannon by naming a destroyer after him. Another was christened in his name in 1942; she sank a Japanese battleship off Guadalcanal, and during the course of World War II earned 16 battle stars.

Captain Bainbridge and the other *Philadelphia* prisoners also were welcomed home as heroes.[6] But with the Barbary War apparently ended, many naval officers and sailors found themselves on the beach as the size of the navy was reduced—most of them grumbling that President Jefferson's only reaction to British arrogance on the high seas was a fleet of useless gunboats and the Embargo.

In the confrontation with England Jefferson played the peacemaker by opting for an embargo on all international trade from American ports, instead of asking Congress for a declaration of war. Most New Englanders complained about the Embargo. (Eaton joined in the chorus.) But it did result in few American merchantmen offering themselves as targets for the Barbary corsairs. And when, just before relinquishing the presidency to James Madison in 1809, Jefferson signed the Nonintercourse Act repealing the Embargo, not many American ships made it to the Mediterranean before being pinned down again by the War of 1812.

President Madison reacted more forcefully to the growing British threat. The frigate veterans of the Barbary War—the *Constitution*, the *Constellation*, the *President*, the *Essex*, and the *United States* as well as the *Chesapeake*—were readied for action; and Jefferson's gunboats, now derisively called the "cockboats or whirligigs of the sage of Monticello," were laid up.

On June 1, 1812, President Madison sent to Congress a declaration of war, protesting that Britain was "trampling on rights which no independent nation can relinquish." Two weeks later England suspended its Orders in Council, which had banned trade with the United States and had been the excuse for attacking American vessels. But the impetus was by now beyond control. On June 30, by a close vote (19 to 13 in the Senate), Congress declared war against Great Britain.

The War of 1812 proved the mettle of the U.S. Navy, Joshua Humphreys's far-seeing ship design, and especially Preble's Boys, when the frigates built for the Barbary War defeated their British opponents in such celebrated sea battles as the *Constitution* vs. the *Guerrière* on Aug. 19, 1812, which in only 30 minutes reduced the *Guerrière* to a smoking wreck while scarcely harming "Old Ironsides." Royal Navy officers complained that Humphreys's frigates, with greater firepower and more speed, were disguised ships of the line.[7] And captains Bainbridge, Hull, Decatur, and Porter demonstrated the prowess they had learned under Edward Preble in the Mediterranean.

Less than a week after the Senate had ratified the Treaty of Ghent, ending the War of 1812, President Madison sent a request up to Capitol Hill: "I recommend to Congress the expediency of an act declaring the existence of a state of war between the United States and the Regency of Algiers, and of such provisions as may be requisite for a vigorous prosecution of it to successful issue." The young United States of America had humbled the greatest navy in the world, and the president and the members of Congress were more than ready to take on the tiny fleet of Algiers. Not only were Americans flushed with victory, but the U.S. Navy still had most of its formidable frigates plus a few captured from the Royal Navy. It took Congress only a week to proclaim another declaration of war on the heels of the War of 1812. And President Madison promptly named Stephen Decatur as the commodore of a new Mediterranean squadron.

● Decatur had returned from the Mediterranean in 1808 to serve as a judge in the court-martial of Captain James Barron after the ignominious *Leopard-Chesapeake* encounter, voting against him and thereby making an enemy of his onetime fellow captain in the Mediterranean. Decatur's capture of the Royal Navy's frigate *Macedonian* was one of the celebrated victories of the War of 1812. But thereafter his frigate *President* was blockaded for the rest of the war.

For his Mediterranean squadron Decatur was given a new flagship, the 44-gun frigate *Guerrière*, fresh from her Philadelphia shipyard, one of many new warships that had still been on the shipways at the end of the war. His fleet included two more frigates and seven smaller vessels.[8] A shining example of Preble's Boys, Decatur had others under him. The captain of his flagship, William Lewis, had been a midshipman on the *New York*, the *Constitution*, and the *John Adams*. Captain John Downes of the *Epervier* had also served in Preble's squadron. Captain Charles Gordon of the *Constellation* had been a gunboat commander in Preble's attacks on Tripoli.

Another veteran of the Mediterranean, with an old score to settle, was Captain William Bainbridge. After his release from the bashaw's prison he had temporarily commanded the New York Navy Yard and had then gone back into the merchant marine. At the outbreak of the War of 1812 he had reentered the navy and had been given command of the *Constitution*, which under Isaac Hull had just demolished Britain's *Guerrière*; as senior to Hull, Bainbridge took her out to defeat and capture Britain's *Java*. Now Bainbridge was named commodore of a second Mediterranean squadron to aid Decatur in finally bringing the Barbary powers to heel. Decatur got away first, sailing in May of 1815, only three months after the ratification of the Treaty of Ghent.

Algiers in the meantime had been in turmoil. Dey Achmet had continued to humiliate Consul Tobias Lear, demanding more naval supplies on the threat of expulsion. But in November of 1808 Achmet had suddenly met his end at the hands of a cabal of Turkish soldiers who replaced him with a figurehead named Ali, who in turn was strangled (with the traditional silken cord) five months later and replaced with another puppet, a vicious old man named Hadji Ali. Hadji Ali reacted favorably to British attempts to stir up the Barbary powers against the Americans during the War of 1812 by declaring war on the United States. Consul Tobias Lear, who was still trying to maintain diplomatic relations with Algiers, was summarily expelled. But there were few American vessels in the Mediterranean for Hadji Ali to harass during the war.

● One vessel he did capture was the Salem brig *Edwin*, whose captain, George Smith, and ten-man crew the dey imprisoned. But Hadji Ali was assassinated in 1814. His prime minister succeeded him for only two weeks before being replaced in the same manner by an overbearing Turk from Lesbos named Omar the Aga, who was on the Algerian throne when Decatur brought his squadron to the Mediterranean in June of 1815. Omar the Aga had done nothing to modify Algiers's war against the United States and his high admiral, Reis Hammida, was cruising the Mediterranean for American prospects.

Decatur lost no time in tracking down Reis and capturing his 46-gun flagship *Mashouda*,[9] killing him in the process. En route to Algiers Decatur also seized another Algerian warship, the 22-gun brig *Estedio*. By June 29 he was off Algiers—31 years from the time the *Betsey* and *Dauphin* had been taken by Algerian cruisers. Decatur presented a letter from President Madison announcing the U.S. declaration of war. If Algiers wanted peace, there would be no tribute paid by the United States; in fact, Algiers would pay the United States $10,000, would release all American property left behind, and would free the Americans from the *Edwin*. Those were the conditions, Decatur said; there would be no negotiations.[10] Dey Omar tried to haggle for a couple of days, but he knew when he was beaten. He signed the new treaty.[11]

Decatur took his fleet on eastward to Tunis. In 1814 Bey Hamouda had choked to death. (The official explanation was that he had gulped down a cup of coffee at the end of the fast of Ramadan.) His successor after a number of revolts, Bey Mahmoud, had evinced scorn for the Tunisian treaty with the United States. One of its provisions permitted American privateers to bring their prizes into Tunisian harbors; but when an American had brought two of them into Tunis during the War of 1812, Tunisian authorities had seized them.

● Decatur sent ashore a demand for Bey Mahmoud to repay the United States $46,000 in compensation. The bey asked for time. Decatur declined. The bey looked again at the massed firepower off his harbor and paid in cash. Decatur raised anchor and went on eastward to Tripoli.

● Bashaw Yusuf Karamanli was 15 years older, down to only three wives (one white, two black), as cantankerous as ever but still on the throne—a remarkable achievement on the Barbary Coast. Yusuf, too, had been beguiled by the British during the War of 1812, and when the same American privateersman had sent two of his prizes into Tripoli, Yusuf had handed them back to their British owners—also in violation of Tripoli's treaty with the United States.

Decatur arrived with his squadron on August 5, and demanded an indemnity of $25,000 for the prize.[12] Yusuf blustered and threatened to tear up the treaty. But the bashaw's navy was not what it had been. High Admiral Murad Reis had fallen into disfavor with his father-in-law and had been exiled to Egypt some years earlier. Evidently at the urging of his daughter, Yusuf had permitted Reis to return, but only as a court interpreter, in which role the bashaw could keep an eye on him. Meanwhile the navy Reis had built had deteriorated, and it was no match for the fleet of U.S. warships assembled in Tripoli Harbor. Yusuf grumbled some more, and paid up.

Bainbridge followed in Decatur's path, reminding the dey, bey, and bashaw of the power the United States could now assemble. The United States continued to patrol the Mediterranean for a few more years. Meanwhile, in August of 1816, Great Britain, humbled by the American example, sent the Royal Navy under Lord Exmouth to join with a Dutch fleet in bombarding Algiers, leveling its shore batteries and forcing the dey to sign a treaty forever renouncing the enslavement of Christians. Britain and most of the European governments ceased paying tribute to the Barbary powers, and peace finally came to the Barbary Coast.[13]

Thomas Jefferson is little remembered as the first president to defy the Barbary pirates, perhaps mainly because of his vacillation at the crucial point. No doubt in his retirement years the Sage of Monticello contemplated the lessons of the Barbary War. In retrospect he was right to insist that force could be met only with force; but he may have regretted wavering at the very time that the bashaw seemed on the verge of surrendering.

• Jefferson did have an excuse. Communications, in the days when a warship moved at about the pace of a walking man, distorted and obscured the view of the action when it was 3,000 miles away in the Mediterranean. The commander in chief never had up-to-date information on which to base his decisions.

But Jefferson's successor, James Madison, did make the decision that ended the Barbary menace. Madison, unlike Jefferson, had the consent of Congress, whose members finally voted a declaration of war. Thus another lesson of the Barbary hostilities, and an early indication of U.S. foreign policy, was that the war-making powers of the president were, as they still are, limited—but that most presidents stretch those powers as far as they can. The authors of the Constitution, whether by accident or design motivated by memories of the Revolutionary War, did not sufficiently reconcile presidential authority with Congress's prerogative to declare war.

There were other lessons:

- That a tyrant unconcerned about his people can withstand a long siege or blockade.
- That all the ramifications of a subversive expedition must be thought through before it is launched, because a cynical plot will sooner or later be exposed for what it is; and promises, to whomever made, must be kept.
- That most such "dirty trick" operations backfire sooner or later.
- That a hostage situation nearly always requires some sort of negotiation, however unpleasant the prospect.
- That negotiation must always be from strength, and that agreements must be enforced.
- That there is no simple solution to a hostage situation, anyway.
- That navy seniority has little relation to fighting ability.
- And that a government must first articulate a set of principles and stand by them ever thereafter.

● It is because not all of these lessons have been learned that, in Santayana's phrase, the United States is repeating history.

As for Jefferson, he is revered by Americans for many other accomplishments; but even today it is a naval tradition to scorn him as the pacifist who sabotaged the U.S. Navy and believed that the mighty Royal Navy could be fought with gunboats. His handling of the Eaton expedition was not his finest hour. But the navy's charge against him is unfair.

Thomas Jefferson and John Adams, his former friend and adversary on the question of how to deal with the Barbary powers, died on the same day, July 4, 1826.

Edward Preble is best remembered for his "Boys," who made the greatest contribution to winning the War of 1812, as is Joshua Humphreys for those big, fast, heavy-gunned frigates. Stephen Decatur was lionized by Congress and the public when he returned from finally subduing the dey, the bey, and the bashaw. From 1815 to 1820 he was one of three highly influential navy commissioners. But his career reached a tragic end when Captain James Barron, still angry over Decatur's court-martial vote against him and his continuing opposition to Barron's reinstatement, challenged him to a duel. They met at Bladensburg, Md., on March 22, 1820, and Decatur was killed. Barron, nicked in the hip, recovered, remained in the navy but in disgrace for the rest of his career. (He lived to be 89.) Nor did William Bainbridge, despite his victory over the *Java* in the War of 1812, ever live down the loss of the *Philadelphia* on Kaliusa Reef.

William Eaton's extraordinary exploit is memorialized by a street in Boston named Derne; hardly anyone on the street knows its origin. What would have pleased "General" Eaton most was the fact that during World War II officers of both the British and German armies fighting in the Libyan Desert made detailed studies of the expedition he had led more than a century earlier.

Perhaps the least-remembered of the Barbary War's *dramatis personae* is Presley Neville O'Bannon—his name misspelled on his trophy sword, his rank incorrect on his grave. Paradoxically, the exploit of O'Bannon and his men is immortalized in a long, proud tradition of the U.S. Marine Corps.

The U.S. Marines won more glory in the War of 1812,[14] and the corps' reputation was so enshrined by 1829 that when President

Andrew Jackson tried to abolish it as a separate service, Congress killed the proposal. In 1834 Congress passed an Act for the Better Organization of the Marine Corps, assuring it separate recognition within the navy. A contrite President Jackson signed the bill.[15] In 1847 the Marine Corps made an even greater name for itself in the Mexican War, leading the American troops into Mexico City where atop the Palacio Nacional Second Lieutenant A. S. Nicholson was first to raise the American flag.[16] So it was that "the Halls of Montezuma" joined the marine liturgy with "the Shores of Tripoli," which had been the marine's battle cry since the Barbary War.[17]

Down the years since the Barbary War the Marine Corps has added to its record for courage and fighting ability—at Belleau Wood and Soissons in World War I, Tarawa and Mount Suribachi in World War II. But the first glorious achievement of the marines is recalled not only in its official hymn. To this day every marine officer in formal uniform carries a sword patterned on the ornate Mameluke scimitar that was presented by a grateful Hamet Karamanli to Lieutenant Presley O'Bannon.

EPILOGUE

★ ★ ★

The U.S. Navy and Marine Corps went back to Tripoli in 1949, nearly a century and a half after Preble's attacks on the city and the explosion of the fireship *Intrepid*.

Of the 13 men who died in the explosion, five were buried (with a short service written by Captain Bainbridge) in a cemetery on a bluff southeast of the city. What happened to the other eight was never known; perhaps there was not enough left of them to inter. Bainbridge's record of the burial was lost; so in 1938 the U.S. State Department instituted a search for the buried remains of the *Intrepid*'s sailors.

The U.S. consul in Tripoli, Orray Taft, Jr., enlisted the help of the city's harbormaster, Mustafa Burchis. Taft studied the available records, letters, and diaries and interviewed descendants of Tripoli's 1804 residents. Burchis searched the waterfront and studied the currents to determine where the bodies might have washed ashore. Together they located the five graves. They were in a burial ground that later (because of the five American sailors, it turned out) was surrounded by a wall, named the Protestant Cemetery, and used for other Christians who died in Tripoli. Taft's and Burchis' reports were sent to the U.S. Embassy in Rome—where they were burned with other State Department files when the United States declared war on Italy in 1941.

The search was resumed in 1949, with Harbormaster Burchis preparing a new report from his notes, and the five graves were located again in the northeast corner of the cemetery. The U.S. Cruiser *Spokane* was dispatched to Tripoli to perform belated honors, and her sailors and marines marched to the cemetery. Leading the 50 Tripolitans attending the ceremony was the city's mayor, Joseph Karamanli, a direct descendant of Bashaw Yusuf.

A formal service was read. Plaques were placed on the grave-stones, each reading, "Here Lies an Unknown American Sailor Lost from the USS *Intrepid* in Tripoli Harbor 1804." Volleys of rifle fire from the honor guard of marines crackled out over the Mediterranean; and the cold, crisp tones of the marine bugler's Taps echoed down the shores of Tripoli.

APPENDIX A

★ ★ ★

This is a typical passport issued by Algiers for American vessels after the 1795 treaty with the United States. Although it would be another two years before Tunis and Tripoli would sign treaties with the United States, the Algiers passport attempted to protect American vessels from all of the Barbary corsairs. The original text of the passport was, of course, in Arabic; the spelling and punctuation suggest that the translation was done by a semiliterate seaman.

This is to certify that the Bearer or possessor of this Passport is a true American and allso the crew—and if navigating on the Seas— he should meet a Corsaire belonging to this Regency—or Tunis Tripolia or Morocca—the[y] shall not be permitted to detain or molest, or stop him his Crew—Cargo—and Vessel—and passengers that might be—on board—but immediately let said Vesel in all Security continue her destined Voyage—and for this purpose the[y] have requested this Passport, which I have given and Signed with my hand—and Sealed with the public Seal of this regency—
So that in case any Algerine Corsaire should in any manner— stop hinder or Molest Said Vessel cargo—& crew—the Commander of said Cruiser—or offender shall be by me severly punished—& restitution made if a Corsaire of Tunis or Tripoly—or Morocco— should in any Manner injure stop or molest said Vessel—thire government shall be obliged to punish Said offender and Make restitution of all damages for this purpose we have given this Passport to be be presented to every Corsaire of the above Mentioned nations that—the Said American Vessel may—meet with.

Signed & Sealed by Hassan Bashaw

Dey—of Algiers

APPENDIX B

★ ★ ★

The "convention," as William Eaton described it when he sent it to the secretary of state on March 4, 1805, is relatively free of legal jargon. This is the full text, complete with its unique spelling and punctuation.

Article I. There shall be a firm and perpetual Peace and free intercourse between the Government of the United States of America, and his Highness Hamet Caramanly, Bashaw the legitimate sovereign of the kingdom of Tripoli, and between the citizens of the one and the subjects of the other.—

Article II. The Government of the United States, shall use their utmost exertions, so far as comports with their own honor and interest, their subsisting treaties, and the acknowledged law of Nations to reestablish the said Hamet Bashaw in the possession of his Sovereignty of Tripoli against the pretensions of Joseph Bashaw who obtained said Sovereignty by treason & now holds it by usurpation, and who is engaged in actual war against the United States.

Article III. The United States shall, as circumstances may require, in addition to the operations they are carrying on by Sea, furnish to said Hamet Bashaw on loan, supplies of cash, ammunition and provisions, and if necessity require, debarkations of troops, also to aid and give effect to the operations of said Hamet Bashaw by land against the common enemy.

Article IV. In consideration of which friendly offices once rendered effectual, His Highness Hamet Caramanly Bashaw, engages on his part, To release to the commander in Chief of the forces of the United States, in the Mediterranean, without ransom, all American prisoners, who are, or may hereafter be in the hands of the Usurper, said Joseph Bashaw.

Article V. In order to indemnify the United States against all expence they have or shall incur, in carrying into execution the engagements expressed in the second and third article of this convention the said Hamet Bashaw, transfers and consigns to the

United States the Tribute stipulated by the last, treaties of his Majesty the King of Denmark, his Majesty the King of Sweden, and the Batavian Republic, as the condition of a peace with the Regency of Tripoli untill such time as said expence Shall be reembursed.—

Article VI. In order to carry into full effect the stipulation expressed in the preceding article, said Hamet Bashaw pledges his faith and honor faithfully to observe and fulfill the treaties now subsisting between the Regency of Tripoli and their Majesties the Kings of Denmark and Sweden and with the Batavian Republic.—

Article VII. In consideration of the friendly dispositions of his Majesty the King of the two Sicilies toward the American Squadrons, his highness Hamet Bashaw, invites his said Sicilian Majesty to renew their ancient friendship; and proffers him a peace on the footing of that to be definitavely concluded with the United States of America, in the fullest extent of its privileges according to the tenor of this convention.—

Article VIII. The better to give effect to the operations to be carried out by Land, in the prosecution of the plan and for the attainment of the object pointed out by this convention, William Eaton, a citizen of the United States, now in Egypt, shall be recognized as General, and Commander in Chief of the land forces, which are, or may be called into service against the common Enemy. And his said Highness Hamet Bashaw, engages that his own Subjects shall respect and obey him as such.—

Article IX. His Highness said Hamet Bashaw grants full amnesty and perpetual oblivion towards the conduct of all such of his Subjects, as may have been seduced by the usurper to abandon his cause and who are disposed to return to their proper allegiance—

Article X. In case of future war between the contracting parties captives on each side, shall be treated as Prisoners of war, and not as Slaves, and shall be entitled to reciprocal and equal exchange, man for man, and grade for grade and in no case, shall a ransom be demanded for prisoners of war, nor a tribute required as the condition of peace, neither on the one part nor the other. All prisoners on both sides shall be given up at the conclusion of peace.

Article XI. The American Consular Flag in Tripoli shall ever be a sacred asylum to all persons who shall desire to take refuge under it except for the crimes of Treason and murder—

Article XII. In case of the faithful observance and fulfillment, on the part of his Highness said Hamet Bashaw, of the agreements and obligations herein stipulated—the said commander in chief of the american forces in the Mediterranean, engages to leave said Hamet Bashaw, in the peaceful possession of the City and the Regency of Tripoli without dismantling its Batteries.

Article XIII. Any article suitable to be introduced in a definitive treaty of Peace between the contracting parties, which may not be comprized in this convention, shall be reciprocally on the footing of the treaties subsisting with the most favored Nations.

Article XIV. This convention shall be submitted to the President of the United States for his ratification in the mean Time there shall be no suspence in its operations.

Signed by HAMET
WILLIAM EATON

and witnessed by

Lt. O'BANNON
Dr. FRANCESCO MENDRICI
PASCAL PAOLI PECK

Done at Alexandria in Egypt Feby. 23rd, 1805 and signed by Hamet Bashaw for himself and successors and by William Eaton on the part of the United States—

Additional Article Secret

His Highness Hamet Bashaw will use his utmost exertions to cause to surrender to the Commander in chief of the American forces in the Mediterranean, the Usurper Joseph Bashaw together with his family and Chief Admiral called Mamad [Murad] Rais, alias Peter Lisle, to be held by the Government of the United States as hostages, and as a guarantee of the faithful observance of the Stipulations entered into by convention of the 23rd February, 1805 with the United States, provided they do not escape by flight—

A Copy, Verbatim of this Convention between the United States of America and His Highness Hamet Caramanly Bashaw of Tripoli, in the English, Arabic & Italian Languages, has been Deposited in the British Consular Office at Alexandria, in Egypt, by desire of William Eaton Esqr. Agent General for the United States of America, at the Several Barbary Regencies—Quod Attestor

Alexandria 1st March 1805
Barthw Gm Mutti
Cancellier

We Samuel Briggs British Consul in Alexandria of Egypt, & it's Dependencies

Certify that the above mentioned Mr. Barthw Gm. Mutti is Cancellier of this Office, & that to all his Deeds, & Writings so Signed, Full faith, & Credit is & ought to be given in Court, & without

Given under our hand, & Seal of Office at Alexandria this first day of March 1805—

Saml. Briggs
British Consul

NOTES

★ ★ ★

Pages 15 to 19

CHAPTER 1

1. His Tripolitan name was Ahmed, but most Americans called him Hamet. Arab names have nearly innumerable varieties of spelling in English. I have used what seemed to be the spellings preferred by most of the American participants.
2. Pasha (ruler) was the title most often given to Turks of high station. Tripoli's Arabic language had no *p*, so pasha became bashaw, the title most Americans used in referring to Yusuf Karamanli, whose name they usually anglicized as Joseph Caramanli or Caramanly.
3. Many Americans in the Mediterranean spelled it as Derne; but Derna was the spelling most often used locally.

CHAPTER 2

1. In 1989 wine merchant William Sokolin took on consignment a bottle of Château Margaux 1787 bearing the label *TJ* and reputed to have come from Jefferson's Paris wine cellar. Offering it for sale at more than half a million dollars, Sokolin took the bottle to a wine tasting at New York's Four Seasons restaurant to show it off to fellow wine fanciers, banged into a metal-topped table, and broke the bottle. Those who caught a few drops said it tasted like Madeira.
   A German wine expert, Hardy Rosenstock, was another collector who claimed to have discovered wine from Jefferson's Paris cellar, in this case hand-blown bottles, also engraved with the *TJ* initials, of Château Lafite and Château Yquem. When he opened one of them at a wine tasting in New Orleans in 1988, it tasted like vinegar.
2. Soon he was shipping home wine cuttings and oak and cork trees as well as hares, pheasants, and partridges. He also was fascinated by the many French inventions he saw—a windlass-operated plow, a screw-propeller steamship, a bright olive-oil-burning cylinder lamp, a machine that duplicated a letter as it was written, and Montgolfier's hot-air balloon.
   One of his favorite finds was the phosphorus match, which he extolled as "a beautiful discovery. . . . The convenience of lighting a candle without getting out of bed, sealing letters without calling a servant, of kindling a fire without flint, steel, punk, etc., are of value." But he warned his correspon-

dent about the matches' propensity to drip burning phosphorus "because it is inextinguishable & will therefore burn to the bone." But, he noted, there was one remedy: "It is said that urine will extinguish it."

3. Jefferson summed up his reasoning in a letter to John Adams: "1. Justice is in favor of this opinion. 2. Honor favors it. 3. It will procure us respect in Europe; and respect is a safeguard to interest. 4. It will arm the federal head with the safest of all instruments of coercion over its delinquent members, and prevent it from using what would be less safe."

4. Caesar's captors were described by Plutarch as "the most bloodthirsty people in the world"; the normal reaction of Cilician pirates to a Roman's demand to be freed was to put a ladder over the side of the ship, tell him to go home, and sarcastically wish him a pleasant journey. But the brash young Caesar treated his captors as underlings. When they announced that the price on his head would be 20 talents, he laughed at them and told them he was worth at least 50. (He was well aware of the Roman proclamation that any Roman captured by pirates was to be ransomed not by his family but by the nearest local government—a penalty for permitting piracy in the area.)

During his 38-day imprisonment while awaiting the ransom payment, according to Plutarch, Caesar "amused himself with joining in their exercises and games, as if they had not been his keepers, but his guards." He spent much of the time composing poetry and orations, which he inflicted on them, berating those who did not appreciate his writing as "illiterate and barbarous." When he napped, he sent word to the pirates to keep quiet so he could sleep. His captors, Plutarch wrote, "were greatly taken with this, and attributed his free talking to a kind of simplicity and boyish playfulness." (Caesar was 26.) Nor did they take him seriously when he promised to return and execute them.

His ransom paid, Caesar went to Miletus, assembled a fleet of ships (presumably manned by other pirates eager for loot), and sailed back to Pharmacussa, where he sank most of his former captors' vessels, landed, and easily defeated them. Looting their base of its treasure, he paid off his crews and pocketed the rest, in one stroke amassing a small fortune. He took the survivors to Pergamum, capital of Roman-occupied Asia Minor, where he ordered all of them crucified. But, perhaps mollified by his humane treatment and knowing the torture of a slow death on the cross, he relented—and had their throats cut instead.

5. The plight of those sold to private families depended on their owners; most became domestic servants. European women proved to be better at sewing, weaving, and embroidery than their Moorish mistresses. Women sold as concubines eventually found their services in bed less onerous, if only because infrequent, than the maddening boredom of harem life, which included a starchy diet to fatten them to the proportions preferred by their masters. Many slaves consigned to public works were permitted to devote their spare time to other jobs. Some managed taverns where non-Muslims could gamble and buy alcoholic beverages; a few acquired enough money in their extra jobs to purchase their freedom.

6. England's protection money had not saved all of its American colonists trading in the Mediterranean. In 1678, Barbary pirates captured the merchantman *Pincke* from New York and held her owner-captain Jacob Leiser, his two sons, and eight crewmen for ransom. New York churchgoers responded with a col-

lection to pay it. Other colonial traders had to be ransomed, and on occasion a congregation collected more money than needed. Trinity Church on Lower Broadway was completed in 1698 with money oversubscribed to ransom American captives. An intriguing aspect of some church subscriptions was a disproportionate participation of New York's black slaves: in one collection 13 percent of the donors were slaves, relatively well-off household servants making their own ironic protest against all slavery.

7. The pass was cut in half laterally; copies of the top half were issued to all of the signatory's vessels, and copies of the bottom half were distributed to the captains of the Barbary "navies." The lateral cut was serrated; and when a pirate captain boarded a European ship, he matched his half of the pass with that of his captive. If the serrations and the wording fitted, he was supposed to let the ship pass without hindrance.

    The system naturally led to abuse: There was a brisk business in forged passports all through the Mediterranean and in Europe and the United States for two centuries.

8. The contemporary xebec was a low-waisted, shallow-draft vessel usually with three masts carrying triangular lateen sails, used by Barbary navies for boarding and close-in fighting in the shoal waters along the coast.

9. Negotiating the Treaty of Paris to end the American Revolution, U.S. diplomats had asked Britain to continue protecting American vessels; they had not been surprised at Britain's refusal. Later attempts to ask for similar protection from other European countries had also been unsuccessful—largely, as France's foreign minister explained, because there was so little respect for the new nation.

10. The Articles of the Confederation read more like a treaty between sovereign nations than a governing federation.

    Article III. The said states hereby severally enter into a firm league of friendship with each other for their common defense, the security of their liberties, and their mutual and general welfare, binding themselves to assist each other against all force offered to, or attacks made upon them, on account of religion, sovereignty, trade, or any other pretense whatever.

    In short, the states agreed to come to one another's aid, but each retained its own sovereignty.

11. When John Adams, the first U.S. minister to Britain, proposed a trade treaty, British diplomats sardonically asked if he meant one or thirteen.

12. The Continental Navy had not exactly covered itself with glory: of its 35 warships, all but one had been sunk or captured by the Royal Navy (which in contrast lost only five). U.S. privateers had helped the cause by harassing British shipping. But it was the French Navy that struck the major blow against Britain by bottling up Chesapeake Bay, cutting off supplies to Cornwallis and forcing him to surrender at Yorktown.

13. Travel was over spine-jarring dirt roads or by stomach-churning schooners Along the coast. As late as 1800, Abigail Adams, en route from Quincy, Mass., to Washington, D.C., got lost south of Baltimore, Md., on a trail through the forest. She and her companion proceeded by "holding down &

breaking bows of trees which we could not pass," she wrote, "untill we met a solitary black fellow with a horse and cart" from whom she was able to get directions toward the nation's capital.

14. Washington reacted to Shays' Rebellion in a letter from Mount Vernon: "For God's sake tell me what is the cause of all these commotions? If they have *real* grievances, redress them if possible. . . . If they have not, employ the force of government against them at once." (When he had been commander in chief outside Boston, Washington had referred to New Englanders as "a nasty people.")

    Jefferson, writing from Paris, had a different reaction: "God forbid we should ever be 20 years without such a rebellion. . . . What country can pre-serve its liberties if their rulers are not warned from time to time that their people preserve the spirit of resistance? . . . What signifies a few lives lost in a century or two? The tree of liberty must be refreshed with the blood of patriots and tyrants. It is its natural manure."

15. Harriet Martineau said of Salem and its seafarers:

    The fruits of the Mediterranean are on every table. They have a large ac-quaintance at Cairo. They . . . have wild tales to tell of Mosambique and Madagascar . . . Anybody will give you anecdotes from Canton and descrip-tions of the Society and Sandwich Islands. . . . They often slip up the west-ern coasts of two of their continents; bring furs from the back regions of their own wide land; glance up at the Andes on their return; double Cape Horn; touch at the ports of Brazil and Guiana, look about them in the West Indies, feeling there almost at home; and land, some fair morning at Salem, and walk home as if they had done nothing very remarkable.

16. Cathcart used his wits to advantage, quickly learning the lingua franca of his captors (a mixture of Arabic, Italian, French, and Spanish) and soon got him-self appointed keeper of the dey's menagerie of lions and tigers. Shortly he was promoted to clerk of the Marine, bookkeeper for the dey's navy. Three years later he was made clerk of one of the bagnios, overseeing the work details and provisions for its slaves. By 1791 he had been promoted to the post of clerk to Algiers's prime minister, who the following year succeeded the dey. Cathcart soon rose to an exalted position for a slave as Christian secretary to the dey and the regency, and became an influential figure in the later negotiations for a U.S.-Algerian treaty.

17. Later Sidi Mohamet's son and successor, Muley Soliman, told a U.S. envoy that the Americans were "the Christian nation my father, who is in glory, most esteemed. I am the same with them as my father was; and I trust they will be so with me."

18. Many American diplomats were convinced that British agents in Algiers were urging the dey to demand an impossible ransom, the British design being to thwart a treaty with Algiers that would permit American shipping to compete with the British in the Mediterranean.

19. During his presidency he kept Mount Vernon from the auctioneer only by selling off parts of his land.

20. He accompanied his half-brother Lawrence, who hoped that the ocean voyage and Barbados's climate would cure his tuberculosis. (Sea voyages were pre-

scribed by doctors to treat all sorts of ills for another century.) It did not help Lawrence, who shortly died.

21. The Constitution provided for secretaries in charge of functions of the administration, and every president after Washington consulted with his secretaries in varying degrees.

22. The other secretaries in Washington's first administration were Edmund Randolph of the Justice Department and Henry Knox, secretary of war (which at the time amounted to secretary of defense; there would not be a Navy Department until 1798).

    Early in his administration Washington also consulted with Vice President John Adams. But he soon tired of Adams's verbosity, and Adams spent most of his time presiding over the Senate, making long speeches, and reminiscing until the senators rolled their eyes skyward with impatience. Adams had been in London too long, had become infatuated with pomp and ceremony, and was particularly concerned about titles for members of the new government. (South Carolina's Senator Ralph Izard called Adams "His Rotundity"; Benjamin Franklin called him "His Superfluous Excellency.") A committee was formed to decide how to address the president when he appeared before the Senate. Adams proposed a canopied presidential seat resembling a throne. And when one senator suggested that they simply call him "Mr. President," Adams rose, his round little body quivering with indignation, to remind everyone that he had witnessed ceremonial functions at Versailles as well as at the Court of St. James's, where the common people had learned respect for their leaders. If the Americans called George Washington nothing more than "Mr. President," Adams warned, "they will despise him to all eternity."

    Treasury Secretary Hamilton had little patience with Vice President Adams, who was easily slighted and resented it. To his intimates Adams sneered at Hamilton as "a bastard Bratt of a Scotch Pedlar."

23. By 1789 he had been a widower for seven years.

24. Jefferson was exaggerating his case slightly. A few brave, if not foolhardy, captains were attempting to slip into some Mediterranean ports.

25. In his classic *John Paul Jones: A Sailor's Biography*, Samuel Eliot Morison writes that an autopsy performed on Jones's remains a century later (1905) "revealed that his kidneys showed signs of glomerulonephritis; and that there were indurated masses in his lungs, some having the appearance of broncho-pneumonic lesions. My friend and neighbor Dr. George C. Shattuck, after reading the account of the autopsy, thinks that, on top of jaundice and nephritis, Jones contracted bronchial pneumonia, which finished him off."

CHAPTER 3

1. The Portuguese captain's report indicated that the Algerian warships were more formidably armed than Jefferson had testified in his message to Congress.

2. Church also discovered that a ninth pirate had followed the original eight into the Atlantic.

3. The eleven vessels were:

The ship *Hope* of New York
The ship *Minerva* of Philadelphia
The ship *Prudent* of Philadelphia
The ship *Thomas* of Newburyport, Mass.
The brig *George* of Rhode Island
The brig *Polly* of Newburyport
The brig *Olive Branch* of Portsmouth, N.H.
The brig *Jane* of Haverhill, Mass.
The brig *Minerva* of New York
The schooner *Jay* of Colchester, Conn.
The schooner *Dispatch* of Petersburg

4. One report had it that Logie persuaded the dey to sign the truce by pointing out the rich American prizes he could capture on the Atlantic side of the Strait.

5. American ship captains heard, and many believed, rumors that a group of British merchants in Cádiz, alerted to the British-arranged truce, had collected a pool of $400,000 to purchase captured American grain from Algiers at bargain prices to sell at a large profit to the intended European recipients of the shipments. A contributing factor to the Algerian captures might have been the undermanned American vessels that had lost sailors to British claiming they were Royal Navy deserters.

6. Church's punctuation was no better than that of most of his contemporaries. But in this instance his lowercase *b* for British may, consciously or unconsciously, have reflected his outrage.

7. *A Journal of the Captivity and Sufferings of John Foss: Several Years as a Prisoner at Algiers.* Foss explained that he made nightly notes in his journal, thus recording every detail of his imprisonment.

8. In a preface to his book Foss states that "my readers ought to be informed that these merciless Barbarians are taught by their religion to treat the Christian captives with unexampled cruelty."

9. It was a curious sign of the dey's ambivalent attitude toward the Christian Americans—or of his cynicism—that he professed to be a great admirer of George Washington and asked for a portrait of this "asserter of independence and liberty." Certainly it was an odd request from so autocratic a potentate.

10. Algiers had wheeled vehicles at the time, but evidently had not developed a braking system strong enough for such heavy loads.

11. The name of this punishment comes from the *bastone,* a five-foot-long stick with a single thong stretching from one end to the other. The victim was thrown on his back and his feet were thrust through the loop formed by the thong. The *bastone* was twisted until the thong gripped his ankles tightly and his bare feet were forced upward. Then, according to another American prisoner, "A Turk sits on his back, and two men, with each a [length of] bamboo or branch of the date tree, as large as a walking staff, and about three feet in length, hard and very heavy, strip or roll up their sleeves and, with all their strength and fury, apply the bruising cudgel to the bottom of the feet." Men had been known to die under the bastinado.

12. The usual method was by driving a stake through the anus until it emerged at the back of the neck.

13. Some Cassandras uttered dire warnings that with the Algerians loose in the Atlantic even the American coast was in danger. Captain Richard O'Brien, captured with his ship *Dauphin*, had written to Jefferson in Paris from his prison in 1786, giving his opinion that the Barbary pirates' activities were confined to the Mediterranean. By 1791, now the spokesman for his fellow captives, O'Brien changed his mind, predicting in a letter to Congress that if allowed into the Atlantic the Algerians might "go on to the coast of America; then, honored sirs, what would be the fatal consequences—what would be the alarm!"

    A similar argument had been used by Hugh Williamson of North Carolina as early as 1789, employing the threat of Barbary attacks on America as one of his arguments for ratifying the Constitution. And in 1791 Robert Montgomery, the U.S. agent in Alicante, Spain, asking to be appointed as a negotiator with Algiers, warned that the American coast was being protected by the Portuguese blockade; if it were removed, he warned, "we must expect to see their [Algiers'] Cruizers on the coast and in Bays of America." But when a similar warning was put to Vice President John Adams, he scoffed that "we are in no more danger than the Empire of China is."

14. It was No. 24 in the collection of *Federalist Papers*.

15. Years later Humphreys and Fox both claimed to have been the sole designer of the six frigates. But Howard I. Chapelle (in his authoritative *The History of the American Sailing Navy*) maintains that "Fox was far better trained than Humphreys in all respects, and was a far superior draftsman." It seems clear that the accolade accorded to Humphreys as "Father of the American Navy" should be shared with the British designer Fox, who of course could not know that the frigates he designed would defeat so many of his native country's frigates in the War of 1812.

    Humphreys and Fox were Quakers, and both were reprimanded by leaders of the sect for their part in building ships of war.

16. And causing some of the frigates, when completed, to "hog," or bend because of the combination of greater length and too many heavy guns.

17. Sample bribes demanded by the dey, as spelled out in a document during negotiations:

    For the Deys Wife and Daughter: $60,000
    For the Deys Casnadar or Chamberlain: $5,000
    For the Deys two Head Cooks: $10,000
    For the two Money Counters: $6,000
    For 13 Officers of Justice: $5,000
    For 62 Officers of the Antient Divan: $13,000

    The ransom eventually agreed upon for ship captains came to $6,000 each, for mates $4,000, for seamen $3,000.

18. Joel Barlow, of Yale's class of 1778, was an amateur poet and a member of a group who called themselves the "Hartford Wits" (oxymoron not intended). After practicing law in Washington, he had gone to Europe in search of his fortune. He settled in Paris, became an international businessman, and stayed in France 17 years. He spoke three languages and, like Secretary of State Jefferson, admired France and its Revolution.

19. His name was variously spelled by the Americans as Bacri, Baccry, Baccri, and Barci in contemporary accounts.

20. What with the new frigate, the annual gift of arms, bribes for assorted officials, and other expenses, the total bill for peace with Algiers came to about $1 million.

21. Barlow returned to the United States in 1805, and in 1811 was asked to go back to France and attempt to persuade Napoleon to stop capturing neutral U.S. ships during his war with Britain. Napoleon refused to see him, but Barlow stubbornly followed the emperor to Poland, then part of Russia, which Napoleon was invading. In the same winter of 1812–13 that defeated Napoleon's army, Barlow caught pneumonia and died. He still lies in a grave near Krakow.

22. The treaty with Tunis contained three provisions to which the U.S. Senate objected: (1) A discriminatory duty on American goods entering Tunis; (2) the right of the bey to commandeer U.S. vessels; and (3) an agreement that the United States would supply to Tunis a barrel of gunpowder for every Tunisian gun fired in salute to an American warship—which would have encouraged a veritable bombardment every time a U.S. man-of-war entered the harbor. All three provisions were later stricken after more negotiations and at further cost to the United States.

23. Isolationists for a century and a half have quoted Washington as warning against "entangling foreign alliances" in his Farewell Address. What Washington actually wrote (with editorial help from Alexander Hamilton) was: "'Tis our policy to steer clear of permanent alliances with any portion of the foreign world, so far, I mean, as we are now at liberty to do it; for let me not be understood as capable of patronizing infidelity to existing engagements." It was Jefferson who in his first inaugural speech proposed "Peace, commerce, and honest friendship with all nations, entangling alliances with none."

24. The Constitution provided for each elector, chosen by his state, to cast two votes, the winner to be president and the runner-up to be vice president. But the Constitution's framers had not forseen the two political parties that had since formed. Thus in the 1796 election Federalist Adams, with 71 electors' votes, became president, while Republican Jefferson, with 68 electors' votes, became vice president.

25. There was much foot-dragging in the naval bureaucracy when the frigate for the dey was ordered. A year after it had been promised, President Washington had to prod Secretary of War James McHenry to get a move on, explaining that "disagreeable as the requisition was found in its reception, and more so in the compliance with it," there would be further trouble with Algiers if the frigate was delayed. (Indeed, it had been promised to compensate for delays in ransom payments.)

    Named the *Crescent* for the motif on the Turkish flag, she was finally launched into the Piscataqua River in Portsmouth, N.H., ironically on the Fourth of July, 1797. Her total cost was $99,727. (Barlow had originally estimated her cost at $45,000.) More delays ensued, and not until January 20, 1798, did she sail for the Mediterranean, her hull loaded with 26 barrels of silver dollars, part of the overdue tribute due the dey—some of which he used to purchase three more warships, which U.S. shipbuilders were glad to sell to him.

26. After the treaty, when the dey became furious over the delays in payment, he threatened to cut Cathcart's and Donaldson's throats. He was not amused when Donaldson pointed out that it would be difficult because both had such bull necks.

27. The ship *Hero*, loaded with naval supplies promised to the bashaw, had sailed from Philadelphia for the Mediterranean with the *Sophia* in the late autumn of 1798. But she had sprung a leak, had put back to Jamaica for repairs, had set out again only to spring another leak, and had gone to New York. Her cargo had been offloaded onto other vessels and had not yet reached Tripoli, where Bashaw Yusuf had been waiting two and a half years for the promised naval stores.

28. Ever since this diverting incident there has been speculation that Cathcart rather than O'Brien attempted to seduce Miss Robinson. But Consul Eaton, in an April 1799 letter describing the 36-day voyage aboard the *Sophia*, paints a picture out of Jane Austen: a ladylike, if not prissy, young Englishwoman offended by the crude behavior of an American ex-sailor.

At first, according to Eaton, Cathcart treated Miss Robinson as an equal, inviting her to sit at the table with him and his bride and seeing to it that she was assigned a cabin rather than a berth in steerage. By the time the *Sophia* reached the Strait of Gibraltar, Eaton reported, Miss Robinson was protesting her "disappointment of the manners of the persons with whom she had engaged . . . I once heard her remark that the rank Mr. C. held under the appointment of the President of the United States had deluded her into a persuasion that his family and manners must have been at least civilised if not refined." The key word seems to be "manners," and Miss Robinson, according to Eaton, declared that "she had such a dislike to Mr. C. that she did not wish an appointment in the same house with him." To which Cathcart reacted with an explosive burst of temper: "A storm arose accompanied with thunder and smut," Eaton recalled. "He later called her many choice names selected from the catalogue of infamies, and demanded her reasons."

Miss Robinson, Eaton wrote, voiced a fear that Cathcart "would not hesitate to discipline her as a slave if occasion suited at a place and time where she could find no protection." Expressing her "contempt for a tyrant," she "now threw herself upon the protection of the consul general." O'Brien promised to find her passage for America and took her in for the time being. Cathcart promptly accused O'Brien of luring his wife's maid away—overlooking, as Eaton pointed out, the fact that Miss Robinson had decided to leave Cathcart's employ "long before she saw the American Consul [O'Brien]."

As for Cathcart being tempted into seduction, Eaton maintained that during all the time he had known Miss Robinson "I observed no single jesture [sic] in her behavior which would justify an impeachment of her honor." She might have been dissembling, Eaton admitted, but he doubted it. "She is a *woman*," he explained, "and cast among *barbarians*." Eaton wrote his letter before O'Brien's marriage proposal, but he predicted, "It would not surprise me if she should find the *end of her travels* in the American house."

Nor was there any indication that Jane Cathcart suspected her husband of attempted infidelity. The couple remained married and had 12 children.

Cathcart had reached Tripoli before he heard of the O'Brien-Robinson marriage. He reacted in an outraged letter to the secretary of state impugning the character of the new Mrs. O'Brien as well as that of the bridegroom. Cathcart never knew how Betsy had reached America from England, he wrote, "as she never told a direct story. I had seen enough of her on the passage [to the Mediterranean] to cause me to form no favorable opinion of her." And when O'Brien offered her refuge, Cathcart maintained, "Betsy wished to be discharged—which I did freely."

He gave a rather different account in a letter to Eaton. O'Brien, he wrote, "took every means to entice her from the service of a young creature [Mrs. Cathcart] in a barbarous community, when it was impossible to procure another female attendant. . . . Why, if he had taken a liking to the girl, he did not declare it openly, why he did not have the candor and request Mrs. Cathcart to part with her as a man of honor should have done?"

29. Evidently O'Brien claimed that the letters must have come open by mistake, eliciting a heavy-handed attempt at sarcasm from Eaton. "It is somewhat extraordinary that letters coming to me . . . should happen to fall open into your hands at the same time. It is equally singular that, as those letters were forwarded to you under strong covers, you should have found it necessary to expend so much time and wax in resealing them."

30. The three frigates reauthorized by Congress were finally nearing completion. But meanwhile the United States was facing an increasing threat from France, whose privateers were attacking American merchantmen, with the excuse that as neutrals in the war between France and Britain the American vessels were aiding France's enemy by trading with Britain.

President Adams attempted to negotiate by sending envoys to France, who were greeted by French diplomats with a demand for a $10 million "loan" and a gift of $250,000 before they could meet with Foreign Minister Charles Maurice de Talleyrand-Périgord. American envoy Charles Pinckney is supposed to have responded with the remembered cry, "Millions for defense, but not a cent for tribute!" What he apparently did say was "No, sir! Not a sixpence!"

When Americans heard the news that the French were behaving like the Barbary pirates, the outcry against the "X,Y,Z Affair" (so-called because Adams identified the French diplomats only as "X., Y. and Z.") led Congress at last in May of 1798 to authorize a Navy Department as separate from the War Department. (A Marine Corps was authorized two months later.) Thus the U.S. Navy, which had almost been stillborn because of the treaty with Algiers, was christened four years later.

31. Bainbridge had interrupted his formal education by going to sea at 15.

32. In a letter to Navy Secretary Benjamin Stoddert Bainbridge tried to explain:

The loss of the frigate, and the fear of slavery for myself and crew, were the least circumstances to be apprehended; but I knew our valued commerce in these seas would fall a sacrifice to the corsairs of this power, as we have here no cruisers to protect it. . . . I hope I may never again be sent to Algiers with tribute, unless I am authorized to deliver it from the mouth of our cannon."

33. Reis Effendi, Turkey's chief civil officer, however, sent aboard an officer demanding that Bainbridge report to him, and professed outrage when the U.S. captain refused to be summoned. Shortly Bainbridge was introduced to Brit-

ain's ambassador, Thomas Bruce, seventh earl of Elgin (late to become famous for the "Elgin Marbles" that he took back to the British Museum from Greece). Elgin explained that Reis Effendi was merely looking for a bribe, which Elgin promised to arrange.

Such British diplomats as Charles Logie in Algiers had been doing what they could to hinder the American presence in the Mediterranean. But Elgin and many other Britons showed little lingering resentment over the American Revolution and aided U.S. diplomats and naval officers whenever they could. In the U.S. naval actions that were to follow in the Mediterranean, the British-controlled port of Malta, for example, offered invaluable assistance and essential supplies to visiting American warships.

CHAPTER 4

1. Jefferson was the presidential candidate of the Republican party, with Aaron Burr as his vice president. John Adams was the presidential candidate of the Federalist party, with Thomas Pinckney of South Carolina as vice president. The Republicans won; but because of the method of ballot-vote-counting, allowing separate votes for president and vice president, Jefferson and Burr were tied. This situation led in 1804 to the Twelfth Amendment to the Constitution, which provided for one vote for the president and his running mate.
2. With his conscience evidently bothering him, Adams wrote to Jefferson blaming the affront on a personal tragedy: One of his sons had drowned at sea. Reflecting the male chauvinism of the time (Jefferson had daughters but no son), Adams wrote, "It is not possible that any thing of the kind should happen to you, and I sincerely wish you may never experience any thing in any degree resembling it." There is no evidence that Jefferson acknowledged Adams's feeble attempt at explanation. At any rate, Jefferson was well aware that Adams's son had died some months earlier.
3. When Senator William Plummer of New Hampshire visited the White House with a congressional delegation, he mistook the president for one of the servants. "He was dressed, or rather undressed," Plummer marveled, "in an old brown coat, red waistcoat, old corduroy small-clothes much soiled, woolen hose, and slippers without heels."
4. Although the Federalists were charging that Jefferson and the Republicans would eviscerate the navy, it was a Federalist-controlled Congress that voted for this reduction.
5. It has become virtually a U.S. Navy tradition that Thomas Jefferson was a pacifist who crippled the navy when he became president. In *The History of the American Sailing Navy* Howard I. Chapelle wrote that Jefferson was "violently anti-naval and anti-military. Doctrinaire in judgment, Jefferson was not influenced by the international state in his time and, in spite of the plain warning of the future trouble given by the numerous incidents including outright attacks on American ships by foreign men-of-war, could not bring himself to prepare for war." Although Chapelle was no doubt referring to the Royal Navy, such criticism overlooks both Jefferson's determination to fight rather

than pay off the Barbary powers, and the fact that it was Congress that denied his requests to declare war against them.

6. The *United States* (44 guns) was launched in Philadelphia on May 10, 1797; she was damaged slightly because the launching ways evidently were at too steep an angle and she plunged into the water faster than planned. The *Chesapeake* (36 guns) had been launched in Norfolk on June 20, 1797; the *Constellation* (36 guns) in Baltimore on September 7, 1797. She was launched without incident but later swung aground while at anchor, fell on her side with the outgoing tide, filled with the next incoming tide, and sank; she was pumped out and refurbished with no major damage.

   The *Constitution* (44 guns) was scheduled for launching on September 20, 1797, a clear, brisk day with whitecaps in Boston's Charles River. At the appointed time whistles blew, church bells rang, and the crowd roared as the big frigate started down the ways. She slid only 27 feet before grinding to a halt. For two hours the shipworkers pried at her in vain with wedges, hammers, and screws. As the tide ebbed, the launch was called off and blocks were driven against her keel to hold her for the next day's high tide.

   Again she did not move. An investigation disclosed that the shipways were not sturdy enough and had sagged under her weight, reducing the angle of inclination. Moreover, when she had settled against the ways, her keel had been damaged. It took another month to replace the keel and strengthen the shipways. Finally, on October 20, she slipped free into the Charles to the relieved cheers of her builders and watchers on shore.

   Not until the following summer, July of 1798, did the *Constitution* put to sea, partly because of difficulties recruiting a crew; her first captain, Samuel Nicholson, was an unpopular martinet. On her shakedown cruise her compasses were mysteriously erratic, until it was found that an ignorant shipyard worker had built her binnacles with iron nails, which distorted the magnetism of the compasses. The binnacles were taken apart and rebuilt with copper nails. Midshipman James Petty, who supervised the repair, happily noted in his log on August 2—eleven months after the frigate's intended launch and more than four years after Congress's appropriation—that he "found our compasses to agree exactly."

   The *Constitution* was followed by the *President* (44 guns) launched in New York on April 1, 1800, and by the *Congress* (36 guns) in Portsmouth, N.H., on the same day.

7. In an act passed June 30, 1798, Congress mandated that warships built by citizens' subscriptions would be accepted into the navy, on the principle that the merchants most affected by the Barbary piracies should do their share to defend their shipping. Many maritime communities responded with frigates and smaller men-of-war, some partially paid for by low-interest government bonds and some presented to the navy as gifts.

8. His engineer's mind at work, Jefferson proposed that these seven vessels be immobilized by an ingenious method of dry-docking: two basins connected by locks as in a canal. The frigates could be floated into a lower basin at high tide. A second, higher basin would be formed by freshwater from a river. The gates of the first basin would be closed and it would be flooded to the level of the upper basin. The locks would be opened; the vessels would be floated into the second basin, which would then be drained off, leaving the

frigates resting on their keels and supported by timbers (much as they had been at their launching). By covering them with a roof, Jefferson argued, they "would last as long as the Interior timbers, doors and floors of a House," and thus would be ready for relaunching when needed. An added advantage to such a dry dock would be the effect of freshwater and exposure to air, killing the barnacles on the vessels' hulls.

But Jefferson's proposal languished in Congress until it was no longer necessary, when the Barbary War escalated to the point that all the frigates were needed in the Mediterranean.

9. Murad Reis was one of the most colorful of the many colorful characters on the Barbary Coast. Born on a farm in Scotland and named Peter Lisle, he went to sea as a youngster, served aboard a Mameluke vessel, learned Arabic, and later worked his way to America, where he shipped as a foremast hand aboard an American vessel sailing back to the Mediterranean. Evidently his experience was unpleasant, because he ever afterward nourished a hatred of Americans. When his ship was captured by a Tripolitan pirate, Lisle became a Mohammedan and joined the Tripolitan Navy.

A handsome blond young man, he courted the bashaw's daughter and won from the bashaw not only his daughter's hand but appointment as high admiral of the Tripolitan Navy and chief of the Marine Department. Lisle also shrewdly chose for his Mohammedan name that of a famous Barbary pirate who had cruised into the Atlantic as far north as Ireland and even Iceland in 1631. The new Murad Reis was also a skilled navigator. But despite his adopted Muslim religion, he was reputed to have a drinking problem. The Americans variously spelled his name as Murad Reis, Marad Rais, Marad Reis, etc.

10. Because tall trees were scarce along the Barbary Coast—and the few available were used for masts—a flagpole was a sign of prestige. So it was a special form of humiliation to chop one down.

11. A century and a half later the United States would send "observers" overseas—a decision that, as in the Mediterranean, inevitably led to full-fledged war.

12. The first secretary of the navy, Benjamin Stoddert, a cavalryman veteran of the Revolution and a peacetime Maryland merchant, had done much to put the new navy department on a sound footing and had argued in vain against the cutbacks mandated by Congress. With Jefferson's Republican administration succeeding Adams's Federalists, Stoddert had submitted his resignation.

13. Secretary Smith's instructions included an admonition that would have later consequences: "Particularly you are not to suffer your own ship to be entered—or your own men examined or taken out, at sea, by any person or power whatsoever; but to resist such attempt to your utmost, yielding only to Superior force, & surrendering, if overcome, your Vessel & men, but never your men without your vessel." It was the growing practice of the British captains seizing crewmen (British-born and often American-born) from U.S. vessels and the growing American resistance to this practice that eventually led to the War of 1812.

14. As a teenager at the outbreak of the Revolution, Dale had some trouble deciding which side to join. A lieutenant in Virginia's state navy, he was captured by a British frigate and while in a prison ship was persuaded by a Tory

schoolmate to join the crew aboard the tender of his captor. Severely injured in another battle, Dale rethought his loyalty while in the hospital, and had the good fortune to be recaptured by the U.S. sloop-of-war *Lexington*, in whose crew he promptly enlisted.

Dale's fortunes turned twice again; in all he was imprisoned by the British three times. During one of his incarcerations he tunneled out of his prison only to be recaptured; defiantly he taunted his guards by singing what they termed "Rebel Songs." Somehow managing to obtain a British uniform, Dale calmly walked out to freedom and to glory as a hero of the Revolution.

15. Commodore was a courtesy rank given to the commander of a U.S. fleet of warships. At the time there was no naval rank above that of captain.

16. The Romans gave the area the Greek name *tripolis* to encompass the three ancient cities of Oea, Sabratha, and Leptis Magna. The Vandals and Saracens laid Sabratha waste; by the nineteenth century Leptis Magna was a crumbling ruin of Roman architecture. Only Oea, now renamed Tripoli, remained inhabited.

17. There was a long-standing Tripolitan legend about Bashaw Hamet's blindness. It was said that at the height of his tyrannical reign, on a visit to a mosque, his eye was caught by the beautiful eldest daughter of the marabut, the mosque's holy man. Hamet demanded that the girl be sent to his harem; and when the marabut protested, Hamet threatened to kill him and his family.

   The marabut consented, and made a great display of his daughter's presentation, dressing her in fine clothes, adorning her with jewels, and sending her to the castle on an ornamented camel. When Bashaw Hamet entered the bedchamber, he found a beautiful corpse. She had agreed to poison herself.

   The bashaw confronted the marabut, who boldly confirmed what he had done and announced that he had also called on Mahomet to strike the bashaw blind. Hamet was too frightened to take revenge, and soon did begin to lose his eyesight.

18. To her added horror, Hassan in his dying words accused his mother of entrapping him.

19. A third class of nineteenth-century warships was designated as a sloop-of-war (sometimes called a corvette). Many were not actually one-masted sloops but full-rigged three-masted ships, though smaller than frigates. Some carried as many as 30 guns each. The fleets of frigates and sloops-of-war were usually supplemented by smaller, two-masted brigs, brigantines, schooners, and ketches and single-masted cutters.

20. A "long" gun, because of its lengthier barrel, provided greater range with more accuracy.

21. Though rated at 44 guns, the *President*, like most warships, carried a few more. Navy captains liked to cram as many guns aboard as the vessel could carry. The *United States*, rated a 44-gun frigate, carried as many as 50; the *Constitution*, rated a 44, had as many as 60.

22. The carronade got its name from the Carron Foundry in Britain where the first such guns were manufactured. The American version was patterned on the British prototype.

23. Langradge usually consisted of a bagful of nails, bolts, razor-sharp bits of

metal, and other junk designed to cut sails and rigging and spray death and destruction along the enemy's deck.

Hammocks stored in the gunwale nettings also provided another safety measure: They could be tossed into the sea as life preservers if a man fell overboard. A well-trussed hammock would float for hours.

24. The *President*'s log at sea observed "nautical time," with each day starting at noon; in the frigate's log, July 2 began at noon of July 1 mainland time. In port the ship's time reverted to land time, occasionally making for confusion when later determining the exact day if one did not take into account whether the vessel was in port or at sea.

25. One of the *Constitution*'s guns was reputed to bounce several feet in the air every time it was fired; its gun crew nicknamed it "Bouncing Billy."

26. According to Tyrone G. Martin (*A Most Fortunate Ship: A Narrative History of "Old Ironsides"*), navy regulations provided a daily ration for each man of a pound of bread and a half-gallon of water, plus a pound of pork, a half-pint of peas or beans, and four ounces of cheese three times a week; a weekly ration of 1½ pounds of beef, a half-pint of rice, 1½ pounds of potatoes or turnips, two ounces of butter, and a pound of fish.

The navy's famous grog was originally named after the Royal Navy's Admiral Edward Vernon, who was known as "Old Grog" because of his custom-tailored grosgrain-lapeled cloak and who in 1740 devised and issued a mixture of three parts water to one part rum. In the U.S. Navy grog generally consisted of a half-pint of watered spirits (usually rum) or a quart of beer per day.

But the amounts were at the discretion of the captain. And if supplies dwindled on a lengthy voyage, he could cut the ration accordingly. The *President*, like the other early U.S. frigates, had narrow hulls near the keel for greater speed, with a corresponding shortage of stowage space for food. Most of the frigates also carried fishing lines, hooks, and seines, and the sailors were encouraged when off watch to supplement their rations from the sea.

For the first few weeks of her transatlantic voyage the *President* was stocked with pigs, sheep, and calves in a special manger forward or in the ship's boats, plus chickens crated in other boats. Newly slaughtered livestock swung in halves or quarters from the beams. Hay and corn to feed the animals was stacked in nearby bales. Occasionally the chickens or livestock would escape their pens or crates and wander about the gun deck, giving it the appearance—and smell—of a floating barnyard.

27. A recipe for duff: Beat the biscuits into the consistency of rough flour. Add raisins and fat. Spoon into a canvas bag. Boil.

28. Discipline aboard a U.S. warship depended on the captain, whose whim was law. The mildest form of punishment was putting a man in irons in the hold under the supervision of the master-at-arms; recalcitrant sailors could spend a couple of weeks or more than a month in confinement. The most frequent offense, perhaps understandably, was drunkenness, followed by an all-embracing charge called neglect of duty. Theft and desertion, the gravest crimes, usually were punished by the lash.

Congress had in 1800 passed an Act for the Better Government of the Navy that limited punishment to 12 lashes. But a sailor frequently was charged with more than one—dereliction of duty, for example, plus disobedience—and given 24. The punishment normally was postponed until more than one man was to be lashed, and then it was scheduled for noon when the frigate's company was assembled to watch the grisly spectacle in the hope that it would teach everyone a lesson.

The transgressor was stripped to the waist and tied to an upended hatch grating. The charge was read, and the captain pronounced the sentence. A pair of boatswain's mates stood on each side of the man; two were assigned, alternating with each other, because one might tire (accordingly left-handed boatswain's mates were in demand among naval recruiters). The boatswain's mates laid on the prescribed number of lashes with the cat-o'-nine-tails, so named because it was composed of nine ropes knotted at the end. (The phrase "not enough room to swing a cat" refers not to a feline but to the space required for this punishment.) With his back reduced to blood-dripping beef, the sailor was cut down and sent to the sick bay for his wounds to be treated so he could return to duty. Ship's boys were usually flogged with the "colt," a three-stranded rope without knots, and were permitted to wear their shirts during the punishment.

Serious crimes such as desertion during battle were court-martial offenses that on conviction were punishable by hanging or as many as 100 lashes, which could be as lethal. The most gruesome punishment (imported from the Royal Navy) was "flogging through the fleet," in which the offender was tied to a section of grating in a ship's boat and rowed from vessel to vessel in the squadron, accompanied by a surgeon. The boatswain's mates of each ship would do the flogging, and the crew of each ship would witness the spectacle as an object lesson. If the surgeon decided that the man could not stand it anymore, he was returned to his ship; when he recovered, he was sent through the rest of the fleet. Although this form of punishment was still used in the Royal Navy, it was banned aboard U.S. warships by Navy Regulations; but the ban was widely ignored by American captains.

29. Marines are as old as navies. As early as 480 B.C., when Themistocles assembled Athens's naval power for defense against the invading Persians, he called for "Marines, twenty to a ship." These *Epitabatae*, fighting aboard Greek triremes, helped turn back Xerxes at the Battle of Salamis. The later Roman navies consisted chiefly of *milites classiari* (soldiers of the fleet) who stormed aboard enemy triremes in close-encounter engagements. By the mid-seventeenth century England's Charles II was organizing "The Duke of York and Albany's Maritime Regiment of the Fleet," soldiers serving aboard ship under the command of the Admiralty to fight the Dutch, who in turn mobilized their own *Korps Mariniers*.

The first American marines were mustered in colonial times: four battalions totaling 3,000 men who were raised in 1740 against the Spanish in the War of Austrian Succession. Because they served under Colonel William Gooch, they were known as "Gooch's Marines." In July of 1741 they stormed ashore at Guantanamo Bay (then called Walthenham Bay) in Cuba and established a base for the Royal Navy. One of Gooch's marine officers, Captain Lawrence Washington, in a rare moment of navy-marine amity, was so inspired by his navy commander, Admiral Edward ("Old Grog") Vernon, that he gave the name Mount Vernon to his family estate in Virginia, which later became the home of Lawrence's half brother George Washington.

30. John Paul Jones was one naval officer who admired the marines, claiming that

they were better disciplined than sailors, most of whom during the Revolution were ex-merchant seamen. (The Continental Marine Corps had been created in November of 1775.) In the *Bonhomme Richard*'s famous battle with the *Serapis* on September 23, 1779, Jones's 140 marines, largely members of the Corps Royeaux d'Infanterie et d'Artillerie de Marine assigned to the *Richard* by Louis XVI, virtually cleared the *Serapis*'s deck with their accurate fire. Sixty-seven of them were killed or wounded in the engagement.

One of Jones's American marines, Lieutenant Samuel Wallingford, who served aboard Jones's *Ranger* on her raiding expedition against St. Mary's Isle, was described by a victim, Countess Selkirk, as "a civil young man in a green uniform . . . [who] seemed naturally well bred." The countess did not think as highly of Jones's naval lieutenant, David Cullum, describing him as having "a vile, blackguard look." On the morning of April 23, 1778, Wallingford and Cullum relieved the countess of her silver (including a teapot, with wet tea leaves from breakfast, which the butler had tried to hide), partook of a glass of wine offered by their cool-headed hostess, and made a hasty retreat before the countryside was aroused. The next day the *Ranger* encountered the British warship *Drake* and defeated her, with the loss of three men, including Wallingford.

31. The slowest of the new frigates was the *United States*, evidently because of the damage to her keel during her launch. Her crewmen promptly gave her the nickname of "Old Waggon."

32. Though categorized as a sloop of war, the *Enterprise* (often spelled *Enterprize* by contemporaries) was an 84-foot-long schooner of 135 tons, recently built on Maryland's Eastern Shore on the plans of the fast, popular pilot schooners of the time.

33. Though a confirmed New England Federalist at heart, Eaton did not share most Federalists' alarm at the prospect of Thomas Jefferson's presidency. Writing home in 1801 before news of the election had reached the Mediterranean, Eaton expressed the hope that Adams had won, but mused that "should the choice fix on Mr. Jefferson we have nothing to apprehend dangerous to our political existence—I never supposed there was a vast difference in the political commitments of those gentlemen."

34. It was accepted practice at the time for warships to fly another nation's flag to deceive a potential enemy. Dale's instructions permitted Sterrett to use this deception but "on no account to fire under any but our Owne."

35. A stern and unforgiving officer, Sterrett had served aboard the *Constellation* in a battle with the *Insurgente* during the Quasi-War with France, and had admitted after the engagement: "One fellow I was obliged to run through the body with my sword, and so put an end to a coward. . . . We would put a man to death for even looking pale on board this ship."

CHAPTER 5

1. He also sent a personal letter of gratitude to Sterrett: "I do myself the pleasure . . . of expressing to you, on behalf of your country, the high satisfaction inspired by your conduct in the late engagement with the Tripolitan cruiser

captured by you. Too long, for the honor of nations, have those barbarians been suffered to trample on the sacred faith of treaties, on the rights and laws of human nature! You have shown to your countrymen that that enemy cannot meet skill and bravery united. In proving to them that our past condescensions were from a love of peace, not a dread of them, you have deserved well of your country, and have merited the high esteem and consideration of which I have now the pleasure of assuring you."

Congress echoed the president's sentiments by passing a resolution awarding Sterrett a commemorative sword and his crew an extra month's pay.

2. Samuel Smith had the previous summer relinquished the post to his brother Robert.

3. Obviously taken aback at Secretary Smith's call of his bluff, Truxton asked to discuss it with the president, and was further abashed at Jefferson's polite—or pretended—indifference: "He never opened his lips to me on the subject of the Squadron or our Mediterranean affairs," Truxton wrote a friend. "I think I can with truth say it was never intended that I should proceed on the command in question."

4. The first that Commodore Morris evidently heard of it was when the secretary wrote him on April 2 granting the permission requested by "your lady."

Women occasionally went to sea aboard U.S. Navy vessels—and Royal Navy warships—in the eighteenth and nineteenth centuries, though there are few official records of their presence. And seldom were they allowed aboard in time of war. Their presence was normally at the discretion of the squadron commodore. Usually they were the wives of warrant and petty officers.

Other women accompanied their husbands aboard Commodore Morris's flagship. One of them, the wife of James Low, captain of the forecastle, gave birth to a son on February 22, 1803, in the Mediterranean. The wife of a gun captain helped officiate at a baptism of the baby, celebrating with wine and fruit. Midshipman Henry Wadsworth reported that the wives of the boatswain, the carpenter, and a marine corporal "got drunk in their own Quarters out of pure spite—not being invited" to the christening.

Babies born on gun decks were the origin of the phrase "son of a gun."

5. Henry Wadsworth was a son of Peleg Wadsworth, a hero of the Revolution and later a member of Congress. In 1807 Henry's sister Zilpah would name her son after him; the son would become famous as the poet Henry Wadsworth Longfellow.

6. The *Betsey-Meshouda* was at length released to the emperor, largely because detaining her in Gibraltar tied down one of the squadron's warships. Muley Soliman immediately loaded her with grain for Tripoli, whereupon she crossed the path of Captain John Rodgers in the *John Adams*, who seized her as a blockade runner.

7. Morris did not endear himself to Cathcart when he later used a clause in his orders authorizing him to negotiate on his own if necessary and informed Cathcart that his services would no longer be needed.

8. One of the additions to Morris's squadron was the *Boston* (28 guns), which had taken Robert R. Livingston to France to be U.S. minister and had been ordered to proceed to the Mediterranean. Her captain, an eccentric and independent officer named Daniel McNeill, did not bother to report to the squadron's commodore but went about the Mediterranean on his own, cap-

turing Tunisians with whom the United States was not at war and ignoring quarantine regulations at the various ports he visited. Nearly deaf, arrogant, and absentminded, McNeill frequently sailed off leaving some of his officers and men ashore, and on one occasion put to sea before three French dinner guests had had time to disembark. McNeill put them ashore on the North African coast, where they managed to find a fisherman to take them back to France. McNeill was finally recalled by the end of the summer of 1803; but he took the *Boston* home with him. On his arrival he was dismissed from the navy.

9. Duels occurred frequently in the new U.S. Navy, whose officers were over-zealous about rank and "honor." Two thirds as many naval officers were killed in duels as by enemy action in all U.S. naval engagements from 1798 until the Civil War.

10. British warships understandably took precedence, and the American squadron's vessels often had to wait their turn for days.

11. In the days before carbon paper correspondents had to make their own copies of their letters. Eaton meticulously preserved a library of letter books containing such copies, most of which are now in the Huntington Library.

12. He also injected himself into an incident that was only momentarily dangerous and did not need anyone fanning the flames. Eaton had been ecstatic at the news of Lieutenant Andrew Sterrett's destruction of the *Tripoli*. But later when the bey of Tunis was angered by Sterrett's interception of the xebec that turned out to be Tunisian, Eaton was quick to castigate his former hero. Sterrett had sent a boarding party aboard the xebec and released her as soon as he found her not to be a Tripolitan warship. But the xebec's captain reported on arrival in Tunis that a few items aboard his vessel had been purloined by the Americans.

When the bey complained to Consul Eaton that Sterrett had committed an act of piracy, Eaton hastily forwarded the charge to Commodore Morris with his own intemperate observation that Sterrett's conduct "exhibits a Scene of debasement as dishonorable to our Arms as it is detrimental to our true interests." Shortly Sterrett brought the *Enterprise* into Tunis and it was discovered that the theft, a minor one, had been committed by three sailors without any American officers' knowledge. The culprits were sent home to be court-martialed, and the bey's anger quickly subsided.

These facts became known just before Eaton sent off his blast to Morris. But instead of tearing up his letter, Eaton merely added a lame postscript reporting the new information without withdrawing his condemnation of Sterrett.

13. Eaton's biographers have characterized his marriage as a loveless union of financial convenience, one even stating that Eaton despised his wife. His long absences from home are usually cited to indicate his lack of affection for her. But in the Eaton papers in the Huntington Library my wife found a number of letters showing that Eaton missed Eliza as well as her children, longed to return to her, and felt sure that she missed him as much.

In July of 1800, for example, he wrote, "Time hurries on . . . I wish I could add to his wings *electric* speed [to] hasten the embrace," signing himself, "Farewell, My Dear Eliza—farewell and think of your exiled William." In another letter he wrote, "I again declare that it is impossible for a man to be more devotedly yours than your William." And to a friend, Stephen Pynchon, Eaton described his absence from home: "I cannot say I am *contented*, not to mention *happy;* I cannot but think of my dear little orphans . . . I cannot help thinking an excellent woman, at least in my opinion, whose goodness & sensibility has deserved a happier life than my untoward fortune has rendered hers."

One example cited to suggest Eaton's estrangement from his wife was his comment on arrival in Tunis when an Italian woman offered to help keep house for him. His response was that he had come "five thousand miles upon a dangerous element and in an inclement season to get rid of my own wife, and would not be embarrassed with a woman here—as I would as soon have the devil in my house." No doubt this was more Eaton's clumsy idea of a diplomatic rejoinder to a woman who may have seemed too forward than a statement of his marital situation. Nor did Eaton admire Tunisian women— what he could see of them in their long dresses and face coverings. "It is an abominable falsehood recorded by geographers," he wrote, "that the women of Tunis are handsome . . . The ladies in the street look like walking ghosts swaddled in rags."

One of Eliza's sons, Eli Danielson, was given a midshipman's appointment, presumably with Eaton's help. Danielson joined his stepfather in his search for Hamet Karamanli, and was devoted to him.

14. The bey claimed that David Vallanzino, owner of part of the *Paulina*'s cargo, was a Tunisian, not a Tripolitan, subject. Morris thought otherwise. With his shipment confiscated, Vallanzino sailed to the United States to demand restitution. Navy Secretary Smith responded with a generous offer: If a court of justice found Vallanzino's claim valid, the United States would repay him for his loss plus damages; meanwhile the United States would pay for his round trip if he returned to the Mediterranean and waited for the case to be adjudicated. Vallanzino insisted on staying and pressing his claim. He little understood the pace of Congress. After waiting for what seemed to him an eternity for the House Committee on Claims to act, Vallanzino made the desperate and dramatic gesture of committing suicide in the lobby of the Capitol.

15. Morris secretly was inclined to agree: "Mr. Cathcart," he later wrote, "has been so unfortunate as neither to command respect nor conciliate esteem. He was considered imperious, quarrelsome, and insincere."

Jefferson also tried to send Cathcart to Tunis when Eaton was expelled. The president wrote to the bey in a letter redolent of the necessary hypocrisy of diplomacy: "Illustrious Friend: Mr. Eaton . . . having requested [sic] leave to return home to visit his family, I have yielded to his request and appointed Mr. James Leander Cathcart to fill the vacancy." The bey also refused to accept Cathcart, calling him an *embroglione* (troublemaker). Cathcart went home, and later served as consul at Madeira and Cádiz. His last 20 years were spent as a clerk in the U.S. Treasury, and he died forgotten in 1843.

16. A Mediterranean vessel somewhat larger than a felucca, usually with two or three masts, one of them square-rigged.

17. While Morris spent nearly a month in Malta getting acquainted with his new son, Admiral Horatio Nelson brought his 32-gun frigate *Amphion* into Valletta Harbor, refitted, resupplied, and left in 36 hours to rendezvous with his flagship.

A similar contrast between the methods of Morris and Nelson occurred the same summer. Attacked by a fleet of Algerian warships evidently mistaking its identity, a Royal Navy frigate escaped into Valletta Harbor. Promptly two British ships of the line and another frigate came out of the harbor, chased down the Algerians, and sank several of them. The incident moved the dey of Algiers to imprison every Englishman in the city and confiscate their property. At the news of this escalation Nelson sailed into Algiers harbor with seven frigates and opened fire with shells and red-hot cannonballs that set fire to half the city. The dey sent a hasty message offering to negotiate. Nelson replied that he could not answer for a while, meanwhile continuing his bombardment. The dey sent a second plea. Nelson responded with a demand for all British prisoners to be freed and indemnified for their losses, plus a substantial fine for misbehavior and a promise never to repeat such an insult to Great Britain. Surrounded by a burning city, the dey capitulated.

CHAPTER 6

1. In an uncharacteristic gesture of vanity he combed his sparse brown hair forward to conceal his growing baldness.
2. Jedediah Preble was even more famous locally as the first white man to reach the summit of Mount Washington and "wash his hands in the clouds," as his friends put it. (No doubt many Indians had preceded him.) One attribute he did not pass along to his third son was an easygoing sense of humor. On an occasion when young Edward was not included in an outing to a nearby island, he bombarded the boat from the shore; his father laughingly returned to pick him up. No such insubordination would later be permitted by Captain Edward Preble.
3. Aboard the *Winthrop* Preble demonstrated the sort of bravado that would pay off later in the Mediterranean. The sloop-of-war was off the Maine coast when her captain, George Little, heard that the 14-gun Royal Navy brig *Allegiance* was on her trail, and decided to seize the initiative by cutting her out at her night anchorage under the British guns at Castine. Little chose Preble to lead a 20-man party, and the *Winthrop* slipped into Castine Harbor at night, easing alongside the anchored *Allegiance*. Only 14 of the 20 men had jumped aboard the British warship when the *Winthrop* fell off. Little, attempting to bring his vessel back in position, shouted to Preble: "Do you need more men?"

   "No," shouted Preble. "We already have too many!" Within minutes he and his boarding party had overpowered the *Allegiance*'s crew; they cut her loose and sailed her out of the harbor before Castine's guns could open up.
4. Before sailing for the Orient, Preble showed another side of his nature in his courtship of Mary Deering of Portland. The hardened sea veteran of 38, when involved in an affair of the heart, did not have the courage to propose directly but instead wrote a pleading letter to Mary's mother, Mrs. Dorcas Deering. "You know how very dear to my heart your amiable daughter is, but I beg leave to assure you she is infinitely more dear to me than my existence," he wrote. "I love her with the tenderest affection, and would sac-

rifice my life to promote her happiness. . . . For heaven's sake, Madam, plead for me, and if she should consent to be mine on my return, my whole future life shall be devoted to a tender and delicate attention to her happiness and your own. . . . If I possessed the world I would give it freely to pass one hour with your amiable family before I go, but that alas is impossible. Adieu."

Mary did consent on his return. But neither she nor Preble even considered following the example of Mrs. Morris by accompanying him to the Mediterranean with the U.S. squadron.

5. Preble wrote to his wife, Mary, at home in Portland: "I am now reduced very low, but hope, if my resignation is accepted, that I shall have strength enough to be on my way home in a fortnight from this. God only knows how much I long to see you. . . . In the meantime I remain your emaciated, sick, but faithful and affectionate husband."

6. He did not, of course, mean American Indians, who were called by many names, mostly derogatory, in 1803, but not native Americans.

7. The U.S. Navy's definitive *Naval Documents Related to the United States Wars with the Barbary Powers* contains a lengthy and detailed list of *Rules and Regulations* issued by Preble aboard the *Constitution*. But in his definitive *Edward Preble: A Naval Biography, 1761–1807*, Christopher McKee offers convincing evidence that it is a misplaced order issued by Captain William Bainbridge for the *Philadelphia*. "How a copy of Bainbridge's general orders found its way into Preble's papers can only be guessed," McKee writes. "Perhaps Preble borrowed the volume and forgot to return it."

In any case every captain issued similar general orders in varying detail; and Preble could be counted on to cover every detail.

8. An extreme example was the case of Thomas Ayscough, who poisoned the frigate's sheep. Ayscough had previously been punished for drunkenness, stealing, insubordination, and neglect of duty; his poisoning prank was discovered when he was caught trying to desert. Clearly regarding him as incorrigible, Preble ordered the maximum punishment, a total of 136 lashes.

Knowing his own volatile temper, Preble usually waited a day or two before decreeing the form and extent of punishment. But when on another occasion the *Constitution*'s Corporal James Wallace set fire to an officer's cabin while attempting to fumigate the ship—without orders to do so—Preble demanded immediate punishment of 36 lashes: 12 for "attempting to fumigate any part of the ship without regular orders," 12 for neglect of duty, and 12 for causing "the rope yarns to blaze." Starting a fire at sea was one of the major transgressions of navy regulations; but the real reason for Preble's hasty decision in this case was his irascibility while awaiting news of two overdue warships.

9. Among ship commanders in the Mediterranean Isaac Hull was noted for his fair-minded leniency. And Preble, though stern, was less notorious than John Rodgers for harsh discipline and administering the lash.

10. He had a library of more than 100 books in his cabin, including such light reading as Carrington Bowles's *Universal Display of the Naval Flags of All Nations in the World*, John Hamilton Moore's *New Practical Navigator*, Robert Liddel's *The Seaman's New Vade Mecum, Containing a Practical Essay on Naval Bookkeeping, with the Method of Keeping the Captain's Books and Complete Instructions in the Duty of a Captain's Clerk*, Emmerich de Vatel's *The Law of Nations*, Vincent

Mignot's *The History of the Turkish Ottoman Empire from Its Foundation in 1300 to the Peace of Belgrade in 1740,* John Payne's *The Naval Commercial and General History of Great Britain,* a few of such travel books as Henry Swinburne's *Travels in the Two Sicilies,* Dominique Vivant Denon's *Travels in Upper and Lower Egypt . . . During the Campaigns of General Bonaparte,* the works of Laurence Sterne and Alexander Pope's translations of Homer.

One well-worn volume was *A Collection of Songs, Selected from the Works of Mr. Dibdin, to Which Are Added the Newest and Most Festive American Patriotic Songs.* On the rare occasions when Preble relaxed with his senior officers after a few glasses of wine, the commodore led a postprandial song or two in a voice that resounded from the beams of the flagship's cabin.

11. Later in the Mediterranean Preble would change his mind, writing to the secretary of the navy a prophetic commendation: "I have on board the *Constitution* many remarkable fine young men whose conduct promises great things for their country."

    In the meantime he held on to one controversial officer because of the man's age and experience. On assuming command of the *Constitution,* he was told by Secretary Smith that he might replace her sailing master, Nathaniel Haraden, who had not been sufficiently subservient. Preble wrote Smith, "I believe he is a good sailing master." As for Haraden's tendency to mild insubordination, Preble confidently added that "he will not attempt it under my command." Haraden kept a journal that provided much detail on the *Constitution*'s actions in the Mediterranean.

12. An incident en route to the Mediterranean impressed those young officers who were still trying to decide if Commodore Preble was more than a hot-tempered tyrant. The *Constitution* was off Cape Trafalgar on a dark night when her lookout reported a flashing light. Preble was on deck instantly, and when a large shape loomed against the horizon, running on a parallel course, he ordered everyone to battle stations. Through his speaking trumpet he hailed the vessel.

    "What ship is that?"

    There was no answer.

    Preble repeated his hail. Silence.

    Preble shouted, "I hail you for the last time. If you do not answer, I'll fire a shot into you."

    Finally there came a booming reply: "If you fire, I will return a broadside."

    Preble answered, "I'd like to see you do it. I now hail you for an answer. What ship is that?"

    "This is His Britannic Majesty's ship *Donegal,* 84 guns; Sir Richard Strahan, an English commodore. Send your boat on board."

    Preble jumped into the mizzen rigging and shouted, "This is the United States ship *Constitution,* 44 guns, Edward Preble, an American commodore, who will be damned before he sends his boat on board any vessel. Blow your matches, boys!"

    In the tense silence that followed, a boat was slung down from the British warship and rowed over to the *Constitution.* An officer climbed aboard, saluted the quarterdeck, and presented an apology from his captain. Actually, he explained, she was the 32-gun Royal Navy frigate *Maidstone.* Under Preble's terse questioning he admitted that her captain had delayed answering Preble's hail to give his men time to rush to their guns.

Preble accepted the apology and dismissed the British officer. The *Constitution*'s officers and men watched the boat return and exchanged smiles of relief and satisfaction. The Old Man had been quite ready to take on a ship of the line twice their size. And more to the point, the *Constitution* had been in battle readiness when the Royal Navy warship had not.

13. The gun carriages, it was later discovered, were the wrong size. U.S. Consul James Simpson reported to the secretary of state that they were for 12-pounder naval guns; the emperor's army used 18- and 24-pounders for his land guns. And one had been lost at sea. Simpson promised to ask for more, of the correct size. This foul-up may have been one reason for the emperor's pique.

14. Perhaps it was a sign of Preble's strict discipline that at Gibraltar a number of the *Constitution*'s sailors swam over to enlist on the nearest Royal Navy warship, many of them evidently, and ironically, Britons who had signed on the *Constitution* to avoid the harsh life of a British man-of-war. Preble tightened security aboard the flagship, and became suspicious when one Royal Navy vessel, the *Termagant*, anchored close to the *Constitution*—"I suppose with an intention of enticing our men to swim to them," Preble noted. He ordered a cutter stationed at night between the two warships to prevent more desertions, with only moderate success.

15. Emperor Muley Soliman was upset over the U.S. blockade of Tripoli, which was a market for Moroccan wheat. U.S. Consul Simpson in Tangier had argued for permitting Morocco to ship foodstuffs to Tripoli, but both Dale and Morris had disagreed, arguing that the blockade was intended to keep shipments out of Tripoli as well as Tripolitan warships in the harbor. But when Muley Soliman threatened war, Commodore Morris gave in, explaining to Secretary Smith in October of 1802, "Knowing the immense injury the commerce of the United States would receive from a war with Morocco, I have authorized . . . passports to vessels bound to Tripoli laden with wheat." Part of Morris's rationalization was that Tripoli had had a good crop that year anyway, so blockading food imports would have had little effect.

The brig accompanying the *Meshouda* was sold in Gibraltar, and her guns were added to the *Meshouda*'s armament when she left for Morocco.

16. Rodgers was 12 years younger than Preble but one step ahead of him on the list mainly because he had been promoted to captain after being the first lieutenant aboard the *Constellation* when she captured *L'Insurgent* in the Quasi War with France.

17. Preble had brought along the officers of the captured *Meshouda*, planning to send them ashore in Tangier to testify to their humane treatment aboard the *Constitution*. But they were enjoying their imprisonment in the flagship's officers' quarters and asked to remain aboard. Shortly Preble found that he had to station a marine guard over the Moroccan officers, "in consequence," explained Sailing Master Haraden, "of their attempting that unnatural crime of sodomy with the boys belonging to the *Constitution*."

18. Simpson had meanwhile assembled an array of gifts—silver tea services, silks, and linens—for the emperor, the governor, the Emperor's Sword-Bearer, his Umbrella-Bearer, his Chief Groom, and nine influential members of the court—at a cost of $1,100.

19. Governor Hashash was "punished" by a fine of 50,000 Moroccan ducats (about $42,000), which confiscated most of the fortune he had amassed in his privileged position. But he remained governor of Tangier, in which office he presumably would not take long to recoup.

20. In what would turn out to be an important decision, he changed captains, assigning the *Enterprise*'s Isaac Hull to the *Argus* and the *Argus*'s commander, Lieutenant Stephen Decatur, to the *Enterprise*.

21. The U.S. schooner *Vixen* was also searching for the *Constitution*, rushing westward with the bad news. But she encountered strong head winds and, tacking toward the Algerian coast, missed the flagship. Because she was running low on water and food, her commander, Lieutenant John Smith, turned back to Malta, where he found that the *Constitution* had put in, had picked up letters from the *Philadelphia*'s imprisoned Captain Bainbridge and had left for Syracuse. The *Constitution* just missed another storm, reaching Syracuse the next day. Still chasing her, the *Vixen* fought the storm for a month before finally catching up.

22. As Porter climbed back down, Ray later wrote, "Lt. P. looked much like the paper on which I am now blackening his name [presumably with no pun intended]."

23. In fact, the widest passage was only a few hundred yards farther along the reef. Had Bainbridge waited a couple more minutes before turning, he might have slipped through.

24. But Bainbridge forgot to destroy his personal papers, which later informed the bashaw of the disposition and details of the other warships in the American squadron. Fortunately for Bainbridge, Preble never discovered this oversight.

25. The *Philadelphia* was not the first ship of the U.S. Navy to surrender to the enemy. In the Quasi War with France the U.S. warship *Retaliation* had struck her colors to a French man-of-war off Guadelupe. Her commander also had been Bainbridge, whose sailors later nicknamed him "Bad Luck Billy."

26. The *Philadelphia*'s surgeon's mate, Dr. Jonathan Cowdery, was surprised when one Tripolitan took him by the hand and led him away from the melee—until he noticed that with the other hand the man was picking his pocket. He got about $10, Cowdery recorded, but missed some gold that the doctor had sewed into the lining of his uniform.

27. Ray claimed that Murad Reis later taunted some of the crew by asking if the captain were a coward or a traitor. "We answered, neither. He replied, 'Who with a frigate of forty-four guns and three hundred men would strike his colours to one solitary gun-boat must surely be one or the other"—conveniently overlooking the other gunboats that had been firing on the *Philadelphia*.

28. Indeed the *Vixen* would have given the Tripolitans pause and might even have helped pull the *Philadelphia* off the reef. At least she could have rescued the frigate's officers and crew. And meanwhile the *Vixen* on her patrol found no enemy warships.

29. Different headcounts have been given for the exact number of officers and men aboard the *Philadelphia* at the time. The ship's roster showed 33 officers, 235 seamen, and 41 marines—total: 309. Bainbridge wrote 306. But most other records of the imprisonment indicate 307.

30. Other reports also described it as lime juice.
31. Between the pages of a book he sent to his counterpart in Malta, who passed it on to Preble in Syracuse, Nissen explained the ruse. Preble quickly adopted it for his own secret messages to Bainbridge, thereby gaining an invaluable spy in the enemy's midst. As more secret messages passed back and forth, Preble was emboldened in one of them to toy with the censors by writing openly to Bainbridge, "I would have you attend to the *juice* of this letter and hope you will find it *sweet to the palate*." Still the bashaw's censors failed to catch on (no doubt because of a shaky command of English).

    At first, however, the messages went only one way, from Bainbridge to Preble. When in one of his letters Bainbridge complained about receiving no response from the commodore, Preble was puzzled because he had replied to all of Bainbridge's reports. He investigated and found a viper in his midst. A Maltese named Joseph Pulis was serving as U.S. consul in Malta. Unable to speak or read English, he had let a pile of correspondence accumulate in his office. Preble suspected more than neglect, and shortly discovered that Pulis had earlier been the Tripolitan consul in Malta.

    Confronting Pulis, Preble found not only his own letters to Bainbridge, which Pulis had not forwarded to the Danish consul in Malta for dispatch to Danish Consul Nissen in Tripoli, but also a number of messages from the secretary of the navy and letters from home addressed to the *Philadelphia* captives, which Pulis was about to return to the United States.

    Preble immediately wrote to Bainbridge explaining what had happened, made sure that his letters would get through, and attempted to revive Bainbridge's spirits: "Keep up a good heart and for God's sake do not despair. Your situation is bad indeed but I hope ere long it will be better."

    Reporting to Secretary Smith, Preble wrote that Pulis "has no respectability attached to his character." The commodore did not have the authority to dismiss a consul, but he appointed a Maltese businessman, William Higgins, as his own agent.
32. Reporting the *Philadelphia*'s loss to his wife, Mary, Preble gloomily wrote that Bainbridge and his crew "are slaves . . . without a prospect of ever again beholding their friends. I hope to God such will never be my fate! The thought of never again seeing you would drive me to distraction. I will not indulge it." Clearly he entertained no fear of being killed in action; indeed, the mortality of senior officers in the early nineteenth-century navy was extremely low.
33. Whatever he told Bainbridge, Preble remained convinced that the loss of the *Philadelphia* was Bainbridge's fault. When a few months later Preble's brother Eben delicately wrote that he had heard that "some slight censure falls on you for having sent this frigate to blockade Tripoli without a consort," Edward Preble answered angrily, "I sent the *Vixen* of sixteen 18-pounders, carronades, in company with her and wholly under the control of Captain Bainbridge, but he thought it proper to send her to look out off the island of Lampedusa. If he had kept her with him, it is probable he would have saved his ship."
34. Rumors reached Preble that the bashaw did not plan to use the *Philadelphia* in his own navy and instead proposed selling her to the bey of Tunis or the dey of Algiers. (In fact, a deal was struck in which the bashaw was to trade her to the bey for two 24-gun xebecs.) But a frigate was a major threat to the U.S. squadron in any Barbary navy, and indeed might tempt the bey or dey to consider joining the bashaw in declaring war against the United States.

CHAPTER 7

1. An older battery of cannon nearby was called "the English Fort" because it had been built mainly by British captives; a similar one west of the city, constructed by French slaves, was called "the French Fort."

2. A group of American prisoners delivering a large copper kettle to another harem met with a different reception. One of the women had to be prevented from attacking the prisoners; a guard explained that her husband had been killed by fire from the *Philadelphia* during its capture—a doubtful claim since the frigate's guns had not been brought to bear on her captors.

3. Three years later, in January of 1807, William Ray, back in the United States, wrote to Captain Bainbridge asking for his help in supplying information for the book Ray was writing on the imprisonment of the *Philadelphia*'s crew. Bainbridge was away on duty and did not reply. Ray's book, *Horrors of Slavery*, criticized Bainbridge for insensitivity to the plight of his crew. When he read it, Bainbridge was outraged, blaming Ray for reacting when his letter was not answered with "an ungrateful heart & unprincipled mind," and called him "an ungrateful wretch with no character to lose." Aware that Navy Secretary Smith would be sure to see the book, Bainbridge promptly wrote him claiming that Ray had written "infamous lies relative to the surrender of the Ship" in an account "replete with calumny & falsehood," and forwarded a file of letters from the prisoners to Bainbridge praising his efforts on their behalf. "He has accused me of a total disregard and derelection of the unfortunate crew in Tripoli," Bainbridge angrily wrote. "The following letters written by Ray himself for the crew, and which beyond doubt expressed his own sentiments at the time—will fully prove his falsehoods."

4. The ringleaders got word to Bainbridge, inviting him to join them if they completed their tunnel. Bainbridge declined, partly because he felt responsible for those who might not escape and partly because, like so many in the navy, he could not swim.

5. Eager for hands, American navy recruiters accepted Britons with few questions. There was also a brisk business in forged U.S. citizenship papers for foreign deserters.

6. Preble knew that his officers and men preferred British-run Malta, but characteristically noted, "I trust we will find amusement enough in the necessary duties of our ship."

7. As usual, Preble spared no time for visiting Syracuse's ancient and crumbling artifacts—a Greek and a Roman amphitheater, temples to the gods, and a statue of Venus recently unearthed by a Sicilian archaeologist. But some of the officers did, though they noted that many of the Greek and Roman marbles and mosaics were defaced with recent graffiti. On a hill near the city was a Capuchin monastery whose monks offered wine tastings; but the wine was not very good.

   Members of the faded Syracusan nobility eagerly entertained—and more eagerly sought entertainment from—the squadron's officers. One Baron Cannarella was caught stealing a couple of silver spoons, a glass, and some sugar at a dinner party given by Lieutenant Decatur. Most of the ordinary citizens were even less attractive to the Americans—shouting beggars following them everywhere, priests working ingenious swindles: "They pretended to show us," *Constitution* purser John Darby wrote, "a piece of dried flesh set in rich diamonds, which they said was a piece of Our Savior's hand."

But as might be expected, the U.S. Navy found that the women of Syracuse helped compensate for the city's drawbacks. The Americans quickly found that when they paraded by a local convent, they were greeted by handkerchief waving from pretty nuns (they claimed) sent to the convent by their strict Sicilian fathers. There was also the daily show of half-naked women washing their clothes in the stream below the Fountain of Aresthusa. Purser Darby wrote that "a breach of the marriage vow is no longer looked upon as one of the deadly sins," and noted that the comparatively wealthy Americans were particularly attractive to the local women.

While Preble spent most of his time off Tripoli, some U.S. Navy officers ashore in Syracuse behaved with such open arrogance that Governor de Gregorio finally sent an appeal to the commodore. By that time Preble had been relieved of command and could only promise to pass the request to his successor.

8. Preble knew that the Navy Department had ordered all prizes to be sent to the United States for condemnation. But he had no time for that lengthy process, and wrote Secretary Smith that he could not send her because "she is not a proper vessel to cross the Atlantic at this season of the year."

9. In another irony the elder Stephen Decatur made his name fighting the French, although *his* father, Etienne, had been a lieutenant in the French Navy who had gone to Newport, R.I., to escape a yellow-fever epidemic in the West Indies and had married a Newport girl, whose parents had insisted on his leaving the sea and settling in America.

The French lieutenant's son (and Stephen Decatur's father) made the first capture of a hostile warship by a vessel of the postwar U.S. Navy when he encountered the French *Croyable*, which had been harassing merchantmen off the U.S. coast. Commander of the sloop-of-war *Delaware*, he lured the *Croyable* to sea by pretending to run; only when the *Croyable* had caught up with him did her captain discover that the supposed merchantman was heavily armed. He tried to escape, but Decatur put a shot across the *Croyable*'s bow, and her captain surrendered. On the *Delaware*'s quarterdeck, watching the Stars and Stripes replace the Tricolor, the French captain muttered, "I wish she had sunk."

"She would have been," Decatur replied, "if you had stood on board and defended her."

10. Later in his career Decatur delivered a phrase that has come down the years in truncated form. At a dinner in his honor he gave a toast: "Our country. In her intercourse with foreign nations, may she always be in the right. But right or wrong, our country!"

11. A sixty-third man was added when our one sailor protested against being excluded. Decatur knew him to be a Quaker who, in the practice of the times, had been absolved from a minor infraction of the law on the condition that he serve in the navy. Questioned by Decatur, the 19-year-old Quaker refused to admit that he longed for action; but he was so insistent about not being left behind by his shipmates that Decatur let him join the expedition.

12. Evidently no one had remembered to stow the *Intrepid*'s anchor below; it was later claimed that the anchor alerted one of the Tripolitans, that Catalans was lying and that it was an American trick.

13. A ship's chain plates, extending down the side of the hull, help secure the standing rigging.

14. Surgeon's Mate Lewis Heerman, one of the boarding party, recalled that "the boarders hung on the ship's side like cluster bees; and in another instant, every man was on board the frigate."

15. Later some of those who boarded the frigate, especially pilot Catalano, claimed that they could have taken her out of the harbor. But the *Philadelphia*'s foremast was still a stump, which meant that she had no fore-and-aft headsails with which to tack out of the harbor against the onshore breeze. Even an offshore wind would have helped little. All of her upper yards were on deck, and she was stripped of her sails; there was no time to bend on new sails. With very little wind at the time, she never could have made it out of the harbor before being sunk by the bashaw's batteries. Nor could the *Intrepid* have towed her out of range in time. Bainbridge, who had studied her through his telescope, had written to Preble recommending to "set her on fire, the only thing to be attempted."

   On his return to the squadron Decatur reported to Preble that the frigate could not have been taken out of the harbor. (Oddly, Decatur's widow many years later wrote that her late husband *had* thought it possible to rescue the *Philadelphia*.) In any case, whether or not Decatur considered the possibility, his explicit orders from Commodore Preble were to set the frigate on fire.

16. Midshipman Morris later wrote a vivid description of the scene: "The appearance of the ship was indeed magnificent. The flames in the interior illuminated her ports and, ascending her rigging and masts, formed columns of fire, which, meeting the tops, were reflected into beautiful capitals."

   Nearly spellbound by the dazzling display, Surgeon's Mate Heerman reported, the men at the sweeps paused to shout and cheer. "But Captain D . . . leapt on the companion and, flourishing his sword, threatened to cut down the first man that was noisy after that."

17. That is, loaded and ready to fire with two cannonballs in each gun.

18. In the same vein Navy Secretary Smith wrote to Decatur forwarding President Jefferson's thanks to "each Individual of your gallant Band."

   And Admiral Nelson, who was aboard the *Victory* blockading the French Navy off Toulon when he heard of the burning of the *Philadelphia*, responded with a sample of the hyperbole he loved, calling it "the most bold and daring act of the age."

19. Lieutenant Stewart of the *Siren*, who was ahead of Decatur on the seniority list, was promoted to master commandant (between lieutenant and captain). And at Decatur's and Preble's recommendation Salvador Catalano, the *Intrepid*'s Sicilian pilot, was granted U.S. citizenship by Congress. Catalano later went to America and became a sailing master in the U.S. Navy.

20. Sterrett may also have been miffed because the ceremonial sword awarded to him by Congress had never arrived; Congress, it turned out, had voted to award it but had not voted the necessary appropriation.

   Secretary Smith tried in vain to calm Sterrett down, and accepted his resignation with sorrow: "Your high reputation as an Officer & a Seaman and your distinguished energy of character, might and probably would ultimately have raised you to the highest honors in the Navy." Sterrett's sword finally reached him after his resignation.

21. Ray and most of the other prisoners, unable to see the harbor, thought that a U.S. assault force was coming ashore to rescue them.

CHAPTER 8

1. There also was a rumor that Jefferson favored fellow Virginian Barron over Preble from Maine.
2. Izard was, however, permitted a short visit with Bainbridge (but with no other *Philadelphia* officer or sailor), and was alarmed at the captain's appearance; confinement had taken its toll. When Preble sent Bainbridge a note of commiseration, the reply confirmed Izard's impression. "I am quite thin," Bainbridge admitted, and rambled on despondently: "in spite of every effort of my own, and your good advice, I cannot prevent sad reflections; my character; my loss of services to my country! and my Family, are painful subjects to contemplate on in a close prison in Tripoli."
3. Secretary of State Madison was meanwhile expressing a similar opinion to Russian envoys. In a letter thanking the czar for also attempting to intercede, Madison made a point—no doubt at Jefferson's insistence—that "the measures taken by the Gov't of the United States, in consequence of the action at Tripoli, and which will be followed up with requisite vigor, promise to repair the loss, and to bring the Bashaw to proper terms of peace." The United States, in short, was quite capable of going it alone.
4. Preble bypassed the U.S. consul, a European named John S. M. Mathieu, a notorious ditherer who entangled American ship captains in red tape while he tried to make up his mind.
5. An incident at this time illustrated Preble's ulcerated anxiety. Nearing Malta on a run from Syracuse at 2:20 P.M. on June 5, the commodore was at dinner when a midshipman came below to report that the flagship was dangerously close to the island. Preble told him to order the helm over to tack out to sea, and went to the cabin window.

   The *Constitution* was under full sail before a fresh breeze. As she swung ponderously into the wind to come about, he saw that she was nearly on the beach. "I sprang on deck," he reported, "and found her in stays [headed into the wind and pausing before turning through it] not a cable's length from the shore, and the Rocks to be seen under her Bottom." Grabbing the speaking trumpet from the officer of the deck, one Lieutenant Tarbell, Preble ordered him below and took charge. Slowly the frigate eased over onto the other tack and moved away from the shore.

   It was a close call—and the *Constitution* was still the only U.S. frigate in the Mediterranean; "had she missed stays or shot her length further a head in stays," Preble wrote, "she would inevitably have struck the Rocks and probably would have been lost, as she was under a great press of canvas with a fresh Breeze."

   Preble got the frigate away from the beach, went below, and wrote an angry note to the officer of the deck. "Sir: The imminent danger which you a few moments since ran this ship into, either through neglect or want of Judgement obliges me to withdraw my confidence in you, so far as to consider it imprudent that you should in future be intrusted with the charge of a watch on board her as her loss would involve incalculable consequence to the U.S.—You will therefore consider yourself as a supernumerary untill ordered to some other Vessel of less consequence."

Three days later, after a petition from the *Constitution*'s officers arguing that the local pilot, not the officer of the deck, was to blame, Preble reinstated Tarbell. It was one of the occasions when Preble's Boys learned that the Old Man could be forgiving as well as strict. Tarbell, Preble concluded, had learned a frightening lesson. The pilot was fired.

6. The attack force:

Frigate *Constitution* (44 guns)
Brig *Argus*** (18 guns)
Brig *Siren* (18 guns)
Brig *Scourge* (16 guns)
Schooner *Vixen* (16 guns)
Schooner *Nautilus* (16 guns)
Schooner *Enterprise* (12 guns)

7. He was the first U.S. commodore to issue such detailed battle orders, spelling out in detail the position of each warship in a concentrated attack on the enemy.

8. A *Philadelphia* prisoner reported that the bashaw had invited a party to the castle roof to watch his gunboats disperse the Americans. With the squadron's cannonballs and bomb shells whistling over their heads, the bashaw and his guests made a hasty retreat to the castle cellar.

9. This was the incident that became a popular story and illustration in many boys' books on the Barbary War. Later there was a dispute over whether the sailor who saved Decatur's life had been Fraser or a shipmate named Reuben James. But Fraser, who survived the war, spent his declining years regaling his listeners with his account of the battle on the deck, stoutly maintaining that he had been the one to step in the way of the Turk's nearly lethal blow.

10. At least that is the navy legend, no doubt somewhat exaggerated. There has always been some question, however, whether or not it was the same gunboat whose captain had shot James Decatur.

11. Describing the battle to a friend later, Decatur revealed a wry sense of humor: "I had eighteen Italians in the boat with me, who claim the honor of the day. While we were fighting, they prayed. They are convinced we would not have been so fortunate unless their prayers had been heard. This might have been the case."

12. Shortly Preble went to his cabin, got his temper under control, sent for Decatur, and apologized.

13. When after the battle it was discovered that Blake's gunboat had fired only two rounds of ball and six of grape, he was held in scorn by many of his fellow officers. A purser wrote in his journal that Blake "is now publickly called a coward by the officers of the Squadron." Blake protested that it was

---

*While the fleet had been towing the Italian gunboats to Tripoli, the *Argus*, at Preble's order, had left her station in the western Mediterranean to join the blockaders.

not his fault, and asked Preble to relieve him from the gunboat forces rather "than to continue under a Suspicious Eye." Preble transferred him to the *Argus* under the guiding hand of Isaac Hull.

14. In the excitement no one remembered to haul down the gunboat's Tripolitan flag, so when the vessel emerged from the clouds of smoke and approached the fleet with her prize crew, the *Vixen* let go a broadside that brought down the flag by dismasting her. The Americans aboard the gunboat shouted their identification just in time before the *Vixen*'s next broadside.

15. Aided by Mrs. John Cannon, wife of the boatswain, who was enthusiastically assisting on deck throughout the action.

16. One of the rare signs that Preble had a sense of sarcastic humor.

17. After the battle some of the naval officers expressed the opinion that gunboat no. 9 had exploded because a piece of smoldering gun wadding had dropped into the powder magazine.

18. Preble promoted Spence to lieutenant and Kennedy to midshipman. Kennedy, who later commanded a fleet, became a rarity: a nineteenth-century sailor who rose all the way through the ranks to commodore.

19. The shells had fuses that were timed to set them off like bombs as they reached their target. Bainbridge claimed that only one of the 41 shells fired that afternoon had exploded. But, confined in his cell, he was in no position to judge. Still, it was clear that the fuses of many shells had failed.

    None of the officers or men of the U.S. squadron had had experience with these flying bombs, though the Neapolitans loaned to the squadron included one Don Antonio Massi who was supposed to train the Americans. Perhaps the other Neapolitans were no great experts either.

    The shells had been provided by the Neapolitans along with the bomb ketches, and scuttlebutt had it that when the shells had been manufactured for use against the French, they had been sabotaged by French spies. Indeed, when Preble examined the remaining shells, he found some with lead packed into the fuse holes.

20. A rank between lieutenant and captain.

21. A warship with her guns dismounted was said to be *en flute* because her empty gunports made her hull look like a flute.

22. The *John Adams* leaked as much as eight inches an hour and yawed badly. Chauncey reported that "we sometimes took a yaw of fifty or sixty miles before we could stop her, and then away she go as far the other way." Because of her condition Secretary Smith expected the later-sailing frigates to catch up with her by the time she reached the Mediterranean.

23. He also took the occasion to make what he considered a formidable threat. He informed the French consul that the United States intended to support Hamet Karamanli in an expedition to overthrow his usurping brother the bashaw. "Mr. Eaton," Preble wrote, "comes out in the Frigate [en route at the time] for that purpose, and brings out arms and ammunition, artillery and cash to enable him [Hamet] to regain the throne of Tripoli—I can assure you, this is a fact, and I have no objection to your acquainting the minister."

24. When Consul O'Brien had come ashore attempting to negotiate, the bashaw had angrily charged that Preble's real reason for sending emissaries into the harbor was to spy on its installations. In fact, Midshipman Charles Morris had discovered during one of these missions a spot near the western entrance

where the bomb ketches would be protected by rock outcroppings. Preble chose this location for the bomb ketches during the attack in the early morning of August 28.

25. The only injury to the American crew came, oddly, a week later when one of the flagship's staysails was loosed and a large chunk of Tripolitan grapeshot that had lodged in the folds fell to the deck and nearly flattened a sailor's foot.

26. She was transporting the sultan's ambassador, who every five years called on the rulers of each city-state for the formality of reappointing them as representatives of the Ottoman Empire.

27. Other, later reports from the city, however, claimed less damage, with nearly all of the American shells falling short of their targets. (And of course the bashaw had plenty of slaves, some of them *Philadelphia* sailors, to make repairs.) But the attackers thought otherwise. The *Constitution*'s sailing master, Nathaniel Haraden, usually a reliable observer, maintained that the bombardment had even blasted open a 40-foot hole in the bashaw's castle.

28. Somers had come to the Mediterranean in the *Boston*, commanded by the erratic Captain Daniel McNeill. When McNeill had been ordered home and had taken the *Boston* with him, Somers had stayed on with the squadron. James Fenimore Cooper, who joined the navy in 1808, met many of Somers's shipmates who, according to Cooper, described the young lieutenant as "a warm-hearted friend, amiable and mild in his ordinary associations, a trained seaman, and a good officer."

   Somers and Stephen Decatur became close friends. When six of their fellow officers insulted Somers, who impulsively challenged all six to a gang duel, Decatur became his second. The duels took place at Sicily. In the first Somers was shot in the right arm. He refused to give up. His second adversary wounded him in the hip. Still insisting on meeting his third, Somers sat on the dueling ground with Decatur beside him holding his right arm. No doubt with Decatur's better marksmanship the third opponent fell. The other three had no stomach for further bloodshed, and Decatur persuaded Somers that his honor had been vindicated. Somers quickly recovered and returned to action.

29. Wadsworth, who had been enjoying the favors of the women of Syracuse, had missed out on the burning of the *Philadelphia* because he had been in the hospital with a venereal disease. "The Devil, or rather my own imprudence," he wrote, "had decreed against me. I was too weak to walk."

30. Another account claims that Israel stowed away and did not reveal his presence until it was too late to send him back.

31. In the autumn of 1805 Bainbridge, released from his Tripolitan prison, read the published comment by Preble, was incensed at what he considered an implied rebuke for his surrender of the *Philadelphia*, and wrote to Preble saying so. Preble managed to mollify him by responding politely, if disingenuously, regretting any such insinuation. "I now declare that neither the expressions which have offended you nor any other made use of in my dispatches were ever intended to reflect, in any degree whatever, either on yourself or [your] officers. . . . The situation of yourself and Somers were very different. I never conceived that you were at liberty to destroy the lives of your officers and crew by blowing up your ship. . . . I value your friendship and should regret that any circumstances should occur to deprive me of it."

Preble was of course fortunate that Bainbridge never saw Preble's immediate reaction in his report to the secretary of the navy: "Would to God that the officers and crew . . . had one and all determined to prefer death to slavery." Secretary Smith had kept this outburst confidential.

32. The *President* had made a fast 15-day crossing to the Azores. But from there on she had fought contrary winds, reaching Gibraltar 37 days from Hampton Roads.

33. Preble, who had urged Decatur's promotion to captain, now wrote to him, "I feel a peculiar pleasure in leaving the *Constitution* under the command of an officer, whose enterprise and manly conduct in battle I have so often witnessed, and whose merit emminently entitles him to so handsome a command. May you ever continue in the pursuit of glory and be crowned with success."

But for Decatur it was a short-lived command. On November 7 Barron ordered him to relinquish the *Constitution* to Captain John Rodgers, who was senior to Decatur, and to replace Rodgers in the smaller *Congress*.

34. Preble sensed that the Napoleonic War was having its effect on the Barbary War. Writing to his friend Decatur, he reported that Acton had agreed as before but that the king had not. "Some more powerful Interest than ours has been the cause," he wrote. "I believe the French have had a hand in the business." Apparently British hospitality to and support for the U.S. squadron in the Mediterranean was angering the French, on the well-known diplomatic assumption that "my enemy's friend is my enemy."

35. A New England Federalist—though nearly apolitical—Preble found that he liked Thomas Jefferson; he later referred to him as "the Chief Magistrate of our nation, whom I esteem and venerate."

36. To his wife, Mary, still awaiting his arrival, he wrote, "I cannot but be a little flattered with the reception I have met with here. The people are disposed to think that I have rendered some service to my country."

37. He had, of course, originally chosen Preble as Mediterranean squadron commodore over John Rodgers, who was one place ahead of him on the seniority list.

Another excuse, which Smith mentioned in his letter relieving Preble of command, was that Congress had mandated that all frigates be commanded by captains; thus the navy could not send any of the new frigates to the Mediterranean with lieutenants on their quarterdecks—which meant using a captain senior to Preble. But the *John Adams* had sailed under the command of Master Commandant Isaac Chauncey, who would not be promoted to captain until 1806. Perhaps that was one reason why the *John Adams* was being used as a transport and supply ship.

38. Smith was popular with many of the navy's senior officers, whom he treated with fairness and consideration. But he also had his critics, one of whom characterized him as "beyond his depth even in tranquil waters." He remained navy secretary into the administration of President James Madison, when he was forced out of office by Treasury Secretary Gallatin, no friend of the navy, who accused him of misuse of government funds.

39. Jefferson endured much public ridicule over his "gunboat navy," but he persevered, and by 1807 had won congressional authorization for 257 of these craft. They were disbanded as useless in the open-ocean warfare of the War of

1812, but half a century later steam-driven gunboats played an important part in the river battles of the Civil War.

40. He had purchased some hunting dogs in Sicily on his way home, but they had died during the winter crossing of the Atlantic.

41. During a visit to Boston the crusty commodore wrote home, "I long to see you and our darling boy. Every morning when I awake my imagination presents him to me, laid by my side on a pillow, smiling and innocent as an angel."

42. Edward Preble's recipe for his special cider (as written to a friend): "Put into each barrel [of apple cider] one quart of French brandy, one pound brown sugar, and the whites of six eggs. Beat to a froth, roll it over a few times, then place in a quiet situation and in a fortnight or sooner it will be sufficiently refined for drawing. And if placed in a cool cellar, well bunged-up and vents stopped, it will keep good for two years."

43. Among the Prebles' Portland neighbors were Mr. and Mrs. Stephen Longfellow and their son (named after one of Preble's Boys), Henry Wadsworth Longfellow. The mansion Preble was building when he died still stands at the corner of Congress and Preble Streets.

44. In a farewell letter to his wife written in Boston Harbor while waiting for the head winds to turn so he could be off to the Mediterranean, Preble had been prayerful: "May the Great God protect and preserve your precious life and health, and to Him do I commend both you and myself. May He in His mercy grant that we may again meet and be long happy in each other's society." After his return they had only two and a half years together.

Mary Deering, heiress to a wealthy Portland shipping family, had been in her early thirties when she married Edward Preble. A handsome woman with blue eyes, brown curls—and a will of iron—she was quite able to stand up to her husband's bursts of temper; her relatives called her "the Grenadier" (but not to her face). Yet as her husband's funeral procession, with his sword atop the black-clothed coffin, proceeded to the cemetery, she fainted and had to be revived in a neighbor's house. She survived her husband by 40 years.

CHAPTER 9

1. His Dartmouth classmates also recalled a couple of examples of Eaton's sophomoric sense of humor. When asked by the college to deliver a new bell, he slung it under his carriage and went clanging through the town. Asked why, he explained to a friend, "I felt *bell*igerent." And when a faculty member questioned his caper, Eaton replied, "I did not forget, sir, I was a member of Dartmouth's *belles*-lettres society."

2. One of Gaither's subordinates scornfully characterized the colonel as "an ignorant, debauched, unprincipled old bachelor." Gaither appeared to be in league with speculators seizing lands from the Indians and was understandably reluctant to have his activities reported to headquarters by an underling.

3. Eaton replaced Joseph Etienne Famin, a Frenchman who had been serving as U.S. consular agent since the treaty with Tunis. Eaton soon found Famin conspiring against him, obviously upset at the loss of a post he had turned to

his financial advantage. Eaton's direct, hardly diplomatic response was to horsewhip Famin in public. The bey, instead of being angry, was amused, though he later pretended that it had been one of Eaton's actions that had made him unacceptable as a consul.

4. This was one reason for Eaton's debts, which so embarrassed Commodore Morris. Eaton also, it later turned out, impulsively spent $12,000 to ransom a Sardinian woman, Countess Maria Anna Porcile, who had been captured and consigned to the harem of Tunis's aged prime minister.

5. Bey Hamouda had taken in Hamet's father and mother; both had died in Tunis. But Hamouda now began to fear the wrath of Yusuf if he continued to shelter Hamet.

6. Perhaps because he had just been ordered to return home, he knew he had no time for such an adventure and was apprehensive over the reception awaiting him at Washington.

7. Eaton's thoughtless anti-Semitism was no worse than that of many nine-teenth-century Americans.

8. The French consul in Tripoli, Bonaventure Beaussier, who worked tirelessly as a middleman to negotiate an agreement to release the *Philadelphia*'s pris-oners, later claimed that he and Foreign Minister Dghies had concealed from the bashaw Preble's threat of American support for Hamet. But the bashaw clearly had already found out from his own sources.

9. Samuel Barron had served in the Mediterranean, had returned home, and had just finished presiding over the navy hearings that had censured ex-Com-modore Morris.

10. Barron was also the first of the American commodores in the Mediterranean to have his own captain (George Cox) aboard his flagship.

11. For reasons best known to himself Hull always claimed that he had been born in 1775 and therefore was two years younger than his actual age.

12. At 18 Isaac wrote to his father, "I having an opertunity of riting to let you no that I enjoy my health." His spelling improved somewhat in later life, but not a great deal.

13. On her arrival in the Mediterranean under the command of Stephen Decatur in November of 1803, Preble wrote Secretary Smith that the *Argus* was "without exception the handsomest vessel of her rate that I have ever seen. She is very much and very justly admired by every Officer." And Midship-man Henry Wadsworth wrote home, "The *Argus* is universally allowed to be the finest vessel floating upon the Mediterranean."

14. In a report to the navy secretary on the *Argus*, Preble also commended the "judgment, prudence and firmness of her Commander Lieut. Hull on whose discretion I rely with confidence."

Barron, the new commodore, could thank the diplomacy of Secretary Smith for Hull's presence in the Mediterranean, or even in the navy. In 1802, when Hull was first lieutenant of the frigate *Adams* and Hugh Campbell was appointed her captain, Hull reacted in an uncharacteristic outburst, writing to the secretary in protest at being passed over and submitting his resignation.

Smith replied by chiding Hull that his action was "unfortunate for the Government and not very honorable to yourself." But in a more mollifying tone he conceded, "I know what the feelings of military men are, and that among them there always exists a jealousy on the subject of rank; this jealousy is by no means an improper one, but it sometimes leads men into hasty & intemperate decisions, incompatible with their own honor."

Smith explained that Hull had been posted as lieutenant aboard the *Adams* because Edward Preble had originally been chosen as commander; because of Preble's illness the navy needed "one of the ablest Lieutenants in the service," adding, "We had no other officers in the country . . . I could so confidently rely on. . . ."

Smith's letter achieved its purpose. Hull withdrew his resignation. The *Adams* sailed for the Mediterranean on June 10, 1802, and had an uneventful voyage until she nearly went aground off the Barbary Coast.

Hull was awakened in his bunk by the cry of "Breakers ahead!" and rushed on deck to find Captain Campbell dithering as the ship bore down on the wave-lashed shore. "Do you see the rocks? Do you see the rocks?" Campbell kept shouting.

With no time for the niceties of naval rank, the lieutenant told the captain, "Keep yourself cool, sir, and the ship will be got off." Hull took the speaking trumpet and called out the orders to get the ship around and off the shore. Only then did he take time to put on the trousers he had grabbed on his dash to the deck.

15. O'Bannon had left a bride in the United States when he had sailed to the Mediterranean, where he earned a shore-leave reputation as a man who attracted the local women.

16. Also aboard was Eli Danielson, Eaton's stepson, a midshipman who happened to be serving aboard the *Argus*. Whether or not this had been arranged through Eaton's influence is not known.

17. Mendrici had been physician to the bey of Tunis, and had been fired because of his intimate bedside manner with one of the bey's wives.

18. After so many months Eaton was not sure that Hamet would even remember him. He wrote:

Excellency:

I am the American Consul who made an agreement with your Excellency previously to your departure from Tunis to Malta. I have since been home: my Government have approved of my conduct; and I am now come out to fulfill my promises. Let me know how I can communicate with your Excellency, without embroiling myself with the Grand Signior [the viceroy], whom I honor and respect. America is at peace with all the world, except your brother Joseph [Yusuf]: we will never make peace with him.

> I am your Excellency's
> sincere friend,
> William Eaton
> Agent-General of the United
> States of America for the
> Barbary States

19. To make matters worse, Eaton had heard that Yusuf had sent hired assassins to Egypt to kill Hamet.

20. Leitensdorfer had a colorful background. His parents, who named him Gervasso Prodasio Santuari when he was born in October of 1772, intended him

to be a Catholic priest. But the young man gave up a theological career to get married, then left his wife to join the Austrian Army. While fighting the French, he deserted to the enemy, assuming the name of Carlo Hossondo. Arrested by the French as a spy while serving in Switzerland, he managed to acquire some opium, which he used on his guards to escape.

He became an itinerant peddler of watches, traveling through Switzerland, France, and Spain. Boldly reenlisting in the French Army (whose records seem to have been in disarray), he followed Napoleon to Egypt, where he deserted again to join the British Army. Soon he was running a coffee shop for British Army officers in Alexandria, making enough money to buy a house and marry a Coptic girl, conveniently ignoring the fact that he had left a wife at home. Branching out, he also managed a theater for the British Army. When the British left Egypt, he deserted his Coptic wife, sailed to Messina, and entered a monastery as a novice Capuchin friar.

Shortly he left the monastery to wander on to Smyrna and Constantinople, where he was making a precarious living as a magician when he discovered that an officer under whom he had served in the French Army was now that country's ambassador. He fled into the Turkish Army, which sent him to Egypt, where he promptly deserted and joined a band of Bedouins.

He next turned up in Constantinople again (where he was careful to avoid the French ambassador) and converted to Islam, circumcising himself with his razor. He joined an order of dervishes, taking yet another name, Murat Aga, and set out along the shores of the Black Sea selling scraps of paper bearing quotations from the Koran.

Because dervishes were known for their healing powers, Murat Aga found himself summoned to the court of the bashaw of Trebizond and commanded to treat the aged monarch's failing eyesight. With an impromptu display of incantations, he blew caustic lime into the bashaw's eyes, washed them with milk, proclaimed his patient cured, and swiftly departed with his gifts before the bashaw could realize that he had been defrauded. Aga joined a caravan, which shortly was ambushed; but in the course of the robbery he overheard one of the brigands regaling his comrades with a tale about a dervish who had cured the bashaw of Trebizond's blindness. He returned even more quickly than he had departed, and was rewarded handsomely by the grateful bashaw.

Soon he was on the road again, joining a pilgrimage to Mecca, then moving on to Jidda, where he decided to become an ex-dervish when offered a job as interpreter for Lord Gordon, a traveling Scot with whom he visited Abyssinia, Nubia, and Cairo, where he deserted again to return to Alexandria. The wife he had left was waiting for him—to ask for a divorce, which he gallantly granted. Then he heard that an American was in Cairo looking for foreign legionnaires. He hurried there, presented himself to Eaton as Eugene Leitensdorfer, and offered his services. Eaton asked him for help in locating Hamet in his Egyptian hideout. And when Leitensdorfer helped reunite them, Eaton gratefully responded by appointing Leitensdorfer his adjutant, in effect his chief of staff.

21. Evidently many of the Mamelukes expressed interest in joining Hamet's expedition, no doubt lured by the prospect of plunder. Eaton reported to Secretary Smith that the local Mameluke chieftain, Osman Bey Berdici, put at least 30 would-be followers in chains to prevent a wholesale defection when he discovered that Hamet had left to join Eaton.

22. It was said that a chief reason the viceroy tried to help Eaton rescue Hamet and supported the expedition against Tripoli was to rid himself of yet another potential troublemaker in Egypt.

23. O'Bannon was clearly regarded aboard the *Argus* as a raconteur. In a letter to Eaton in Cairo Hull wrote, "Tell Mr. O'Bannon all his shipmates are well and very anxious to hear his description of the Nile." They obviously anticipated that O'Bannon's adventure would lose nothing in the telling.

24. Not until recent years have military historians established the names of the marines accompanying O'Bannon:

Acting Sgt. Arthur Campbell
Pvt. Bernard O'Brian
Pvt. David Thomas
Pvt. James Owens
Pvt. John Whitten
Pvt. Edward Steward

The name of the eighth marine in the contingent remains unknown.

25. Midshipman Eli Danielson, Eaton's stepson who had accompanied him to Cairo, went back aboard the *Argus*. Certainly he could have joined the march to Tripoli if Eaton had insisted, and there can be little doubt that Danielson wanted to. Perhaps Eaton, considering the dangers ahead, forbade him to.

26. In English variously spelled el Taiib, el Tayib, il Tayib, il Tahib, etc.

CHAPTER 10

1. In his biography of Eaton, Francis Rennell Rodd traces each leg of the long march and makes a good case that Eaton's estimate of mileage was off by a few miles in his earliest entries.

2. On some days the supply caravan, usually accompanied by one or two of O'Bannon's marines to make sure they did not desert, straggled as many as 15 miles behind the lead column.

3. Although Cowdery did not specify which son-in-law, it probably was Grand Admiral Murad Reis.

4. How O'Bannon had failed to notice the missing buttons at daily inspection is not explained. Perhaps the marines carried extra buttons in their kits. Eaton later wrote that the exchanges between the marines and the local girls were detected when someone noticed the women wearing necklaces made of brass buttons.

    There evidently were other exchanges, or at least attempts. Eaton's interpreter was attracted to a Bedouin girl in the marketplace whose parents offered her to him for a sack of rice. Eaton apparently inspected her, because he wrote that the girl "was a well-proportioned, handsome brownette of about thirteen or fourteen years, with an expressive hazel eye inclining to black, arched eyebrows, perfect teeth, and lips formed for voluptuousness. —A bargain would have been concluded if my consent could have been accorded; prudence forbade it."

5. Nevertheless Eaton was given to frequent anti-Semitic remarks about the Jews of the Barbary Coast, perhaps partly because of their influence in the money markets and his constant need for loans.

6. Eaton wrote in his journal—and then crossed it out—that the matrons would "perform the office of examining her ability for this final ceremony, and in fact prepare the ground for easy access by artificial operations. The husband has three other wives for his amusement."

7. In his journal that night Eaton wrote, "Some of the Bashaw's officers exclaimed 'For God's sake do not fire! The Christians are our friends!'" No doubt their exclamations suffered in translation.

8. Lieutenant O'Bannon later recounted a more colorful version of the mutiny. Eaton, he recalled, handed him his rifle, pistols, and scimitar before approaching the rebellious Arabs, so O'Bannon became concerned when Eaton disappeared into the milling horde. O'Bannon considered charging the Arabs but held back because he realized they could kill Eaton before he could reach him.

After the mutiny had subsided, O'Bannon claimed, Eaton told him that he had derided Hamet and his followers as women afraid of battle, who would rather turn back than have the glory of capturing Derna. At that, Eaton supposedly told O'Bannon, Hamet broke down and sobbed, as did some of his Arabs. Before Eaton could lead Hamet away, O'Bannon said, some of the Arabs lifted their "general" onto their shoulders and paraded about until he demanded to be put down.

After the talk with Hamet, according to O'Bannon, Eaton summoned two of the Arab ringleaders to his tent, informed them that they had broken a cardinal military law and would have to pay the price, at which he swiftly decapitated both of them with his scimitar. He then displayed their dripping heads on pikes as a warning to the rest of the Arabs.

O'Bannon's account has the true flavor of the hero-worshiping marine. Eaton, he said, performed "this grisly act with a tranquility of spirit astonishing in one who so frequently displayed a tenderness to all his fellow human beings." But it is unlikely that Eaton himself would have omitted such dramatic scenes from the account in his journal.

That evening, according to O'Bannon, he chided Eaton for his rash bravery in walking unarmed into the midst of the hostile Arabs. "Such action, I told him, was not courage but foolhardiness of the blindest and most stubborn sort." Eaton's response, O'Bannon recalled, was to laugh and raise his sleeves to reveal two knives strapped to his forearms. Again, it is difficult to believe that Eaton did not mention this subterfuge in his journal. In any case, two knives, even in the unusually accurate hands of Eaton, would hardly have stemmed the mob of Arabs had they attacked.

9. Eaton's journal is not clear about which day his army met these Arabs; he mentions them only after his arrival at Bomba.

CHAPTER 11

1. From Pope Pius VII came a statement that carried great weight in the Christian European nations that had been implacably opposed to Muslims in the

Mediterranean ever since the Crusades. "The American commander," Pius wrote of Preble, "with a small force and in a short space of time, has done more for the cause of Christianity than the most powerful nations of Christendom have done for ages."

Pius VII may also have been making a sideswipe at Napoleon, with whom he had had a running battle for more than a decade. It was Pius VII from whose hands Napoleon had grabbed the crown to place on his own head in the famous coronation scene the same year. Pius also expressed great interest in the new United States of America (and no doubt in the missionary possibilities there for the Church of Rome).

2. She had just arrived in the Mediterranean under the command of Lieutenant John Dent, who called her "one of the finest vessels of her class in any service." When Lieutenant Evans was given command of the *Hornet*, Dent was transferred to the *Nautilus*.

3. He may have been one of the men who reported to Eaton that there were American ships waiting at Bomba.

4. The occasional misspellings were the fault of one of Barron's aides; the ailing commodore was dictating all his correspondence.

5. It is an interesting coincidence that at about the time Barron was writing this letter Hamet was telling Eaton in his desert tent that he suspected the Americans of using him as a foil to strike a deal with his brother.

6. Glenn Tucker, in his excellent book on the Barbary War, *Dawn Like Thunder*, correctly points out that marines could have been much more effective in Eaton's army than aboard ship during a bombardment of Derna, and questions Barron's orders that restricted Eaton to only eight marines in an ambitious land campaign against Tripoli.

7. The single piece of artillery Eaton's army had started out with evidently had been lost or abandoned somewhere in the desert.

8. Private John Whitten was killed in action; Private Edward Steward died of his wounds two days later. Privates David Thomas and Bernard O'Brian were wounded but survived. Perhaps significantly, Eaton reported 12 other Christians killed but made no mention of Arab casualties.

9. In his report to the commodore Eaton made a point of praising Hull and his naval officers: "I would be going out of my sphere to comment on the conduct of naval commanders in the field. Yet I should do violence to my own sense of duty & obligation were I not to observe they could not have taken better positions for their vessels nor managed their fire with more skill and advantage."

   But he reserved his highest praise for Lieutenant O'Bannon: "The detail I have given [in his account of the battle] of Mr. O'Bannon's conduct needs no encomium. —And it is believed the disposition our government have always discovered to encouragement will be extended to this intrepid, judicious and enterprising officer." Nor did Eaton forget Midshipman Mann: "Mr. Mann's conduct is equally meritorious."

10. From Fort Enterprise Eaton sent a gloating message to Hull: "The Enemy are shamefully flogged, we have collected twenty of their heads, besides those you killed."

11. A manifest in the Eaton papers in the Huntington Library listing some of the goods "delivered from on board the United States Brig Argus to William

Eaton," indicates the city's need for clothing, especially turbans.

May 15. A Bale containing
   40 pieces striped glazed cotton cloth
   2 pieces blue linen
   26 pieces white linen
   10 pieces cotton hand kerchiefs
   A Bale containing
   49 pieces white linen
   20 pieces striped linen
   42 bundles thread
   32 Silk Turbans
May 17 a Chest containing
   10 pieces Silk
   25 Silk Turbans
   9 pair Shoes
   6 check Shawls
   2 White Silk Turbans
   A Chest containing
   2 white turbans
   13 red Caps
   5 pair Shoes
   6 gun Locks
   2 muskets

12. The copy among the Eaton papers in the Huntington Library is dated "April 29." The *Hornet* with Barron's letter did not reach Derna until June 1. Presumably Eaton meant May 29 and in his distress wrote the wrong date. He had made a similar mistake before in his journal. Still, how could he be answering a letter three days before receiving it?

   A likely answer is offered by Francis Rennel Rodd (who gives the date as May 28) in his book *General William Eaton*. The news must have reached Derna from Tripoli that Bashaw Yusuf was negotiating with Consul Lear. Actually, because no U.S. warships returned to Malta or Syracuse immediately, Eaton continued to add to his letter for nearly two more weeks.

13. The stilted phraseology of Eaton's letter to Barron is unlike the straightforward entries in his journal. Evidently he felt it might help convince Barron if he resorted to the sort of pretentious prose the commodore used in his own dispatches. And Eaton's handwriting in this letter is neater than in his journal; clearly he considered this one of the most important documents of his career.

14. On the 7th, however, Hassen learned as Eaton had that money and Arabs could be a bad combination. Just as some of Eaton's camel drivers had disappeared as soon as they had been paid, Hassen's deputy, put in charge of the money chest, absconded with it to Egypt.

15. Captain Campbell was one of the navy officers who disapproved of Eaton's expedition. When Eaton came aboard the *Constellation* at Derna, Campbell coldly informed the "general" that all he could provide for him was a cot.

CHAPTER 12

1. In his journal on October 20, 1804, William Eaton made an entry suggesting that Lear was hardly a devotee of Jefferson. Consul General Richard O'Brien, whom Lear replaced, once regaled Eaton, according to the journal, with a curious and not entirely believable scene that O'Brien claimed Lear had described to him. After becoming president, Jefferson asked Lear to be his secretary of state, to which Lear claimed he replied, "Do you suppose, Sir, that I would accept this appointment to serve under you! No, Sir, I will not abandon my principles for any preferment that is within your gift— Confer your favors on devotees who count them—but leave me to enjoy my purity of conscience and my independence of mind, that while I pity your weakness I may despise your administration!"

   Almost surely this expostulation became exaggerated as it was passed along. It does not sound like the pragmatic, crafty Tobias Lear. Eaton's reaction was more characteristic: "If this be true, it is manly— If it is false it is not out of character."

2. When the scuttlebutt had reached the Mediterranean that Preble was being considered as secretary of the navy, Decatur had written to congratulate him and had reported on Lear's direction of the negotiations, no doubt reflecting his own as well as Commodore Rodgers's dismay. Preble replied, "That a Col. should command our Squadron as you inform me must be a matter most of surprise . . . abroad as well as at home."

3. Discouraged by the refusal of King Ferdinand to supply gunboats, Barron had discounted the efforts of Master Commandant Thomas Robinson, who had been searching for more of them in the Adriatic. Barron did not yet know that Robinson had just concluded a deal for four gunboats and two other small warships. Meanwhile nine gunboats and two merchantmen converted into bomb ketches were on their way across the Atlantic from the United States. All but one, which was lost with all hands, would make it to the Mediterranean. But they arrived too late; even the message from Washington announcing their departure did not reach Barron until May 26, when preliminary peace talks were already under way.

4. In his prison journal Dr. Cowdery reported an encounter with Yusuf that included a more sinister threat. The bashaw, he wrote, "swore by the prophet of Mecca, that if the Americans brought his brother against him, he would burn to death all the American prisoners except me; that my life would be spared, because I saved the life of his child when very sick. He went off in a great passion and mounted his horse."

   Cowdery also recorded a somewhat lighter note: Yusuf had not yet sent his harem and children into the countryside because they were pleading that they would rather fall into the hands of the Americans than the rebellious Arabs outside the capital.

5. Although Baron may not have known it, the governor of Benghazi had joined Hassen's forces attempting to retake Derna.

6. The clumsy punctuation evidently indicated Barron's illness and muddled state of mind in May of 1805 as he dictated and read his correspondence.

   And Barron's conscience was bothering him. Quite aware that President Jefferson had approved Eaton's project, he was preparing his case against

Eaton's angry accusations of breaking faith with Hamet. In the same letter to Lear, Barron rationalized that the lives of Bainbridge and the other American prisoners were more important. He had been impressed by Yusuf's threats against them. "I must contend," he argued, "that the liberty and perhaps the lives of so many valuable & estimable Americans ought not to be sacrificed to points of honor, taken in the abstract."

7. Eaton, for his part, had only praise for Rodgers because of his aggressive actions against all of the Barbary rulers.

8. The dey of Algiers also projected himself into the proceedings. Perhaps at Lear's instigation, the dey wrote to the bashaw that he was sending Lear to Tripoli to discuss terms for peace. "I am sending him to you myself," he wrote. "Consul Lear is a man of great erudition and knows how things go; hence I beg you not to let him return without satisfying him in respect to all that I have asked."

9. Dr. Cowdery had noted in his journal two weeks earlier that de Souza had donated 300 guns to the bashaw for use in defending the city.

10. Of the 307 *Philadelphia* prisoners, six had died. One—John Wilson—had elected to remain in Tripoli and four others who had turned Muslim had been detained. That left 296 men who returned to the squadron. The United States had 89 Tripolitans to exchange, leaving 207 Americans to be ransomed. So the $60,000 worked out to a ransom of $290 per American.

11. Some other provisions of the treaty:

   • No religious differences would be considered reason for further hostilities. Consuls and agents of both the United States and Tripoli would be permitted freely to observe their own religious ceremonies.

   • In cases of dispute, neither nation would declare war on the other for one year, providing time for negotiations.

   • If war were declared, the consuls of both countries would be allowed to embark their personnel and effects on whatever vessel they wanted.

   • No prisoners would be considered as slaves; they would be exchanged as prisoners of war, rank for rank. If one nation had more prisoners than the other, they would be ransomed at the rate of $500 per captain, $300 per mate or supercargo, and $100 per seaman.

   • If any U.S. citizen died in Tripoli, his property would be released under the direction of the U.S. consul. If there was no consul in office at the time, the property would be held until a party with the right to it could appear to claim it. Tripoli's government would be liable to render an account of the effects, and neither the bashaw nor any of his subjects would intervene in the execution of the deceased's will.

12. Eaton could not, however, resist the temptation to take a potshot at Commodore Barron's announcement that the time was "highly favorable to treat of peace." What Barron considered the favorable moment, Eaton snorted, was a time when the commodore "had not seen Tripoli during the last eight months, not even within gun shot; some of his frigates had not ever been nearer it than Malta; seldom, if ever, more than two of them cruising off that port, and generally not but one; his squadron had never been displayed to the enemy's view; nor a shot exchanged with the batteries of Tripoli . . . except

en passant." Eaton made clear the invidious comparison with Commodore Preble's constant attacks on Tripoli.

13. Eaton also assured his friend (Congressman Thomas Dwight): "If the 60,000 dollars [ransom] had, instead of going to Joseph, been sent to Hamet Bashaw at the moment of the Argus rejoining us at Bomba on the 15th April, and correspondent vigorous operations pursued elsewhere, we should have started the usurper from his capital before this date and *wrested* our captives from his chains."

14. The American gunboats had finally arrived by midsummer, after the signing of the peace treaty.

15. Rodgers's Mediterranean squadron included:

Frigate *Constitution* (44 guns)
Frigate *President* (44 guns)
Frigate *Constellation* (36 guns)
Frigate *Congress* (36 guns)
Frigate *Essex* (32 guns)
Frigate *John Adams* (32 guns)
Brig *Argus* (18 guns)
Brig *Siren* (18 guns)
Brig *Vixen* (14 guns)
Brig *Franklin* (8 guns)
Schooner *Enterprise* (14 guns)
Schooner *Nautilus* (14 guns)
Sloop *Hornet* (8 guns)

Plus seven gunboats and ketches newly arrived from the United States; two captured Tripolitan gunboats; and six Adriatic gunboats. The total force was nearly three times what Commodore Preble had had the year before.

16. Ambassador Mellimelli took with him four Arabian stallions as a gift from the bey to President Jefferson. The president felt it improper to accept them and donated them to the Treasury Department. For a while they were kept in the presidential stables, and their stud fees were used to help pay for U.S. hospitality to Ambassador Mellimelli. Soon the ambassador's expenses required selling the horses.

Mellimelli obviously was accustomed to a luxurious life-style. He had brought along an entourage of 11 retainers who were housed at U.S. expense, including an Italian orchestra to serenade his guests at the series of lavish parties that he gave also at U.S. expense.

When it was discovered that the U.S. government was paying for prostitutes for Mellimelli's retinue as well, Secretary of State Madison primly responded to the criticism with an excellent example of early diplomatese: "Appropriations to foreign intercourse are terms of great latitude and may be drawn on by very urgent and unforseen circumstances."

Meanwhile Treasury Secretary Gallatin saw to it that Ambassador Mellimelli got no tribute from the United States for the Tunisian prizes. Finally the ambassador was urged aboard a ship sailing from Boston for the Mediterranean. Later, however, Consul Lear came through with a "gift" of

$10,000 when Mellimelli pleaded that he would be killed if he returned to Bey Hamouda with nothing to show for his efforts.

17. When Edward Preble heard of the encounter, he was struck dumb (after one bristling oath). Secretary Smith shortly wrote asking if he would preside over the court-martial of Captain Barron, but by that time Preble was too ill. He was glad to have an excuse not to be the man to condemn (as he was sure he would have to) an old friend from his Mediterranean squadron.

18. Some time later, after an appeal by President Jefferson, the Royal Navy returned two of the four *Chesapeake* sailors, Daniel Martin and John Strachen. A third man, Jenkin Ratford, had been found guilty of desertion and had been hanged from the yardarm of H.M.S. *Halifax*. The fourth, William Ware, the navy claimed, had taken ill and died.

CHAPTER 13

1. Edward Preble wrote to Eaton, "The arduous and dangerous services you have performed have justly immortalized your name, and astonished not only your country but the world. If pecuniary sources and naval strength had been at your command, what could you not have done." Another of history's "What-ifs": Clearly Preble was hinting that if he had still been commodore, Eaton would have had full cooperation.

2. A thousand acres were also included for Midshipman George W. Mann, who had fought beside O'Bannon and his marines at Derna. The marine survivors were Arthur Campbell, Bernard O'Brian, David Thomas, and James Owen.

    Today the United States has a few towns named Eaton and a couple of hamlets named O'Bannon but no town named Derna.

3. Jefferson did indeed see the agreement signed by Eaton and Hamet, which Eaton sent to Washington (via Barron) from the Arab's Tower. But it did not follow that Jefferson approved of every provision in it. And if he did not, it was too late; Eaton and Hamet were on the march across the desert by the time the agreement reached the president.

4. In 1813 Prentiss published his own biography: *The Life of the Late General William Eaton.*

5. Eugene Leitensdorfer, Eaton's peripatetic adjutant, was paid off at Syracuse and attempted to return to his homeland in the Tyrol, only to be captured and enslaved by Turks in Albania. As resourceful as ever, he set about healing Turkish sailors, with such success that he won his freedom. He gravitated to Palermo, Italy, where he married yet again and again left his wife to sign on aboard a merchantman bound for the United States. He landed at Salem, Mass., in 1809, and presented himself to a surprised William Eaton, asking for a job.

    Eaton gave him letters of introduction to various persons of prominence and sent him to Washington where Leitensdorfer was hired by Jefferson's chief architect, Benjamin Henry Latrobe, and given the title of surveyor of public buildings, evidently a euphemism for night watchman. Leitensdorfer also turned his ready hand to making and selling everything from maps to shoes. And with his characteristic abilities at persuasion, abetted by Eaton's friend Senator Bradley, Leitensdorfer won a congressional land grant of 320 acres in Missouri, plus pay as a U.S. Army colonel for the time he had served with Eaton—including a mileage allowance for the march across the desert.

6. At their urging Congress passed a resolution of official U.S. gratitude to Danish Consul Nicholas Nissen, who had been the prisoners' chief aid and comfort during their incarceration.

7. When officers of the Royal Navy had first seen Humphreys's big frigates in the Mediterranean, they had derided them as big, clumsy warships "built of pine" rather than the hard oak of England. Only Admiral Nelson had predicted that these new American frigates could one day cause the Royal Navy grief.

8. Decatur's squadron:

Frigate *Guerrière* (44 guns)
Frigate *Macedonian* (38 guns)*
Frigate *Constellation* (36 guns)
Sloop of War *Epervier* (18 guns)*
Sloop of War *Ontario* (16 guns)
Brig *Firefly* (14 guns)
Brig *Spark* (14 guns)
Brig *Flambeau* (14 guns)
Schooner *Torch* (12 guns)
Schooner *Spitfire* (12 guns)

9. A new Algerian frigate, not the *Meshouda* (former *Betsey*) that had caused so much trouble between the United States and Morocco.

10. An Algerian minister, studying the U.S. squadron in the harbor, bitterly reminded the British consul that Algiers had declared war on the United States at England's urging, and complained, "You told us that the Americans would be swept from the seas in six months by your navy, and now they make war upon us with some of your own vessels which they have taken."

11. The new treaty freed the crew of the captured *Edwin*, and Decatur put them aboard the *Epervier*, which he was sending back to the United States. It happened that two of his officers, Lieutenant Benedict Neale and Captain Lewis of the flagship, had recently married sisters, so Decatur gave them leave to return home. Lewis carried the treaty with him to present to Navy Secretary Benjamin Crowninshield with Decatur's covering message: "I beg to express to you my opinion that the presence of a respectable naval force in the area will be the only certain guarantee for its observance."

The *Epervier* left the Mediterranean on July 15, 1815, and was never seen again.

12. Decatur originally calculated the value of the two prizes at $30,000, but the U.S. consul persuaded him that $25,000 was a more accurate figure. Decatur agreed to lower the price—in return for the release of ten European captives in the bashaw's prison. Eight were to be Neapolitans, as an American gesture of thanks for the use of King Ferdinand's gunboats; and two were to be

*Captured from the British in the War of 1812.

Danes, in gratitude for Consul Nicholas Nissen's selfless efforts in behalf of the *Philadelphia* prisoners.

13. Yusuf Karamanli held onto his throne for another two decades, when one of his sons (as Yusuf had) revolted against his father. Yusuf had annointed a younger son, Ali, as his successor; and his eldest son, Muhammad, attempted to assassinate Yusuf. He failed, retreated into the countryside, formed his own army, and initiated a civil war.

At the behest of the British and French consuls, the sultan in Constantinople sent a Turkish general, Mejib Pasha, with 22 warships and 6,000 troops to restore order. Pretending to favor Ali, Nejib Pasha lured him and some 30 of his retainers aboard a warship, arrested them, and transported them to Constantinople.

The Turkish Army meanwhile stormed ashore and seized the shore batteries from Yusuf's soldiers. The sultan then issued an order placing Tripoli under the direct control of Nejib Pasha, and the century-old Karamanli dynasty ended. Yusuf survived for another two years and was buried with full honors. Tripoli remained a province of the Ottoman Empire until it was occupied by Italy in 1911.

Tunis was invaded by France in 1851; Bey Muhammad VI was forced out of power but permitted to sit on the throne as a figurehead. In 1871 the former regency became a French protectorate. France had a tougher time subduing Algiers. Despite an invasion of 37,000 French troops in 1830, the Algerians fought on for years. It took some 100,000 French soldiers to end the resistance, and Algiers was not entirely subdued until 1848.

In the end it was the European subjugation of the North African regencies that helped nurture the xenophobic animosities and anti-Christian fervor of modern Arabs in the Mediterranean.

14. It was during the War of 1812 that the first woman marine saw action. A Bostonian named Lucy Brewer befriended one of the marines assigned to the *Constitution* when the frigate put into the city just before the battle with the British *Guerrière*. Miss Brewer was so enchanted by her friend's accounts of life aboard a warship (and perhaps by this particular marine) that she masqueraded as a man, successfully enlisted, and took part in the battle, later writing an account of it that was as accurate as Captain Isaac Hull's official report.

15. One of the Marine Corps' major claims to presidential favor was the Marine Corps Band, which had been formed by the first commandant, William Burrows (for the expenses of which he assessed his officers $10 a month). The musicians quickly became popular at the White House, where they played for President John Adams on New Year's Day 1801. President Jefferson was delighted with the Marine Band when on his inauguration day two months later it serenaded him with a composition written for the occasion, "Jefferson's March." From Jefferson's time the band has been known as "the President's Own," and it greatly enhanced marine prestige with the Executive Office and in Congress, which assumed its expenses in 1805.

Just before he retired, Commandant Burrows, at Jefferson's suggestion, asked Captain John Hall, who was about to sail as commander of the marines aboard the *Constitution*, to enlist a second marine band among the well-known musicians of Italy. (Whether or not the example of Tunisian ambassador

Mellimelli's Italian orchestra stimulated Jefferson's idea is not known.) According to marine legend, Hall sent ashore a sergeant's guard at Catania, Italy, virtually kidnapped 14 strolling musicians, and sent a self-congratulatory message that got a cold reception in Washington. Burrows, it developed, had not mentioned his request to his successor, Franklin Wharton, who was nonplussed when he received Hall's announcement that he "had been fortunate enough to enlist 14 good Musicians for the Marine Corps" in Italy. Moreover, by this time Burrows had died, and there was no record of his request.

Wharton coldly replied to Hall, "I have received your letter. . . . The part of it which relates to a band of music I cannot comprehend. . . . I have never given any orders for the collection of a band in the Mediterranean, and it will not be mentioned as belonging to the Corps." Furthermore, Wharton had no intention of adding 14 musicians and their families to his budget. "The expenses already arising," he wrote, "will not be paid." Wharton could imagine the reaction at navy headquarters. "The Secretary of the Navy," he icily informed Hall, "can never assent to two bands for one Corps."

But Wharton was too late. Captain Hall and his Italian musicians arrived in the United States in September of 1805. Grudgingly accepted into the Marine Band, they formed an "Italian Group" that became popular with the Washington audiences. Hall had officially enlisted the musicians in the Marine Corps. But as soon as their term had expired, they were disbanded, and the navy offered them and their families passage to Sicily. Some accepted; in fact, when the frigate *Chesapeake* was crippled by the *Leopard* and had to return to port, she brought back some badly frightened musicians who had been on their way home.

Others reenlisted, including a 12-year-old clarinetist named Venerando Pulizzi, who rose from music boy through the ranks to fife major (at 19) and eventually to drum major (at 31), and led the Marine Band for three years. He then resigned, enlisted in the Corps as a fighting marine, and rose from line sergeant to sergeant major, serving until his death, at 62, in 1852, after 47 years in the Marine Corps.

Captain Hall survived the displeasure of the commandant, and was promoted to major in 1814.

16. Some army adherents claimed that it was Captain B. S. Roberts of the army's Mounted Rifles who hauled up the first Stars and Stripes in Mexico City in his capacity as Officer of the Day. But Lieutenant Nicholson was Roberts's officer of the guard, and was ordered by Roberts to raise the flag.

17. For a while the new marine motto was "From Tripoli to the Halls of Montezuma." No one seems to know when the marine hymn's now-famous opening lines were officially adopted. The melody comes from Jacques Offenbach's opera *Geneviève de Brabant*, which had its premiere on November 19, 1859, featuring a duet, "The Gendarmes of the Queen," from which the marine hymn takes its tune. Not until 1898 did it make its first recorded appearance, on a recruiting poster proudly proclaiming: "From the Halls of Montezuma/ To the Shores of Tripoli."

The marine hymn is not to be confused with the marine march *Semper Fidelis*, which was composed by John Philip Sousa, leader of the Marine Band from 1880 to 1892.

BIBLIOGRAPHY

★ ★ ★

The major source of information on the Barbary War at sea is *Naval Documents Related to the United States Wars with the Barbary Powers*, a seven-volume compendium of letters, reports, orders, and other communications assembled by U.S. Navy historians. *Naval Documents* includes some of the papers of William Eaton recounting his remarkable expedition by land. But the complete collection of Eaton's papers, as mentioned in Acknowledgments, is at the Huntington Library in San Marino, California.

Here are the books, articles, and other sources that I found most useful and recommend for further reading.

Abbatt, William. *A Forgotten Hero: The Magazine of History with Notes and Queries.* 1907 and 1911. A reprint of William Ray's diary (see below) with a biographical note on William Eaton.

Adams, Henry. *The Life of Albert Gallatin.* New York: 1943.

Albion, R. G., and J. B. Pope. *Sea Lanes in Wartime: The American Experience, 1775–1945.* 1942, reprinted 1968. An excellent account of the effect of various wars on merchant shipping.

Allen, Gardner W. *Our Navy and the Barbary Corsairs.* Boston: Houghton Mifflin, 1905.

Angle, Paul M. *By These Words: Great Documents of American Liberty, Selected and Placed in Their Contemporary Settings.* New York: Rand, McNally, 1954.

Anthony, Irvin. *Decatur.* New York: Scribners.

Baldwin, Leland D. *The Stream of American History.* New York: Richard R. Smith Publisher, 1952.

Bennet, Marion T. *Lt. Presley Neville O'Bannon, USMC.* An annotated MS about O'Bannon's career.

Bergerac, J. M. de. *Memoirs d'un Protestant Condamné aux Galères.* 1757.

Blyth, Stephen, C. *History of the War Between the U.S. and Tripoli.* 1806.

Botting, Douglas. *The Pirates.* Alexandria, Va.: Time-Life Books, 1978.

Boyd, Julian P., ed. *The Papers of Thomas Jefferson*, 12 vols. Princeton, N.J.: Princeton University Press, 1955.

Bradford, Ernle. *Julius Caesar: The Pursuit of Power.* New York: William Morrow, 1984.

———. *The Sultan's Admiral: The Life of Barbarossa.* London: Hodder & Stoughton, 1968.

Broadley, A. M. *Tunis Past and Present.* 1882.

Bruns, James H. "Neither snow nor rain. . . ." Constitution magazine, Winter 1989.

Buchanan, John E. *American Merchantmen and the Barbary Powers: 1783–1815.* Thesis for Munson Institute of American Maritime History; G. W. Blunt White Library, Mystic Seaport Museum, Mystic, Conn. Aug. 17, 1959.

Casson, Lionel. *The Ancient Mariners.* New York: Macmillan, 1959.

Cathcart, James Leander. *The Captives, Eleven Years a Prisoner in Algiers*, compiled by his daughter, J. B. Cathcart Newkirk: Herald Point, La Porte, Ind.: 1899.

———. *Tripoli. The First War with the United States*, letter book compiled by his daughter, J. B. Cathcart Newkirk. Herald Point, La Porte, Ind.: 1901.

Channing, Edward. *A History of the United States*, 6 vols. New York: Macmillan, 1920.

Chapelle, Howard I. *The History of the American Sailing Navy.* New York: W. W. Norton, 1949.

Chenier, L. S. *Cruelties of the Algerian Pirates.* 1816.

Chidsey, Donald Barr. *The Wars in Barbary.* New York: Crown, 1971.

Clark, Thomas. *Naval History of the U.S. from the Commencement of the Revolutionary War to Present Time*, 2 vols. Philadelphia, 1814.

―――. *Sketches of the Naval History of the U.S.*

Cleveland, Stephen. *History of the War Between the U.S. and Tripoli.* Salem: 1806.

Commager, Henry Steele, and Allan Nevins. *The Heritage of America.* Boston: Little, Brown, 1949.

Cooke, F. O. "O'Bannon in Libya." *The Leatherneck*, Aug. 1942.

Cooper, James Fenimore. *History of the Navy of the United States*, 2 vols. Philadelphia: Lea & Blanchard, 1839.

―――. *Lives of Distinguished Naval Officers.* Auburn, N.Y.: 1846.

Cowdery, Jonathan. *American Captives in Tripoli—or, Dr. Cowdery's Journal.* Boston: 1806. Journal of the *Philadelphia*'s surgeon's mate.

Currey, E. H. *Sea Wolves of the Mediterranean: The Grand Period of the Modern Corsairs.* 1910.

Dan, Père F. *Histoire de Barbarie et de ses Corsaires.* 1649.

Davidson, Marshall B. *Life in America*, 2 vols. Boston: Houghton Mifflin, 1951.

Deardon, Seton. *A Nest of Corsairs.* London: John Murray, 1976.

Eaton, Rev. Arthur W.H.A. *Memorial Sketch of William Eaton.* 1893.

Eaton, William. *Interesting Details of the Operations of the American Fleet in the Mediterranean.* 1805.

Edwards, Samuel. *Barbary General: The Life of William H. Eaton.* Englewood Cliffs, N.J.: Prentice-Hall, 1968.

Eller, E. M. *To the Shores of Tripoli.* Proceedings, U.S. Naval Institute, March 1933.

Emerson, Edwin, Jr. *A History of the Nineteenth Century Year by Year*, 3 vols. New York: P. F. Collier & Son, 1901.

Felton, Cornelius C. *Life of William Eaton.* Sparks Library of American Biography, 1st Series, Vol. IX. New York: 1844.

Field, James A. *America and the Mediterranean World, 1776–1882.* 1969.

Fisher, Sir G. *Barbary Legend: War, Trade and Piracy in North Africa,*

1415–1830. 1958. An interesting revisionist view of Mediterranean piracy.

Flexner, James Thomas. *George Washington and the New Nation*. Boston: Little, Brown, 1969.

———. "Washington's Inaugural." *Constitution* magazine, Winter 1989.

Folsom, Benjamin. *A Compilation of Biographical Sketches of Distinguished Officers of the American Navy*. 1814.

Forester, C. S. *The Barbary Pirates*. New York: Random House, 1953.

Foss, John. *A Journal of the Captivity and Suffering of John Foss*. Newburyport, Mass.: 1798.

Geer, Andrew. "To the Shores." *The Leatherneck*, Nov. 1952.

Gerson, Noel B. *Barbary General, the Life of William H. Eaton*. 1963.

Glubb, Bagot. *A Short History of the Arab Peoples*. New York: Stein & Day, 1969.

Gooding, Judson. "An American in Paris." *Constitution* magazine, Winter 1989. Jefferson as minister to France.

Grant, Bruce. *Captain of Old Ironsides: The Life and Fighting Times of Isaac Hull and the U.S. Frigate Constitution*. Chicago: Pellegrini & Cudahy, 1947.

Gruppe, Henry E. *The Frigates*. Alexandria, Va.: Time-Life Books, 1979.

Guttridge, Leonard F. and Jay D. Smith. *The Commodores: The U.S. Navy in the Age of Sail*. New York: Harper & Row, 1969.

Hajji, Khalifa. *History of the Maritime Wars of the Turks*. Trans. 1831.

Hamilton, Alexander, James Madison, and John Jay. *The Federalist Papers*. New York: Heritage Press, 1945.

Hammer, J. von. *History of the Ottoman Empire*. 1836.

Harris, Thomas, M.D. *Life and Services of Commodore William Bainbridge*. Philadelphia: 1837.

Heinl, Robert Debs. *Soldiers of the Sea: The United States Marine Corps, 1775–1962*. Annapolis, Md.: U.S. Naval Institute Press, 1962.

Hill, Frederick Stanhope. *Twenty-six Historic Ships.*

Hoffman, Carl W. "The Marine Band—The President's Own." *Marine Corps Gazette,* Nov. 1950.

Hofstadter, Richard, William Miller, and Daniel Aaron. *The United States: The History of a Republic* Englewood Cliffs, N.J.: Prentice-Hall, 1957.

Hollis, Ira N. *The Frigate Constitution, the Central Figure of the Navy Under Sail.*

Hooper, Bayard. "'To the Polls, Ye Sons of Freedom!'" *Constitution* magazine, Fall 1988.

Howland, Felix. "Tripolitan Background of the War of 1801–1805." *The Marine Corps Gazette.* March 1938.

Hyman, Harold M. "Arms, Men and the Constitution." *Constitution* magazine, Spring 1989.

Irwin, Ray W. *The Diplomatic Relations of the United States with the Barbary Powers.* 1970.

Jennings, John. *Tattered Ensign.* New York: Thomas Y. Crowell, 1966. A history of the frigate *Constitution.*

Johnston, Harry A. *A History of the Colonization of Africas by Alien Races.* Cambridge, England: 1930.

Kahn, Arthur D. *The Education of Julius Caesar.* New York: Schocken Books, 1986.

Keegan, John. *The Price of Admiralty: The Evolution of Naval Warfare.* New York: Viking, 1989.

Knox, Dudley W. *A History of the United States Navy.* 1936. Meticulous operational detail.

Koch, Adrienne. *Jefferson and Madison; The Great Collaboration.* New York: Alfred A. Knopf, 1950.

Lane-Poole, Stanley. *The Story of the Barbary Corsairs.* New York & London: 1890.

Lewis, Charles Lee. *Famous American Marines.* Boston: L.C. Page, 1950.

———. *The Romantic Decatur.* Philadelphia, Pa.: University of Pennsylvania Press, 1937.

Lincoln, C. H. *The Hull-Eaton Correspondence During the Tripoli Expedition of 1804–5. Proceedings of the American Antiquarian Society*, Vol. XI: 1901.

McKee, Christopher. *Edward Preble: A Naval Biography, 1761–1807*. Annapolis, Md.: U.S. Naval Institute Press, 1972.

Mackenzie, Alexander Slidell. *Life of Stephen Decatur*. Boston: 1846.

MacNeil, Neil. "The First Congress." *Constitution* magazine, Spring-Fall, 1989.

Malone, Dumas. *Jefferson and His Time*, 6 vols. Boston: Little, Brown, 1948–1981.

Martin, Mary. *History of the Captivity and Sufferings of Mrs. M. Martin, who was Six Years a Captive in Algiers*. Boston: 1807.

Martin, Tyrone. *A Most Fortunate Ship: A Narrative History of "Old Ironsides."* Chester, Conn.: Globe Pequot Press, 1980. Martin was captain of the *Constitution* from 1974 to 1978.

Mee, Charles L., Jr. "Ratified: A Constitution Subject to Change." *Constitution* magazine, Fall 1988.

Mercier, Henry. *Life in a Man-of-war*. Boston: Houghton Mifflin, 1927 reprinted from 1841 edition.

Merriman, Roger B. *Suleiman the Magnificent, 1520–1566*. Cambridge, Mass.: 1944.

Metcalf, Clyde H. A. *A History of the Marine Corps*. New York: 1939.

Miller, Lt. (J.G.) Arthur P., Jr. *Tripoli Graves Discovered. Proceedings, U.S. Naval Institute*, April 1950.

Millett, Allen R. *Semper Fidelis: The History of the United States Marine Corps*. New York: Macmillan, 1980.

Minnigerode, Meade. *Lives and Times; Four Informal American Portraits*. 1925. Includes a chapter on William Eaton.

Morgan, John. *A Complete History of Algiers*. 1731.

Morison, Samuel Eliot. *John Paul Jones: A Sailor's Biography*. Boston: Atlantic Monthly Press, 1959.

———. *"Old Bruin": Commodore Matthew C. Perry, 1794–1858*. Boston: Atlantic Monthly Press, 1967.

Morris, Richard B. "Decision to Fight Again." *Constitution* magazine, Fall 1988.

————. *The Making of a Nation*, Vol. 2 of *Life History of the United States*. New York: Time-Life Books, 1963.

Morris, Richard Valentine. *A Defence of the Conduct of Commodore Morris During His Command in the Mediterranean with Strictures on the Report of the Court of Inquiry Held at Washington*. New York: I. Riley & Co., 1804.

Nash, H. P. *The Forgotten Wars: The Quasi-War with France and the Tripolitan War*. 1968.

Naval Documents Related to the United States Wars with the Barbary Powers, 7 vols., Washington: 1939–1944.

Neeser, Robert W. *The Ships of the U.S. Navy.*

————. *Statistical and Chronological History of the United States Navy, 1775–1907.*

New Hampshire Patriot & State Gazette, Sept. 21, 1835. Profile of William Eaton.

Newman, P. H. *Ancient Sea Galleys*. 1915.

Nicolay, Helen: *Decatur of the Old Navy*. New York: D. Appleton Century, 1942.

Noah, M. M. *Travels in England, France, Spain and the Barbary States*. New York: 1819. Noah was U.S. consul to Tunis after the Barbary War.

Nordhoff, Charles. *Man-of-war Life*. Cincinnati, Ohio: Moore, Wilstack, Keys, 1856.

Ormerod, Henry A. *Piracy in the Ancient World*. New York: Dorset Press, 1987.

Paullin, Charles Oscar. *Commodore John Rodgers*. 1910.

Perkins, Roger. *Gunfire in Barbary.*

Pierce, Lt. Col. Philip, and Lt. Col. Frank O. Hough. *The Compact History of the United States Marine Corps*. New York: Hawthorn Books, 1960.

Playfair, Sir Robert Lambert. *The Scourge of Christendom*. London: 1884.

Plutarch. *Lives of the Noble Grecians and Romans*, trans. John Dryden. Chicago: Encyclopedia Britannica, 1952.

Powell, E. Alender; *Gentlemen Rovers*. 1913. Includes a profile on William Eaton.

Pratt, Fletcher. *Preble's Boys*. New York: William Sloane Associates, 1950.

Prentiss, Charles. *Life of the Late General William Eaton*. Brookfield, Mass.: 1813.

Rankin, Robert H. *Small Arms of the Sea Services.*

————. *Uniforms of the Sea Services, A Pictorial History*. 1962. Includes Marines & Navy.

Ray, William. *Horrors of Slavery; or, the American Tars in Tripoli*. Troy, N.Y.: 1808. Reprinted in *The Magazine of History With Notes and Queries*. One of the *Philadelphia's* imprisoned marines.

Rentfrow, Frank Hunt. "To the Shores of Tripoli." *The Leatherneck*, Dec. 1929.

Rodd, Francis Rennell. *General William Eaton*. New York: Minton, Balch, 1932.

Rousseau, Baron A. *History of the Conquest of Tunis by the Ottomans*. 1883.

Roscoe, Theodore, and Fred Freeman. *Picture History of the U.S. Navy*. New York: Charles Scribner's Sons, 1956.

Ross, Frank E. "James Leander Cathcart—'Troublesome, Litigious Trifler.'" *Americana* magazine, Oct. 1934.

Sabine, Lorenzo. *Life of Edward Preble*. Boston: 1847.

Schachner, Nathan. *Thomas Jefferson: A Biography*, 2 vols. New York: Appleton-Century Crofts, 1951.

Schuon, Karl, ed. *The Leathernecks: An Informal History of the U.S. Marine Corps*. New York: Franklin Watts, 1944.

Skippen, E. "A Forgotten General." *The United Service*, Vol. V, No. 1, 1881.

Smelser, Marshall. *The Congress Founds the Navy, 1787–1798*. South Bend, Ind.: Notre Dame University Press, 1959.

Smith, Jay D. *Commodore James Barron: Guilty as Charged?*. *Proceedings, U.S. Naval Institute*, Nov. 1967.

Smith, Myron J. Jr. *The American Navy 1789–1860. American Navy Bibliography, Vol. II.*

Sparks, Jered, ed. *Library of American Biography*. Includes a chapter on William Eaton.

Sprout, H. & M. *The Rise of American Naval Power, 1776–1918.* 1939.

Stanford, Peter. "The *USS Constitution*: Reaching Out Over the Horizon." *Sea History* magazine, Summer 1987.

Stein, R. Conrad. *The Story of the Barbary Pirates*. Chicago, Ill.: Childrens Press, 1982.

Thubron, Colin. *The Ancient Mariners*. Alexandria, Va.: Time-Life Books, 1981.

Tucker, Glenn. *Dawn Like Thunder: The Barbary Wars and the Birth of the U.S. Navy*. Indianapolis: Bobbs-Merrill, 1963.

Tully, Richard. *Narrative of Ten Years Residence at Tripoli*. New limited edition, ed. Seaton Durden: London: Arthur Barker, 1957. Original edition, London: Coburn, 1819.

Van Doren, Carl. *The Great Rehearsal: The Story of the Making and Ratifying of the Constitution of the United States*. New York: Viking Press, 1948.

Wadsworth, Henry. *Letters Written on Board the United States Ship Constitution During a Cruise in the Mediterranean . . . to Miss Hashtash and Others. . . .*

Waldo, Samuel Putnam. *Biographical Sketches of Distinguished American Naval Heroes*. 1823.

Welch, Galbraith. *North African Prelude*.

Whipple, A.B.C. *Fighting Sail*. Alexandria, Va.: Time-Life Books, 1978.

Wood, Gordon S. *The Creation of the American Republic, 1776–1787.* New York: W. W. Norton, 1969.

Wood, Peter. *The Spanish Main*. Alexandria, Va.: Time-Life Books, 1979.

Wright, Louis Booker, and Julia H. Macleod. *The First Americans in North America*. Princeton, N.J.: Princeton University Press, 1945.

INDEX

★ ★ ★

The Naval Institute Press is the book-publishing arm of the U.S. Naval Institute, a private, nonprofit, membership society for sea service professionals and others who share an interest in naval and maritime affairs. Established in 1873 at the U.S. Naval Academy in Annapolis, Maryland, where its offices remain today, the Naval Institute has members worldwide.

Members of the Naval Institute support the education programs of the society and receive the influential monthly magazine *Proceedings* and discounts on fine nautical prints and on ship and aircraft photos. They also have access to the transcripts of the Institute's Oral History Program and get discounted admission to any of the Institute-sponsored seminars offered around the country.

The Naval Institute also publishes *Naval History* magazine. This colorful bimonthly is filled with entertaining and thought-provoking articles, first-person reminiscences, and dramatic art and photography. Members receive a discount on Naval History subscriptions.

The Naval Institute's book-publishing program, begun in 1898 with basic guides to naval practices, has broadened its scope to include books of more general interest. Now the Naval Institute Press publishes about one hundred titles each year, ranging from how-to books on boating and navigation to battle histories, biographies, ship and aircraft guides, and novels. Institute members receive significant discounts on the Press's more than eight hundred books in print.

Full-time students are eligible for special half-price membership rates. Life memberships are also available.

For a free catalog describing Naval Institute Press books currently available, and for further information about subscribing to *Naval History* magazine or about joining the U.S. Naval Institute, please write to:

Membership Department
U.S. Naval Institute
291 Wood Road
Annapolis, MD 21402-5034
Telephone: (800) 233-8764
Fax: (410) 269-7940
Web address: www.navalinstitute.org